WITHDRAWN

National Deconstruction

National Deconstruction

Violence, Identity, and Justice in Bosnia

David Campbell

University of Minnesota Press

Minneapolis

London

Published by the University of Minnesota Press
111 Third Avenue South, Suite 290
Minneapolis, MN 55401-2520
http://www.upress.umn.edu

Library of Congress Cataloging-in-Publication Data

Campbell, David, 1961–
    National deconstruction : violence, identity, and justice in
Bosnia / David Campbell.
        p.   cm.
    Includes index.
    ISBN 0-8166-2936-6 (hardcover : alk. paper). — ISBN 0-8166-2937-4
(pbk. : alk. paper)
    1. Social psychology. 2. War — Psychological aspects. 3. Fear.
4. Yugoslav War, 1991– — Bosnia and Hercegovina — Psychological
aspects. I. Title.
HM291.C277   1998
302 — dc21   98-17006
                                                           CIP

Printed in the United States of America on acid-free paper

The University of Minnesota is an equal-opportunity educator and employer.

10 09 08 07 06 05 04 03 02 01 00 99 98   10 9 8 7 6 5 4 3 2 1

For Elena, Amira, Ziad, our Sarajevo taxi driver, and the many others

Contents

Preface
Problematizing Bosnia

The morning after the assassination of the Bosnian deputy prime minister, Hakija Turajlić, the UN's commander in Sarajevo, General Philippe Morillon, read a statement to the assembled press corps. "Bosnia Herzegovina is afflicted by a human illness — fear of others, fear of the other," he said. One journalist wondered whether this statement, which "sounded like a college term paper on existentialism," was an indication of the general's "madness or enlightenment."[1]

Foregrounding the question of the relationship to the other in order to explore provocations called up by the Bosnian war and occluded by more conventional accounts, this book moves beyond the journalist's puzzlement and the general's views. Although suggestive, Morillon's observation captures barely half the picture. Fear of others is not a pathology possessed by others alone. It afflicts "us" as well. Indeed, the relationship to the other that can sometimes turn septic encompasses "us" and "them," for the relationship to the other is the condition of possibility for the self. Justice is the relationship to the other; it is justice when we are open to the surprise of the other, acknowledge the other's summons, or are willing to be unsettled by our encounters with others. The relationship to the other is the context of the political, it is the site of an irreducible responsibility, and yet it is in the relationship to the other that responsibility is often suppressed or effaced by violence.

Although emphatically concerned with Bosnia, this book is not, however, about Bosnia per se. While it details often underappreciated events and issues implicated in the course of the violence, it offers (assuming such things might be possible) neither a comprehensive account of the conflict nor a full explanation of its cause. Rather than assuming a pregiven, externally existing entity called Bosnia, this book is concerned primarily with "metaBosnia," the array of practices through which Bosnia (indeed, competing "Bosnias") comes to be. Positioned in the above ethico-political terms made possible by the thought of Derrida and Lévinas, which permeates the argument, this book concentrates on the way the relationship to the other is variously effaced or enacted in those constitutive practices.

This contrast between Bosnia and metaBosnia recalls an important Foucauldian point that frames the argument. When we operate from a position that argues that cultural practices make forms of experience historically possible through the marginalization and exclusion of others, the analysis of practices concerned with the representation of violence and the violence of representation takes on a different form. As Foucault argues, "The proper task of a history of thought... [is] to define the conditions in which human beings 'problematize' what they are, what they do, and the world in which they live."[2] Analysis proceeds, therefore, not on the basis of examining behavior and ideas as foundational or causal concepts, but rather on "the *problematizations* through which being offers itself to be, necessarily, thought — and the *practices* on the basis of which these problematizations are formed."[3]

A problematization is something that has made it possible to think in terms of problems and solutions; it is something that "has made possible the transformations of the difficulties and obstacles of a practice into a general problem for which one proposes diverse practical solutions." A problematization "develops the conditions in which possible responses can be given; it defines the elements that will constitute what the different solutions attempt to respond to."[4] In seeking to show how different solutions to a problem have been constructed and made possible by the way the problem is posed in the first place, it demonstrates how different solutions result from a specific form of problematization.

The problematization of Bosnia has occurred along and through a continuum of political spaces and transnational surfaces, from the bodies of individuals, to the corporate body of the former Yugoslavia, the representational bodies of academic and media workers, the international bodies of the world community, and back again. No matter what assumptions or proclivities we bring to bear on the situation, we are always dealing with metaBosnia rather than a priori Bosnia. Some problematizations are more powerful and deeply entrenched than others, but no one escapes the discursive realm of a problematization to find themselves in an extra-discursive realm of pregiven problems and ready-made solutions. The latter always depends on the former.

To be sure, the dominant discourses of international relations, security studies, and the like make such claims, but they are dependent on a range of epistemological conceits. As a result, these more conventional approaches are unable to recognize the manner in which their diagnostic modes involve relations of power that bring a particular problematization into being. Disciplinary power effects a problematization through strategies of normalization. These strategies work on people and places so as to compare, differentiate, hierarchize, and homogenize them in ways that map them as manageable problems amenable to solutions that more often than not involve distribution, enclosure, and surveillance.[5] In the case of Bosnia, perhaps the most prevalent problematization involves the ethnicization of the political field. With its array of historical, statistical, cartographic, and other procedures, this has helped organize Bosnia into an "intractable" problem such that the apartheid politics of partition could be proposed as the most "realistic" solution. In bowing to the force of conceptual determination, those who operated in such terms replicated and reproduced the strategies of violence they ostensibly sought to ameliorate.

Drawing out these representational issues so we can better appreciate our imbrication in the relationship to the other and invent better political responses attuned to the relationship to the other is the overriding purpose of this book. As such, it can be read as the problematization of the problematizations that reduce Bosnia to a problem, thereby bringing to the fore the necessary concern with ethics, politics, and responsibility contained by more traditional accounts.

Acknowledgments

In the course of its development, the argument in this book has been iterated and reiterated in a number of papers presented in a variety of places. On every occasion I have benefited greatly from the questions of audiences and the commentaries of discussants too numerous to mention individually. To honor those contributions requires something like a travelogue detailing the relevant presentations.

The first outing for some of the key conceptual notions, which picked up where my study of the Gulf War had left off, was in a paper titled "A Question of Responsibility: Ethical Engagement and the Practice of U.S. Foreign Policy," presented at the American Political Science Association's 1993 annual meeting, and later that year at the International Relations Seminar at Columbia University. A portion of this paper, which in revised form provides the basis of chapter 6, was published as "The Deterritorialization of Responsibility: Lévinas, Derrida, and Ethics after the End of Philosophy," *Alternatives: Social Transformation and Humane Governance* 19 (fall 1994), 455–84; copyright 1994 by *Alternatives* and used with permission of Lynne Rienner Publishers, Inc.

The discussion of Derrida's *coup de force* and the rethinking of "ethnic/nationalist" violence was articulated in "Violent Performances: Identity and the State in the Bosnian Conflict," a paper presented to the seminar series on Identity and Governmentality organized by research students in the Faculties at the Australian National University in August 1994, and the MA International Relations Program at Flinders University, Adelaide, in September 1994. Providing sections in chapters 2 and 4, a version of this paper was published as "Identity, Sovereignty, Responsibility: Reflections on Post–Cold War Moral Cartography," in *The Return of Culture and Identity in International Re-*

lations Theory, edited by Yosef Lapid and Friedrich Kratochwil (Boulder: Lynne Rienner Publishers, 1996); copyright 1996 by Lynne Rienner Publishers, Inc., and used with permission of the publisher.

In February 1995, following a beneficent invitation from the organizers in Canada, I delivered a talk called "The Necessary Impossibility of Democracy: An Articulation of the Political Possibilities of 'Postmodernism'" to the Eleventh Annual Political Studies Students Conference at the University of Manitoba. Subsequent to that, a paper titled "Ontopology: Violence, Identity, and Justice in Bosnia" was presented to the Applied Derrida conference at the University of Luton in July 1995; the Aberystwyth PostInternational Group conference "Sovereignty and Subjectivity" at the University of Wales in September 1995; the International Theory Group at Keele University in October 1995; and the Centre for Theoretical Studies in the Humanities and the Social Sciences, University of Essex, and the Department of Politics, University of Bristol, in November 1995. Containing elements of chapter 2 and the final section of chapter 3, a version has been published as "Ontopology: Violence, Identity, and Justice in the Bosnian Conflict," in *Sovereignty and Subjectivity,* edited by Jenny Edkins, Nalini Persram, and Veronique Pin-Fat (Boulder: Lynne Rienner Publishers, 1998); copyright 1998 by Lynne Rienner Publishers, Inc., and used with permission of the publisher. For permission to use this material, along with the above publications, I am grateful to Lynne Rienner. Thanks are due also to the *Review of International Studies* for permission to use material from "MetaBosnia: The Narratives of the Bosnian War" for a section in chapter 3.

The documentary exegesis of the Bosnian peace process that makes up chapter 5 was, in shortened form, the subject of a paper titled " 'Ethnic' Bosnia and Its Partition: The Political Anthropology of International Diplomacy," which was presented to the 1996 British International Studies Association annual conference, the Graduate Institute of International Studies in Geneva, and the Department of Geography, Loughborough University, in March 1997, the 1997 International Studies Association meeting in Toronto, as well as the International Theory Group at Keele University in May 1997. Finally, the implications of the argument for representing and responding to the Bosnian war, detailed in chapter 7, were aired in "Alternative Spaces: The Case of Bosnia," a paper presented to the SSRC Workshop on Sovereignty, Security, and Modernity, at the University of Notre Dame, Indiana, in April 1997, and the RECIPE Lecture Series at the University of Amsterdam the following month.

Special mention needs to be made of those who gave of their time and effort to build upon encounters from the above chronology and offer detailed comments or provide valuable references. Debts are owed to Roland Bleiker, Bill Connolly, Martin Coward, Alex Danchev, James Der Derian, Mick Dillon, Jasna Dragovic, Kevin Frost, Larry George, Eric Herring, David Howarth, Andrew Linklater, Debbie Lisle, John Louth, David Mutimer, Ashis Nandy, Paul Patton, Simon Philpott, Hidemi Suganami, Gearóid Ó Tuathail, Rob Walker, and Michael Waller. My apologies are forthcoming to those who might have been overlooked in my recollected memory or recorded notes of the past four years. For their helpful reports on the original proposal for this book, I am grateful to Simon Critchley and Ernesto Laclau. A Keele University Research Award, which provided a semester's leave in the autumn of 1996 and a small grant toward travel expenses incurred in Bosnia, enabled drafts of the first five chapters to be completed. Marla Stone contributed a reader's report with important reflections, and I am greatly obliged to the acute insights Peggy Kamuf provided in her engagement with both the proposal and the manuscript. The final version benefited substantially from the generous reading of Michael Shapiro.

To the members of Foundation YSY in Amsterdam who enabled our participation in the Summer University Project at the University of Tuzla during July and August 1996, I could not be more appreciative. The commitment and energy of Issa Niemeijer, Yannick du Pont, Michel Richter, Hugh Griffiths, and Jochem Beunderman (among others unknown) provided experiences and insights that had many repercussions for this and future projects. In Tuzla, the classroom contributions of our students were significant, the interaction with fellow faculty was insightful, the assistance and information provided by Miriam Struyk and Miralim Tursinović was invaluable, while the hospitality of Branka Radića's residents was unforgettable. To Kate Manzo goes the infinite thanks to a partner who helped make all that is here possible, not the least of which is our pleasure in Elena's enjoyment of her other headings.

One
Ethics, Politics, and Responsibility: The Bosnian Challenge

The Demand of Face-to-Face Encounters

For Amira Muharemović, the spread of the Bosnian war to Tuzla on 15 May 1992 came as a surprise. Although aware of the events that were central to the dissolution of the former Yugoslavia — such as the independence of Slovenia and Croatia, the Bosnian referendum over its future, and the local tensions between the mayor and the Yugoslav Army (JNA) — Amira did not expect war. And when it did come, in the form of an organized Serbian withdrawal from Tuzla in the week prior to the first shelling on Friday the fifteenth, another revelation was in store. Amira, like many in Tuzla (the only city to have voted in the majority for nonnationalist candidates in Bosnia's 1990 elections) paid little attention to manifestations of particular identities. Until the mass departure of Serbs, the knowledge that those individuals — many of whom she knew personally — were Serbs was either absent or unimportant. Indeed, the idea that she might have a particular identity representable in exclusive ethnic terms was opaque to Amira. "I am a Muslim," she told us, "but I didn't know that before the war. Before the war, of course, we were all atheists!"[1] Given this relaxed disposition, it came as something of a surprise when, in giving accounts of the fighting around Tuzla, which included the shelling of her neighborhood, Amira started to speak of "the Chetniks." But she did so rather self-consciously and was at pains to point out her reasoning behind this representation. It was, she said, so that a distinction could be made between Serbs as a whole and those who waged war against Tuzla. "It's just like the distinction you draw between Germans and Nazis," Amira observed.

On the bus from Tuzla to Sarajevo, we found ourselves sitting next to Ziad, who identified himself as a refugee from Srebrenica. A mine engineer who once had two houses in that now infamous town, Ziad was currently living in a small apartment in the Sarajevo suburb of Ilidza. His experience on fleeing Srebrenica was extraordinary: detained in a camp in Serbia proper for some months, he then ended up in Minneapolis for medical treatment, before returning to his family in Bosnia. Ziad joked about his experiences in the United States, where his hosts asked him questions that revealed an orientalist perspective on Bosnia; they were stunned to learn that he had only one wife and amazed that he had no trouble working the washing machine. When I asked Ziad for his thoughts on the paradox of his current existence — whereby those Serbs who vacated the apartment he now lives in could in all likelihood be residing in his houses in Srebrenica — he shrugged his shoulders, gave a weak smile, and remarked that all of them were caught up in a situation brought on by "a few crazy people."[2]

In Sarajevo itself we experienced perhaps the most moving encounter. Wanting to see more than just those parts of the city that one could easily walk around, we found without difficulty a taxi driver, whose name we sadly did not catch, prepared to spend an afternoon showing us the former frontline areas. This driver's twelve-year-old son had been killed by a shell the year before while playing on the streets outside the family apartment. Yet on more than one occasion during that tour, unprompted by any particular question, he turned to us with genuine puzzlement and asked why the many other foreigners he met always assumed that because he was a Muslim, he would naturally hate all Serbs. "I presume *a* Serb fired the shell that killed my son," he said, "but I do not know which one. So why would I hate all Serbs? I live with them, I walk with them, I work with them, many are my friends."

These three face-to-face encounters in Bosnia demand a rethinking of both our understanding of the conflict and the way in which we approach the questions of ethics, politics, and responsibility. They do not by themselves legitimize and secure one particular interpretation over another. After all, it would not be difficult to quote exclusively hard-line nationalist views from the many media accounts of the Bosnian war to sustain the common narrative of inevitable and natural conflict. But these encounters do permit nonetheless a significant conceptual observation.

It is that even in the most difficult circumstances individuals exercise the capacity for ongoing and ever present judgment, evaluation, and discrimination that problematizes the chauvinistic and xenophobic rationales offered as accounts for those extreme situations.

Distinguishing between "Chetniks" and Serbs so as to absolve the latter for the actions of the former, refusing the temptation to blame all members of one side and instead holding a "few crazy people" on all sides responsible, and resisting the pain of personal loss brought on by nationalist violence to endorse a multicultural existence are moments of an ethos that render other understandings of the Bosnian war as manifestly partisan. As such, these moments exhibit an ethos that exceeds and overflows the categories and containments of the dominant narratives of identity politics used to comprehend the Bosnian war. And, as such, they put paid to the notion that the hybrid condition of Bosnian life and politics could simply be dismissed as the product of mythic displacements by misguided European intellectuals.[3]

Coming from these face-to-face encounters is a call for the appreciation of alterity that makes them possible. Responding to the demand that issues forth from these moments, this book seeks to intervene in a range of issues. Prominent among them is that international politics in the post–Cold War era is said to have been marked by new forms of violence, most often understood in terms of "ethnic" and "nationalist" conflict. This project is animated by two concerns relevant to that context. Firstly, it focuses on a prominent but specific instance of this emergent violence, the conflict in Bosnia-Herzegovina. As part of the disintegration of the former Yugoslavia, the violence in Bosnia is widely regarded as perhaps the most bewildering manifestation of this larger phenomenon. Marked by violence incomprehensible from a standard strategic calculus, and with its resonances of the Holocaust, the war in Bosnia has exposed the shortcomings of conventional understandings of "intra-state" versus "inter-state" violence, and left in their place the self-serving morality of pity and victimhood that reassures us that its horrors are ethically and spatially distant.[4]

Which leads to the second impetus for this project: if conventional understandings of international violence have little purchase on the complexity of the war in Bosnia, can alternative interpretations offer more, both analytically and politically? In recent years, the discipline of international relations has been characterized by extensive debates on the merits of critical thought. Within those debates, the question of the ethical and political implications of poststructuralist thought has featured prominently. It is a question that has an importance that extends well beyond the field of international relations, and this project seeks to explore the ethical and political possibilities enabled by poststructuralist thought in the context of the Bosnian war unconstrained by disciplinary concerns.

The Ethos of Political Criticism

The logic of inquiry that informs the argument of this book is encapsulated by the idea of *political criticism* constituting an *ethos*. Although the terms *deconstruction* and *poststructuralism* have been used to this point to indicate the assumptions behind and the direction of this argument (and the former will figure significantly in subsequent chapters), thinking in terms of an ethos of political criticism best captures a crucial feature of the argument. Undertaking a critique involves an intervention or series of interventions in established modes of thought and action. Such interventions are thus positioned in a particular relationship to those practices they wish to critique. They involve an effort to disturb those practices that are settled, untie what appears to be sewn up, and render as produced that which claims to be naturally emergent. The positioning of the interventions means that there is an ethico-political imperative inherent to them, not a predetermined or established politics, but a desire to explore and perhaps foster the possibilities being foreclosed or suppressed by that which exists or is being put in place. Intervening necessarily involves a questioning of that which is established, and that questioning betrays a concern or dissatisfaction with what is settled and creates the conditions of possibility for the formulation of alternatives. It is in this context that the notion of *ethos* — which Foucault identifies as a "manner of being" or "practice" implicated in the philosophical life of Enlightenment criticism — is pivotal for the idea of political criticism.[5] Critique is not just something for the academic observer; critique is a lived experience, even for those in the most extreme circumstances, as the face-to-face encounters suggested.

Writing this argument in terms of an ethos of political criticism, for which the strategies of deconstructive thought and poststructuralism play an important part, also has an immediate practical concern. It is an attempt to resist the label of "postmodernism" being applied to the argument. Of course, given that I have no control over that, and given the increasing frequency with which "postmodernism" is used to identify an important strand of the new critical debates in international relations, this may be a forlorn hope. Nonetheless, I hope it will give pause for thought to those who would so easily place a body of disparate work under one umbrella so as to ready it for dismissal.

Reading the face-to-face encounters as moments in a deconstructive ethos signifies that what is urgently required is not the construction of a theory, much less a theory of international relations, or perhaps even less a theory of ethics for international relations. What is required is an ethos of political criticism, for those encounters reveal the attitude that Foucault understood as a "mode of relating to contemporary reality; a voluntary choice made by certain people; in the end, a way of thinking and feeling; a way, too, of acting and behaving that at one and the same time marks a relation of belonging and presents itself as a task."[6]

Concerned with assumptions, limits, their historical production, social and political effects, and the possibility of going beyond them in thought and action, the ethos of political criticism presupposes a logic of inquiry markedly different from more conventional approaches in international relations. Its function, to paraphrase Susan Sontag, is to show *how* something is what it is rather than what it means (or *why* it is what it is).[7] Which is not to suggest that the question of meaning is without importance; it is, rather, to direct our attention away from a preoccupation with a search for *the* cause or origin of something, and focus instead on the political consequences and effects of particular representations and how they came to be.

The Ethics of Political Criticism

This concern with representation is sometimes seized on by critics to argue that if the foundations of intellectual and political certainty are questioned, then there is little basis for opposing some of the worst excesses of our time. Two recent interventions by established North American international relations scholars demonstrate this.

John Ruggie, in an argument designed to bracket off any contribution so-called postmodern theorists might make to (what he termed) postmodernity, claimed via secondhand sources that within international relations postmodern theorizing has been at best "symptomatic," "preoccupied with style and method," and offers "limited substantive insight." But Ruggie attempts to drive the nail into the postmodern coffin by declaring that the "the Paul de Man saga, especially the shameful defense of de Man by several leading deconstructivists, shows poignantly how deleterious the political consequences can be that follow from the moral vacuum — if not moral vacuity — the French fries would have us inhabit."[8]

It is revealing that for one so concerned with methodology, it is the alleged ethico-politics of the position that he seeks to delegitimize that is the killer point. However, one hardly need be a defender of de Man's offensively fascist and sometimes openly anti-Semitic writings for the (then German-controlled) Belgian newspaper *Le Soir* between December 1940 and November 1942 — writings that Derrida painfully noted manifested "an alliance with what has always been for me the very worst"[9] — to recognize the anti-intellectual and highly polemical nature of Ruggie's caricature. Two brief observations on the de Man affair are pertinent to understanding Ruggie's dismissive gesture.

The first is that de Man and his wartime writings are taken by the critics (including, it seems, Ruggie) to be indissolubly linked with a body of theory, such that "the primary goal of the rage in question is a settling of accounts with 'deconstruction.' "[10] It is for this reason that the entire first half of David Lehman's book — which Ruggie cites as the basis for his argument — is concerned with deconstructive thought rather than de Man. But logic of this type, even assuming that de Man as a thinker can be said to stand in for a varied tradition assembled under the heading "deconstruction," is far from being shared by all those justifiably critical of the wartime politics of de Man (and Heidegger). With respect to the latter, Jürgen Habermas, certainly no apologist for Heidegger's politics, has argued that "Illumination of the political conduct of Martin Heidegger cannot and should not serve the purpose of a global depreciation of his thought."[11]

At the same time — and somewhat paradoxically — it can be said that deconstructive thought is not really on trial, for "it has already approved its usefulness, even in the work of many who now attack it."[12] This is, one suspects with unintended irony, abundantly evident in Lehman's book, where for all the lamentations about the perfidious influence of textuality as one of deconstruction's central ideas,[13] the focus of his argument and the target of his wrath are texts and their politics: de Man's wartime writings, and the responses of those, like Derrida, who have so outraged the critics. In this vein, it is interesting that the same angry critics who are so keen to maintain a sharp distinction between the world and the text have no hesitation in referring to de Man as an "academic Waldheim," an act of moral leveling that equates the actions of an officer in a German army unit known for its record of atrocities with the words of a newspaper columnist and reviewer.[14]

Likewise, in defending a social science epistemology (part of what Searle called "the Western Rationalist Tradition") as the best and only way for the study of international political economy, Stephen Krasner has invoked ethico-political arguments not dissimilar to Ruggie's. Krasner, although convinced of the superiority of theory building via empirical testing, is nonetheless concerned that results are partial, the findings weak, and the superiority of one paradigm over another not yet established. "Why not throw it all up," he asks, "Adopt a post-modern stance. It would be more fun if it were not necessary to muck through all that messy and ambiguous data."[15] To accept Krasner's framing of the argument—so-called postmodernism versus empirical work—in the absence of any citations to support the claim would be somewhat paradoxical. Had he been prepared to muck through all that messy and ambiguous literature, he might not have been able to make his grand assertion. To accept Krasner's framing of the argument would also involve overlooking the normativity—concealed by the "non-normative" category of the "empirical"—that is the condition of possibility for this distinction.

But what is most interesting about Krasner's argument is the way he uses ethico-political concerns to make the much-hoped-for telling blow against so-called postmodernism: "the Western Rationalistic Tradition can contest claims by testing them against empirical data. This check on the assertions of the mighty is one of the bulwarks that modern society has constructed against the ravages of political extremism. None of the evil regimes of the twentieth century—Hitler's Germany, Stalin's Soviet Union, Mao's China—has supported the Western Rationalistic Tradition." In contrast, "post-modernism provides no methodology for adjudicating among competing claims. There is no reason to think that post-modern pronouncements will exercise any constraint over those with power."[16] Krasner then concedes that "the Western Rationalistic Tradition . . . is no panacea for the prevention of evil." But

> it does offer the best hope for academicians to make a positive contribution to the larger society because it can in some instances suggest a wise course for public policy and in others demonstrate that a policy is wrong. Post-modernism, in contrast, in its more extreme versions provides no such check. On the contrary, it leads directly to nihilism which can produce an intense and burning flame but which hardly moves society towards peace and justice.[17]

It is hard to know where to begin when confronted with such statements, for they beg numerous questions and rely on various unexplicated assumptions. To be so authoritative Krasner had to avoid an engagement with any of the literature he criticizes, to overlook the reams of work in the philosophy of the natural and social sciences that problematize his account of rationalism, and to sidestep thorny historical issues concerning the way in which the political regimes he names employed scientific and social-scientific methodologies in pursuit of their unethical objectives. To wrap it up, Krasner had to assert that the goals of "peace" and "justice" govern his concern, even though most would recognize them as incapable of being determined by the methodologies he advances.

In addition to their invocation of ethico-political concerns to resolve epistemological issues, the polemics of Ruggie and Krasner illustrate the way in which responding to the policies of Nazi Germany, particularly the Holocaust, has become the test case for legitimizing some approaches over others. Arguing in support of the ethics of political criticism—an ethos employing the strategies of deconstructive thought and poststructuralism—means confronting this challenge. It is one that this book readily accepts. Indeed, the argument here will be that the ethos of political criticism and its attendant strategies are indispensable if we are to meet the ethical imperative of confronting events akin to the Holocaust.

Bosnia, the Holocaust, and Responsibility

Bosnia provides an important contemporary site for illuminating these issues, and these issues will serve as important means of understanding the war there. All parties to the violence in Bosnia, both inside and out, have at one time or another invoked the image of the Holocaust and its context to justify their actions and make demands on others for a response.

For the Bosnians the representation of the conflict as genocide was common. In the midst of the fighting, Mustafa Spahlic, a Muslim cleric, was moved to declare that "Bosnia's Muslims are the new Jews of Europe."[18] During attempts to persuade the United States and others to lift the arms embargo against Bosnia, the then prime minister Haris Silajdžić countered arguments that this would simply increase the level of violence by declaring that "this is the same argument used back in 1940, 1941, when some people wanted to bomb the rails leading to Auschwitz." Silajdžić noted that at the time some had opposed the move because it would lead to greater Nazi violence. "So, they did not bomb the rails, so the Nazis killed only six million people.... This is the same argument and the same result." The embargo, said Silajdžić, tied "the hands of a victim country.... We are trying to preserve not only Bosnia, but democracy, and that democracy is attacked by fascism."[19] The Bosnian president, Alia Izetbegović, likened Geneva negotiations to those that took place between Germany and Czechoslovakia in 1938: "Instead of Munich it is Geneva. Instead of little Czechoslovakia it is little Bosnia. Instead of negotiating for a real peace, they are negotiating for an imaginary one. And instead of Beneš, it is me."[20] In the aftermath of the war, references to the Holocaust via the notion of genocide have become the new narrative of national identity for Bosnia. Exhibitions of artwork and photos, television programs, and historical accounts designed to show the continuity of genocide document the violence against Bosnia during the war.[21]

While the Bosnians deployed the notion of genocide and cast the Serbs as the Nazis, the Serbs were busy invoking World War II analogies to shift that mantle to the Croats and the Bosnians. In a March 1992 speech to the last Congress of Serbian Intellectuals in Sarajevo, Milorad Ekmecic declared that "in the history of the world, only the Jews have paid a higher price for their freedoms than the Serbs."[22] The breakup of Yugoslavia was thus portrayed as the beginning of another Holocaust in the making for the Serbs. To ensure the responsibility for that prospect was historically located, the Serb Ministry of Information in Belgrade distributed an "expensively produced brochure... [with] page after page of old photographs of severed Serbian heads." Its title, "Never Again," invoked the purported lesson of the Holocaust, though the particular lesson they had in mind concerned atrocities committed by the Independent State of Croatia during World War II.[23] To reinforce the message, Belgrade television was much concerned in the early days of the conflict with Croatia to broadcast nightly archival footage of the Jasenovac concentration camp.[24] The return to World War II was also evident in the way the Bosnian Serb General Ratko Mladić saw the war as an effort by Germany to reinstall a sphere of influence that had been resisted fifty years earlier: "Germany sponsored the war.... It turned the Croats and the Muslims against the Serbs and set them in motion to achieve the German aim to Germanize the Balkans."[25]

Invoking World War II imagery has been an integral part of Croatia's reemergent nationalism, with the result that their opponents have been handed at least a symbolic cause for concern. Although some have objected to the scripting of the post-1991 Croatia as a reiteration of the wartime fascist regime in the Independent State of Croatia, the appropriation of Ustaša symbols—such as the name for the currency (Kuna) and the red-and-white checkerboard shield (the savhonica) on the flag—have helped produce this interpretation.[26] Moreover, among the political leadership of Croatia there has been little critical accounting for the excesses of Croatia's past. President Tudjman, a historian whose work has been overtly revisionist in its attempt to downplay the number of those killed at the Jasenovac concentration camp run by Ustaša forces, generated renewed anger with his attempt to turn the camp into a memorial for Croatian war victims, along with his suggestion that the communists were also responsible for the mass slaughter at the camp.[27] Although Tudjman has condemned the Ustaša leader Ante Pavelić for his "mistakes," he has argued that Pavelić understood Croatia's aspiration for independence and should thus be reburied along with other national figures in Croatia.[28] For external analysts, be they historians or journalists, the rich resource of World War II representations that are the obverse of those invoked in Croatian discourse—Munich, the Sudetenland, and appeasement—has been widely utilized to frame the war and the international community's (in)action.[29]

Despite the prevalence of these representations, the major diplomatic players in the Bosnian war went to great lengths to avoid invoking genocide and the Holocaust as ways of understanding the conflict. The response that would have been demanded, even legally required, had they done so was not one they cared to meet. But at one critical juncture in the war, the way in which representations are saturated by ethics became obvious for many. As the Croatian writer Slavenka Drakulić observed:

> After a year of violence, with the dead numbering approximately 200,000, with many more wounded and over two million refugees flooding Europe, there came the story of the concentration camps. And all of a sudden in a thin desperate man behind the barbed wire the world recognized not a Moslem, but a human being. The picture, the words "concentration camp" and "holocaust" finally translated the true meaning of "ethnic cleansing." At last people in the West began to grasp what was going on. It was suddenly clear that Europe hadn't learnt its lesson, that history always repeats itself and that someone is always a Jew. Once the concept of "otherness" takes root, the unimaginable becomes possible. Not in some mythological country but to ordinary urban citizens, as I discovered all too painfully.[30]

For Drakulić, this moment and its ramifications posed the ethico-political dilemma that this books takes up. How was the Holocaust possible? If we vowed "never again" and had the capacity to witness similar events fifty years later, how was it that we could once more be overcome by inaction? Why did rationalist faith not provide insurance against its historical repetition?

> Now I think I understand what I couldn't understand before: how it happened that people who lived near German concentration camps didn't do anything, didn't help... maybe the best explanation as to why people didn't stop the massacre is given by a Polish villager from present-day Treblinka [in Claude Lanzmann's documentary *Shoah*] who, in answer to the question whether they were afraid for the Jews, answered that if he cut his finger it hurt him, not the other person. Yes, they knew about the Jews, the convoys, the fact that they were taken into the camp and vanished. Poles worked their

land right next to the barbed wire and heard awful screams. "At first it was unbearable. Then you got used to it," said yet another villager, a Pole. They were Jews, others, not-us. What had a Pole to do with the fact that Germans were killing Jews?

So we all get used to it. I understand now that nothing but "otherness" killed Jews, and it began with naming them, by reducing them to the other. Then everything became possible. Even the worst atrocities like concentration camps or the slaughtering of civilians in Croatia or Bosnia. For Serbians, as for Germans, they are all others, not-us.... For Europe, the "other" is the lawless "Balkans" they pretend not to understand. For the USA it's more or less a "European problem": why should they bother with the screams of thousands of people being bombed or simply dying of hunger, when the screams can hardly be heard? Let Europe do something, aren't they working the land next to the barbed wire?

I don't think our responsibility is the same — and I'm not trying to equate the victims with those who murdered them in cold blood — all I'm saying is that it exists, this complicity: that out of opportunism and fear we are all becoming collaborators or accomplices in the perpetuation of a war. For by closing our eyes, by continuing our shopping, by working our land, by pretending that nothing is happening, by thinking it is not our problem, we are betraying those "others" — and I don't know if there's a way out. What we fail to realize is that by such divisions we deceive ourselves too, exposing ourselves to the same possibility of becoming the "others" in a different situation.... We all make it possible, we allow it to happen. Our defence is weak, as is our consciousness of it. There are no them and us, there are no grand categories, abstract numbers, black and white truths, simple facts. There is only us — and, yes, we are responsible for each other.[31]

Otherness, representation, violence, complicity, responsibility — these are some of the many provocations forced upon us by Bosnia. These are the concerns we need to find a way to address. These are the demands invoked by face-to-face encounters in extreme circumstances. These are imperatives that call forth, not an ungrounded faith in the testing of theory via evidence, but an ethically and politically committed ethos of criticism.

Can conventional approaches to ethics in international relations embody the ethos of criticism I have outlined here? It would take a sustained exercise, perhaps a book in itself, to explicate in full the limitations of more conventional approaches that I suspect exist. Two things fuel this doubt and encourage me to move ahead with an exploration of the ethical and political possibilities enabled by the ethos of political criticism. The first reservation is prompted by reading the encounters that open this book. They are moments heavily theorized in a richly prosaic manner, even though they would not be recognized as being so theorized by conventional ethical discourse.[32] They manifest an unceasing commitment to evaluation and judgment designed to encourage a nonviolent relation with others. They help demonstrate that the question of ethics in a context like the Bosnian war is always already present, not something waiting to be imported from outside.

In contrast, many if not most arguments concerning ethics and international relations exhibit a predilection for the future tense and thus imply that moral action is some way off. In the oft-heard demand for an ethical theory of international relations there is the suggestion that once we, the external analysts, find the codes, norms, or rules to guide moral action, *then* we will be able to impart them for the benefit of the relevant participants.[33] This is explicit in one of the few accounts of international ethics that discuss the Bosnian war, where Mervyn Frost has written that *"from a moral point of view the task of outsiders in a dispute like the Bosnian one is to provide a dynamic framework . . . within which the people may constitute themselves as citizens in a state or states."*[34] By adopting a traditional perspective on the stance of the analysts and the purpose of their work—that we should be external to our domain of concern and offer up theories to guide solutions for those on the inside—arguments like this diminish the way in which the attitude, ethos, or philosophical life of which Foucault speaks is an ongoing and ever present disposition for those directly involved as well as those more distanced, even if some recognize it more than others. Equally, given understandings to be developed in this book, arguments like Frost's displace the ethical as they proclaim a theory of ethics.[35]

The second concern comes from the fact that most accounts of the (im)probability of ethical action in international relations depend on the notion of a prior and autonomous sovereign subjectivity—whether it be the individual, the state, or some other corporate actor—deploying either a putatively universal moral code (the deontological view) or muddling through the situation in order to achieve what might be thought of as the best possible outcome (the consequentialist account).[36] The problem of responsibility that situations such as the Bosnian war bring to the fore—how response-ability can be fostered and exercised—cannot be fully engaged by perspectives with these commitments. That is because the normal foundations for ethical considerations in international relations—sovereign states in an anarchic realm—are often the very objects of violence in such contexts and can no longer be theoretically considered sufficient as a basis for resolution, even if their illusory permanence remains efficacious within political discourse.[37]

This limitation is apparent also in Frost's argument, which is indebted to certain assumptions about sovereignty being both desirable as a good in itself and realizable as a basis for ethical conduct. This is evident in that the most important "settled norms" he identifies as criteria for ethical action involve the always contentious and intrinsically contestable notions of state sovereignty and the preservation of the society of states.[38] When it comes to working from these commitments to an ethical perspective on Bosnia, Frost is led to conclude that "what constitutive theory recommends as the appropriate ethically grounded forms of action in cases such as Bosnia, in fact, quite closely matches the policies which have been pursued by the major external actors involved there (the United Nations, Britain, the European Union, Russia and France)."[39] This conclusion is quite breathtaking, and it reveals the problems encountered when one relies on contingent settlements of the ethical (such as state sovereignty) as supposedly secure foundations for ethical theory. What Frost is arguing with respect to Bosnia is not just that the policies of these external states were necessary, or the best options in difficult circumstances, but that they were the appropriate ethically grounded forms of action. He would find little support for that conclusion among any of the actors in Bosnia, be they combatants from any side, civil political groups overlooked by the international community, nongovernmental organizations engaged in humanitarian work, the various UN agencies, or even a good number of the representatives of those external states.

In contrast, this book aims to demonstrate that the settled norms of international society—in particular, the idea that the national community requires the nexus of demarcated territory and fixed identity—were not only insufficient to enable a response to the Bosnian war, they were complicit in and necessary for the conduct of the war itself. This is because inscribing the boundaries that make the installation of the nationalist imaginary possible requires the expulsion from the resultant "domestic" space of all that comes to be regarded as alien, foreign, and dangerous. The nationalist imaginary thus demands a violent relationship with the other. Given that all forms of community are bounded to at least some extent, no form of community is going to be totally free of such violence. But insofar as nonethnic and nonnational forms of community are more at home with difference and abjure less, they involve a less violent relationship with the other.

Making the case for this proposition requires a substantial rethinking of the categories and relationships that constitute the political imaginary of international society. This is begun in chapter 2 with a refiguring of the relationship between violence, identity, and the political. Undertaken in terms of the deconstruction of Yugoslavia, the argument outlines how an understanding of the performative constitution of identity is required to appreciate the way in which the foundations of authority for political action and community are constructed. That leads to a reconceptualization of "ethnic" and "nationalist" conflict that highlights its violent enactment of the grounds from which it claims to flow. Because there is thus buried within every naturalized rendering of political community the space for its dissimulation and transformation, it is argued that deconstructive thought is a necessary prerequisite for historical and political progress.

Not surprisingly, conventional representations of the Bosnian war do not allow for this interpretation. Indeed, because they deploy an ethnically structured way of seeing, the "Bosnia" that is materialized at the intersection of political, media, and academic accounts is a tightly ordered world expunged of contingency and flux. This misrecognition of "Bosnia" as other is bound up with a misrecognition of the self that flows from the repeated denial of the radical contingency of "our" identities and territorialities. Chapter 3 reviews the dominant narrativizations of the Bosnian war and, by exploring the politics of historical narrative in the work of Hayden White, demonstrates the exclusions on which they depend. Importantly, the criteria by which judgments can be made about and between competing narratives are also articulated. Those issues overlooked in the narratives of chapter 3 are explored in chapter 4, where different notions of ethnicity, history, and violence are detailed, and events from the Bosnian war that problematize those narratives are discussed.

In chapter 5, the response of the international community to the Bosnian war is analyzed in some detail. Through a review of the documents in which the various peace proposals were articulated, the anthropological and political assumptions behind the international community's thinking are exposed. Beginning with a consideration of the terms in which some well-known neorealist scholars of international relations proposed the partition of Bosnia, this chapter demonstrates how a specific problematization of Bosnia produced a particular solution. As this problematization was shared with at least two of the nationalist parties engaged in the Bosnian war, this chapter reveals how the peacemakers of the international community were in an alliance of political logic with some of the paramilitaries, and thus failed to provide a space for, let alone to encourage, nonnationalist forms of social and political life.

Detailing an alternative political account of Bosnia, one that would permit the ethos exhibited in the face-to-face encounters and problematize the naturalized notions of ethnic conflict and territorialized division, requires a sustained theorization of ethics, politics, and subjectivity. This is undertaken in chapter 6, through the work of Derrida and Lévinas. Its goal is to outline the political consequences of a deconstructive approach, with an emphasis on the radically democratic and multicultural possibilities it enables. Chapter 7 explicates some of what this means for the practice of politics in Bosnia, both during and after the war.

All in all, this book works from the premise that the "task of outsiders" in relation to a situation like the Bosnian war is not to prescribe analyses whose logic is implicated in the crisis, or enforce remedies that foreclose alternatives. The task for outsiders is to think outside of the political discourses through which the representation, conduct, and resolution of the war were sought. Only then can the call that issues from the face-to-face encounter with the other be addressed and better possibilities be fostered.

Two
Violence and the Political

The Deconstruction of Yugoslavia

Lord Carrington, chair of the first international conference dealing with the crisis in Yugoslavia, wrote on 20 November 1991 to the Arbitration Commission established by the European Community (EC) to deal with legal issues arising from the conflict, seeking guidance on an important matter:

> We find ourselves with a major legal question: Serbia considers that those Republics which have declared or would declare themselves independent or sovereign have seceded or would secede from the SFRY [Socialist Federal Republic of Yugoslavia] which would otherwise continue to exist.
>
> Other Republics on the contrary consider that there is no question of secession, but the question is one of a disintegration or breaking-up of the SFRY as the result of the concurring will of a number of Republics. They consider that the six Republics are to be considered equal successors to the SFRY, without any one of them or group of them being able to claim to be the continuation thereof.
>
> I should like the Arbitration Committee to consider the matter in order to formulate any opinion or recommendation which it might deem useful.[1]

When does a state exist, and how does it end? This was the issue at the heart of Carrington's questions and dealt with by the commission's work.

For the commission, the opening premise in any consideration of this matter was that "the existence or disappearance of the State is a question of fact" and thus not dependent on the declaratory policies of other states.[2] Easy though that sounds, given Carrington was forced to ask the questions he did, and that the commission was required to provide a reasoned response dependent on a range of judg-

17

ments, the issues of a state's existence are not so cut and dried. In positing the factual nature of existence and disappearance, the commission was referring to the principles of public international law that set forth the requirements of statehood. According to the Montevideo Convention on Rights and Duties of States (26 December 1933), "the State as a person of international law should possess the following qualifications: (a) a permanent population; (b) a defined territory; (c) government; and (d) capacity to enter into relations with other States."[3] As a ground for determining the course of action and argumentation in the Yugoslav context, however, these principles proved insufficient to account for developments. In the commission's reasoning, partly because of the instructions given it by the EC, political judgments rather than international legal principles came to the fore. By demanding adherence to an array of substantive policy positions—democracy, human rights, established frontiers, nuclear nonproliferation, and the peaceful settlement of disputes—and insisting on commitment to a variety of international agreements and charters, the criteria for statehood against which the claims of the former Yugoslav republics were judged went well beyond the mere application of international law.[4] Moreover, the political nature of the exercise was reaffirmed by the uneven application of the commission's conclusions, something most obvious when the EC ignored part of its advice on the recognition of Slovenia and Croatia.[5]

The political nature of the Arbitration Commission's judgment about the existence and end of Yugoslavia makes its reasoning more interesting. In the opinion requested by Carrington's questions, the commission argued that because Yugoslavia was a federal state in which the essential organs of the federation were inoperative, and because there had been a recourse to force that showed the authorities were powerless to enforce cease-fires, "the Socialist Federal Republic of Yugoslavia is in the process of dissolution."[6] In other words, Yugoslavia neither existed nor had ended.

This ambiguity was recognized by the Yugoslav authorities themselves. In a letter dated 24 September 1991 to the UN Security Council seeking a hearing on the conflict, the Yugoslav delegate asserted that "Yugoslavia can no longer simply be repaired. It should be redefined."[7] Central to this concern was the notion of state succession: if the republics were thought of as seceding, what international subject would succeed the SFRY? As the commission had noted in its first opinion on the status of the SFRY, " 'state succession' means the replacement of one State by another in the responsibility for the international relations of territory."[8] The authorities in Serbia and Montenegro wanted to constitute the succeeding subject, so on 27 April 1992 a joint session of the three parliamentary bodies from the state in question—the Parliamentary Assembly of the SFRY, the National Assembly of the Republic of Serbia, and the Assembly of the Republic of Montenegro—passed a resolution proclaiming the foundation of the "Federal Republic of Yugoslavia" as the entity that would continue "the State, international legal and political personality of the Socialist Federal Republic of Yugoslavia."[9]

This proclamation was unrecognized by the majority of other states, with the struggle over the constitution of the succeeding state represented by the battle for the international seats occupied by the former (though not formerly finished) SFRY. To try and clarify this situation, Carrington wrote again to the Arbitration Commission on 18 May 1992 and asked whether the SFRY's fluid status had been resolved such that its "dissolution [could] now be regarded as complete?"[10] After taking into account the range of political developments in the period since its prior opinion, the Arbitration Commission concluded on 4 July 1992 "that the process of dissolution of the SFRY referred to in Opinion No. 1 of 29 November 1991 is now complete and ... the SFRY no longer exists."[11] In the same vein, UN Security Council resolution 777 (19 September 1992) declared that Serbia and Montenegro should apply for UN membership, as they were unable to take over the UN seat vacated by the fact that "the State formerly known as the Socialist Federal Republic of Yugoslavia has ceased to exist."[12]

Nonetheless, active traces of the SFRY could still be found at the United Nations. This uncertainty was evident in a letter from the Under-Secretary-General and Legal Counsel of the United Nations (dated 29 September 1992) to the Bosnian UN ambassador. The Legal Counsel pointed out that while the newly proclaimed "Federal Republic of Yugoslavia" cannot participate in the work of the UN General Assembly and its various bodies, General Assembly resolution 47/1 (22 September 1992) did not terminate the SFRY's membership in the United Nations:

> Consequently, the seat and nameplate remain as before, but in Assembly bodies representatives of the Federal Republic of Yugoslavia cannot sit behind the sign "Yugoslavia." Yugoslav missions at United Nations Headquarters and offices may continue to function and may receive and circulate documents. At Headquarters, the Secretariat will continue to fly the flag of the old Yugoslavia as it is the last flag of Yugoslavia used by the Secretariat. The resolution does not take

away the right of Yugoslavia to participate in the work of organs other than Assembly bodies. The admission to the United Nations of a new Yugoslavia under Article 4 of the Charter will terminate the situation created by resolution 47/1.[13]

Contrary to the UN Security Council resolution, therefore, the SFRY neither existed fully nor had ended completely. Indeed, although there were proclamations about the end of the SFRY, the state had no end, insofar as "the end" would imply its complete dissolution prior to and separate from the inauguration of another state or states. The end of the SFRY was inextricably bound up with the emergence of five new states, none of whom could be the state to automatically succeed the SFRY. And the existence of the SFRY at the United Nations was not terminated until such time as "a new Yugoslavia" was admitted.

The advent of the new was the only thing that could finish off the old. There was thus no destruction of Yugoslavia. The process of dissolution continued after it had been declared at an end, and long after it had already given rise to new formations and different possibilities. In this sense, Yugoslavia was *deconstructed*.

To say as much is not simply to engage in a different description. It is, rather, to indicate the homologous relationship between the deconstruction of an identity like "Yugoslavia" and the precepts of philosophical deconstruction. From earliest writings, Derrida has contrasted the notion of identity as self-contained with an understanding of identity as being the effect of a contingent set of relations.[14] In terms of the latter notion, identities are negations of the multiplicity of selves and their relations with others that inhabit the settlement of the supposedly autonomous self. Accordingly, the deconstruction of Yugoslavia is a condition best understood in terms of deconstructive thought.

Deconstructive Thought and Politics

Deconstruction is a term that has entered the popular lexicon, and from there reentered academic discourse, as a synonym for nihilism and destruction.[15] To think of it as wholly negative — as simply a form of critical political practice that destroys and levels — is to miss the productive complexities it signifies, most obviously through the linkage of *de-* and *construction*. The above reading of the international legal debate that pondered the status of the Socialist Federal Republic of Yugoslavia and the new states to which it gave rise served to demonstrate that ends and beginnings, dissolutions and reconstitutions are not discrete and separate events. As such, this complex interdependence of conditions and possibilities is better represented by the idea of deconstruction than it is by the notion of destruction.[16] Which is *not* to suggest that thinking this through in these terms links deconstruction with the violence and injustice of the conflict in the former Yugoslavia in anything like a causal relationship. The latter is not the offspring of the former, despite the inclination of some to put the onus for political developments they do not like on theoretical projects they wish to oppose.[17] It is to suggest, in the first place, the need for a more nuanced understanding of deconstruction.

There can surely be no more difficult aspiration. Not because deconstruction per se is difficult to understand; rather, because it is difficult to speak of deconstructive thought as something, let alone something understandable through the formula that deconstruction *is* X or Y or Z. As Derrida has observed, "perhaps deconstruction would consist, if at least it did consist, in precisely that: deconstructing, dislocating, displacing, disarticulating, disjoining, putting 'out of joint' the authority of the 'is.' "[18] Even more, linking the name of Derrida with deconstruction is not something done without thought: "I have never claimed to identify myself with what may be designated by this name [deconstruction]. It has always seemed strange to me, it always left me cold. Moreover, I have never stopped having doubts about the very identity of what is referred to by such a nickname."[19]

Such admonitions, however, are perhaps best seen as integral to deconstructive thought rather than as cautions against "it." For what marks Derrida's various ruminations on the theme is that deconstruction signifies, on the one hand, the determinate strategies that can be variously deployed to disturb and unsettle, while, on the other hand, it marks the undecidable nature of the context in which those strategies are required to operate — as well as the process and provocation that take place in between. As Derrida has observed (albeit in a formulation that he might also disavow), "one of the definitions of what is called deconstruction would be the effort to take this limitless context [the "real-history-of-the-world"] into account, to pay the sharpest and broadest attention possible to context, and thus to an incessant movement of recontextualization."[20]

Among the procedures we can find reference to as deconstruction are "two ways or two styles, although it most often grafts one on to the other. One takes on the demonstrative and apparently ahistorical allure of logico-formal paradoxes. The other, more historical or more anamnesic, seems to proceed through readings of texts, meticulous interpretations and genealogies." In this context an important "deconstructive procedure" involves rethinking of history such that "the onto-theo- but also archeo-teleological concept of history —

in Hegel, Marx, or even in the epochal thinking of Heidegger" is subject to critical scrutiny. Such questioning has a positive intent, for it
aims not to diminish historicity "but, on the contrary, to show that
this onto-theo-archeo-teleology locks up, neutralizes, and finally cancels historicity."[21]

There are others — any number of others — that might contribute
to a denaturalization of "the real." But they are all animated by an
ethico-political concern:

> to put it in a word, they have always represented, as I see it, the at
> least necessary condition for identifying and combatting the totali-
> tarian risk.... without deconstructive procedures, a vigilant politi-
> cal practice could not even get very far in the analysis of all these
> political discourses, philosophemes, ideologemes, events, or struc-
> tures, in the reelaboration of all these questions on literature, his-
> tory, politics, culture and the university. I am not saying that, *inversely*,
> one must organize trials in the name of (singular) deconstruction!
> But rather that what I have practiced under that name has always
> seemed to me favorable, indeed destined (it is no doubt my princi-
> pal motivation) to the analysis of the conditions of totalitarianism
> in all its forms.[22]

Those strategies, animated by an antiauthoritarian spirit, are more
than just tools to be utilized by an interested bystander or a distanced
analyst. They are also elements in modes of being embodied — as the
face-to-face encounters with which the book opened demonstrate —
in the lives of individuals, even in extreme circumstances. They are
present in any number of prosaic practices that problematize through
their actions the often violent claims of self-enclosed identities. Although Amira, Ziad, and the Sarajevo taxi driver (and many of the
others mentioned in subsequent chapters) might never have read the
philosophical treatises of deconstructive thought, aspects of their
daily lives have enacted its ethos.

In this sense, the radical strategies of deconstructive thought are
required by what might be called "the ontology of deconstruction."
Perhaps a better formulation, following William Connolly, is that we
might say the procedures, tactics, and strategies associated with deconstructive thought are fostered by the onto-political assumptions
made by a deconstructive ethos. To say political interpretation is "onto-
political" highlights the way in which "it contains fundamental presumptions that establish the possibilities within which its assessment
of actuality is presented."[23] This dimension is more often than not
occluded within the human sciences, particularly by those accounts
that depend upon unacknowledged assumptions about an unprob-

lematic reality. In contrast, deconstruction is a form of "projectional interpretation" that "proceeds by projecting ontological presumptions explicitly into detailed interpretations of actuality, acknowledging that its implicit projections surely exceed its explicit formulation of them and that its explicit formulation — constructed relative to other identifiable positions — always exceeds its current capacity to demonstrate its truth."[24]

It is this form of interpretation that enables the argument in this book. One of its claims is that the projectional character of interpretation is either ignored or overlooked by conventional renderings of the Bosnian war: they inject ontological presumptions (about ethnicity, nationalism, identity, violence, etc.) into their claims of actuality without disclosing their complicity in the representational process. In contrast, the logic of inquiry embodied in this argument does not simply assert a new reality in opposition to an old account no matter how impoverished. Rather, "it challenges closure... first, by affirming the contestable character of its own projections, second, by offering readings of particular features of contemporary life that compete with detailed accounts offered by others, and, third, by moving back and forth between these two levels as it introduces alternative interpretations onto the established field of discourse."[25]

The onto-political character of deconstructive thought is manifested in those moments where Derrida speaks of deconstruction's ontology. When asked by Richard Kearney whether deconstruction can "ever surmount its role of iconoclastic negation and become a form of affirmation," Derrida's response was that "deconstruction certainly entails a moment of affirmation" not the least reason for which is that he "cannot conceive of a radical critique which would not be ultimately motivated by some sort of affirmation, acknowledged or not." The affirmation, however, does not derive from the conscious desires or intentions of a subject interested in deconstruction, but from the fact that "deconstruction is, in itself, a positive response to an alterity which necessarily calls, summons or motivates it. Deconstruction is therefore vocation — a response to a call."[26] In the Bosnian war, the call of the other has rung out loud and clear.

As the vocation roused by alterity, deconstruction's onto-political claim is that our condition can be characterized by the problematic of identity/difference, where neither term can be understood except in relation to the other, and because of which claims about secure identities, traditionally authorized grounds, and the political necessities said to flow from them are met with a critical skepticism. It is in this context that Derrida has asserted "deconstruction is neither a theory nor a philosophy. It is neither a school nor a method. It is not even a discourse, nor an act, nor a practice. It is what happens, what is happening today in what they call society, politics, diplomacy, economics, historical reality, and so on and so forth. Deconstruction is the case."[27] Deconstruction is "at bottom *what happens or comes to pass* [ce qui arrive]."[28] In the case of the former Yugoslavia, its deconstruction—as the reading that opened this chapter suggested—is what happened and came to pass. And in its passing, the deconstructive ethos of those who have contested the nationalist imaginary and its violence responded to the call that emanated from that moment.

How then might we build on this recognition and reclaim politics from the pitiful account of Bosnia discussed in chapter 1 so that we can better enable the exercise of responsibility, while at the same time paying respect to those small steps that have already been taken? The first requirement is what might be called a "properly political analysis" of the conflict in Bosnia. At issue in that context is the question of the relationship between violence, identity, and the political. The next section seeks to rethink the relationship of violence to the political along lines suggested by some of Derrida's more overtly political writings.[29] The intention is to show how the intensification of so-called ethnic and nationalist conflict in places such as Bosnia, while clearly horrific, is an exacerbation rather than an aberration of the logic behind the constitution of political community. As we shall see in chapter 4, this refigures our understanding of violence in circumstances like Bosnia.

Violent Performances

First and foremost among the onto-political assumptions of deconstructive thought is the concept of the performative constitution of identity. Rather than viewing identity—which is an inescapable prerequisite of being—as either given by intentional human activity or granted by natural extra-human forces, the idea of performativity draws attention to "the reiterative and citational practice by which discourse produces the effects that it names."[30]

Care needs to be taken, however, to distinguish this position from those concerned with the concept of "construction." To argue for the centrality of the performative constitution of identity is different from maintaining that some form of constructivism—often articulated as "all things are socially constructed"—needs to be accounted for.[31] As Judith Butler has argued, constructivist arguments tend to operate in two predominant ways. In the first, discourse becomes an omnipotent force so deterministic that "it" acts as the governing subject such that all accounts of human agency are expunged. In the second — which maintains the logic of the first, but changes the character of the subject — the volitional human agent reigns supreme and willfully engages in construction without constraint.[32]

What both these lines of argument depend on is faith in an idealist/materialist dichotomy, whereby the former (as discourse) works on and alters the latter (the material world). Such faith — commonly exhibited in those reactions to "postmodernism" that suggest it is all about ideas and language — seems quaintly anachronistic given the course of debates in political theory throughout the twentieth century. But it is a frequently iterated faith that arguing in terms of the performative constitution of identity seeks to move beyond. Identity should not be seen as an epiphenomenal product of a more substantive, material substructure. Identity functions within discourse, but in so doing, it transgresses and erases the discursive/extradiscursive distinction. As Ernesto Laclau and Chantal Mouffe have argued,

> the fact that every object is constituted as an object of discourse has *nothing to do* with whether there is a world external to thought, or with the realism/idealism opposition. . . . What is denied is not that . . . objects exist externally to thought, but the rather different assertion that they could constitute themselves as objects outside of any discursive condition of emergence.[33]

To put it in an overly simple manner, while this means that nothing exists outside of discourse, it still recognizes important distinctions between linguistic and nonlinguistic phenomena. It is just that there is no way of bringing into being and comprehending nonlinguistic phenomena except through discursive practices. It is for reasons akin to this that instead of construction we should think in terms of *materialization*, as a performative process that *"stabilizes over time to produce the effect of boundary, fixity, and surface,"* thereby moving beyond the metaphysical oppositions of idealism and materialism.[34]

The performative constitution of identity is central to rethinking the relationship between violence and the political, especially in the context of the state. Although the many discourses surrounding the state that invoke its name and declare its purpose give the appearance of simply reflecting a reality awaiting apprehension, such discourses bring that reality into being through the process(es) of materialization. From foreign and security policies to crises of intervention, immigration strategies, the protocols of treaty-making, representational politics at the United Nations, and beyond, the sites of the state's performative constitution of identity are many and varied.[35]

What all of them have in common, however, is that when pursued with respect to the grounds that give them legitimacy, the sources of authority upon which those discourses rest can be considered "mystical."[36] This is most evident in those exceptional circumstances when an entity is inaugurated. By whose authority and by what right did, for example, those who signed the American Declaration of Independence act? We might think that it was because they acted in the name of "the people." But as Derrida argues in a short but insightful reading, before the declaration invokes the authority of the people, they do not exist as a people, and those who sign have no pre-established basis for doing so:

> they do *not* exist as an entity; it does *not* exist, *before* this declaration, not as *such*. If it gives birth to itself, as free and independent subject, as possible signer, this can only hold in the act of the signature. The signature invents the signer. This signer can only authorize him- or herself, to sign once he or she has come to the end ... if one can say this, of his or her own signature, in a sort of fabulous retroactivity.[37]

The same considerations are evident in the 27 April 1992 parliamentary resolution (discussed at the outset) proclaiming the foundation of the "Federal Republic of Yugoslavia" as the entity that would succeed the Socialist Federal Republic of Yugoslavia.

What this fabulous retroactivity of authority brings to light is the way in which the founding moment that institutes the law, a constitution, or the state involves an interpretive and performative force, a *coup de force*:

> It is probable, as it might be said, that such a coup de force always marks the founding of a nation, state, or nation-state. In the event of such a founding of institution, the properly *performative* act must produce (proclaim) what in the form of a *constative* act it merely claims, declares, assures it is describing. The simulacrum or fiction then consists in bringing to daylight, *in giving birth to*, that which one claims to reflect so as to take note of it, as though it were a matter of recording what *will have been there*, the unity of a nation, the founding of a state, while one is in the act of producing that event.[38]

In this sense, the crucial point that flows from the notion of performance in the *coup de force* is temporal. It highlights the way in which something receives its interpretive justification as true after the fact.

The *coup de force* can take any number of forms. It can involve an interpretive act, a violent performance, or a symbolic enactment. In the Bosnian war, all these forms and more have been evident (as chapters 3, 4, and 5 will demonstrate). A good example of the *coup de force* as symbolic enactment is the rediscovery by Serbian populism of an Orthodox burial custom in which the mortal remains of a ruler are carried through all monasteries in the country prior to burial. In 1989 this ritual was practiced to great effect if somewhat anachronistically. The remains of King Lazar, the Serbian leader during the defeat inflicted by the Ottomans at the Battle of Kosovo six hundred years previously, were disinterred and paraded from monastery to monastery across Serbian territory. This was the "new birth of the Serbian symbolic community" that brought something into being as though it had always been there.[39] Such communal inscriptions were bolstered by other historical appropriations, and in the Serbian community, none was more important than the remembering of the genocide against its people during the Ustaša regime in Croatia.[40]

No matter how historically secure it appears, the *coup de force* remains violence without a ground "since the origin of authority, the foundation or ground, the position of the law can't by definition rest on anything but themselves."[41] Even if earlier laws, resolutions, or conditions are successfully appealed to, "the same 'mystical' limit will reappear at the supposed origin of said conditions, rules or conventions, and at the origin of their dominant interpretation."[42] Indeed, at each self-declared point of origin, at each supposedly secure ground, the discourse of primary and stable identity "comes up against its limit: in itself, in its performative power itself.... Here [at the limit] a silence is walled up in the violent structure of the founding act."[43] These features are prevalent in the context of states:

> The foundation of all states occurs in a situation that we can thus call revolutionary. It inaugurates new laws, it always does so in violence. Always, which is to say even when there haven't been those spectacular genocides, expulsions or deportations that so often accompany the foundation of states, great or small, old or new, right near us or far away. In these situations said to found law (*droit*) or state, the grammatical category of the future anterior all too well resembles a modification of the present to describe the violence in progress. It consists, precisely, in feigning the presence or simple modalization of presence. These moments, supposing we can isolate them, are terrifying moments. Because of the sufferings, the crimes, the tortures that rarely fail to accompany them, no doubt,

but just as much because they are in themselves, and in their very violence, uninterpretable or indecipherable. That is what I am calling "mystique."[44]

Bosnia is one such terrifying moment in which we have witnessed "spectacular genocides, expulsions or deportations that so often accompany the foundation of states." It is, moreover, a terrifying moment many have found "uninterpretable or indecipherable." But do the concepts of "simulacrum," "fiction," "violence without a ground," "the absence of foundations," and "mystique" offer an incisive understanding? Such notions would appear at first sight to confirm the worst fears of deconstruction's detractors, that it is beyond reason and nothing more than (in Derrida's words) "a quasi-nihilistic abdication before the ethico-political-juridical question of justice and before the opposition between just and unjust."[45] But appearances at first sight can be deceptive, particularly if they themselves are motivated by a certain desire to go beyond reasoned argument and simply dismiss that which appears alien, foreign, and strange. For at least three reasons, to speak of the interpretive and performative basis of authority is not to advocate irrationalism, injustice, or any other form of licentious anarchy.

The first reason is that within the frame of Derrida's argument, the proposition that the interpretive and performative *coup de force* gives birth to grounds that must be considered either "illegal" or "inauthentic" is rethought. To say that the foundation of authority cannot rest on anything but itself, that it is therefore violence without a ground, "is not to say that they [the grounds constituted in the *coup de force*] are in themselves unjust, in the sense of 'illegal.' They are neither legal nor illegal in their founding moment. They exceed the opposition between founded and unfounded, or between any foundationalism or anti-foundationalism."[46]

The second reason is that just as the founding of the law, or any similar foundation of authority, exceeds the normal confines of either/ or logic, so too *the authority of reason* as that which itself supposedly governs the logic of the either/or — for it is the powers of reason that are said to enable us to distinguish between the just and the unjust, and so on — exceeds these confines. Simply put (though this is very difficult to put simply), this is because reason cannot ground the authority of reason. In other words, the authority of reason itself — by which it is said that the argument above might be quasi-nihilistic, irrational, and so on — depends on a similar interpretive and performative *coup de force*.[47] This feature of reason has been forgotten (or, better, it has become a silence walled up) because of the transformation of Leibnitz's principle that "nothing is without reason" into the situation, identified by Heidegger, in which "the principle now says that every thing counts as existing when and only when it has been securely established as a calculable object for cognition."[48] This transformation-cum-deformation has meant the erosion of the distinction enabled by reason between "calculative thinking" and "reflective thinking." But, Heidegger asks, "may we give up what is worthy of thought in favor of the recklessness of exclusively calculative thinking and its immense achievements? Or are we obliged to find paths upon which thinking is capable of responding to what is worthy of thought instead of, enchanted by calculative thinking, mindlessly passing over what is worthy of thought?"[49]

For Derrida, finding those paths of thought avoided by calculative thinking is integral to uncovering the "silence . . . walled up in the violent structure of the founding act." Following explicitly both Leibnitz and Heidegger, Derrida argues that "to respond to the call of the principle of reason is to 'render reason,' to explain effects through their causes, rationally; it is also to ground, to justify, to account for on the basis of principles or roots."[50] This responding means that the first path avoided by calculative thinking that needs to be taken is to ask, "what grounds this principle [reason] which is itself a principle of grounding?" Taking that path, however, uncovers the disturbing thought that there is an "impossibility for a principle of grounding to ground itself," such that "this very grounding, then, would have to hold itself suspended above a most spectacular void."[51] Are we just left hanging? Is the much feared abyss of nihilism that critics think haunts Derrida's work inescapable at this juncture? Derrida responds to this in two ways. The first is to ask a question in the name of reason: "Who is more faithful to reason's call, who hears it with a keener ear, who better sees the difference, the one who offers questions in return and tries to think through the possibility of that summons, or the one who does not want to hear any question about the reason of reason?"[52] The answer is implicit in the question. Which produces the second response, one that tries to grapple with the necessary principle of reason and the void over which it dangles. In a spirit akin to Heidegger's view on that which is worthy of thought, Derrida argues that " 'Thought' requires *both* the principle of reason *and* what is beyond the principle of reason, the *arkhe* and an-archy."[53] It is in this context, of both invoking and questioning the limit of reason, that Derrida's thought manifests the ethos of the Enlightenment akin to the idea of political criticism discussed in chapter 1.

But what politics and what understanding of justice and responsibility, even if we accept that they flow from an adherence to thought faithful to reason, might reasonably respond to the *coup de force* that produced the silence walled up in the violence of its founding act(s)? Here—and this is the third reason—Derrida offers hope. In his view, the logical result of the walls of authority containing concealed silences is that the resultant structure (be it the law or the state) is "essentially deconstructible, whether because it is founded, constructed on interpretable and transformable textual strata ... or because its ultimate foundation is by definition unfounded."[54] In other words, necessarily built into such structures, through a founding act that has no recourse to established, prior grounds, are moments of potential undoing. This potential for dissimulation, however, is not necessarily negative. That the law or the state "is deconstructible is not bad news. We may even see in this a stroke of luck for politics, for all historical progress."[55]

How so? The argument of chapters 6 and 7, in addition to the critique that precedes them, is one response, albeit in the specific context of Bosnia. More generally, the way in which the affirmative and just character of deconstruction can be appreciated is to understand its critical relationship to the traditional grounds of authority that have restricted justice in the past. Indeed,

> a deconstructionist approach to the boundaries that institute the human subject ... as the measure of the just and the unjust, does not necessarily lead to injustice, not to the effacement of an opposition between just and unjust but may, in the name of a demand more insatiable than justice, lead us to a reinterpretation of the whole apparatus of boundaries within which a history and a culture have been able to confine their criteriology.[56]

In other words, a deconstructive approach involves critically examining the discursive processes of materialization that produce settlements—such as the idea of pre-given subjects—upon which the criteria for judgment are based. This points us down the path our thoughts need to travel and toward the goal we have in mind: how, upon recognizing the dissolution of the traditional grounds of responsibility, there remains the possibility of an ethical course that can be chartered by deconstructible subjects, particularly those who want to respond to the call of reason contained within the cry for reason emanating from the situation in the Balkans.

The next task is to consider how this understanding of violence and the political—where the violence of the *coup de force* is integral to the political, and not just located in those instances regarded as exceptional—relates to the Bosnian war. The first step is to demonstrate, as chapter 3 will argue, that the relationship between violence and the political articulated by this deconstructive account is effaced by the conventional readings of that conflict.

Three
Ontopology: Representing the Violence in Bosnia

A Clash of Narratives

During the Summer University Project in Tuzla a number of forums were held to explore current events in Bosnia. At the conclusion of one such occasion, which had been concerned with the question of refugees, a summation was offered by one of the panelists, a North American professor of the social sciences. Drawing his thoughts together, the professor talked of the difficulties encountered in "post-ethnic conflict situations." Although he used this concept without prejudice—indeed, the professor thought that it was no more than an obvious piece of social science terminology—he was somewhat taken aback to find that it provoked an immediate and angry response from one of his fellow panelists, a professor of medicine at the University of Tuzla. "What are you calling a 'post-ethnic conflict situation'? Bosnia?" With increasing vehemence, the Bosnian professor declared that such a concept was wholly mistaken. Given the conduct of the Yugoslav Army and Milošević, among others, he said, the war was clearly the product of "fascism." One could find moments of ethnic conflict as the war progressed, he conceded, but they were not the cause of the disaster.[1]

This encounter was a stark reminder of how the same events can be represented in markedly different ways with significantly different effects. For the Bosnian professor, as for many in Bosnia generally, to understand the war in terms of "fascism" is an essential element in foregrounding the political nature of the conflict. Events such as the café massacre in Tuzla—where seventy-two young people were killed by a shell on 25 May 1995—are blamed on the "Srpski fasisticki agresor."[2] For many others—be they participants in the conflict, members of the media, or academic analysts—the ideas of an "ethnic conflict," "ethnonationalist war," "ethnoreligious struggle," or the like have been seemingly natural ways of accounting for the incomprehensible. Because these representations obscure the relationship between violence, identity, and the political theorized in chapter 2, they are ultimately depoliticizing.

The angry encounter at the Tuzla forum illustrates the centrality of narrative to any understanding of complex events such as "Bosnia." The present always passes us by to become the past. Once it does, our relationship to the past, even the ever so immediate past (let alone that from which we are either spatially or temporally distanced) is necessarily mediated. More often than not, that mediation takes the form of a narrative, whereby contested events are connected in such a way as to give some meaning. In the context of the argument being made here, the narrativizing of reality is integral to the performative constitution of identity.

Introducing the concept of narrative to an appreciation of political issues requires an exploration of the arguments of Hayden White, whose philosophy of history is the touchstone for such considerations.[3] This partial but critical review of White's position will serve as the basis for appraising the various accounts of the Bosnian war.

Narrative and Its Limits

The historical profession, if it has paid any attention to White, has reacted with hostility to his philosophy. White's arguments have been tarred with the brush of "postmodernism" in a manner that echoes the conventional response to positions so represented in international relations. In his review of the sustained challenge to the goal of objectivity in American historiography, Peter Novick argues that White was caught up in the denunciations of a "neo-objectivist" or "hyper-objectivist" minority who, reacting to the wickedness associated with "the sixties," were influential in their ability to lump together "various relativistic, 'postmodern' currents into an undifferentiated and monstrous Other which had to be combatted if liberal rationalism was to survive."[4]

Given the assumptions that inform White's philosophy of history, the antagonistic reception is puzzling. Rather than being a card-carrying "pomo" (as the detractors might be want to say), White has stressed on any number of occasions the formalist and structuralist nature of his enterprise. His work is a major critique of historical realism and thoroughly antipositivist. Though some argue he has been moving in recent times in poststructuralist directions, it is far from embodying the anarchical tendencies that so frighten the critics.[5]

White's work is animated by a concern with the structure of historical consciousness, the forms of historical representation, and the authority they claim.[6] Narrative, far from being one mode of historical representation among many, is for White a "meta-code" or "human universal" for the creation of shared meaning.[7] This position is held consciously or otherwise by historians in general, he argues, as narrativity has become the sign of the profession's maturity and the paradigmatic form of reality.[8] In contrast to the annals or the chronicle—where the unadorned chronological ordering of reality is, in varying degrees, sufficient to qualify as an account of the real—history proper requires the narration of events so that they are "revealed as possessing a structure, an order of meaning, that they do not possess as mere sequence."[9] One can then distinguish between historical accounts on the basis of their reflexivity about the place of the narrative. A historical discourse that narrates—that is, "openly adopts a perspective that looks out on the world and reports it"—can be contrasted to one that narrativizes—that is, "feigns to make the world speak itself and speak itself as a story."[10]

For White, narratives are a performance. Through the operation of "emplotment," facts are structured in such a way that they become components in a particular story.[11] While White is careful to argue that historical events are different from fictional ones—the former "can be assigned to specific time-space locations, events that are (or were) in principle observable or perceivable," while the latter are "imagined, hypothetical, or invented"[12]—he wants to insist on the point that historical narratives are "verbal fictions, the contents of which are as much *invented as found* and the forms of which have more in common with their counterparts in literature than they have with those in the sciences."[13] This comes from recognizing that

> any given set of real events can be emplotted in a number of different ways, can bear the weight of being told as any number of different kind of stories. Since no given set or sequence of real events is intrinsically tragic, comic, farcical, and so on, but can be constructed as such only by the imposition of the structure of a given story type on the events, it is the choice of the story type and its imposition upon the events that endow them with meaning. The effect of such emplotment may be regarded as an explanation, but it would have to be recognized that the generalizations that serve the function of universals in any given version of a nomological-deductive argument are the *topoi* of literary plots, rather than the causal laws of science.[14]

Emplotment is thus what White terms the "fictional function" in nonfiction discourse.[15] Contrary to those who believe that a narrative simply reveals the structure that was immanent in events all along, White is concerned with the constructed nature of that immanence. The events that come to be real "are real not because they occurred but because, first, they were remembered and, second, they are capable of finding a place in a chronologically ordered sequence."[16] This recognition is occluded in conventional accounts because of the overriding impulse to moralize reality:

> this value attached to narrativity in the representation of real events arises out of a desire to have real events display the coherence, integrity, fullness, and closure of an image of life that is and can only be imaginary. The notion that sequences of real events possess the formal attributes of stories we tell about imaginary events could only have its origins in wishes, daydreams, reveries. Does the world really present itself to perception in the form of well-made stories, with central subjects, proper beginnings, middles, and ends, and a coherence that permits us to see "the end" in every beginning?[17]

Despite the plausibility of White's focus on the disjuncture between the non-narrativized state of the world and the common impulse to plot events into a story structure—a focus that recalls Foucault's injunction about the world not turning a legible face toward us—it is not difficult to see how his argument causes so much concern among those convinced that there have to be limits on the representations we can proffer for any series of events. White's conclusion—whereby foregrounding the role of narrative means facing the fact (his term) "that when it comes to apprehending the historical record there are no grounds to be found in the historical record itself for preferring one way of construing its meaning over another"—is like a red rag to the objectivist bull.[18]

But there is a paradox contained within the formulation of some events as historical that means, even if one is to disagree with large elements of White's argument, the undecidability of historical narratives and the possibility of different figurations cannot be overlooked. As White argues, for an event to be historical in the first place, it has to be open to at least two narrations of its occurrence: "Unless at least two versions of the same set of events can be imagined, there is no reason for the historian to take upon himself the authority of giving the true account of what really happened."[19] Were only one narrative to be possible, events would simply be apprehended with their true meaning automatically apparent to all. However, if—as is the case—

more than one narrative is possible, this calls forth not only a narrative rendering of reality but also the very grounds for questioning that particular narrative as only one among other possibilities. Contained within the conditions of possibility for historical narratives, therefore, is the logic by which their authenticity can be interrogated.

This paradox, and in particular White's negotiation of it, is a major problem when it is claimed that specific events — most obviously, the Holocaust — are such that they should not be treated "as constructs of the historical imaginary."[20] But as Saul Friedlander has argued, in the introduction to a seminal collection of essays on this issue, the Holocaust is an event that requires a global approach and a sustained reflection on the politics of its representation.[21] Friedlander recognizes that the need for truth is in tension with the ambiguous nature of events and language, but he is skeptical of the contribution arguments such as White's make: "notwithstanding the importance one may attach to postmodern attempts at confronting what escapes, at least in part, established historical and artistic categories of representation, the equivocation of postmodernism concerning 'reality' and 'truth' — that is, ultimately, its fundamental relativism — confronts any discourse about Nazism and the Shoah with considerable difficulties."[22] As an account of something general called "postmodernism," and White's purported links to such a project, this is more than a little problematic. But its ethico-representational concern is a useful hinge for this argument.

What Friedlander reveals is that, although most critics of White would contest his argument on epistemological grounds, in the end ethico-political assumptions and concerns are paramount. In other words, the same regulative ideals deployed by those in international relations hostile to "postmodernism" are at work here. To achieve this, Friedlander contrasts the uncertainties of representation prompted by the Holocaust with the clarity of a position stated by Pierre Vidal-Naquet. As a historian involved in public resistance to revisionist accounts that sought to deny the Holocaust, Vidal-Naquet acknowledges that historians construct — "we have become aware that the historian *writes*; that he produces space and time, being himself intrinsically embedded into a specific space and time" — but nonetheless does not want to dispense with the governing idea of reality. Vidal-Naquet is convinced that "everything should necessarily go through to a discourse; but beyond this, or before this, there was something irreducible which, for better or worse I would still call reality. Without this reality, how could we make a difference between fiction and history?"[23] To which Friedlander added, "how, indeed, can one not *wish* to ascertain the distinction between fiction and history when extreme events such as the Shoah are concerned?"[24] In both cases, it is the widely shared ethico-political *desire* that there *should* be such a distinction, rather than the conviction that such a distinction exists, or that the increasingly vulnerable epistemological criteria for such a distinction can be set forth, which secures the argument.

One of the reasons that the ethico-political has moved to the fore in place of the epistemological is that particular outcomes cannot be guaranteed by the use of specific methods. For example, in legal cases concerned with the revisionist debates about the Holocaust, Robert Faurisson, a deactivated professor of literature at the University of Lyon, has acted as an "expert witness" in the defense of Holocaust denials and neo-Nazi publishers because of his alleged authority in "text criticism." Faurisson's argument has been that because of recent literary theories that show that specific terms cannot be understood via reference to historical context, and because all meaning is indeterminate, it is not possible to see words like "resettlement" or "special treatment" in Nazi documents as code for extermination and liquidation.[25]

Such developments would seem to give grounds for those who are sure that deconstruction (presumably among the theories Faurisson had in mind) knows no bounds. But such a conclusion would be hasty, for revisionism relies heavily on objectivist logics. As Christopher Browning argues, Faurisson also works the other side of the positivist coin by claiming that such words ("resettlement," etc.) mean no more than what they literally state, a point dependent on correspondence notions of truth antithetical to deconstruction. Indeed, as Vidal-Naquet has acknowledged and White recognized, the revisionist case relies heavily on those stalwarts of rigorous empirical method, archival research, and documentary testimonies.[26] Rationalist methodologies thus offer no firm insurance against fascism.

White has confronted these issues directly, but in a way that is less than satisfactory, though for less than expected reasons. As he writes:

> It is often alleged that "formalists" such as myself, who hold that any historical object can sustain a number of equally plausible descriptions or narratives of its processes, effectively deny the reality of the referent, promote a debilitating relativism that permits any manipulation of the evidence as long as the account produced is structurally coherent, and thereby allow the kind of perspectivism that permits even a Nazi version of Nazism's history to claim a certain minimal credibility. Such formalists are typically confronted with

questions such as the following: Do you mean to say the occurrence and nature of the Holocaust is only a matter of opinion and that one can write its history in whatever way one pleases? Do you imply that any account of the event is as valid as any other account so long as it meets certain formal requirements of discursive practices?[27]

"In such questions," declares White, "we come to the bottom line of the politics of interpretation which informs not only historical studies but the human and social sciences in general." The first bottom line is ethico-political and unsurprising—the revisionist account of the Holocaust is "as morally offensive as it is intellectually bewildering."[28] The second, coming from the preeminent critic of naive historical realism, is more surprising. White, following Vidal-Naquet, suggests that the revisionists engage in "a total lie" because they often deny the very existence of the Holocaust. From that, White draws a theoretical conclusion: "an interpretation falls into the category of a lie when it denies the reality of the events of which it treats, and into the category of an untruth when it draws false conclusions from reflection on events whose reality remains attestable on the level of 'positive' historical inquiry."[29] But as others have noted, how is this notion of "positive" historical inquiry different from the objectivist historical methodology White's project undermines?[30]

White's remark recalls other moments in his writings where the seemingly boundless possibilities of narrative emplotment he often champions are instead signaled as having definite limits. For example, he has argued one such limit comes from the sense a historian has of the types of plots "that can be recognized as stories by the audience for which he is writing."[31] In this context, White says, the Kennedy assassination was unlikely to be narrated as a comedy. In a similar vein, in his own essay directly confronting the representation of the Holocaust, White declares that "in the case of an emplotment of the events of the Third Reich in a 'comic' or 'pastoral' mode, we would be eminently justified in appealing to 'the facts' in order to dismiss it from the lists of 'competing narratives' of the Third Reich."[32] This position stems from White's assertion that historical discourse can be "properly assessed in the truth value of its factual (singular existential) statements taken individually and the logical conjunction of the whole set of such arguments taken distributively." Were historical discourse to be immune to this, "it would lose all justification for its claim to represent and provide explanations of specifically real events."[33] In the end, these elements of White's position are not unlike those of critics such as Perry Anderson, who maintains that narratives are not "plenipotentiaries over the past" because of the exterior and interior limits set by a combination of the evidence and the applicability of emplotment styles.[34]

These statements provide evidence in White's arguments of "a timidity which holds him back from recognizing the discursive character of historical facts."[35] Such a situation is all the more odd when we consider that "the theory-ladenness of facts, as the jargon has it, is almost a basic postulate of philosophy of science."[36] This timidity seems to derive from White's structuralism, which assumes there are two levels of meaning in historical discourse—on the surface, the facts and their formal interpretation, combined with a deeper level of figurative language that plots those facts.[37] There is thus in White a structuralist-inspired claim that the discursive/extradiscursive opposition—exceeded in this argument by the concern with the performative constitution of identity—holds and secures the limits.

Such faith is misplaced, not least because of the common recognition that the documentary record to which historians turn for their grounded interpretations is itself linguistically mediated and imbricated with narrativized meanings, either by prior historians or the actors themselves.[38] Two examples help illustrate this. To consider the historical meaning of the Holocaust is in itself to invoke what Martin Jay calls "a post facto conceptual entity." That is, the idea of "the Holocaust" was not in use during the events that it now signifies.[39] No single person can be said to have witnessed the whole marked by this term, which counsels us to recognize that its "truth or meaning, however we fashion the relation between those two very different concepts, cannot be proved by stitching together all of the individual testimonies."[40] However, the issue of narrative is not restricted to a *post factum* shaping of events, for it was not straightforward "facts" that shaped the actions of both killers and victims in the Holocaust: "it was the structural, mythological, and figurative apprehension of these facts that led to action taken on their behalf," which means that "world views may have both generated the catastrophe and narrated it afterwards."[41]

Likewise, to think about the events that took place at Srebrenica in July 1995 is to confront the impossibility of escaping narrativity. Aside from the recognition that "Srebrenica" has become, because of the events, one of those historically pregnant names that mark much more than a place on a map, any encounter with the events symbolized by it involves an indebtedness to narrativity. For Bosnians, it was an instance of "ethnic cleansing" or "genocide"; for Serbs it was a "battle." For nobody was it simply a place where people "were killed," a figuration, bland though it seems, that nonetheless implies different entailments and responsibilities than saying, for example, "people died there." These considerations and situations might lead us to draw a distinction between the "micronarratives" of the participant-interpreters and the "macronarratives" of the observer-interpreters, but they do not license us to posit a narrative-free and interpreterless zone of reference to legitimize and stabilize particular understandings.[42]

White's invocation of the limits that allegedly avoid the seemingly boundless possibilities of plots is thus an unsatisfactory and unsustainable resolution to an important dilemma. Given the inevitability of narrativization at both participant and observer levels, not to mention the frequent involvement of observer accounts in participant practices, how can we judge between competing interpretations? This is perhaps *the* most significant conceptual point raised by this discussion, and it is a central concern of this argument. It will receive its most sustained treatment in chapter 6, but some reflections, which will help direct the later analysis, need to be made here. Somewhat paradoxically, White's argument can provide a starting point.

What led White to posit limits to narrative possibilities was the concern that his much quoted argument about evaluation and justification — in short, that one can find no grounds within the historical record for preferring one account over another — was insufficient in the face of historical events like the Holocaust. However, if we go back to his earlier formulations of this argument, an interesting point emerges. In *Metahistory,* White wrote that "when it is a matter of choosing among these alternative visions of history, the only grounds for preferring one over another are *moral* or *aesthetic* ones. . . . Placed before the alternative visions that history's interpreters offer for our consideration, and without any apodictically provided theoretical grounds for preferring one over another, we are driven back to moral and aesthetic reasons for the choice of one vision over another as the more 'realistic.' "[43] Similarly, in the context of exploring the ideological implications of different emplotments, White declares that "in my view there are no extra-ideological grounds on which to arbitrate among the conflicting conceptions of the historical process and of historical knowledge appealed to by different ideologies. For, since these conceptions have their origins in ethical considerations, the assumption of a given epistemological position by which to judge their cognitive adequacy would itself represent only another ethical choice."[44]

The suggestion that aesthetic grounds might constitute an appropriate arena for appeal has been widely criticized, not least because, as White concedes, it is usually associated with fascist ideologies.[45] But the alternative site of *moral* grounds that White mentions has not attracted much direct attention. This is something of a mystery when one considers that those critical of the epistemological dimensions of approaches such as White's—I have in mind the critics of "postmodernism" in international relations discussed in chapter 1, as well as the contributions of Friedlander and Vidal-Naquet mentioned above—invoke ethico-political considerations (invariably with reference to the Holocaust) to finalize their claims. If moral grounds operate effectively and ethically in those circumstances, could they not do so in others?

This, of course, begs the question of what would constitute moral grounds. Let us turn to an argument made by Amos Funkenstein for possible direction in this regard. Funkenstein asks the crucial question: "what makes one story more 'real' than another? Or, in another variation, what distinguishes a legitimate revision from a revisionist confabulation?" His thoughts prompted by this bear the traces of both White and Vidal-Naquet:

> No historiographical endeavour may presume to "represent" reality—if by representation we mean a corresponding system of things and their signs. Every narrative is, in its way, an exercise in "worldmaking." But it is not arbitrary. If the narrative is true, reality, whatever its definition *must* "shine through it" like Heidegger's being—and, like the latter, without ever appearing directly.... Closeness to reality can be neither measured nor proven by a waterproof algorithm. It must be decided from case to case without universal criteria. Everything in a narrative—factual content, form, images, language—may serve as indicators.[46]

Once more we can note the desire rather than the certainty associated with this notion of reality. But while everything within a narrative may be means for that narrative's closeness to reality, in the end Funkenstein poses the rhetorical question, "how could we discriminate between a genuine narrative and a counternarrative unless by a criterion outside the narrative?"[47] This question is motivated by the need to respond to a historiographical genre Funkenstein calls "counterhistories"—those accounts that use their opponents' key sources against their grain for polemical purposes.[48] At first glance, such narratives might seem to embody an important element of the critical ethos, except that what Funkenstein is focusing on are those counterhistories that aim to distort their opponents' self-image, identity, and memory. In this context, the revisionist accounts of the Holocaust are exemplary instances of violent counterhistories. The issue, then, is how can such a counterhistory be judged and by what criterion external to the narrative? Funkenstein can be read as positing a moral ground of the sort White might have intended: *these narratives should be judged in terms of the relationship with the other they embody.* Revisionist accounts of the Holocaust seek to destroy the identity of the other, and this should be the grounds upon which they are delegitimized. Political arguments within Israel that negate Palestinian political identity are, says Funkenstein (a Zionist and a historian), to be abhorred and opposed. For in all instances "by destroying the identity of the other we will destroy our own."[49]

In this ethical imperative, one consistent with the impulse that animates deconstruction, lies the potential basis for evaluating and judging competing narrative interpretations of the Bosnian war. Which should not surprise us, for it is this ethical imperative that flowed through the face-to-face encounters with which this book opened.

The Narratives of Participant-Interpreters

The inescapability of narrativity is the condition that has made it necessary to explore the ethico-political criteria for evaluation and judgment of competing narratives. This condition, an especially acute condition in the realm of politics, requires us to reconsider the way in which we understand the relationship between political practices and our interpretations of them. We can no longer place faith in the epistemological security of an extradiscursive domain, a narrative-free and interpreterless zone of reference, to stabilize particular understandings via their correspondence to "facts." Therefore, as suggested above, it might be useful to draw a distinction between the "micronarratives" of the participant-interpreters (the political actors) and the "macronarratives" of the observer-interpreters (the media and academics) and explore the relationship between them.

Such a formulation is not without a number of difficulties. The spatial implications of micro-/macro-levels might draw us toward the notions of correspondence we are trying to overcome. And the suggestion of a difference between "participants" and "observers" (while insisting that both are nonetheless "interpreters") could delineate more clearly than is either necessary or possible a distinction between two realms of discursive practice. That said, this formulation can usefully direct our attention to the way in which the evaluation of narratives involves some form of negotiation between different orders of narrativity so as to ensure — as both White and his critics desire — that historical and political representation is not "an utterly arbitrary concoction."[50] As Jay argues, however, "the *telos* of the process of negotiation is not . . . perfect congruence between the two narratives, that of the actors and that of the historian, for such a goal is impossible to obtain."[51] This is the case because meaning is not uniform for those involved in the historical events we are considering, and the accounts of later observers are shaped by considerations unknown to the participants. There is thus no escaping the difficulty and necessity of intersubjective judgment, both in relationship to the community of participants about whom one is writing as well as to the community of citizens and/or scholars for whom such accounts are written. Whether that process of judgment can be best rendered in terms of Habermas's communicative account (as Jay argues) or Derrida's deconstructive decision (as is argued here) is also a matter for debate.

With these concerns in mind, the following sections will consider how the disparate narrative orders — micronarratives of the political participants (whether local, regional, or international) and the macronarratives of the media and academic analysts — have represented the conflict in Bosnia. In considering the relationship between these disparate orders, the argument will be concerned with whether the macronarratives go beyond the limits suggested by the micronarratives, or whether they have been restricted by their sense of the limits associated with the latter, such that other narrativizations of the political and historical field have been underplayed or ignored.

The Bosnian Actors: Serbs versus the Government

For the Bosnian Serb community, the conflict has been a "civil war" involving an "ethnic struggle" between groups who cannot, and do not want to, live together.[52] It leads not to "ethnic cleansing" but to "ethnic displacement — people want to leave."[53] This is the official line, as the various counsel putting the Serbian/Yugoslav position to the International Court of Justice in 1993 made clear. Responding to the arguments of the Bosnian representatives — who were seeking an order preventing Serbia and its allies from enacting genocide — Ljubinko Zivkovic (a diplomat at the Yugoslav embassy in The Hague) told the court that the conflict was a "civil war" in which the "ferociousness of the international and inter-religious fighting ... has taken on immense proportions. . . . what we have on our hand is a clear-cut case of civil war among the peoples of a former Yugoslav republic, which is composed of Muslim, Serbian and Croat population." "Ethnic cleansing," argued Zivkovic, is therefore no more than "plain violence, perpetrated by all sides in this civil war."[54] Once the fighting had been halted by the Dayton accords, Milošević concluded that "in a civil war like the one in Bosnia, there are no winners and there can be no winners. . . . All are losers and peace is the only victory."[55]

But before the Bosnian Serbs were sidelined by the diplomatic maneuvering at Dayton, they had made clear the way in which the "civil/ethnic" war involved an assertion of the nexus between territory and identity. As the deputy commander of Bosnian Serb nationalist forces, General Milan Gvero, has proclaimed, "We say everybody has to live on his own territory, Muslims on Muslim territory, Serbs on Serbian.... This [Serb areas in Bosnia] is pure Serbian territory, and there is no power on earth that can make us surrender it."[56] To reinforce the point, the Bosnian Serb commander General Mladić has declared that "borders are drawn with blood."[57]

While this sounds like an implicit admission of responsibility for the conflict, the Serbian view—both in Serbia proper and Bosnia—is that they are victims, not aggressors; liberators, not conquerors. If conflict is required, it is because Germany, the Vatican, and the United States have supported an independent Catholic Croatia and a Muslim Bosnia, thereby threatening the Serbs as before.[58] Indeed, General Ratko Mladić claimed that the NATO air strikes of August 1995 were more brutal than Hitler's April 1941 raid on Belgrade.[59] To keep the connection in front of their soldiers, Bosnian Serb barracks in Bosnia have been adorned with posters showing soldiers in swastika-adorned uniforms and declaring, "Are You Ready for Deutschmocracy?" alongside others with the green paint signifying Islam spilling over the blue flag of the European Union.[60]

Religious symbolism has figured prominently in Serbian rationales for the fighting. Although it is "the Muslims" who have been made synonymous with one faith, it is the Serbs who have most vigorously connected religion and nationalism, especially in their use of the Serbian Orthodox cross bracketed by the Cyrillic letters for their motto "Only Unity Can Save the Serbs."[61] Serbian Orthodox church leaders—most notably the head of the church, Patriarch Pavle—have given their blessing to Bosnian Serb strategies.[62] Such endorsements brought Greek military volunteers to fight alongside the Bosnian Serbs "in the name of Orthodoxy."[63] In the aftermath of Serbia's acceptance of the Vance-Owen plan and its rejection by the Bosnian Serbs, Radovan Karadžić argued that the struggle was along the fault lines of faith: "we realize that now we are completely alone and that only God is with us, although we are defending Christianity against militant Muslim fundamentalism."[64] When the Dayton agreement retained the town of Gorazde as part of the Federation of Bosnia-Herzegovina, with a narrow corridor running through Republika Srpska and connecting it to Sarajevo, the senior Serbian leader of a neighboring town expressed his opposition to the arrangement by asking an American journalist, "would you allow Iran to run a corridor through the heartland of the United States?"[65]

It is because of, and in response to, such external provocations that Borislav Jović (then vice president of Milošević's Serbian Socialist Party) argued that "the Serbs fought for centuries to live in one state.... That state was Yugoslavia. We suffered great injustices in it—economic and political—but it was ours, and we sought to protect it."[66] In a similar vein, Vojislav Šešelj, commander of a Serbian nationalist paramilitary organization, declared that "we have been fighting for 1,000 years, 1 million Serbs gave their lives, and what is ours, we will not give up." And to underscore that commitment, Šešelj threatened that "each dead Serb should be paid for with the lives of at least 100 Muslims."[67]

Not all Bosnian Serbs were represented by Karadžić and the Serbian Democratic Party (SDS), and those outside that orbit held some rather different views. The Serb Civic Council, an organization that supported both the sovereignty of the Bosnian republic and the government led by Alija Izetbegović throughout the war, issued a statement in July 1995 that exhibited rather different understandings. It is worth quoting in its entirety:

> The Serb Civic Council [SGV] of Bosnia-Hercegovina has issued a proclamation to the Serb people in Bosnia-Hercegovina. This is a time of historic change for all the people of Bosnia-Hercegovina. The fate of all its citizens is to be decided, regardless of their political beliefs, ethnicity and religion. The war has set Bosnia back severely. It has set back and made difficult the tradition of tolerance, it has distorted the human face and reduced human dignity to below the [words indistinct]. Only peace brings hope, and opens the possibility for a better future. Serb people of Bosnia-Hercegovina, join the struggle for peace, for the end to the war, for a just and peaceful solution to the Bosnian drama, for the return of the expelled and displaced, for a Bosnia-Hercegovina as our common home. This means the acceptance of the Contact Group peace plan, and the construction of Bosnia-Hercegovina as the common state of equal citizens and nations living there. It is well known that the Pale regime, isolated from the entire world, is not supported by the entire Serb nation, or the leadership in Serbia. Is it not senseless for Serb sons to continue dying for the insane idea of an ethnically clean Serb state in Bosnia-Hercegovina, and beyond in the Yugoslav region? It is senseless since this same Serbia is populated by 35% of non-Serbs. Serb people of Bosnia-Hercegovina, reject the policy of war and ethnic cleansing, and support those who are for peace and against war, for justice against injustice, for return against expul-

sion, for a quiet life against crime. Act in the best tradition of your people, justly and humanely.

Do you know, you legion of Serb women in black, why your children have died, why your husbands and brothers have died, and who is hunting down your dearest in Serbia, and forcing them into the Bosnian slaughterhouse? Those who have dragged them into the war will stop at nothing to stay in power, escape justice and hold on to their stolen and cursed war booty. Do you know where their children are now? Serbian people, protect your hearths and help others to return to theirs; no-one needs ghost towns and villages, overflowing with graveyards, closed factories and deserted schoolhouses. Ask yourself: Is it not the Pale policy that is leading you precisely in this direction? The peoples of Bosnia-Hercegovina have freedom-loving and honourable anti-fascist traditions; we call on you to turn to these traditions. Bosnia-Hercegovina is an internationally recognized state, its legitimate authorities guarantee equal human and civil rights for all people, irrespective of their ethnic allegiance and religious belief. The sooner you opt for mutual coexistence and put your trust in the multinational, common and legitimate authorities of the Republic of Bosnia-Hercegovina, the sooner we will see peace for all peoples in the country and state of Bosnia-Hercegovina.[68]

The SGV statement rejects the ethnicization of Bosnian politics, supports the sovereignty of the Republic of Bosnia-Herzegovina, and endorses the rights guaranteed to all citizens of the state by its legitimate authorities. As such, the SGV's representation of the conflict is contrary to the notion of a "civil/ethnic war." It is more akin to the view expressed by a Bosnian army commander. The war, he said, is "about civilization. It's not an ethnic war; it's a war of ordinary people against primitive men who want to carry us back to tribalism."[69]

Contrary to the Bosnian Serb nationalists who saw in an Izetbegović-led Bosnia the emergence of a Muslim state, the official statements of Izetbegović and the Bosnian government have stressed the nonethnic, multireligious character of the state. Speaking in 1990, Izetbegović declared that "we are not on the road to a national state, our only way out is toward a free civic union. This is the future. Some people may want that [to make Bosnia a Muslim state] but this is not a realistic wish. Even though the Muslims are the most numerous nation in the republic, there are not enough of them. They would have to comprise about seventy per cent of the population."[70] Speaking in Sarajevo at the presentation of the Hagaddah (an invaluable fourteenth-century Jewish prayer book), attended by Jewish, Islamic, Catholic, and Orthodox leaders in April 1995, Izetbegović called on

them to "stay in this country, because this is your country. . . . Our goal
is that this becomes a tolerant community of all religions and nationalities."[71] This possibility rested on resistance to those enemies who
insisted on "one-national, one-religious and one-party states."[72] The
constant invocation of this position is sometimes mocked by Sarajevans who speak of "multi-multi-multi-" to refer to the ethos enunciated by Izetbegović.[73] Although some officials no doubt deployed the
notion of multiculturalism for rhetorical effect, the complex and hybrid nature of Bosnian identity (to be discussed in chapter 7) embodies a commitment to heterogeneity that exceeds such tactics.

The Bosnian government's representation of the conflict is thus
markedly different from the Bosnian Serbs, and involves two aspects.
The first is evident in the use of terms like "terrorism," "aggressor terrorist Serbs," and "terrorist Serb military forces" to characterize the
enemy.[74] The implication is that legitimacy and statehood rest with
one side, the initiative for unlawful aggression with the other. As a
result, humanitarian aid alone was insufficient because Bosnia "is
not facing a natural disaster."[75] The second representation, as noted
in chapter 1, is that of "genocide."

As the application to the International Court of Justice by the Bosnian government representative argued, invoking the formulation of
the Genocide Convention of 1948, "not since the end of the Second
World War and the revelations of the horrors of Nazi Germany's 'Final Solution' has Europe witnessed the utter destruction of a People,
for no other reason than they belong to a particular national, ethnical, racial and religious group as such."[76] The specific argument was
that "the rump Yugoslavia, with its agents and surrogates, has killed
Bosnian citizens because of their Bosnian nationality or because of
their Muslim religion, or both."[77] The motive for this aggression was
articulated by the Bosnian Foreign Minister Muhamed Sacirbey in
these terms: "As the Communist regimes of Eastern Europe began to
crumble, the political, military and bureaucratic power structure in
Belgrade needed to identify a new philosophy that would allow it to
maintain its absolute power and privilege. The answer was fascism."[78]

Official Bosnian representations, and those that supported them,
have rarely departed from the political register to make points concerning ethnicity. But in response to an extraordinary intervention by
the UN negotiator Thorvald Stoltenberg, an argument that had exclusive ethnic connotations did emerge. Stoltenberg, who was working
in tandem with Lord Owen (who himself had observed the conflict
was "a civil war with elements of aggression") to negotiate a settle-

ment to the war, gave a lecture in Norway on 31 May 1995 in which he endorsed a civil war view by saying that most if not all of the people in Bosnia were Serbs: Serbs who had converted to Islam or dress like Croats.[79] In response, one outraged Sarajevan wrote that "you would know that Muslims (Bosnians) and Croats have their ethnic origin, their past, their present, and that they are not Serbs."[80] As with all exclusivist projects, it is claims about the past, designed to naturalize the present, that are often the most important, and the response to Stoltenberg brings out an important representation for Bosnia; that is, the idea of a polity ever present through historical time called Bosnia. It has been represented pictorially by the stamp designers for Bosnia, who have issued a "a regular-sized, thirty-five Bosnian dinar stamp . . . [which] shows a map representing 'The Bosnian State's Development in the Middle Ages' with no less than five color-coded territories and two dozen medieval towns marked, along with today's Bosnian borders."[81] Likewise, in various arguments supporting Bosnian sovereignty in relation to Serbian aggression, the claim is made of "centuries of a common Bosnian identity," with "its own very distinct history and culture," a state that has existed as a "coherent entity for centuries," a country that has been multicultural "for six hundred years."[82] Many who have argued the pro-Bosnian position have thus often engaged in a logic of identity politics similar in form if not content to those they are opposing.

The International Community

As a set of actors, the international community—in this case, the politicians and military who were engaged with the Bosnian war—is as diverse as could be imagined. Yet in their interpretation of the conflict, they adhered to and invoked a very limited range of representations. Moreover, they are representations that have had more in common with the Serbian position than that of the Bosnian government. As Anthony Borden argued in 1993, "the official peace process under the auspices of the United Nations and the European Community has become deeply infected with the view of the conflict as among three ethnic 'sides' with ancient and essentially irresolvable animosities."[83]

This was evident from President Bill Clinton's inaugural address in January 1993, where he spoke of a world "threatened still by ancient hatreds and new plagues."[84] Secretary of State Warren Christopher opined that the conflict is "really a tragic problem. The hatred between all three groups—the Bosnians and the Serbs and the Croatians—is almost unbelievable. It's almost terrifying, and it's centuries old. That really is a problem from hell."[85] After failing to convince the Europeans of the virtue of the "lift and strike" policy—the proposition that the arms embargo against Bosnia should be lifted and allied airpower used to threaten and/or strike Serbian positions—Christopher expanded on this theme in congressional testimony. He told the House Foreign Affairs Committee that the conflict was a "morass" with "atrocities on all sides," and a manifestation of "ancient ethnic hatreds." As were his remarks on television two months previously, Christopher's account was premeditated. A few hours before going to Capitol Hill, Christopher's staff asked the relevant desk in the State Department to provide examples of atrocities committed by Muslims in Bosnia. Those who dealt with the request pointed out the differences between the isolated war crimes of individual Bosnians and the systematic policy of the Bosnian Serbs, but these objections did not deflect Christopher from assigning equal culpability to all.[86] In response to a congressman who argued that ethnic cleansing was akin to genocide, Christopher maintained that "it's been easy to analogize this to the Holocaust, but I've never heard of any genocide by the Jews against the German people."[87]

In distancing official American understandings of the Bosnian war from the Holocaust, Christopher was moving away from a position argued on occasions by Clinton. As a presidential candidate, in the wake of international publicity revealing the Serbian camps in August 1992, Clinton had argued that "if the horrors of the Holocaust taught us anything, it is the high cost of remaining silent and paralyzed in the face of genocide."[88] Similarly, when asked at a press conference on 23 April 1993 whether as president he saw a parallel between ethnic cleansing in Bosnia and the Holocaust, Clinton replied that "ethnic cleansing is the kind of inhumanity that the Holocaust took to the nth degree. The idea of moving people around and abusing them and often killing them, solely because of their ethnicity, is an abhorrent thing, and it is especially troublesome in that area where people of different ethnic groups lived side by side for so long together."[89] Having articulated this position, which was also contrary to the historical determinism of Christopher's later arguments, Clinton nonetheless argued that the United States should not become involved as a partisan in the conflict. When pressed to account for the contradictory notion that in the face of Holocaust-like activity the world power the President claimed should lead could not take a partisan stand, Clinton argued that the goal of U.S. policy was "to figure out whether there is some way, consistent with forcing the people to resolve their own difficulties, we can stand up to and stop ethnic cleansing."[90]

The remarks of Clinton and Christopher were made after the International Court of Justice issued an order on 8 April 1993 containing three provisional measures relating to the Genocide Convention. The order was given little coverage in the United States and was not referred to by the administration to support its position. Indeed, when the order was made, the State Department argued in prepared responses that there was in the order "no finding whether acts of genocide have in fact been committed." In this and other circumstances, the administration continued to emphasize its opposition to ethnic cleansing but went no further than arguing Serbian crimes "border[ed] on genocide," were "tantamount to genocide," or constituted "acts of genocide" — anything other than being genocide itself.[91] While a good number of American politicians outside the administration represented the conflict in terms of genocide, the administration's desire to avoid the obligations associated with the concept was supported by other rationales.[92] One argument, made in a now infamous State Department lunch on 28 April 1993 between Peter Tarnoff, Tim Wirth, and Elie Wiesel (the latter of whom was pressing the ethical case concerning Bosnia), was that "'the survival of the fragile liberal coalition represented by this Presidency' was a higher stake than any moral obligation to intervene" in the conflict produced by understanding it as genocide.[93] Another argument, made by Christopher in June 1993, was to emphasize that Bosnia "involves our humanitarian concerns, but it does not involve our vital interests."[94]

Highlighting "ethnic cleansing" and "humanitarian concerns," rather than "genocide" and "vital interests," was a manifestation of the privilege accorded to the notion of "civil war" in place of "international aggression." Throughout 1994 and 1995, it remained prominent in American accounts. Prior to the February 1994 market bombing in Sarajevo, when the French government was calling on the United States to press the Bosnian government to accept a partition plan, Clinton expressed his administration's hesitation to do so by saying, "I don't think the international community has the capacity to stop people within that nation from their civil war until they decide to do it."[95] At the end of that year, when U.S. Secretary of Defense William Perry declared that the Serbs had effectively won the conflict with their capture of 70 percent of the republic, the White House Chief of Staff told reporters after a National Security Council meeting that the United States had concluded that Bosnia was nothing other than a "civil war."[96] And only a month before the violence of Srebrenica, Clinton was reinvoking notions of ancient hatred and historical fatalism.[97]

The representational components of the civil war discourse—
"ethnic hatreds," "warring factions," "ancient animosities," and so
on—remained prominent even after the United States made the running to negotiate an end to the conflict in the latter stages of 1995,
and even after events at Srebrenica had spurred the reinvocation of the
genocide script. The chief U.S. negotiator in that process, Richard Holbrooke, maintained that the war "is about land . . . and, of course, ethnic hatreds."[98] In his address to the nation rallying support for the
Dayton agreement, Clinton emphasized the civil/ethnic dimensions
but also invoked the World War II script of the Holocaust. He began by
noting that "last week the warring factions in Bosnia reached a peace
agreement as a result of our efforts in Dayton, Ohio." The four years of
"terrible war" in Bosnia called forth the past: "horrors we prayed had
been banished from Europe forever have been seared into our minds
again: skeletal prisoners caged behind barbed-wire fences, women and
girls raped as a tool of war, defenseless men and boys shot down in
the mass graves, evoking visions of World War II concentration camps,
and endless lines of refugees marching toward a future of despair."[99]
Congressional opposition to the administration's decision to send
U.S. forces to Bosnia to police the Dayton agreement invoked history
to support their position. According to one Republican who was a
spokesperson chosen by the leadership: "I see no reason to send
young men over there to lose their lives over something we can do
nothing about. These people have been fighting for centuries."[100]

Throughout the conflict, one fear held by American and European leaders resonated with Serbian rationales for their activities in
Bosnia and underscored the civil/ethnic war representation: the notion that Bosnia might become an Islamic force in or near Europe. This
idea was indirectly invoked by U.S. analysts when they expressed concern that the UN plan for safe havens in Bosnia might create "six little
West Banks in Western Europe with enormous problems."[101] In France,
Gaullist leaders worried about "the emergence of a kind of Gaza strip
in the midst of the Balkans." Anxiety about "Bosnian fundamentalism" has also been invoked by those who sought to use the arguments to build support for Bosnia. Thus, Margaret Thatcher argued
that if the West failed to intervene, "embittered Bosnians will be driven
toward fundamentalism, forming an 'Islamic timebomb' in the soft
underbelly of Europe."[102] Revelations about the Clinton administration's decision to acquiesce in or encourage arms shipments to the
Bosnian government from Iran, Saudi Arabia, Pakistan, and Turkey
and the presence in Bosnia of small numbers of *mujahideen* and Iran-

ian special forces provoked angry responses that emphasized the Islamic threat this was said to have encouraged.[103]

If the closer proximity of military forces to the Bosnian war might suggest their representations of the conflict were less mediated by the figurations favored by the politicians, there is good reason to believe otherwise. In his repeated clashes with American officials who favored the use of airpower, UN Protection Force (UNPROFOR) commander General Michael Rose's opposition was founded on the assumption that the United Nations could not be used to alter the military balance in a civil war, much less a "confused civil war situation."[104] This understanding was manifest each time the United Nations referred to the protagonists in Bosnia as "the warring factions."[105] More often than not, those "factions" were identified on an ethnic register. When UNPROFOR released leaflets in airdrops throughout Bosnia on 31 December 1994 in support of a recently signed cease-fire, the leaflets explained that "Bosnian Serbs" and "Bosnian Muslims" signed a historic agreement and urged people everywhere to respect the truce, thereby denying legitimacy to the Bosnian government.[106]

The invisibility of Bosnia made possible by the "civil/ethnic" war account has been underscored in strategic assessments by the invocation of the ancient animosities thesis. The *New York Times* reported in February 1994 that UN commanders considering a peace plan for Sarajevo "acknowledge that they face fears and hatreds going back not just the last 22 months of combat, but hundreds of years of mountain traditions of banditry and guerrilla warfare, intensified by fierce bonds of religion and nationalism."[107] During a U.S. Senate Armed Services Committee hearing, the senior intelligence officer for the Joint Chiefs of Staff was asked why the people in Bosnia have a propensity for conflict. He replied: "Sir, I wish I had the answer to your question . . . but there is certainly a history going back, at least in my study of the problem, as far back as the thirteenth century, of constant ethnic and religious fighting among and between these groups."[108]

Narratives of Observer-Interpreters
The Media

That "hatred is the only constant" has been as pervasive a tendency among observers as the military and politicians alike.[109] News reports have repeatedly spoken of the way in which "Serbs savor ancient hatreds," how "Balkan hatreds defy centuries of outside meddling," the way the end of the Cold War has seen a "conflict born of old grievances" such that "the contagion" of "Europe's new tribalism could infect us all."[110] Tellingly, such representations persisted in the run-up to, and analysis of, the Dayton agreement. The *New York Times* editorialized that Dayton represents "the imperfect political resolution of a conflict that, while launched by cynical politicians, quickly brought into play ancient ethnic animosities."[111]

The media's representations thus go beyond simply repeating those on whom they rely for the story. They authorize and circulate representations in their own right, sometimes through editorials, other times through the journalist's voice (as in news stories that begin with statements like, "Efforts to persuade Bosnia's warring factions to resume peace talks...").[112] Commentators are especially significant in this regard, though whether they are arguing for or against a particular proposition does not always matter. Thus, A. M. Rosenthal sought to explain away the conflict with the argument—not dissimilar to that of Thorvald Stoltenberg, noted earlier—that it was a war between "Serbian Muslims" and "Serbian Christians."[113] Rosenthal's fellow *New York Times* columnist William Safire argued some two weeks later in a piece sympathetic to Bosnia (with terms reminiscent of Samuel Huntington's "clash of civilizations" thesis) that its "choice, in extremis, is stark: surrender or fight. The Muslim decision, to the irritation of the Christian West, is to fight."[114] The contrasting intentions but shared terms of these interventions manifest the media's reliance on and perpetuation of a geopolitical discourse to comprehend Bosnia, one that effects "a structured way of seeing" that foregrounds essentialist categories and testifies to the lack of a language for hybridity.[115]

The seeming need to categorize Bosnia in terms of one or more fixed identities is, of course, hardly restricted to the print media.[116] The "civil/ethnic" representation has flourished just as well in the electronic domain. One instance from British television, told by Lee Bryant (the former press officer for the Bosnian embassy in London) to a newspaper columnist, provides an illuminating example. Although Bryant found it difficult to get Bosnians interviewed by BBC television's *Newsnight* program, he

> did manage to get one of his Bosnian friends on to *Newsnight* recently. The man was ethnically a Croat, as Bryant informed the producers several times; nevertheless, when the programme went on Kirsty Wark [the presenter] referred to her interviewee as a Muslim. Bryant objected, but to no avail. Viewers, he was told, believe that the terms "Bosnian" and "Muslim" are synonymous, and any departure from this rule would only confuse them.[117]

The Academy

The representations that have dominated political, military, and media discourse are more limited than those offered by the participants in the conflict. The predominance of an ethnic register, with its associated historical assumptions and religious associations, has marginalized the political account offered by the Bosnian government as well as nonnationalist forces, such as the Serb Civic Council. Most strikingly, this reliance on a largely ethnic account of autonomous and settled identities has been shared by many who have sought to argue the case in favor of the Bosnian government. To see if a more pluralistic account of the conflict and its dynamics can be offered, this section deals with the largely academic narratives striving for an explanation.

Coming to grips with the conflicts in the former Yugoslavia, argues Bogdan Denitch, requires a knowledge of history. In his view, however, the possibility for historical understanding has been weakened, especially in the United States:

> History unfortunately involves dull and specific facts, sometimes even dates. History and facts are unfashionable in advanced academic circles nowadays. Popular culture in the United States has long accepted the vulgar statement that history is bunk; currently the know-nothing prejudice is confirmed by the latest trends in the academy. Deconstructionism and postmodernism have apparently convinced an entire generation that it is sufficient to be acquainted with a powerful and, above all, fashionable and contemporary general theory. The important thing is that the theory seems to be new. These overarching abstract theories enable their adherents to generalize glibly about most everything, including politics in lands they know nothing about.[118]

Denitch's prejudice (as per usual, a sweeping condemnation unburdened by argument or references) is not uncommon, though his faith in naive historical realism is perhaps a little rarer than it once was. It nonetheless allows Denitch to bemoan the allegedly common idea that "facts can be relativized to fit any pet theory" and to call for renewed attention to the general and historical context of events.[119] Historical interpretation and controversy, however, are not absent from Denitch's own argument. In the course of exploring the political manipulation of data concerning World War II massacres in the former Yugoslavia, Denitch offers his own *"valid* ways to calculate losses." The conclusion he reaches on the vexed issue of how many died at the Ustaša camp at Jasenovac is that "it is not possible" for the number of casualties to have exceeded one hundred thousand, thereby mak-

ing improbable the claims of "extreme [Serbian] nationalists." Such
an estimate puts him closer to Franjo Tudjman's much criticized partisan assessment than to other accounts.[120] The point, of course, is
not to resolve the debate for or against an argument like Denitch's,
but simply to demonstrate that the logic of inquiry claimed by historical realists is rarely applied in their own arguments. The political
nature of historical argumentation insinuates even the positions of
those who think they are immune from such considerations.[121]

Various accounts of the recent political history of the Bosnian war
can amply support this contention. To make this case and explore the
way in which some interpretations of the Bosnian war have become
established to the exclusion of others, I want to focus on the narrativizing strategies of ostensibly objectivist works dealing with the Bosnian war, and demonstrate how many of the major assessments of the
conflict have reduced this complexity to the banalities of ethnic essentialism in order to attribute responsibility to particular individuals or groups. As such, they have been complicit in the constitution
of realities they merely claim to describe. What follows, then, focuses
only on a small selection of available writing: single-authored monographs that aim to offer a comprehensive account of the Bosnian war
(or at least its place in the many conflicts of the former Yugoslavia).[122]
This is an arbitrary and restrictive criterion that excludes a range of
interesting literature, but it enables the question of comparing narratives to be pursued with greater clarity.

To achieve that goal, I want to return to an important aspect of
Hayden White's argument discussed earlier. White maintained that
narrative was the paradigmatic form of proper history because of the
insufficiency of an account in the form of an annals or chronicle to
encapsulate a story. In the annals, a diarist simply records events for
each year in the period covered (often leaving some years blank), without any suggestion of a connection between events.[123] As the subsequent stage in the development of historical representation, the chronicle maintains the priority accorded temporal ordering, but through
its concern with a specific issue or area, provides more detail than an
annals, and thereby suggests meaning even as it refuses closure.[124]

To analyze how these accounts narrativize events and issues, we
need to be able to judge them in relation to a set of events the accounts consider important; that is, rather than imposing an external
criterion upon them and seeing how they measure up, we need to
isolate the events the selected narratives deal with, consider how those
events are included in some narratives while excluded from others,
and reveal the ways in which those events are represented and the
manner in which they are articulated so as to construct an argument.

Given White's contention that narrative has become the accepted historiographical mode because of its superiority to the annals and chronicles, isolating the work that narrativizing strategies do means considering those elements in particular accounts that supplement the simple description and temporal location of specific events. Isolating those events thus requires the retrospective construction of a chronology of specific events from a period important to the understanding of the Bosnian war. Any number of historical periods could be suitable candidates for this exercise, but the period between 1990 and 1992 provides a good basis for comparison.

The period August 1990 through April 1992, which covers the political debates about Bosnia's future in the collapsing Yugoslavia up until its international recognition as a state and the commencement of large-scale fighting in Sarajevo, is widely identified in these accounts to be pivotal for their various interpretations. That is because the character of the accounts depends in large part on how they assign responsibility for the fracturing of Bosnia, and assigning responsibility in this context depends in large part on whom or what they regard as pursuing a different political arrangement in this period. The importance of this parameter can be judged by Lord Owen's claim that "the recognition of Bosnia and Herzegovina was the trigger that many had predicted it would be to the formal outbreak of a war that was already simmering in the background before recognition."[125]

Of course, in the context of White's argument, the events selected for inclusion in the chronology neither exist unproblematically in an extradiscursive domain nor are they independently deemed to be important. Nor is the language used to describe them necessarily neutral. As such, *they are included here because they have been identified as significant by the various narratives in the monographs considered.* Moreover, *the events are described in the terms used by the particular narratives from which they are drawn.* But no narrative covers all these events, and there is considerable variation in who covers what and how. As we shall see, that variation illuminates clearly the inescapable politics of representation involved in the narration of events.

Chronology: Bosnia 1990–92

(1) August 1990	Brawl between Serbs and Muslims, near Foča
(2) September 1990	Bosnian Serbs establish paramilitaries
(3) November 1990	Bosnian elections; national coalition government formed

(4) March 1991	Tudjman and Milošević meet at Karadjordjevo and discuss the partition of Bosnia
(5) April 1991	Autonomist Serbs declare the formation of a regional parliament for *Bosanska Krajina* based in Banja Luka
(6) June 1991	More than 50,000 Muslims, Serbs, and Croats demonstrate in Sarajevo for the unity of Yugoslavia and Bosnia
(7) 11 July 1991	Bosnian Serbs (SDS) release a party statement announcing a boycott of parliament and denounce Izetbegović as an illegitimate ruler
(8) 16 August 1991	Izetbegović announces a referendum on the future of Bosnia within Yugoslavia
(9) September 1991	Four Serb Autonomous Regions established; request JNA aid
(10) 14/15 October 1991	Bosnian parliament debates and adopts a declaration of sovereignty; Serb delegates walk out before vote
(11) 17 October 1991	Bosnian government creates a new coat of arms and flag for the republic
(12) 24 October 1991	Bosnian Serbs leave power-sharing coalition and establish their own parliamentary assembly
(13) 29 October 1991	Bosnian government informs Yugoslav federal parliament that it is a sovereign state
(14) November 1991	Assembly of Bosnian Serbs holds first session

(15) 9–11 November 1991   Assembly of Bosnian Serbs conducts referendum for Serbs in which an overwhelming majority vote to remain part of Yugoslavia

(16) 12 November 1991   The *Posavina* community of eight communes establishes a Bosnian Croat autonomous entity in northern Bosnia

(17) 18 November 1991   Eighteen Bosnian Croat communes set up Herzeg-Bosnia in western Herzegovina

(18) 15 December 1991   EC makes a provisional offer of recognition to Bosnia

(19) 20 December 1991   Bosnian presidency requests diplomatic recognition from the EC

(20) 21 December 1991   Assembly of Bosnian Serbs announces the creation of the Serbian Republic of Bosnia-Herzegovina

(21) December 1991   A separate Croatian state in western Herzegovina — "Herzeg-Bosnia" — is declared after Tudjman makes Mate Boban leader of the Croatian Democratic Union (HDZ) in Bosnia

(22) January 1992   Milošević issues secret order to transfer Bosnian-born JNA officers back to their republic

(23) 9 January 1992   The independence of the Serbian Republic of Bosnia-Herzegovina proclaimed

(24) 27 January 1992   Another Bosnian Croat entity is formed from four communities in central Bosnia

(25) 26 February 1992   Bosnian Serbs and Bosnian Croats meet secretly in Graz,

		Austria, to discuss territorial partition
(26)	29 February–March 1992	Referendum on Bosnian independence
(27)	1 March 1992	Shots fired at a Serb wedding party in Sarajevo
(28)	2 March 1992	Serbs set up barricades in Sarajevo
(29)	3 March 1992	Bosnian government declares independence
(30)	18 March 1992	First international agreement to partition Bosnia
(31)	5/6/7 April 1992	Bosnia recognized by United States and EC
(32)	6 April 1992	War in Bosnia begins

This composite chronology demonstrates immediately two important facets of the argument concerning the centrality of narrative. First, it does not (and, therefore, the narratives from which it is derived do not) encompass everything that happened in or pertaining to Bosnia between 1990 and 1992. After all, are we to believe that nothing occurred between November 1990 and March 1991 (points 3 and 4)? Nothing between 27 January 1992 and 26 February 1992 (points 24 and 25)? Or in any of the other numerous gaps? The historical field is simply too heterogeneous and too disparate for any account to encompass everything. White's observation, therefore, that the events in a chronicle are real not because they occurred but because they are remembered by ex post facto accounts is thus vividly demonstrated.[126]

Second, the act of recording the thirty-two events in a sequential record does not in itself constitute a historical account. Listing the events in this form does not provide a narrative account for the events and cannot reveal either the existence or salience of one story over another. To confirm White's general thesis, therefore, we can see that for there to be a historical account of the above events, their emplotment in a narrative—the form of which is neither given nor determined by the events themselves—is required. (Which is not surprising, because the placing of the various points in the above chronology is derived from their being remembered and posited as events by the narratives in the first place.) More particularly, the necessity of emplotment is manifested by the fact that nothing in the above list points unproblematically toward the notions of *tragedy, inferno, death,* or *drama* so common in the titles of books on Bosnia. The consequence of this is that, as White argues, a recourse to the historical record will not by itself resolve the issue of which is better or worse. However, this suspends neither the importance nor possibility of judgment. It means that an attentiveness to the way these monographs handle the negotiation between micronarratives and macronarratives against the backdrop of the relationship to the other they embody becomes important.

What, then, do the various narratives concerning the Bosnian war make of these and other events, and what does that allow us to say about those narratives? Those accounts sensitive to the possibility of different interpretations of the Bosnian war identify two predominant stories. One is the tale of a *civil war* in which antagonism between various groups emerges for a variety of reasons. The other is of *international conflict,* in which aggression from one state threatens another.[127] Other elements — ethnicity, historical hatred, aggressive nationalism, religious ideologies, or political and economic failures — are mobilized in the respective narratives to support their overall explanation. A close examination of the monographs in question will demonstrate the different narrative arguments and the way they figure the heterogeneity of the historical record so as to support those arguments.

The first story is obvious in Edgar O'Ballance's *Civil War in Bosnia,* where the conflict is understood as a "vicious three-sided . . . civil war," a "confused struggle between territorial warlords and rival militias" (ix). At the center of O'Ballance's account stands the figure of the Bosnian president Alija Izetbegović, "a dedicated Muslim who had almost single-handedly worked and planned to turn his multiethnic country... into a unitary sovereign state, while his secret agenda was to give it a predominantly Islamic-oriented character" (vii). Izetbegović's "Islamic fixation" was most apparent, according to O'Ballance, in the *Islamic Declaration,* which supposedly advocated a "united Islamic Community from Morocco to Indonesia," and for which he was imprisoned by the Tito regime (3). Similar opprobrium was not forthcoming when discussing other leaders' deficiencies; with regard to Tudjman, O'Ballance offers an account laced with equanimity. After noting Tudjman's imprisonment, O'Ballance writes that the future Croatian president "wrote books reassessing Croatian history, one being *Wasteland,* which caused him to be accused of being a fascist and anti-Jewish, which he denied" (21).

As a result of the centering of one leader, O'Ballance writes the story of Bosnia as the story of Izetbegović, with everything done or not done so as to enhance, in order of priority, his power, the power of his political party, the Party of Democratic Action (SDA), and the power of the Muslims (6). As a consequence, O'Ballance begins his account with event 1 from the chronology, although he maintains the clashes took place in September 1990. More importantly, he asserts that "the clashes were alleged to have been instigated by Izetbegovic's SDA" (5). In contrast, Susan Woodward provides a rather different account in *Balkan Tragedy* (276), where she writes that "since early September [1991], paramilitary gangs from Serbia had stirred up interethnic conflict in towns of eastern Bosnia such as Bijeljina, Foča, Višegrad, and Bratunac."

The concern to demonstrate at every opportunity that Izetbegović sought to expand his power base leads O'Ballance to make particular judgments. With regard to the elections of 1990 (event 3), he has Izetbegović elected as president on 18 November 1990, but the multiparty parliamentary elections not taking place until 2 and 9 December 1990 (6). O'Ballance then argues that

> a representative government was formed, including Serb and Croat ministers as well as Muslim ones, dominated by Izetbegovic and his SDA. At this uncertain moment a national-coalition power-sharing government of the three main ethnic groups, instead of a unitary one, might have had a unifying and calming effect on restless ethnic activists, and stultified swings toward separatism; but it was not part of Izetbegovic's plan to share power with any of them." (6–7)

Others, however, explicitly contradict his understanding. In *The Death of Yugoslavia*, Laura Silber and Allan Little (210) state that despite their differences, the three nationalist parties formed a united front against the Communists before the poll and maintained that agreement afterwards despite electoral results that made it unnecessary. As a result, the Bosnian collective presidency had two places each for Muslims, Serbs, and Croats, and one for a Yugoslav, with Izetbegović (as leader of the largest party) elected president of the presidency, with the Serb Krajišnik Speaker of the Parliament, and Jure Pelivan, a Croat, Prime Minister (211).

To enable his story of a civil war driven by the self-interested calculations of one central actor, O'Ballance's account makes no mention of events 4 to 9, recording only a brief mention of events 11 and 12 before focusing on the moves toward Bosnian sovereignty (events 18, 23, 26, 27, 28, and 30). As a result, his narrative does not take a sustained look at any of the events (especially 5 and 9) that indicated unilateral Serbian moves toward autonomy in advance of the Bosnian government's pursuit of sovereignty and international recognition. Having given preeminence to the latter, and placed the personality and political program of Izetbegović to the fore, such omissions were necessary. As Sabrina Petra Ramet argues—in a narrative that makes a contrary argument—by paying attention to Serbian moves of this kind, it is not possible to script Serbian policy as simply reacting to (so-called) Muslim initiatives. As she notes in *Balkan Babel* (243–44), with regard to event 2, "these formations were set up, thus, *before* the elections that would place Muslim leader Alija Izetbegović in the presidency and cannot, therefore, be portrayed as a response to his election." This ordering of responsibility goes against the central thrust of O'Ballance's account of the Bosnian war, which shares with a number of other interpretations the desire to diminish the culpability of the Serbs by casting their activities as responses to provocations by the non-Serbs. As O'Ballance argues with respect to the first Bosnian parliamentary declaration of sovereignty (event 10), "this was a direct challenge and the inevitable watershed toward eventual civil war" (7). But the same could equally be said of earlier Serbian moves for autonomy that challenged the government elected in November 1990 (events 2, 5, 7, and 9).

O'Ballance's criticisms of Izetbegović persist to such an extent that the Bosnian president is portrayed as the major obstacle to all the peace initiatives, supposedly rejecting earlier proposals and making insistent and repeated demands for revisions (207). But this partisan account does also have moments where the criticisms are shared around. In a moral leveling that is common to the "civil war" accounts, the participants are cast as "factional leaders" of "warring militias," with all sides said to be equally guilty of atrocities such that there is "little to choose between them" (viii, ix, x). Equally common is the notion that the character of the violence can be explained in terms of "old hatreds and prejudices, involving slaughter reminiscent of medieval times" (xi), such that the war showed "tribalism and ethnic nationalism" were victorious over regionalism (245). History was crucial here: "When aroused, the Bosnian combatants reacted in much the same way as their forebears, as confirmed by events in Yugoslavia during the Second World War. King Alexander's rule and Tito's firm administration were misleading interludes of comparatively peaceful coexistence—but old hatreds, feuds and prejudices had not been eradicated, they simply lay dormant" (245–46).

John Zametica's *The Yugoslav Conflict* offers some interesting reflections on the nature of history. In its conclusions, Zametica writes that "of course, history, with its infinity of facts, will always be subject to selective interpretation" (75). Nowhere more so than in the former Yugoslavia, where complexity required added care, he noted. Which leads Zametica to a particular recommendation: "Analysis as a guide to policy which is divorced from self-interest is presumably of the utmost importance to the international community. If the international community, benevolently inclined, continues its growing involvement in conflict areas around the world, its principal weapon must be knowledge" (76). Few have been better placed than Zametica to fulminate on the relationship between knowledge and self-interest. Shortly after completing this *Adelphi Paper*, Zametica restored his Serbian forename (Jovan) and went off to Pale as a senior adviser and spokesperson for Radovan Karadžić.

Zametica's self-interest is amply evident in his monograph. Politics and its participants are represented solely in ethnic and religious terms, with special attention paid to the "strong streak of clericalism" in "the Muslim Party" (37), and to the negative resonances supposedly to be found in Izetbegović's *Islamic Declaration*, points that Zametica provided for O'Ballance's argument. All of this is wrapped up by the observation that "there was nothing secular" in Izetbegović's outlook (38) and the resultant conclusion that all "this was quite enough for the Serbs" (39).

The narrative of *The Yugoslav Conflict*, although it notes the elections of 1990 (event 3), does not begin a discussion of Bosnian's troubles until the EC offer of international recognition (event 18), which it claims "provided the deadly catalyst for the Bosnian *dénouement*" (38). While the result of the elections is said to have produced a power-sharing arrangement that furthered the notions of constitutional equality central to Tito's Yugoslavia—whereby decisions that affected national groups could not be taken without the consent of those groups—Zametica argues that the situation after the end of 1991 violated this important code (37): "Once the Muslim-Croat coalition made an effective attempt to hijack Bosnia-Herzegovina through the dubious legitimacy of a referendum, followed by international recognition, it brushed aside—to its own peril—the only principle that in the past held the republic together: the constitutional equality of all three constituent nations" (39–40). Zametica was there referring to event 26, the EC-mandated referendum that was a prerequisite for international recognition. But if that was contrary to constitutional equality, could not the same be said of the exclusive Bosnian Serb referendum (event 15) held three months earlier? Or any of the Serbian autonomist initiatives (events 5, 7, 9, 12, and 14) in the period prior to that? Or those of the Croat community (events 16, 17, 21, and 24)? Not surprisingly, these events are absent from Zametica's monograph. Had they been considered, it would not have been possible to speak of one side "hijacking" the republic to the detriment of the others.

Zametica, however, is not the only one to maintain that in these matters culpability rests with the Bosnian government. In *Broken Bonds*, the inflections of Lenard Cohen's narrative clearly assign responsibility. In the context of the Bosnian presidency requesting the diplomatic recognition that the EC had offered (event 19), Cohen argues that Izetbegović ignored Serbian protests, went ahead "irrespective of Serbian fears," and thus contributed to heightening the anxiety of Bosnian Serb leaders, which Cohen describes as "perfectly understandable" (242, 243). The referendum that the EC required (event 26) was thus "a red flag to most members of the Bosnian Serb community" (242). Once recognition came (event 32), Cohen observes that "for the Serbs, the fact that EC recognition came precisely on April 6, 1992, the anniversary of the date in 1941 that the Germans bombed Belgrade, added insult to injury" (245). But like Zametica's and O'Ballance's narratives, Cohen's pays no attention to either of the prior unilateral Serb or Croat initiatives to wrest sovereignty from Bosnia (events 5, 7, 9, 12, 14, 16, 17, 21, and 24).[128] Moreover, his representations of the political participants in the conflict, including the Bosnian government, as "ethnic delegations" (260) engaged in a "savage ethnic and political conflict on the territory of the former Yugoslavia" (xvii) effect certain claims concerning legitimacy.

Like O'Ballance's account of the civil war, Cohen's argument recurs to notions of historical hatred to try and make sense of the conflict and explain why international recognition would not put a damper on the crisis. Although he argues that the "various ethnoreligious groups" had maintained some sense of coexistence under Tito's authoritarianism, he says that "intense latent hatred and psychological distance existed among the various groups." Indeed, "glib media claims" about good group relations were said by Cohen "to [have] seriously misjudged the real situation of underlying interethnic animosities" (245). All this meant that in 1992 and 1993 the fighting in Bosnia was especially violent because "just as half a century earlier," the citizens "were intent on 'settling accounts of centuries of hatred.'"

Explaining how the cycle of violence came about is a task, says Cohen, for "systematic psychological research." And while all nationalist political leaders whipped up hatred and intolerance, "the historically conditioned proclivities of large segments of each ethnoreligious community... to embrace programs of aggressive nationalism must also be taken into account" (246). This is not, argues Cohen, impressions to the contrary notwithstanding, to suggest that the fighting was a spontaneous continuation of history. Accounts that focus only on peaceful coexistence or permanent hatred are equally blind to "the region's complex pattern of ethnic relations and reciprocal fear" (247). Nonetheless, Cohen is adamant that attention be focused on "the important historical factors that have conditioned Balkan and South Slav political life" (331).

Paul Mojzes's *Yugoslavian Inferno*, though sensitive to the political implications of the "civil war" versus "international conflict" narratives (87–91), nonetheless promotes a particular reading of history that favors the former over the latter. Mojzes's specific concern is to consider the significance of religion for the region and the conflict. Hence the choice of his title: " 'Inferno' suggests a situation of real and symbolic conflagration, unrelenting suffering, the prevalence of unmitigated evil, futility and hopelessness. It can be appropriately applied to the former Yugoslavia, where ethnoreligious warfare has consigned millions to hell and where a return from hell is by no means assured" (xv). Later in the book, Mojzes stresses that "the fear and hatred-induced acts that brought about the war cannot be explained rationally. They were evoked by human destructiveness and self-centredness. Sinfulness and intransigence are at the motivating core of the war" (153).

The irrationality of the Balkan "cataclysm" is a product for Mojzes of a number of historical and psychological dispositions. He notes that historically "the Balkan economies are perpetual war economies" with "no tradition of nonviolent resistance or pacifism" (41). A long-established situation of "colonial dependency" has meant that the peoples of the Balkans, now that they are in a position to take charge of their destiny, "act belatedly like juvenile delinquents" (52). As a result, psychologically the people "oscillate between extremes, with little propensity for moderation" (43), manifest a cultural norm of revenge, and exhibit the character traits of obstinacy, stubbornness, loathing, and inflexibility (50–51). In consequence, "life in the Balkans has never been intrinsically respected, because the individual is relatively unimportant in a collectivist climate" (60).

With the conflict overdetermined in this manner, it is thus not surprising to note that *Yugoslavian Inferno* is largely uninterested in the historical and political field signified by the chronology, mentioning only events 31 and 32 in its account. Mojzes does, however, list a number of secular developments central to the conflict—the unresolved national question, politicians manipulating nationalism, and intellectuals providing the rationalization for it being the key three—

which he regards as comprising a hierarchy of culpability (152–75). They derive their responsibility from the fact that "ethnic nationalism" has been the preeminent historical force in the Balkans throughout the nineteenth and twentieth centuries (83). This combination of historical determination and political volition leads Mojzes to a general conclusion. "This accursed land," he writes, "was always prone to tectonic collisions . . . and those who have reignited the ethnoreligious hatreds have hurled entire nations into the inferno" (86). With respect to Bosnia, this intersection of forces is summarized by way of a revealing metaphor:

> There is a popular dish in Bosnia called "Bosnian Pot." It is made of a variety of vegetables with meat and it is greatly spiced with red-hot paprika. It is slowly baked in a ceramic pot. It is quite tasty, but for some unaccustomed stomachs it can create considerable indigestion. This dish is analogous to the war in Bosnia and Herzegovina. The variety of nations there are as mixed as the vegetables in the pot. Hatred has made them fiery-hot, both in spice and in heat. They have simmered for a long time, but now the pot has boiled over and has brought quite an indigestion to the international community. The pot has broken, too, and the ingredients are scattered all over the place, bringing a tragedy to the inhabitants which is, thus far, the greatest in Europe since the termination of World War II. (106–7)

The orientalism of Mojzes's argument is all the more extraordinary given the personal reflections he offers at the beginning of his book. Mojzes recognizes the "many contradictory narratives" about the conflict but argues that the interpretations "vary according to the background of the author. Serbian authors tend to write pro-Serbian narratives, Croatian pro-Croatian, Muslims pro-Muslim, and so forth" (xvi). In this context, Mojzes argues it is important he set forth his background and biases. Somewhat surprisingly, given the Balkan character argument he offers, we find he was born in Croatia to a religious but nonnationalist family, was raised in Serbia, but considered himself a Yugoslav admiring of Tito's socialist policies of brotherhood and unity. Even more astonishingly, he then "reject[s] the notion that we are determined by our past — not *in spite of* being an historian but because I *am* an historian" (xvii). It seems, in a somewhat contradictory manner, that what applies to him does not apply to the Balkans (at least in his argument), and while the past is not personally determinate, ethnicity nonetheless governs interpretations.

Personal authorizations for narratives on the conflict in the former Yugoslavia are not uncommon. In *The Yugoslav Drama*, Mihailo

Crnobrnja writes from the perspective of a Yugoslav ambassador to the European Community who served during the conflict. Crnobrnja is conscious of the implications invoked by the notion of "drama," though he argues that the title "was, in a way, forced on me by events, rather than a matter of deliberate selection" (xii). Cast in four parts— the stage, the actors, the plot, and the final curtain—Crnobrnja's account is a story of "national awakening and the victory of aggressive nationalism" (3). As such, and particularly in the case of the Bosnian war—where it was "a confrontation among three ethnic communities within a state that has been internationally recognized" —Crnobrnja argues it is not possible to understand the conflict as an international war. It might not have been "civil" insofar as it was "ethnic," but it was at the beginning no more than "an internal confrontation of the people of one country" (160).

Whether that "one country" was Yugoslavia or Bosnia does not matter for Crnobrnja, because the issue was whether either could avoid "the ugly virus" of aggressive nationalism (176). Once the former had unraveled, the latter was imperiled. The danger came not from any pseudo-naturalistic working out of history or hatreds—for all ethnic groups had "lived together for centuries without warring with each other" (174)—but from the political ambitions of the representatives of those groups. Unlike Mojzes's *Yugoslavian Inferno*, therefore, Crnobrnja's *The Yugoslav Drama* pays attention to some of the key political developments within Bosnia in the run-up to large-scale fighting (events 3, 4, 6, 9, 10, 14, and 15).

Crnobrnja's invocation of those events, however, is not designed to discriminate between sides. While O'Ballance's *Civil War in Bosnia*, Zametica's *The Yugoslav Conflict*, and Cohen's *Broken Bonds* ignore these and other such events as a means of directing responsibility for the ethnic conflict toward the (so-called) Muslims, and Izetbegović in particular, Crnobrnja does not seek to redress the balance by utilizing the events for reassigning responsibility. This thereby supports the contention that the events do not, in and by themselves, give rise to a particular interpretation. Rather, *The Yugoslav Drama* seeks to diminish the need for a judgment about responsibility by maintaining all ethnic groups played an equal part (178).

This forced impartiality is central to Crnobrnja's argument and figures in a number of subsequent places. For example, after noting that it is difficult to establish who gave the orders for ethnic cleansing operations, he argues that "the entire chain of command, up to and including the principal leaders—Milošević, Tudjman and Izetbegović—bears heavy responsibility for not putting an end to these gruesome methods of 'cleansing' and for not publicly denouncing them" (186).

When Crnobrnja departs from his strategy of treating all sides equally regardless, it is to redress what he sees as the bias of Western media "which set out to report only on Serb brutality in the first place." The visibility of Serb atrocities was made all the more easy, Crnobrnja argues, because although Croats and Muslims "engaged in similar atrocities," Serbs had "conquered a larger territory" (182). That this greater conquest was the product of a disproportionate level of violence, rather than an unrelated outcome that simply heightened "visibility," seems not to have disturbed the author of *The Yugoslav Drama*. Indeed, the Serbs' right to an amount of territory well beyond their proportion of the population (which was how it was usually calculated) is justified by Crnobrnja as follows:

> The media often reported that the Serbs had won almost 70 per cent of the territory of BiH. There was no mention of the fact that in times of peace the Serbs populated well over 50 percent of the territory, choosing to reside in less well-populated areas, in contrast to the Muslims, who were typically concentrated in towns and cities. The Serb territories were always proportionately larger than their numbers in the population. Of the Muslims, the opposite was the case. Thus, the Serb gain was not from 0 to 70 per cent, as many reports would imply, but was rather a matter of much more limited territorial expansion to meet strategic goals, mostly concerning the corridor and territories in the east of BiH. (187)

Highlighting ethnic patterns of land ownership said to have preceded the war was a common feature of Bosnian Serb arguments. Zametica employed similar points in an effort to diminish the charge that, in their opposition to the Vance-Owen plan, they were "flouting" the international community:

> Please understand those whom you wish to destroy: Bosnian Serbs do not imagine they are conquering anything. Most of the land in Bosnia is theirs, legally, farm by farm. They have tried to secure its possession—within some form of Serbian state, statelet or set of cantons. . . . Before the war, 64 per cent of land was registered to Serbs as most lived in rural areas.[129]

Not surprisingly given his later role, Zametica's argument and figures were deployed by Radovan Karadžić in his opposition to various peace initiatives.[130] All of this leads Crnobrnja to note somewhat defensively that "all of the above is not meant to minimize the responsibility of the Serbs. Theirs is by far the greatest" (188). His even-handedness to that point, however, is justified with the proposition that a resolution to the conflict will not be possible unless the role of *all* sides in furthering it is understood.

In coming to terms with the Bosnian war, one of the most common dispositions, when faced with the option of "civil war" or "international aggression," is to avoid a decision and argue—as does *The Yugoslav Drama*—that it is either a combination of the two, or that a focus on one to the exclusion of the other is a half-truth (the position of Mojzes's *Yugoslavian Inferno*). Bogdan Denitch's *Ethnic Nationalism* evinces a similar ambivalence. On the one hand, it talks of the second Yugoslavia (1945–91) being "murdered" rather than simply ending (69), and argues that the leaders of Serbia and Croatia are "tearing apart and partitioning Bosnia-Herzegovina, a sovereign member of the United Nations" (2). On the other hand, it speaks of a "civil war" (62, 72).

Denitch's essay, which is concerned with the rise and use of ethnic nationalism in Yugoslavia as a basis for considering the general relationship between nationalism and democracy, contains other equivocations. While he favors a focus on the political manipulation of ethnicity and nationalism, and thus seeks to avoid the determinism of a Balkan character or history that runs counter to such an argument, Denitch nonetheless gestures toward the latter position by talking of a "Rip Van Winkle [which] staggered back to life in 1989 and has had a desperately difficult time in trying to catch up with the long lost years." Denitch writes, in a style more complex but nonetheless akin to Mojzes's "Bosnian pot" metaphor, that "it is as if all the predemocratic political movements, folkish sentiments, populist prejudices, and vaguely religious nationalist identities had been preserved in amber during the long years of Communist power in Eastern Europe and the Soviet Union" (128).

Denitch's concern is less with the political history of the Yugoslav conflict and its Bosnian manifestation, and more with the thematic consequences pertaining to ethnicity, nationalism, multiculturalism, and democracy they suggest. His main object of concern, therefore, is with the way in which the political construction of the *demos* has been limited to claims about the supremacy of the *ethnos*. This exclusivist categorization is a problem because, although he is suspicious of "essentialist talk about mentalities," he sees ethnicity as being something ascribed ("you are born with it or you are not") rather than acquired, like citizenship (136, 141). The political salience of even an ascribed ethnicity is not automatic, however. As Denitch argues with respect to the 1990 Bosnian elections (event 3), in a point overlooked by all other accounts, some 28 percent of the electorate voted for non-nationalist parties, giving power to their representatives in Tuzla and the center of Sarajevo. Given that another quarter of the electorate did not vote at all, Denitch concludes that it is wrong to suggest the ethnic nationalist leaders represent a majority of the Bosnian people (193).

Denitch's *Ethnic Nationalism* introduces one interpretation of the conflict not found elsewhere. He argues that the war and its promotion of nationalism as collective identity can be seen as a response to the collapse of the old universalisms associated with Communist rule. In the face of this "red meat of the organic, 'authentic' Heideggerian national community" the " 'cool,' legal and rational democratic universalism" has been insufficiently powerful (128). As such, the conflict has been "a postmodern, disintegrative war of particularisms against both the reality and imagery of an orderly if repressive modern society" (72). This has been made possible, Denitch argues, because there has been a retreat from rationalism that has enabled both a paranoid political culture and the emergence of irregular Yugoslav paramilitaries that share cultural links with German skinheads and French racists (73, 75). This postrational, postmodern condition has been fostered by a consumer culture that devalues and replaces "boring 'cool' values — like tolerance and democracy — with 'hot' values like ethnic identity and possessive individualism" (73).[131]

Understanding the Yugoslav conflicts as instances of "civil" and/or "ethnic" war does not necessarily result in responsibility being shared equally by all parties to the fighting. Sabrina Petra Ramet's *Balkan Babel*, which figures the struggle in that manner (243), is a good example of the way in which this common interpretive focus can produce different accounts of the historical field. Although, as a revised collective of previously published essays, this book does not have the narrative coherence and purpose of a more integrated text, the introduction nonetheless leaves the reader with little doubt as to its preeminent concern. While noting it is not the only source of instability, Ramet declares that "since 1918, there has been a constant tension between Serbs and non-Serbs in this polyglot country, as Serbs have repeatedly tried to Serbianize and/or dominate the non-Serbs, and non-Serbs have doggedly fought such domination. This struggle between Serbs and non-Serbs lies at the heart of the instability for which Yugoslavia was famous" (1).

This struggle, however, is not located simply in the political domain, and Ramet's greatest contribution is in drawing attention to the other sites in which it is located. As she notes in the conclusion,

> this book has argued that political dynamics are reflected in, and
> even adumbrated by, changes in the cultural sphere and that the re-
> ligious sphere underpins and legitimizes actions and decisions taken
> in the political sphere. The political, cultural and religious spheres
> do not exist apart from each other; they are, rather, organic parts of
> a religio-politico-cultural system in which activity in one part has
> intentions, reflections, and consequences in other parts. (320)

Ramet's understanding of the "civil" or "domestic" domain is thus
inherently more complex than narratives that restrict themselves to
an institutional political register. Her detailed concern with gender
relations, cultural products such as music and literature, the media,
and religious practices (which includes the important point that Yugoslav society was progressively secularized, to such an extent that
levels of belief were well below those reported in the United States)[132]
demonstrates the complexity of social and political life in the former
Yugoslavia so often overlooked by other narratives operating within
a "civil" frame.

Ramet's account of the Bosnian war begins with a reversal of the
argument that interethnic conflict in the republic was persistent. Employing a historical generalization common to those who wish to challenge Serb policy without disturbing the parameters of their analysis,
Ramet argues that "Muslims, Serbs and Croats had lived in peace for
most of the 500 years they cohabited in Bosnia-Herzegovina. The intercommunal violence that accompanied World War II was an important deviation from this pattern, but even then the situation was
complicated." Shattering this peace required, therefore, the sowing
of seeds of hatred, for which "the Serbian Orthodox Church certainly
deserves credit." Arguing that "a sense of Bosnianness began to un-
ravel in the latter half of the 1980s," Ramet points to events 1 and 2
of the chronology to shift responsibility for the fracture from Izetbegović to the Bosnian Serbs (243).

Whereas narratives such as Cohen's *Broken Bonds* and O'Ballance's
Civil War in Bosnia downplay or ignore Serbian initiatives to establish
autonomy so as to make their reaction appear defensive, Ramet's
concern with those events (e.g., 9 and 20) achieves the reverse and
casts the Bosnian government and the republic as subject to pressure
and seeking recognition for security. To underscore who was pursuing ethnic exclusivism, Ramet points out that after sovereignty was
granted by the international community, "the UN and EC mediators,
along with the Western media, began to treat the Bosnian government
as if it represented only Muslims, even though, as of 12 February 1993,
the Bosnian cabinet still included six Serbs and five Croats, along-

side nine Muslims" (248). Such reminders were necessary, Ramet argues, because the inability or unwillingness to distinguish between the parties means "everything is relativized to the point where everyone becomes equally guilty. In consequence, the only 'rational' response seems, to relativists, to be total indifference or studied 'evenhandedness'" (259). The attention she pays to points unrecorded by others — such as the $1.176 billion in war material the Federal Republic of Yugoslavia supplied in 1993 to Serbian militias in Bosnia and Croatia (204), and the more than 4,000 Russian freight cars loaded with arms sent to the same groups toward the end of 1994 (254–55) — effectively demonstrates the points that contest such an approach.

Relativist hesitations of the kind opposed by Ramet, or doubts about the grounds for argumentation and ethico-political purpose evident in stories such as Mestrović's *The Balkanization of the West*, are not to be found in those narratives that view the Bosnian war as an instance of international aggression. Christopher Bennett's *Yugoslavia's Bloody Conflict* opens with a revealing story. Bennett relates his experience being mugged on the London underground to Bosnia's and Croatia's fate after 1991: "they, too, have been assaulted by a powerful and deranged assailant, wielding not only a knife but also an array of sophisticated weaponry" (vii). The identity of the international assailant is not much in doubt. But in case it was, Bennett makes it clear in his chapter on Bosnia. Noting that the elections of 1990 (event 3) produced a coalition government, he writes that "had the fate of the Bosnia-Hercegovina been left to Bosnians there was still a chance that they could have come to an understanding among themselves. But it was not left to Bosnians and conflict was imported from outside, principally from Serbia" (182–83).

To establish that this is the case, Bennett refers to all the initiatives undertaken by Bosnian Serbs to undermine the sovereignty of the new republic (events 1, 4, 5, 7, 9, 10, 12, 14, and 15), noting that they replicated strategies already used to good effect in the war against Croatia (183). A good number of these same events are discussed in Crnobrnja's *The Yugoslav Drama*. But there they function as part of an argument that distributes responsibility to three constituent groups equally. In contrast, Bennett reads these events as local evidence of the overall plan for a Greater Serbia: "the Yugoslav wars were not the consequence of an unfortunate series of events and misunderstandings, but of a calculated attempt to forge a Greater Serbia out of Yugoslavia" (238). Moreover, he highlights the significance of discussing these events in this manner: "though Serb apologists consider the recognition of Bosnia-Hercegovina the spark which ignited the conflict, this explanation ignores the order of events. The war had already begun before the international community recognized Bosnia-Hercegovina; the events were not the other way around" (187–88).

Whereas O'Ballance's narrative placed Izetbegović at the critical center, for Bennett, Milošević is the culprit. Yugoslavia was destroyed rather than just fell apart, and "it was destroyed by at most a handful of people, and to a great extent by a single man, Slobodan Milošević" (247). That "militant Serbs set out in a *blitzkrieg*-style operation to exterminate the non-Serb population as well as any Serbs who refused to go along with the Greater Serbian vision of the republic's future" (245) meant that Milošević could—in an invocation of the politically resonant and culturally powerful World War II script—only be compared to Hitler, and the international community's response could only be compared to Europe's in the 1930s (243–44).

If there is one event that anchors a narrative of Serb nationalism's responsibility and Milošević's complicity, it is his statement to Kosovo Serbs in April 1987. According to Bennett (94), it was on 27 April and went "nobody will ever beat you again." For Laura Silber and Allan Little, in *The Death of Yugoslavia* (37), it was on 24 April and was "no one should dare to beat you." *The Death of Yugoslavia*, which accompanies the BBC television series of the same name, thus has a theme similar to Bennett's *Yugoslavia's Bloody Collapse*, albeit phrased more mildly. "One of the central themes of our book," the authors write, "is that under Milošević's stewardship, the Serbs were, from the beginning of Yugoslavia's disintegration, the key secessionists. This is not to say that Milošević was uniquely malign or solely guilty. The foot soldiers of Yugoslavia's march to war were legion and were drawn from all nationalities in the country" (26).[133]

The great virtue of *The Death of Yugoslavia* is its rich reportage of the complexity of the Yugoslav conflicts. To support their central contention, Silber and Little are able to deploy indigenous political voices to make their points. Thus, we hear Ivan Stambolić, the Serbian president ousted by Milošević, declare that Milošević's populist methods were "the red rag to the bull of other nationalisms. When the biggest nation begins to wave flags, the smaller nations were obviously afraid" (47). Although the Serb leadership is center stage, their Croatian counterparts are not exonerated in the same way that Tudjman is dismissed by Bennett (242) as no more than a scapegoat for the country's disintegration. The telling case of Josip Reihl-Kir, the moderate Croat police chief in Slavonia, is testament to this. Kir was unable to prevent an April 1991 military raid organized by Gojko Šušak designed to provoke conflict around Borovo Selo, a Serb village near Vukovar.

Nonetheless, because of this and other efforts at moderation, he was assassinated by his political compatriots. As Silber and Little conclude, "it is a striking commentary on the direction in which Croatia was moving during those crucial weeks leading to the outbreak of full-scale war, that Kir's moderation, his conciliatory approaches to the Serbs, had cost him his life, while Šušak's activities, stoking tension and provoking conflict, were to win him one of the most prominent places in Tudjman's government [as defense minister]" (144).

The Death of Yugoslavia, like Cohen's Broken Bonds, also contains important points that question those "civil war" narratives, which emphasize credible Serb fears as a rationale for the actions. Although the insensitivities of the Croatian authorities in relation to the Krajina Serbs are well documented by Silber and Little (98–103), they nonetheless point out that Lord Carrington's 1991 peace plan contained important initiatives with respect to the desires of the Serb communities in Croatia and Bosnia.

In a similar vein, Silber and Little (208–9) offer an account of Izetbegović's religious convictions and political aspirations markedly different from that in O'Ballance's Civil War in Bosnia or Zametica's The Yugoslav Conflict. According to Silber and Little, Izetbegović's Islamic Declaration "was a work of scholarship, not politics, intended to promote philosophical discourse among Muslims. In it, he excluded 'the use of violence in the creation of a Muslim state, because it defiles the beauty of the name of Islam.'"

The comprehensiveness of The Death of Yugoslavia can be seen in the fact that its narrative encompasses more events (3, 4, 7, 9, 10, 12, 14, 15, 18, 19, 20, 22, 25, 26, 27, 28, 30, and 31) from the chronology than most others (208–21). That it does so does not make it impartial, or free from contestation, for those events are still read in terms of the narrative's central plot of the Serbs being the primary secessionists. But it does mean that it is superior to less complete and obviously more partial narratives, such as O'Ballance's and the contrasting but equally particular account of Bennett.

Susan Woodward's Balkan Tragedy is even more comprehensive than Silber and Little's account. Although it shares with The Death of Yugoslavia a concern for the international context and dimension of the conflict, the understanding of the international employed by Woodward's narrative is somewhat different. Woodward's initial concern is to differentiate Balkan Tragedy from arguments that either focus on the conflict as a war of aggression committed by one state (Serbia) against another (Bosnia)—the interpretation that Woodward identifies, somewhat surprisingly, with the U.S. government—or stress "that the Yugoslav and Bosnian conflicts constituted a civil war based on the revival of ethnic conflict after the fall of communism" — a view more common in Europe and Canada, Woodward notes (7). Instead, *Balkan Tragedy* aims to demonstrate the manner in which "the Yugoslav conflict is inseparable from international change and interdependence" such that it is not something "confined to the Balkans but is part of a more widespread phenomenon of political disintegration" (3). As a result, Woodward writes that "the story recorded and analyzed in this book begins a decade before the fall of the Berlin Wall, when the economic austerity and reforms required by a foreign debt crisis triggered a slide toward political disintegration" (4).

Woodward notes that insofar as the Yugoslav conflict has been understood as an instance of a more general phenomenon, this has been done in terms of "ethnic conflict," whether internally generated or externally sourced. Such a rendering, Woodward argues, had the politically disastrous consequence of promoting an ethnically defined solution (14).

Woodward does not doubt that the Yugoslav wars are a form of aggression. But against that representation and what she sees as its capacity to distract attention from the immediate causes, Woodward wants to articulate "real origins and fundamental issues" of the conflict. For *Balkan Tragedy*, these are to be found at the intersection of domestic upheavals brought on by transformations in the European and international orders. This involves "the collapse of states, the problematic meaning of national self-determination in relation to human rights and borders, and the process of incorporating (or excluding) former socialist states into the West" (13). More specifically, Woodward maintains the real origin of the Yugoslav conflict derives from "the politics of transforming a socialist society to a market economy and democracy" and the way in which that meant for Yugoslavia "the disintegration of governmental authority and the breakdown of political and civil order" that resulted in the collapse of the Yugoslav state (15, 378).

The argument in *Balkan Tragedy* rests on an economic logic allegedly common to the dynamic of disintegration evident in Eastern Europe, Yugoslavia, the Soviet Union, and Czechoslovakia in 1989–91 (349–50). Nationalist politics is said to have emerged in those areas closer to and more integrated with Western markets, and to have been pushed by politicians in those wealthier regions who had support from Western sources for their reforms. However, once this drive overflowed into areas less able to cope with the austerity measures required by liberalization strategies, adverse political consequences emerged (35).

Whether such economistic mechanisms can comprehensively account for the numerous developments examined in the study is a matter of judgment. After all, if economic deprivation is what fuels nationalist politics, why (as the argument claims) does nationalist politics emerge in the first instance in regions of relative affluence? Moreover, a reliance on an economic logic of this kind diminishes the insightful analysis Woodward offers with respect to, for example, the way the politics of national self-determination governed both indigenous and international strategies (see chapters 7 and 9). There can be no doubt, though, that *Balkan Tragedy* is right to correct the lack of attention to the regional and global political economy in other accounts, with chapter 3 being a detailed account of the conditions that preceded and embraced the conflict. Similarly, the thorough consideration of the prewar bases of stability in Yugoslav society in chapter 2 puts paid to the common cliché that it was either the iron hand of Tito or the firm lid of communism that suppressed tensions. Woodward's analysis demonstrates that the country "was not held together by Tito's charisma, political dictatorship, or repression of national sentiments but by a complex balancing act at the international level and an extensive system of rights and overlapping sovereignties" (45).

However, given *Balkan Tragedy*'s fundamental concern with the economic logic apparent in the dynamic of disintegration, its account of the Bosnian war is, despite attention to many of the same events as are in Silber and Little's account, somewhat different from their narrative in *The Death of Yugoslavia*. Although Woodward also deals in her narrative with many of the events (1, 3, 4, 5, 8, 10, 11, 12, 13, 15, 16, 17, 20, 24, 25, 27, 29, 30, and 31) that encompass autonomist moves, they function not as threats to one side or another but rather as manifestations of the politics of national self-determination enabled by the larger context of disintegration and transformation. This is most obvious in the sustained attention that *Balkan Tragedy* alone pays to the establishment of Croatian enclaves within Bosnia (events 16, 17, 21, and 24). As a result of this different treatment, Woodward concludes — in contrast to the emphasis in Silber and Little's core thesis — that "the Serbian leadership in Belgrade was only one of the participants aiming to create national states in a territory that was nationally mixed and contested. Nor were the Serbs as unified as their slogan proclaimed" (334). Nonetheless, her analysis offers few if any of the comforts for the Serbian position manifest in narratives such as Cohen's and O'Ballance's.

The Ontopology Effect: The Cartographic Logo, Ethnic Frame, and Historical Precedent

Given the diversity of readings of the disparate events offered by the various narratives of the Bosnian war—thereby demonstrating White's key points that events can be emplotted in a number of different ways, and that this emplotment stems from the story type rather than the essential character of the events—there would seem to be little that they share in common. However, as Timothy Mitchell has argued, "fields of analysis often develop a convention for introducing their object," and that convention is often manifested in seemingly obvious formulations and naturalistic descriptions.[134]

By taking a step back to consider the form rather than content of the observer narratives, three crucial features they all exhibit can be revealed. The first is that each is usually fronted by, or at least incorporates somewhere, a map of the Yugoslav federation showing the boundaries of the various republics with their respective capitals. The second is that they often begin with, or at least discuss at crucial times, a statistical survey of the Yugoslav population, which uses census data to report on the ethnic/national composition of the population. And the third is that their narrative of the Bosnian war is always preceded by a consideration of the historical horizon in such a manner as to suggest, implicitly or explicitly, that there is a linear teleology between the past and the present.

To frame one's narrative with a map of the former Yugoslavia would seem to be no more than an unremarkable act of description.[135] However, maps are not simply inert records or passive reflections of the world of objects but "refracted images contributing to dialogue in a socially constructed world."[136] As J. B. Harley argues, we should recognize that "both in the selectivity of their content and in their signs and styles of representation maps are a way of conceiving, articulating, and structuring the human world which is biased toward, promoted by, and exerts influence upon particular sets of social relations."[137] Most importantly, nationalism is the set of social relations with which maps have historically the greatest affinity. As representations of a bounded imaginary, maps have become logos for nationalist struggles in areas as diverse as the Basque country and the Philippines.[138] When the Yugoslav federation is represented with its internal republican borders clearly marked, the lines of nationalist cleavage and fracture appear as predetermined, and the latent but ever present existence of new national sovereignties awaiting their fulfillment is suggested. The map thus indicates the possibility of a particular narrative. What the map cannot represent is something other than a nexus between territory and identity, such as multiculturalism.

Similarly, to cite Yugoslav census statistics might seem to involve no more than drawing attention to an objective accounting of the population. But as Foucault has reminded us, to conceive of society as "a population" is to construct the social in a particular manner that is not naturally given.[139] Statistics then play a crucial role in materializing society as a population bearing certain characteristics. As a technology of power/knowledge, "counting practices carve up the population in a myriad of ways, sorting and dividing people, things, or behaviors into groups, leaving in their wake a host of categories and classifications. . . . more than an administrative technique for the extraction and distribution of resources, statistics have become tools in the crafting of modern subjectivity and social reality."[140] As a means of performing national subjectivities, few statistical genres have greater impact than the census that, through its mutually exclusive yet shifting national categorizations, "fill[s] in politically the formal topography of the map."[141]

The constructed character of the Yugoslav census is revealed by considering the emergence of "Muslim" as a national category (a discussion to be pursued further in chapter 7). Although contemporary discourse has made "Muslim" synonymous with "Bosnian," the former term was not a separate category (and then only with "quasi-national status") until the 1961 census. In 1965 the League of Communists in Bosnia-Herzegovina granted Muslims the right to national self-determination, after they had entered the federal constitution's list of constituent nations two years earlier. It was not until 1971 that the census categorization firmly established "Muslim" as a nationality.[142] This genealogy is obscured, however, by the constant citation of the 1991 census statistics for Yugoslavia that predominate in the narratives.[143] With regard to Bosnia, these statistics materialize Bosnia as "44% Muslim, 31% Serb, 17% Croats, 6% Yugoslav," with a small remainder. The effect is to establish these markers of identity as socially salient, the community fault lines around which politics will revolve. Just as the republican borders on the map signal the immanent becoming of new national sovereignties, so these statistics symbolize the future ethnic divisions that will populate and politicize the emergent entities. Sometimes census and map come together in the cartographic representation of ethnic/national composition, thereby naturalizing a territorialized politics of ethnic/national self-determination.[144] Even in arguments where it is asserted, rightly, that "ethnic differences, even substantial differences, do not set a society inexorably on the path toward war," the symbolizations of map and census work to establish the contrary position.

If the map enacts immanent national units, and the census populates those entities with fractured subjects, then the writing of a historical horizon that locates these features in a linear narrative secures the teleology of conflict. Each of the monographs considered engages in such a historical scripting, albeit with different time frames. Some focus on political and economic developments of the past decade or two as a way of locating the current conflict.[145] More commonly, others turn their attention back more than a century in order to uncover actors, events, and issues that function as the precedents for the present period.[146] Although there are not unimportant differences among these accounts, more often than not they are concerned with the Ottoman empire, the Habsburgs, the Balkan Wars of 1912–13, World War I, the Kingdom of Serbs, Croats, and Slovenes, World War II, Tito, and finally the post-Tito era. The contemporary struggle is thereby located as but the latest episode.

This conjunction of territorial representation, population identification, and historical determination means that for all the significant differences in the narratives examined here, they give rise to an order of representation we might understand in terms of what Derrida calls "ontopology."

Ontopology is a neologism that signifies the connection of the "ontological value of present-being to its *situation,* to the stable and presentable determination of a locality, the *topos* of territory, native soil, city, body in general."[147] A key assumption—if not *the* most important assumption—that informs the dominant understandings of the Bosnian war discussed above is that the political possibilities have been limited by the alignment between territory and identity, state and nation, all under the sign of "ethnicity," supported by a particular account of history. Moreover, this account is central not only to the macronarratives of the observer-interpreters but to the micronarratives of at least one of the protagonists in the conflict. As such, whether explicitly or implicitly (through markers like the map and the census that frame their arguments), we can conclude that the dominant narratives of the media and the academy have operated in terms that have helped legitimize and sustain the geopolitical positions of extreme nationalists. Important elements of the conflict, along with influential accounts of the conflict, are thus driven by "a *primitive conceptual phantasm* of community, the nation-State, sovereignty, borders, native soil and blood."[148] Indeed, the conventional understandings of the conflict have been "as essentialist, if not ferocious, as the nationalisms of ex-Yugoslavia."[149] They have thus been an element in the *coup de force* through which the Bosnian war has been materialized.

In this context, the notion that the responsibility to the other can serve as an ethical imperative that allows for the evaluation and judgment of competing narratives seems more pertinent than ever. The failure of the international community, the media, and the academy to heed the plurality of political positions and the nonnationalist voices that contested the identity politics of those prosecuting the war is testament to the way in which the responsibility to the other was not enacted. Although alternative representations of the conflict—such as it being the product of a genocidal politics or international aggression—were far from absent, they were even further from displacing the "civil/ethnic" account from its privileged position in both political discourse and public policy. In part this was because those arguments focusing on genocide or aggression were often framed by civil/ethnic parameters, such that their ability to contest the dominant accounts was dissipated.

According to the process of judgment identified above, the possibility of disparate emplotments does not lead to purely arbitrary histories, because the relationship between micronarratives and macronarratives has to be considered. This negotiation between the two orders of narrative establishes that many of the observer accounts are overdetermined by their reliance on the logic of the argument enunciated by only some of the participants. The heterogeneity, hybridity, and anti-geopolitical nature of the historical and political field have been overlooked or underplayed by the search for a cause that could either absolve ourselves of any responsibility or secure strategies for managing the crisis.

This proclivity stems from our desire, according to Michael André Bernstein, to "try to make sense of a historical disaster by interpreting it, according to the strictest teleological model, as the climax of a bitter trajectory whose inevitable outcome it must be."[150] Narratives of tragedy thus abound, and accounts that emphasize historical undecidability and alternative political possibilities are pushed to the side. Enacting our responsibility to the other involves recovering those different figurations that contest fixed understandings. The next chapter attempts to do that with counternarratives that seek to disturb the ontopological certainties of the dominant representations of the Bosnian war.

Four
Violence and Identity in Bosnia

Inscribing History and Identity

When a Croatian militiaman stitched an Ustaša symbol to his uniform before going into battle with Serbian forces, he was doing more than acting out a preordained history or exercising a pregiven subjectivity: he was reproducing and rearticulating a historical representation and violently deploying it in the present to constitute his (individual and/or collective) subjectivity. In such moments it is possible to appreciate how individual practices render one not only as an ethno-nationalist but also as an ethno-historian who naturalizes his nationalism historically.

Although this constitutive process can be caught up in the partisan impulses of new regimes — and Croatia seems to have enacted measures after independence in 1991 that resulted in conflict with others, especially Serbs within its territory[1] — such a stimulus is far removed from the purposive calculation of popular understanding. While these moments are often portrayed as manifesting an instrumental rationality in the form of conscious manipulation by elites, a more reflective account of the character of political violence in a place like the former Yugoslavia can demonstrate that it is as modern as it is premodern, for it constitutes the identities in whose name it is deployed. In particular, what can be disclosed is the way in which there is a continuum of political spaces and transnational surfaces along which "Bosnia" is violently constituted, from the bodies of individuals, through the corporate body of the former Yugoslavia, to the international bodies of the world community.

Disclosures of this kind require, as chapter 2 noted, an important deconstructive strategy: the problematization of teleological accounts of history. The purpose of so doing, as Derrida argues, is not to banish or finalize history but, rather, to show that teleology "locks up, neutralizes, and finally cancels historicity."[2] The deconstruction of historical teleologies is thus the condition of possibility for an appreciation of historicity and how it has been banished. This is a crucial theme with respect to Bosnia because most if not all interpretations of the conflict concern themselves with the relationship between history and violence.

This is obvious in those that deploy some variation of the "ancient animosities thesis," but is also evident when a focus on the historically constituted nature of the conflict is deployed as an effort to get away from at least some elements of the primordialist understandings. Focusing on historical constitution suggests the conflict was constituted *in history,* which implies that the hostility has an identifiable point of origin and is transmitted from generation to generation until it reaches the present. History is thus naturalized, and historicity extinguished.

A deconstructive reading would open the way for suggesting that the conflict is constituted *in the present,* and that "history" is a resource in the contemporary struggle. This proposition would be consistent with Benedict Anderson's provocative question: "Supposing 'antiquity' were, at a certain historical juncture, the *necessary consequence* of 'novelty'?"[3] That is, in the foundation of the new, claims about the old, in which it is said to precede and provide the heritage for the present, are required.

Historical representations have political consequences. One of the principal effects of the historical fatalism associated with the ontopological rendering of the Bosnian war has been to disenable calls for political or military action, to the despair of those who think we have witnessed a genocidal conflict, and to the relief, if not satisfaction, of those who prefer to sidestep responsibility. If conflicts represented as "ethnic" are understood as no more than settled history or human nature rearing its ugly head, then there is nothing that can be done in the present to resolve the tension except repress or ignore such struggles. In this view, the historical animus has to be enacted according to its script, with human agency in suspension while nature violently plays itself out. The only alternative consistent with this understanding would be for nature to be miraculously overcome as the result of an idealistic transformation at the hands of reason.

Not all accounts that depend on ontopological assumptions exhibit their logic as clearly as this.[4] Except in the most primordialist renderings—of which there nonetheless are quite a few—there is less a notion of predetermined nature and more a belief in the way the past makes likely the tragic nature of the present. Concomitantly, the role for human agency is not so completely diminished, though the plurality of possibilities that might be thought to exist at any given present are severely constricted.[5] However, even granting these differences, it is possible to posit a different logic by which to represent conflicts such as Bosnia. Following the argument concerning the relationship between violence and the political in chapter 2, this would involve seeing the violence in Bosnia as perhaps as the most extreme version of a *coup de force* designed to found that without foundation: in this case, to found an ethnically homogeneous state when polyethnicity and national heterogeneity prevailed.

The claim of the argument here is that such a deconstructive account of violence and the political in Bosnia offers a greater potential for understanding. Moreover, by politicizing the nature of the conflict, the range of possibilities for responding will be increased, for in demonstrating the mystical foundations of authority on which such conflicts are constructed, deconstructive thought is a necessary precondition for transformation. As such, deconstructive thought is more than an approach that problematizes seemingly coherent narratives and identities; it is an ethos that contests the way violence is implicated in all dimensions of the political and its representation.

Inscribing Violence and Its Intelligibility

This rethinking of history realigns our understanding of violence along the lines suggested by the idea of the *coup de force*. Violence is normally treated as a surface expression of a deeper cause—what Allen Feldman calls the "psychogenetic schema that begins in grievance (material or ideational), moves to expression, and culminates in violence in the absence of redress."[6] Regardless of the alleged nature of the cause—economic deprivation, virulent nationalism, or political manipulation, among others—many if not most conventional accounts of "ethnic/nationalist" struggles share the "narrative model of linear history," as chapter 3 demonstrated with respect to Bosnia. As a result, Feldman's contention that "sites of legitimation and authorization suppress historicity through linear, teleological, eschatological, or progressive temporalities" is easily supported.[7]

In contrast, if we pursue Derrida's notion of "thinking another historicity,"[8] we can recast the conflict in Bosnia as "an ethnography of surfaces—those sites, stages, and templates upon which history is constructed as a cultural object." In this context, "the historiographic surface is a place for reenactment, for the simulation of power and for making power manageable as a material force," and political violence is "a mode of transcription" that "circulates codes from one prescribed historiographic surface to another."[9] In Ann Norton's terms, this means that "violence is taken as a species of inscription and an act of authority. Acts of violence, like acts of speech and writing, invest the material with meaning by giving it structure.... In its inscription of will on the world, violence is a signifying act, giving expression and authority to identity and will."[10]

Conceiving of violence as a form of political inscription and transcription, rather than the product of a "psychogenetic" cause, as a performance rather than a purely instrumental practice, highlights its constitutive role in identity politics and means the claims about a recent intensification of "ethnic/nationalist" conflict can take on a very different character. Far from being a natural outgrowth of historical animosities and earlier conflicts, we can think of these issues of ethnicity and nationalism as *questions of history violently deployed in the present for contemporary political goals.*

This rendering of violence and its relationship to the constitution of political community is occluded by the prevalence, as chapter 3 illustrated, of ontopological assumptions in the major narrativizations of the Bosnian war. That these accounts have become readily and powerfully established, despite elements of the historical and political field that they survey, should not surprise us. That is because, as Derrida argues, the intelligibility of violence is also produced by the order it seeks to establish:

> One can say that the order of intelligibility depends in its turn on the established order that it serves to interpret. This readability will then be as little neutral as it is non-violent. A "successful" revolution, the "successful foundation of a state" (in somewhat the same sense that one speaks of a "felicitous performative speech act") will produce *après coup* what it was destined to produce in advance, namely, proper interpretative models to read in return, to give sense, necessity and above all legitimacy to the violence that has produced, among others, the interpretative model in question, that is, the discourse of its self-legitimation.[11]

In other words, the "civil/ethnic" discourse, infused with ontopological assumptions and identified in chapter 3 as dominant, although it appears as simply a description of the situation in Bosnia, is better understood as a discourse of self-legitimation produced by the violence it appears to merely represent. In line with the emphasis Derrida has given the violence of representation, which Richard Beardsworth refers to as "thinking the political in terms of the violence of conceptual determination" — this outcome is not entirely surprising.[12] In consequence—because of the continuum of political spaces and transnational surfaces along which "Bosnia" is constituted—the performative nature of the discourse of ethnic violence encompasses within the same logic, albeit in very different ways, those observing at a distance as much as those fighting close-up. While there is undoubtedly a substantial difference between, say, a military commander engaged in ethnic cleansing, an international diplomat using census data to map a political solution to that ethnic cleansing, and an academic analyst deploying rhetorics of ethnicization, the difference is one of how a particular logic is operationalized. It is not a difference of competing logics, for all those characters are working within the same nationalist imaginary. This is not to suggest that there is a necessary and inexorable progression from a rendering of community in ethnic terms to the politics of genocide. It is to suggest, however, that those different practices do not reflect distinct nationalist imaginaries.[13]

As such, there are many sites at which the conventional order of intelligibility concerning Bosnia can be contested. Conceptually, as has already been indicated, this can be done in terms of rethinking violence and history. Likewise, as will be argued below, the notion of *ethnicity* can be critically explored. Politically, we can turn to the narrativizations of the Bosnian war overlooked by the ontopological stories. In a series of counternarratives, therefore, this chapter will demonstrate alternative renderings of some important aspects of the conflict.

These counternarratives do not function as simple assertions of "the truth" in order to overcome all distortions and/or falsehoods, for they are neither free from nor beyond the politics of historical representation outlined in chapter 3. Instead, in line with the ethos of political criticism outlined in the first chapter, the purpose of constructing counternarratives is to offer up those dimensions of the historical and political field marginalized by ontopological narratives that contest and disturb the certainties of the "civil/ethnic/nationalist" accounts. Through their destabilizing interventions, these counternarratives embody a different relationship to the other and thus help effect a better interpretation.

Any number of arguments could contribute to counternarratives and be significant here, but a select range that disturb key points in the ontopological order of intelligibility will be considered. Therefore, in contrast to the centrality accorded essentialist accounts of ethnicity and the natural antagonism it is said to cause, we will look at the claims of coexistence and the politics of genocide. Instead of reading the materializations of violence as the working out of preordained cleavages and tensions, we will consider the symbolic character of the violence and its identity politics. And in place of notions about the settled religious differences and their role, we will examine the contested character of Islamicization in Bosnia. In each of these instances the argument is framed in terms of the deconstructive ethos. They have also been selected because they are located in the immediate context of the Bosnian war, and thus emphasize the way in which national deconstruction is best appreciated, and its pathologies best contested, by deconstructive thought. And as the first section of the final chapter will argue, issues of identity politics that are beyond the immediate context of the war problematize the ontopological order of intelligibility even further.

Concerning Ethnicity

Ethnicity is a concept that in its own right has a curious double life. As its salience in anthropological discourse has declined, its importance to the political world has increased.[14] This is most obvious in accounts of forms of violence supposedly new to the post–Cold War world, which have often cast them as "ethnic" — as in the case of Bosnia — no matter the other possibilities that exist. This efflorescence notwithstanding, "the 'ethnicity' that lives in public...discourse is no less chimerical than its academic sibling."[15]

The anthropological literature on ethnicity has conventionally been understood in terms of primordialist accounts versus instrumental arguments, followed by attempts to go beyond these positions. The primordialist position is that ethnicity is "a brute social fact" expressing the essential or innate character of group. While held overtly by few, its casting of "ethnicity" as an independent variable, the "first cause" from which often violent consequences are derived, means that elements of this conception can often be smuggled back into social scientific arguments.[16] The instrumentalist position holds instead that ethnicity is a resource created by members of a community to bring people together and mobilize them. Sometimes referred to as constructionist, in this position ethnicity is taken to be a response to particular circumstances. According to John Comaroff, in addition to these two orientations, a position that "tempers primordialism with a careful measure of constructionism" has emerged and become common. Sometimes understood as "perennialist," this position considers ethnicity to be a universal potential, but one that is realized only in certain circumstances.[17]

Contributions on ethnicity that have been significant in international relations and political science have embodied elements of this synthesis. Milton Esman's *Ethnic Politics* declares that "the concept of ethnic identity and solidarity that informs this study is drawn from both the primordialist and instrumentalist positions."[18] With a primordialist air, Esman writes that the notion that ethnicity is a "free-standing reality" or "societal phenomena" that draws on an "underlying core of memories [and] experience," has meant that "from the dawn of history communities organized on putative common descent, culture, and destiny have coexisted, competed, and clashed."[19] In an instrumental or constructionist cast (though he would resist the latter term, having expressed an antipathy to the supposedly fictive dimensions of social construction), Esman argues that "ethnicity" is not "so palpable a reality [that] it is an existential fact of life," but rather something that is meaningful only in a relational context where it is influenced by a range of catalysts and constraints.[20] Similarly, Anthony Smith's many works, much cited in international relations as *the* theorization of the issue, claim to resist the notion of primordialism but argue that the *ethnie* that precedes the nation and nationalism (understood in terms of a collective name, common myth of descent, shared history and culture, association with territory and a sense of solidarity) can be observed in diverse communities, even those that existed thousands of years ago.[21]

Traces of primordialism are not difficult to locate in arguments that claim to be free of them, especially when the conflict in the former Yugoslavia and Bosnia is the issue. Few of the narratives examined in chapter 3 explicitly deal with ethnicity as an abstract concept, but their ethnicization of politics in the region means that few would disagree with Denitch's claim that "ethnicity is ascribed, not acquired. You are born with it or you are not."[22] Even overtly instrumental accounts of the conflict can invoke primordial-like notions of ethnicity, and when the concern is history rather than ethnicity, a similar fixity can be observed.[23] Barry Posen's argument concerning the importance of the security dilemma in the emergence of nationalist, ethnic, and religious conflict in Eurasia styles itself as going beyond the notion that the release of age-old antipathies is a sufficient explanation. Yet, when it comes to considering the former Yugoslavia, the argument shifts unselfconsciously to maintain that Croat and Serb history "goes back hundreds of years, although intense Croat-Serb conflict is only about 125 years old. The history of the region is quite warlike."[24]

Posen's argument points to the way in which references to the Balkan region can do the work of a primordialist understanding of ethnicity, even when those terms are not directly invoked. Indeed, the idea that the Balkans is an atypical region with a distinct and historically determined character has been prevalent in a plethora of analyses and pronouncements. Thus, Malcolm Rifkind, the British Defense Secretary, explained the hopelessness of the Bosnian crisis during a NATO meeting by saying simply, "It's the Balkans."[25] According to a senior alliance military officer, "the problem is that NATO has not adapted to fighting against serpents, and they happen to be swarming all over the Balkans."[26] We can note, similarly, the way in which one Western diplomat observed in relation to the future of Milošević that "of course, there's no accountability in the Balkans," or the observation of another that while Milošević would enforce UN sanctions against the Bosnian Serbs, "it's impossible to totally close a border in the Balkans." We can observe the description of the conflict as a "Balkan imbroglio," of the Bosnian prime minister as "part Balkan wheeler-dealer," or hear a journalist's narrative speak of "the political passivity that is a hallmark of the Balkans" and of a politician who "dodged the question in best Balkan style."[27] And we can find many of these prejudicial formulations in the memoir of one of the international community's chief negotiators charged with the responsibility of finding a solution to the conflict.[28]

These and other absolutist generalizations, encompassing characteristics that are all equally applicable to other circumstances, serve to mark the Balkans as backward, foreign, barbaric, uncivilized, fundamentally different—any of the significations that can be applied to "our" orientalized others. Indeed, some have argued that there is so prevalent a rhetoric for this region that we should speak of "Balkanism" as a subset of orientalism.[29] Whatever the merits of such an argument, the more interesting point is the way in which orientalist discourse has migrated to the regions marked as other, only to be redeployed by those so marked. This can come in the form of general self-disparagement—the pathetic remarks of one who wanted to explain away Srebrenica because "we are Balkan people and we are uncivilised"—or self-discipline, where, in academic accounts as much as public discourse, those in areas of the former Yugoslavia once ruled by the Hapsburg monarchy look down upon those in former Ottoman-ruled areas.[30]

Such representational practices stem in part from the invention of "Eastern Europe" as a distinct area. As Larry Wolff has argued, the division of Europe's symbolic geography into West/East—replacing the Renaissance boundary of North/South—was a product of the Enlightenment, during which time the idea of "civilization" was appropriated to the West and denied to the East by influential essayists and philosophers (including Voltaire and Rousseau) who eschewed the need to travel to the regions they mapped.[31]

This notion of a cultural and political significance to the geography of West/East recurs in the literature on ethnicity and nationalism. Many recent contributions have sought to draw a distinction between "civic" and "ethnic" nationalism, with the latter regarded as being prevalent in non-Western contexts where, it is argued by the likes of Smith, the birth community and native culture are emphasized to the detriment of contractual notions of citizenship said to characterize Western communities. The effect is to reimport into sociological analyses the rarely used dictionary understanding of *ethnicity* as meaning "pagan" or "heathen," and instantiate an assumption of political modernization whereby the less-developed polities of the East will one day catch up to the West.[32] At the same time, this understanding obscures the extent to which racialized notions of identity are integral to the supposedly nonracial "civic" societies of the West.[33]

What is striking about much of the literature in international relations and political science dealing with ethnicity is its almost complete ignorance of the subtleties of the anthropological literature on the subject. Thus, Marcus Banks observes that in political science there has been a preference for "clearly defined, objective definitions of ethnicity and ethnic groups."[34] Likewise, Katherine Verdery has argued that "the pedestrian efforts that persisted in sociology and political science" failed to heed the insights of Fredrik Barth's seminal essay in *Ethnic Groups and Boundaries*. Published in 1969, and the progenitor to a long line of anthropological research, Barth's argument shifted the focus on ethnicity away from seemingly objective and shared cultural content to the organization of cultural difference through the boundaries that dichotomize groups.[35] As we shall see in chapter 5, this lacuna in political thought is easily visible in the anthropological assumptions that enable the peace plans that sought to end the Bosnian war.

Heeding the thrust of much anthropological literature in the wake of Barth would cast doubt on some of the central tenets of arguments such as Smith's. As Comaroff notes, to believe that the origins of a nation can be found in a premodern *ethnie* requires overlooking the way in which some of the supposedly most essentialized ethnicities — such as the Yoruba of Nigeria, and the Zulu and Tswana of southern Africa — made their transition from "humanity" to "ethnicity" only in the context of European colonialism. The conclusion to draw from this, says Comaroff, is that "far from being an abstract property or a universal potentiality, a thing or an immanent capacity... ethnicity is a set of relations, its content constructed in the course of historical processes."[36]

The impetus for ethnicity as an essentialized category, then, has nothing to do with the prevalence of characteristics said to be associated with ethnicity. Definitions of *ethnicity* claim that it comprises language, culture, nation, race, religion, or some other property. But they reveal no property that was ethnicity and *not* some other contingent and contestable aspect of identity such as language, culture, nation, race, or religion. This suggests that *ethnicity* is a term that signifies relationships of power in the problematic of identity/difference rather than being a signifier for which there is a stable referent. Those who are marked as "ethnic" are rendered as "not European"; the term *ethnic* rarely if ever applies to white Europeans.[37] As a result, argues Comaroff, "ethnicity is not an ontological feature of human life" and thus cannot be — contrary to the way it is deployed with respect to situations such as Bosnia — "an 'independent' explanatory principle."[38]

Given this, it would be better to follow Verdery's account of ethnicity as one of the "basic ordering principles which, singly or in combination, organize the social universe of humankind," and suggest that the limitations associated with the discursive economy of identity politics are an issue for participants and observers alike.[39] This is because the key categories of the discursive economy of identity (which include age, race, gender, caste, class, kinship, nation, and ethnicity), particularly when they are institutionalized in systems of social classification, "also establish grounds for authority and legitimacy through the categories they set down, and . . . make their categories seem both natural and socially real," thereby making the question of purposive action secondary for all concerned.[40] Ethnicity is therefore better understood as a component of the representational politics of identity — particularly the identity of "others" — and attempts to naturalize ethnicity are best regarded as efforts to remove the question of identity/difference and its materialization from the realm of politics. Given the obvious importance of issues of identity to conflicts such as that in Bosnia, this interpretive move is deeply flawed.

Violence, history, and ethnicity are concepts central to the conventional narrativizations of the conflict in Bosnia. The refiguring of these concepts suggested here, which results in being able to appreciate the central role of traditional theorizations in the performative constitution of identity, opens up the space for a consideration of alternative narrativizations that run counter to many of the ontopological renderings examined in chapter 3. What is presented, however, is not one unitary position designed to overcome its antithesis. Rather, an effort will be made to convey the complexities and tensions that revolve around and cut through the issues under consideration. Portraying the flux inherent in these moments is more than sufficient to contest the totalizing claims of ontopological narratives. Indeed, this strategy can be thought of in terms of Michael André Bernstein's call for "a new kind of anti-totalitarian narrative" whereby "a prosaic, quotidian voice can contest at the formal as well as the thematic level the absolutist ideology that makes mass murder conceivable."[41]

We will begin with one of the most obvious ways of contesting the view that ethnicity in Bosnia was deeply felt and inevitably conflictual—the counterclaims of multicultural and multiethnic coexistence. This reading is important for two reasons. First, it will demonstrate the way in which particular claims about what exists embody metaphysical commitments that effect specific inclusions or exclusions, thereby recalling themes concerning the violence of representation and the order of intelligibility. Second, these arguments suggest that the level of violence in Bosnia was brought on not by the clash of autonomous and settled identities but by the attempt to produce a society in which the divisions between people could be clearly seen and enforced. As one commentator remarked during the escalation of the war, "those who now say that Bosnia is being carved along its seams are wrong: Bosnia is being cut right through its living flesh, hence all the blood."[42]

The Claims of Coexistence

The official Bosnian political narrative of an open state opposed to exclusionary ideologies was discussed in chapter 3, and its central themes were reiterated throughout the conflict. Often the same media accounts, and certainly the same media outlets, that rendered the Bosnian war in terms of ethnic exclusivity carried stories of communal coexistence that contested those premises. In one such report, a ("Muslim") Bosnian army commander who spoke with a group of (Serbian) Bosnians declared that "we have all lived together here for centuries, and we want to go on living together." Responding for the gathering, one of the (Serbian) Bosnians proclaimed that "it's impossible to divide us, we are simply too mixed. Politics are one thing. Real life is another."[43] Similarly, an elderly (Serbian) Bosnian—whose own son, a doctor, was killed by Serb nationalist forces because he refused to join ethnic cleansing operations—was reported as being mystified at the Vance-Owen plan: "We have lived together for a thousand years.... Where did they come up with this crazy plan to divide us up? Why don't they come and talk to us?"[44]

In one sense, these micronarratives of the participant-interpreters are as nationalist as those of their opponents: they project back into history — back "hundreds of years" if not "a thousand years" — an imperative drawn from the present to justify the form of the nation they believe should exist. However, the shared logic cannot disguise the markedly different political results of their argument, manifested in a variety of concrete and different ways. In a chess club in Tuzla, the multiethnic members resisted a reporter's questions about the categories of their identities: "When we are shelled together we go to the cellar together, we share the food together. This was all started by a few mad people who did not care what happened to ordinary people."[45] Faced with similar views, and noting the way mixed marriages more than complicated ethnic categorization, one reporter observed that "people recall the time when they lived together and often did not know or did not care whether their neighbor was a Serb, a Croat, a Muslim or a Montenegrin."[46] Throughout the conflict that lack of regard for exclusive identities was evident in the way secret networks comprising large numbers of Serbian individuals assisted those targeted for ethnic cleansing.[47] And in the wake of the Dayton agreement, one angry teenager denounced the partition of the peace plan: "Do you think we were fighting for just a percentage of land?. . . We fought for one Bosnia, with everyone living in it, and people here feel that all those people died for nothing."[48]

Those who fled Bosnia for a refugee existence in Europe found themselves in the paradoxical circumstance of having been forced from a hybrid polity by chauvinist policies only to end up in an equally plural and varied site. According to the proprietor of a café in Düsseldorf, which had become a retreat for Bosnians, "we've got Muslims, Serbs, Croats, Macedonians, Albanians. This place is a mini-Yugoslavia." Sometimes the multicultural ethos expressed by Bosnians combined with the refugee experience to produce a series of dislocations. Reflecting on his circumstances, one Bosnian in Germany remarked, "I can't live somewhere I can't identity with. I can't identify with the government in Bosnia and I can't identity with Germany either. I'm someone from the former Yugoslavia, but that no longer exists. First I'm a human being, then a Bosnian, then someone from Bosnia of the Muslim religious. But I'm not religious. I don't feel Muslim."[49]

That said, the image of communal harmony or nonessentialist identities often disclosed by Bosnians cannot disguise the divisions that altered the lives of others. As one account of the conflict in Croatia reported, the war has torn apart ethnically mixed families. Fathers, sons and brothers have volunteered for rival militias, only to face each other gun in hand. In Borovo Selo one son of a Croatian mother says he is ready to shoot his Serbian father over the barricades. "I am sure that would kill me as well," he told the Zagreb weekly *Danas*. "My uncles sent a message that they have nothing but the bullet for me."[50]

Such feelings were realized in the case of a Serb man who shot his daughter and Croat wife once war broke out. Although sporadic episodes of this kind have been used to buttress a simple tale of inevitable ethnic conflict, they reflect a more complex political issue. As Kenneth Anderson notes of the last case, the implication to be drawn is that "he had no other identity, no identity given to him by modernity, with which to counter-balance his sudden, horrifying discovery of 'outsidedness.' Neither individual identity nor identity with his family was enough to save him or them."[51]

Had it been fostered and supported, perhaps a discourse of identity politics organized around some notion of multiculturalism might have benefited those people. And if there is one symbol of the multicultural ethos of Bosnia, it is Sarajevo. Even the most unlikely of its citizens experienced that ethos directly. When Radovan Karadžić married into a Sarajevan family, "he moved in with his new wife's family in an apartment building that housed 11 families — one Croat-Hungarian, five Muslim, four Serb, one Croat. It remains a metaphor for the Sarajevo spirit of coexistence. Even though Karadžić himself has been saying for four years that Bosnia's three nations 'cannot live together,' all but Karadžić and his Serb in-laws still reside at Sutjeska 2."[52] As one analyst noted, because of this coexistence and its persistence throughout the conflict, "Sarajevo is an irrefutable rebuttal to the Serbian war refrain that it is impossible to live together. This is why it must be completely ravaged."[53] The enormity of the devastation inflicted on Sarajevo is, therefore, testament *not* to the impossibility of coexistence *but* to its persistence. Which is why two-thirds of the population signed a petition in January 1995 calling for the capital to remain open and undivided, why a delegation of Sarajevo Serbs traveled to Belgrade in March 1995 to stress that they enjoyed the same rights as other citizens and demanded an end to the war, and why after Dayton thousands of Sarajevans continued to protest publicly in support of coexistence.[54] At the same time, disillusion with the international community's timidity in responding to their situation, combined with the population transformation in which many who fled the city have been replaced by people from rural areas overrun by Serbian forces, has fueled a bitter skepticism among some toward the multicultural ethos. As one refugee in Sarajevo explained, "we are not interested in these intellectuals who talk of living together.... They have all left Bosnia. It is the poor who remain to fight. This country belongs to us now, not them."[55]

This remark points to a common, though problematic, explanation in Bosnia for the conflict. The idea that an urban/rural divide, between the cosmopolitan outlook of the city and the xenophobic view of the village, with attendant assumptions about class and education, has political consequences more significant than anything to do with ethnicity is sometimes suggested. It is claimed that the most extreme nationalists are rural folk, and that the influx into Sarajevo and Tuzla of refugees from the rural areas has hardened nationalist proclivities in Bosnia.[56] Similarly, Serbs opposed to the Serb nationalism of those who wanted to partition Sarajevo believe, as one who is married to a Muslim declared, that "they are country people who lost their homes in Karadžić's war and now pretend Grbavica [a suburb of Sarajevo] is theirs.... All this nonsense about Serbs not being able to live together with Muslims and Croats was invented by Karadžić who persuaded ignorant people it was true."[57] Prevalent though it is, this rendering overlooks the complexities of identity even in nonurban Bosnia (which will be considered in chapter 7) as well as the fact that the desire for reintegration in postwar Bosnia can be found outside Sarajevo as well as in it.[58]

The "foreign minister" of the then unrecognized Bosnian Serb republic, Aleksha Buha, implicitly recognized that coexistence was the norm when he declared in 1993 that it was better for his people "to commit collective suicide than to live with others any longer."[59] In the period of reassessment that Dayton has allowed for, a good number of Serbs have come to question this. While "multi-culturalism is not politically correct in Pale," even some residents of the Republika Srpska capital concede that they had Muslim friends in the past. But they cannot envisage a mixed life in the future: "It's not because we hate Muslims. It's because they hate us."[60] For those who have ventured into Sarajevo, there is palpable surprise that the image of a city overrun by Islamic fundamentalism that had been broadcast by Pale television — with all women in head scarves and the Orthodox church destroyed — failed to materialize. Likewise, there is disappointment that the family and friends they left behind are sometimes not as welcoming as they had hoped. The conclusion reached is that because of the war, "it will take at least five years before we can live together again."[61]

Such concerns about the possibility or otherwise of future living arrangements are an untimely issue for the tens of thousands of Bosnian Serbs who remain of their own volition within the ("Muslim-Croat") Federation of Bosnia-Herzegovina, as well as the non-Serbs remaining in what is now Republika Srpska. As shall be argued in chapter 7, while the war has produced greater homogenization of the population than existed before, such statistics counter the oft-repeated notion that Bosnia is now composed only of ethnically exclusive territories. They also illustrate the folly of assuming that all Bosnian Serbs can be placed in the orbit of and represented by the SDS leadership in Republika Srpska.[62]

This contention is ably demonstrated by reference to the event many assume signifies the monocultural future for Bosnia's entities. The handover to federation control in early 1996 of the Sarajevo suburbs formerly occupied by Bosnian Serb forces, which was required by the Dayton agreement, saw the population transfer of thousands. Although often understood as an inevitable and understandable development given the horrors of the war, specific acts of commission and omission by important parties made it happen.

The major act of commission was the Bosnian Serb leadership's decision to prompt the exodus of tens of thousands of Serbs from suburbs such as Grbavica, Ilidza, Ilijas, and Vogosca. According to the UN High Commission for Refugees (UNHCR) spokesperson, Kris Janowski, "they didn't have to go. They were incited to go by their own authorities. There were incited by a regime previously responsible for expelling tens of thousands of people and killing many others."[63] The transfer of the Serbian population from Sarajevo was deemed by the Bosnian Serb leadership to be necessary for the fulfillment of their long-standing desire for the ethnic partition of the city and the creation of a "Serbian Sarajevo."[64] Ensuring that Serbs *did not* live in areas governed by non-Serbs was also necessary for the argument that Serbs *could not* be governed by non-Serbs.[65]

During a six-day period in February 1996 between fifty thousand and sixty thousand Serbs either left or were forced out of their residences and transferred to Republika Srpska. Following an unrecognized plebiscite in December 1995, the operation was not totally successful, as they left behind more than ten thousand of their compatriots. But in the face of an unrelenting propaganda campaign against the possibility of coexistence, backed up by arson strikes, violent attacks, the removal of industrial plants, and the cutting off of essential utilities, the pressure on citizens to conform was great.[66] The Serbian Civic Council even claimed that the children of those expressing a desire to remain were being kidnapped in order to force their parents to relent.[67] There was additionally an inducement from the Pale leadership to encourage the flight. Plans for the construction of a new Serbian Sarajevo in Republika Srpska territory were announced. Dubbed "Paleopolis," the scheme called for a new urban complex, estimated to cost $15 billion, to house those who gave up their Sarajevo residences.[68]

To counter the separatist rallying cry, a number of organizations encouraged Serbs to remain in Sarajevo. The Serbian mayor of Ilidza, the Serbian Civic Council, the Democratic Initiative of Sarajevo Serbs (which represented those who supported Karadžić during the war but nonetheless wished to remain), and even the Belgrade regime all sought to contest the Pale leadership's strategy.[69] These declarations were matched by similar statements from the federation authorities, especially when they had to condemn the unsanctioned activities of "Muslim gangs" (as opposed to the officially organized violence of the Serbian authorities) who were contributing to the atmosphere of intimidation.[70]

That the fear that had been induced could not be overcome was anything but inevitable. Above all else, the international community could have directed its representatives in the area to counter in practice the separatist strategies. In particular, NATO's Implementation Force (IFOR) could have responded more decisively to the acts of violence being perpetrated. On one of the very few occasions when they did other than stand back and observe the "scorched earth" policy unfolding before them, the arsonists they temporarily detained were handed over to the Serbian authorities, who released them immediately.[71] But instead of working against separatism, IFOR actually worked for it. In late February 1996 the IFOR commander Admiral Leighton Smith provided IFOR military escorts for Bosnian Serb forces implementing the exodus from Sarajevo.[72]

Equally, the federation authorities could have done a good deal more than simply offer soothing statements. For example, at the height of the exodus, new policing arrangements for the suburbs concerned could have been more sensitive to local anxieties (although this would have required greater assistance from the International Police Task Force established by the Dayton agreement).[73] Nonetheless, in the three months immediately after the organized exodus, some five thousand of those Serbs who left wanted to return. But in doing so they encountered obstacles from the federation side that indicated the acts of omission that ensured the acts of commission were not effectively countered.[74] At the Inter-Entity Boundary Line, some vehicles with "unrecognised license plates" have been prevented from crossing into the federation, forcing those returning to transfer to buses and trucks. Once they make it back to Sarajevo—despite promises that all vacated property would be sealed for six months—they often find that refugees from Srebrenica and elsewhere have occupied their apartments, that their community's doctors have not been employed in local hospitals, and that local schools do not welcome their children. Whether or not this adds up to an official policy opposing reintegration, or is the product of both a lack of enthusiasm to promote reintegration and the practical problem of where to house the thousands of Bosnian refugees, the federation's (in)action rightly attracted serious criticism.[75]

The Politics of Genocide

Those accounts that have emphasized the claim of coexistence do not deny that mass violence of a horrific kind has been perpetrated in Bosnia. However, those accounts view that violence as the consequence of a strategic plan to produce political domination and cultural homogeneity instead of as resulting from the mechanical operation of a historically inevitable ethnic antagonism. Understood in terms of genocide (as chapter 1 made clear), this argument involves an array of complex conceptual questions. These will help demonstrate the way in which the rationale for violence inheres even in the structures of intelligibility and response strategies that claim to contain it.

The UN Convention on the Prevention and Punishment of the Crime of Genocide (signed in December 1948, and in force from January 1951) provides the currently accepted definition:

Article II

In the present Convention, genocide means any of the following acts committed with intent to destroy, in whole or in part, a national, ethnical, racial or religious group, as such:

(a) Killing members of the group;

(b) Causing serious bodily or mental harm to members of the group;

(c) Deliberately inflicting on the group conditions of life calculated to bring about its physical destruction in whole or in part;

(d) Imposing measures intended to prevent births within the group;

(e) Forcibly transferring children of the group to another group.

Article III

The following acts shall be punishable:

(a) Genocide;

(b) Conspiracy to commit genocide;

(c) Direct and public incitement to commit genocide;

(d) Attempt to commit genocide;

(e) Complicity in genocide.[76]

As with all international legal instruments, a number of interpretive questions arise. Three are especially important. First, what constitutes "intent to destroy"? Second, what sort of quantification is implied by the notion of "in whole or in part"? Does the discussion in the UN Legal Committee, where there was a debate during drafting about whether the killing of an individual could constitute genocide, mean that "in part" should be "an appreciable part"?[77] Third, is the exclusion of political and social groups from protection warranted by the objections of the British and Soviet bloc delegates, who during the convention's negotiation claimed that "because of their mutability and lack of distinguishing characteristics," the inclusion of such groups would diminish and dilute the convention?[78] Not surprisingly, these issues have promoted numerous debates, the interesting details of which need not detain us here.[79] The immediate concern is to keep the above questions in mind while considering the way in which the charge of genocide has been debated in relation to Bosnia.

The international community, especially the United States (as was noted in chapter 3), went to considerable lengths to avoid casting the Bosnian war in terms of genocide. This provoked the publication of internal dissent from within the State Department. Having resigned to protest U.S. policy, George Kenney argued that U.S. policy "borders on complicity in genocide" because "anyone is guilty who watches genocide and does nothing."[80] One of Kenney's predecessors on the Yugoslav desk circulated a paper in early 1994 titled "The Pin-Stripe Approach to Genocide," in which it was argued that the president, the secretary of state, and other senior officials knew that genocide was being waged by Serbs against Muslims but sought to downplay the evidence.[81]

One counter to this view claimed that while war crimes were being committed in Bosnia, genocide had a "very specific meaning: the systematic annihilation of a racial, political or cultural group."[82] Aside from mistakenly including political groups within the convention's remit, this opinion rewrote the proviso of "intent to destroy, in whole or in part" as "systematic annihilation." These errors were essential for an argument that wanted to claim that "the goal of the combatants in the former Yugoslavia is to drive the enemy from the land, not to capture and kill every man, woman and child." In a public intervention that shared some of these concerns, Kenney stepped back from his earlier view to argue that Bosnia was analogous to Lebanon, rather than to Rwanda or the Holocaust, because a recalculation of the overall death toll and the absence of "systematic killing" in the detention camps meant that the charge of genocide was misplaced.[83]

What these arguments demonstrate is the way our understanding of genocide is largely determined by the shadow of the Holocaust rather than the articles of the UN Convention. While the convention does not entail any requirements about the scale or systematic nature of the killing — other than those associated with the intent to destroy, in whole or in part — popular understanding of the Holocaust's uniqueness determines for many what does or does not count as genocide. Unless there is a similarly organized bureaucratic production of mass death, in which one side consists entirely of perpetrators while the other side is without question defenseless victims pursuing nonviolent strategies, the charge of genocide and the obligations that flow from it are avoided.[84]

The international community's sensitivity to the question of genocide has been exacerbated by the evidence amassed to support the claim. While the Bosnian war is anything but a black-and-white situation, there can be little doubt that the overwhelming majority of observers have concluded that the leadership of one party is predominantly responsible for the brutal strategies of ethnic cleansing. According to a CIA report in early 1995, "the Serbs" committed 90 percent of the acts of ethnic cleansing. As one official said of the leaked report, "to those who think the parties are equally guilty, this report is pretty devastating. . . . the scale of what the Serbs did is so different. But more than that, it makes clear, with concrete evidence, that there was a conscious, coherent, and systematic Serbian policy to get rid of Muslims, through murders, torture, and imprisonment."[85]

Moreover, because ethnic cleansing has been viewed as the objective of the war, rather than merely an unfortunate side effect, the conclusion that Bosnia has suffered genocide has been reached by many nongovernment sources. Amnesty International, Helsinki Watch, the UN Commission of Experts on the Former Yugoslavia, and the UN Special Rapporteur on the Former Yugoslavia (former Polish prime minister Tadeusz Mazowiecki) concur on this general point, and have at least indirectly supported the overall conclusions of the aforementioned CIA report. In that conclusion they have been joined by a large body of international reportage.[86]

One qualification to that consensus highlights an important point. Although influential in arguing that ethnic cleansing was the political objective, Mazowiecki refrained in his UN reports from using the term *genocide* to cover the atrocities he condemned. This reservation was not the product of substantive doubts but a caution brought on by his belief that such a determination could only be made by an international legal authority. As such, Mazowiecki regarded the determination of genocide to be a matter for The Hague tribunal.[87]

The International Criminal Tribunal for the Former Yugoslavia (ICTY) has indicted a number of individuals for genocide, and their work is likely to establish their responsibility for genocide in legal terms.[88] But before the ICTY was established, the 1993 rulings by the International Court of Justice (ICJ) in response to an application from Bosnia calling Serbia to account in terms of the Genocide Convention cast important light on the argument. The ICJ's decisions involve significant judgments about the nature of the Bosnian war and the evidence available for its conclusions. As such, those decisions and the reasoning behind them illustrate conceptual and political themes central to the argument of this book. To date few if any accounts of the Bosnian war have given these decisions the attention they merit.

In its application, based on documentary sources akin to those noted above, Bosnia asked the ICJ for an order that would have declared primarily that Yugoslavia (Serbia and Montenegro) had breached the Genocide Convention, violated the Geneva conventions, and contravened the Universal Declaration of Human Rights and the UN Charter by engaging in the killing of and violence toward Bosnian citizens. In response, Yugoslavia requested an order citing Bosnia for genocide, and called into question Bosnia's use of press reports to substantiate its case. Yugoslavia's counsel maintained that "the allegations made against the Federal Republic in the stream of documents that have been sent to the court by the other side are unsupported by any hard evidence. Press reports, often tendentious, are not adequate as a basis for such serious charges against a sovereign State."[89]

The nub of the Bosnian argument was that in terms of the Genocide Convention, "the rump Yugoslavia, with its agents and surrogates, has killed Bosnian citizens because of their Bosnian nationality or because of their Muslim religion, or both."[90] Bosnia's counsel agreed that the convention meant Bosnia had to establish not only that Yugoslavia's actions had resulted in the deaths of people but also that an intent to destroy Bosnian Muslims as a group in whole or in part had to be established.

To that end, Bosnia relied on the evidence accumulated by other governments, international organizations, NGOs, and the media. In a subsequent application for provisional measures, Bosnia buttressed that claim with additional sources of information, two of which were crucial. The first was an official communiqué from the Serbian diplomatic mission in New York, while the second was a statement from the Serbian government published in an official newspaper. Both were aimed at pressurizing the Bosnian Serbs into accepting the Vance-Owen peace initiative, and it was stated in the latter that "Serbia has lent a great, great deal of assistance to the Serbs in Bosnia. Owing to that assistance they have achieved most of what they wanted." Most of this assistance, it said, "was sent to people and fighters in Bosnia-Herzegovina." In contrast, Yugoslavia supported its claim for an order against Bosnia with documents from the "Yugoslav State Commission for War Crimes and Genocide." In an April 1993 memorandum cataloging alleged Bosnian atrocities, this organization noted that much of its evidence came from the army of (the then unrecognized) Republika Srpska.[91]

In making an application against Yugoslavia for contravening the Genocide Convention, Bosnia was asking the ICJ to hear a full case, which is pending.[92] But Bosnia also argued that the circumstances warranted a consideration of provisional measures prior to a full hearing. In so doing, Bosnia was relying on the court's "power to indicate, if it considers that circumstances so require, any provisional measure which ought to be taken to preserve the respective rights of either party."[93] The ICJ accepted that the Genocide Convention and its statute provided legitimate grounds for the case, and on 8 April 1993 issued an order for provisional measures.

By unanimous vote the court ordered that "The Government of the Federal Republic of Yugoslavia (Serbia and Montenegro) should immediately, in pursuance of its undertaking in the Convention on the Prevention and Punishment of the Crime of Genocide of 9 December 1948, take all measures ... within its power to prevent commission of the crime of genocide." By a vote of thirteen to one, the court ordered that

> The Government of the Federal Republic of Yugoslavia (Serbia and Montenegro) should in particular ensure that any military, paramilitary or irregular armed units which may be directed or supported by it, as well as any organizations and persons which may

be subject to its control, direction or influence, do not commit any acts of genocide, or conspiracy to commit genocide, of direct and public incitement to commit genocide, or of complicity in genocide, whether directed against the Muslim population of Bosnia and Herzegovina or against any other nationality, ethnical, racial or religious group.

And by another unanimous vote, the court ordered that "the Government of the Federal Republic of Yugoslavia (Serbia and Montenegro) and the Government of the Republic of Bosnia and Herzegovina should not take any action and should ensure that no action is taken which may aggravate or extend the existing dispute over the prevention or punishment of the crime of genocide, or render it more difficult to solution."[94]

While neither Bosnia nor Yugoslavia won precisely the order each had requested, and notwithstanding U.S. attempts to argue that this order made no determination about genocide actually taking place, the result was a political vindication of much of Bosnia's position and a repudiation of Yugoslavia's. As much was recognized by the judge who dissented from the second part of the order. According to Judge Nikolai K. Tarassov, "these passages of the Order are open to the interpretation that the court believes that the Government of the Federal Republic of Yugoslavia is indeed involved in such genocidal acts, or at least that it may very well be so involved."[95]

Tarassov's dissent stemmed from his concern that the court's order involved a de facto judgment on the merits of the substantive case prior to its being heard in full. He was concerned despite the formal proviso contained in the order that while the court can consider the circumstances drawn to its attention, it "cannot make definitive findings of fact or of imputability."[96] Similarly, the court emphasized that it was not called upon to establish the existence of breaches of the Genocide Convention by either party, "but to determine whether the circumstances require the indication of provisional measures to be taken by the Parties for the protection of rights under the Genocide Convention." A fine legal distinction with unclear political implications was being made: although there was no final determination of fact, the circumstances were such that provisional measures were warranted.

This paradox was even more prominent in the court's consideration of Bosnia's second request (which included the evidence of Serbian involvement noted above) and Yugoslavia's additional request for the measures it was denied in the April order.[97] Once again the court did not grant the details of either Bosnia's or Yugoslavia's applications. But it did reaffirm the April order, and in so doing it strengthened the argument that it was making a de facto substantive determination on the issue of genocide in Bosnia.

Although, in its order of 13 September 1993, the court noted again that it could not make definitive findings of fact, it nonetheless argued that

> since the Order of 8 April 1993 was made, and despite that Order, and despite many resolutions of the Security Council of the United Nations, great suffering and loss of life has been sustained by the population of Bosnia and Herzegovina in circumstances which shock the conscience of mankind and flagrantly conflict with moral law and the spirit and aims of the United Nations.[98]

While a view of the circumstances influenced its reaffirmation of the April order, a similar view led the court to deny Yugoslavia's request for an order against Bosnia. The court argued that although it must "recognize the existence of some risk to the persons whose protection Yugoslavia seeks," and reminded both parties of those elements of the earlier order applicable to each of them, it did "not find that the circumstances, as they now present themselves to the court, are such as to require a more specific indication of measures addressed to Bosnia-Herzegovina."[99]

In reaching their rulings, the judges illustrated an important point about the prevailing judicial epistemology in this case. Whether arguing for or against Bosnia's position, the judges spoke freely in objectivist-sounding terms about "facts." Yet the logic of their position is closer to Hayden White's understanding of narrative (discussed in chapter 3) than might first appear to be the case. The majority opinions endorsed the legitimacy of the Bosnian government's sources, as well as the overall proposition derived from them. Given that those sources consist of media accounts as well as government and NGO reports, the majority of the ICJ's bench have in effect come out in favor of intertextuality, and rejected the notion that there is an extradiscursive realm of evidentiary authority to which they could appeal.[100]

In support of the ICJ's determinations of actuality, there is an accumulating body of evidence concerning the assistance, planning, and matériel Yugoslavia provided the Bosnian Serbs. Evidence for military assistance includes intelligence intercepts of consultations between the Yugoslav army's general staff in Belgrade and the officers directing operations in Bosnia, the appointment of a senior Yugoslav officer to command the Croatian Serb army in Krajina just prior to Croatia's successful Operation Storm, financial records that show Serb military personnel in Bosnia and Croatia being paid from Belgrade, the use of buses with Belgrade registrations to expel people from the "safe havens" in eastern Bosnia, the repairs to Bosnian Serb military infrastructure carried out by the Yugoslav army after the NATO air strikes of August 1995, and the regular reports of UN military observers recording flights with military cargo from Serbia into Bosnian Serb territory.[101]

The thorny issue of intent required by the Genocide Convention is also being illuminated by new thinking and new accounts. An example of the thinking can be found in the UN Commission of Experts' report, where the following is noted:

> It is the element of intent to destroy a designated group in whole or in part, which makes crimes of mass murder and crimes against humanity qualify as genocide. To be genocide within the meaning of the Convention, the crimes against a number of individuals must be directed at their collectivity or at them in their collective character or capacity.... The necessary element of intent may be inferred from sufficient facts. In certain cases, there will be evidence of actions or omissions of such a degree that the defendant may reasonably be assumed to have been aware of the consequences of his or her conduct, which goes to the establishment of intent, but not necessarily motive.[102]

The new accounts, including the publication in late 1995 of a revealing book by Borislav Jović, a former confidant of Milošević, have provided many details on the strategic plans for Bosnia of the Serbian leadership.[103] These involved the formation of "Chetnik militias" in the spring of 1991, the establishment of fortifications around Sarajevo in the autumn of 1991 by the Yugoslav Army (JNA) (which were observed by U.S. intelligence), the organized exodus of Serb families from Sarajevo in March 1992 (and Tuzla some weeks later), and the disciplined tactics of the Bosnian Serb army (in contrast to their rabblelike image).[104] More than a year after the Dayton agreement was signed, the testimony of Serbian paramilitaries on their role in ethnic cleansing operations, and the lawsuits of JNA soldiers injured in the covert war in Bosnia seeking compensation for service the authorities wish to cover up, have added to this knowledge.[105]

Sidestepping the charge of genocide, and the importance of intent, would involve — as one of the newspaper columns referred to above argued — the proposition that the war was about territory rather than the destruction of a community. In this view, "ethnic cleansing" would have been the "collateral damage" Mazowiecki maintained it was not. But one aspect of the ICJ deliberations further challenged this view. As Judge Elihu Lauterpacht noted, this defense of the Yugoslav position was made virtually impossible by Yugoslavia's commitment to the idea that ethnic cleansing and genocide were comparable and linked. This admission came in that party's first request for provisional measures to be ordered against Bosnia. In the context of arguing that the court should be restricted to the Genocide Convention, Yugoslavia asked the court to order the end of the practice of ethnic cleansing. In so doing, Yugoslavia at least implicitly took the position that ethnic cleansing was relevant to the Genocide Convention, and vice versa.[106]

Although territory was not there an issue, there was a spatial dimension to genocide identified by Lauterpacht that both ran counter to the Bosnian argument and demonstrated the prevalence of certain assumptions about identity politics in thinking about the Genocide Convention. Bosnia had argued in its second request for provisional measures that Yugoslavia should be ordered to "cease and desist from any and all efforts . . . to partition, dismember, annex or incorporate the sovereign territory of Bosnia and Herzegovina." Sustaining this request required Bosnia to argue that these strategies could be subsumed by the Genocide Convention, which, in turn, meant Bosnia had to demonstrate that those practices are aimed at destroying, in whole or in part, a national, ethnical, racial, or religious group. The issue this raises for Bosnia is, Which formulation of political community and identity would be affected?

In the first request for provisional measures, the Bosnian counsel had argued that Yugoslavia was killing "Bosnian citizens because of their Bosnian nationality or because of their Muslim religion, or both." This conception ran together, in an ontopological manner, national and religious dimensions of identity. But according to Lauterpacht, of all the groups identified by the convention (which had excluded political and social formations), the only one that could be threatened by territorial dismemberment and partition was the *national* group. The question this prompted was thus, What national group is being threatened in Bosnia? This produces an interesting reflection by the judge on Bosnian nationality (or the lack of it):

> Once one speaks of a "national" group defined by reference to the people resident within the territory of Bosnia-Herzegovina, one immediately excludes any "national" group that may be described by reference exclusively to a single ethnical, racial or religious qualification. The population of Bosnia-Herzegovina includes not only Muslim elements, but also Serbs, Croats and other minority religious or ethnical groups. Since the conduct which is the subject of

the evidence produced by the Applicant is aimed not at all the people of Bosnia-Herzegovina, but principally at the Muslim population, it cannot be said to be aimed at the "nation," i.e., the totality
of the people, that live in the territory of that country.[107]

In other words, because the Bosnian "nation" was multinational
and multireligious, it could not be the subject of protection under the
Genocide Convention. When considering the sixth part of Bosnia's
second request—that the People and State of Bosnia and Herzegovina
must have the means to protect themselves from "acts of genocide
and partition and dismemberment by means of genocide," this restrictive understanding was developed. While arguing that this conclusion
does not diminish a finding that genocide is taking place, Lauterpacht dismisses Bosnia's contention that partition is being achieved
by genocide. He does so because, picking up on the Bosnian counsel's
original argument,

the object of the genocide is the Muslim population of Bosnia not
"the People and State of Bosnia-Herzegovina" as a whole. The latter concept must comprise all elements of the population of Bosnia
and Herzegovina, of which the Muslim population forms no more
than 40 per cent. So, though the Government of Bosnia and Herzegovina is entitled to the means to protect its population, or part of
its population, from genocide, that entitlement does not extend to
the protection of the State from dismemberment where the population of the state is evidently divided within itself and cannot be
said to compose a "national group" within the meaning of that expression as used in Article I of the Convention.[108]

This reasoning reveals a cruel paradox in the Genocide Convention. Lauterpacht maintains that once one starts thinking about Bosnian identity, any notion of its being defined in terms of a particular
group ("national" or otherwise) is excluded because the polity is multicultural. As a result, to receive protection from partition under the
Genocide Convention would effectively mean constituting Bosnia in
terms of a homogeneous population with a particular territory. Therefore, because a "national" group has to be ethnically, racially, or religiously specific, and only a singularity of this type has status for the
convention, for a multicultural state to protect itself from partition
would require submitting itself to the very identity politics and territorial division it is seeking to resist. In the guise of a "civic" conception—the national group—we find the convention depends on "ethnic" formulations, recalling the way these terms have been conflated

in the literature on nationalism. Ontopological formulations have thus governed both the remedies available to those subject to nationalist violence as well as the argument marshaled in their favor.

This demonstrates that the Genocide Convention, and the identity politics it manifests, cannot accommodate threats to a hybrid, multi-cultural polity. As we shall see in chapter 5—and explore further in chapter 7, with respect to the deterritorialized nature of Bosnian/Muslim identity—the incapacity of the discourses and institutions of international politics to accommodate multicultural identities has been one of the most significant shortcomings exposed by the Bosnian war. That this limitation was shared in part by the Bosnian counsel in the presentation of that country's case offers no comfort. It has, at least, been identified as a problem by the UN Commission of Experts: "Genocide . . . would as a legal concept be a weak or even useless instrument if the overall circumstances of mixed groups were not covered."[109] But overcoming this restriction involves conceptualizations of identity and politics previously foreign to international thought.

Violence against Bodies and the Body Politic

As the UN Commission of Experts on the Former Yugoslavia argued in its final report, the all-important question of intent could "be inferred from sufficient facts. In certain cases, there will be evidence of actions or omissions of such a degree that the defendant may reasonably be assumed to have been aware of the consequences of his or her conduct."[110] This formulation echoes the epistemological issues invoked by the ICJ judges, but there can be little doubt that with four years of war leaving upwards of a quarter of a million people dead, four million displaced, and thousands raped, the sufficiency of "facts" is not in short supply. In Bosnia, the scope of the violence left almost no area untouched by population transfers, with more than 80 percent of the non-Serb population having been expelled from areas under Serb military control.[111]

The organized character of ethnic cleansing can be illustrated in a number of ways. Through official bureaus to conduct "population exchanges," those targeted for removal required documentation permitting them to leave and were often charged "exit fees" for the bus services provided for that purpose. If they had to sell property in order to raise the money, that too necessitated authorization. When pressure needed to be increased on target populations, those in charge barred them from selling their goods at market as previously required.[112] And when the manpower for these and other operations needed to be bolstered toward the end of the war, Serb authorities (in Bosnia and Serbia proper) press-ganged Serbian refugees from the Krajina into military service.[113]

Had ethnic cleansing been no more than a symptom of territorial expansion, then one would have expected it to have diminished toward the end of the Bosnian war, when Bosnian Serb forces had to retreat from the 70 percent of the country they once held to territory they had previously conquered. Instead, ethnic cleansing intensified in the latter stages of the conflict, with some of the most extreme cases taking place only hours before the cease-fire in October 1995.[114] The massacre at Srebrenica, which also exemplifies tragically the issues of intent and planning, is but the best-known instance of this.[115] As we shall see in chapter 7, ethnic cleansing has continued even in the wake of the Dayton agreement.

But it is the nature of the violence imbricated in ethnic cleansing that reveals that the conflict in Bosnia was more about political identities and their constitution than their inevitable antagonism. In line with the Genocide Convention's requirement that what is important is not just the fact that people are killed but that they are killed because they constitute or symbolize a particular community, the purpose of this section is to demonstrate the way in which the violence of Bosnia can be thought of in terms of the *coup de force* (as outlined in chapter 2). As the means by which identity is inscribed and transcribed across a range of surfaces, violence can be thought of as the practice through which questions of history are deployed in the present for contemporary political goals. The result is the performative enactment of the identities subsequently regarded as preexisting and the source of the conflict. In these terms, the strategically bizarre cultural violence against symbols of identity in Bosnia — mosques, churches, museums, and memorials — and the horrific violence against bodies — mass rape of women and the disfiguration and rape of men — become comprehensible if no less justifiable.

The symbolization of violence is an effect that involves both the perpetrator and the victim. It can be all too vividly demonstrated by those incidents where the bodies of victims, both living and dead, have been scarred with religious markings. The gender dimensions of the violence — whereby males are selected for death, and females are systematically raped — testify to the entailments of identity at work.[116] Similarly, the organized and widespread destruction of libraries, museums, and religious buildings exceeds any possible account of "collateral damage" and is testament to the war on identity, history, and memory that has been integral to the Bosnian war.[117] To recall Feldman's conception of violence, the bodies and buildings constitute the sites and stages upon which history has been constructed as a cultural object through the Bosnian war.

The Advent of Islamicization?

The rhetoric of the Bosnian Serbs (and to a lesser extent the Bosnian Croats, along with elements of the international community) has often cast the Bosnian war in religious terms, as a clash between Christianity and Islam. Thereby rationalizing violent practices as justifiable self-defense in the face of a fundamentalist onslaught, this representation (as noted in chapter 3) produced an alignment between their position and those European leaders who expressed concern about the possibility of an Islamic state within Europe.

The official Bosnian position, often underscored by expressions of popular opinion, has been that of defending a nonnationalist and multiethnic option. There have been, however, strong political undercurrents within Bosnia that have dissented from the official position, often appearing to confirm some elements of Bosnian Serb propaganda. By and large, those undercurrents have come not from a constituency that wished to pursue a Muslim nationalism prior to the war but, rather, from those who have argued since the outbreak of war that the success of chauvinism made a defense of multiculturalism untenable.[118]

Tensions of this kind first emerged publicly in response to the peace plans pushed by the international community after the collapse of the Vance-Owen proposal. As we shall see in the following chapter, those plans proposed the effective partition of Bosnia. They thereby undermined the possibility of a nonnationalist solution emerging from the international arena, strengthening at the same time the hand of exclusivists within Bosnia. As a result, some argued that the Bosnian authorities should discard their ethos of tolerance and start doing unto others as was being done unto them. This would have meant military forces should have been nationalized. That this did not become official policy can be inferred from the fact that Bosnian Croat (HVO) units in Sarajevo continued to fight alongside and for the Bosnian army, even though there was serious fighting between Bosnian and HVO forces in the central regions of the country. But it did mean that a Serbo-Croat partition plan was denounced by a Muslim assembly before Bosnia's parliament had met to consider it.[119]

In this context, there emerged a clash between "Bosnians" and some "Muslims." This distinction, conflated in the dominant representations, marked the political fault line between those who wanted to maintain and defend the multicultural polity and those who wanted to promote a new form of exclusion given the progress of other exclusionary projects. To this end, a few significant leaders of the religious constituency argued toward the end of 1994 that mixed marriages (which amounted to 45 percent of those in the city) were bound to fail and should be opposed. Derided by one *Oslobodjenje* editorial as constituting "racism and fascism," this view was exacerbated by the leader of the Islamic community, Mustafa Ceric, when he declared that the "horrible and incomprehensible" policy of systematic rape carried out by the Bosnian Serb forces was "less painful and easier to accept than all these mixed marriages and all these children born of mixed marriages." As one report of Ceric's views observed, Sarajevo was "stunned" by this. A young woman, "weeping with rage" retorted that "I am half-Muslim, half-Croatian. . . . After two years of shelling by nationalist Serbs, here I am attacked by my own side. It's a shame. . . . I'm not afraid to say I miss the Serbs who have left the city and that I would like us to live together again as before."[120]

Ceric's prejudice was driven by resentment at the failure of the international community to come to Bosnia's aid, a resentment driven by a paradoxical view. "We are being killed," he declared, "because we want to live together. You see, we Bosnians are defending your principles in Europe. We are defending the principles of the United Nations and its Secretary-General — and he is the one who is breaking those principles. I ask you, is there anything left of humanity in the West? Is there anything left of justice or humanism?"[121] A similar bitterness pervaded the views of the culture and education minister, Enes Karic, who derided the attention given to mixed marriages as "an attempt to recreate the myth of the past." Noting that he was once a scholar who argued against Islamic fundamentalism in favor of democracy, the minister observed that "I've changed my mind about democracy. We experience European democracy here as bombs."[122]

The sentiments of Ceric and Karic presaged an attempt to institute a *kulturkampf* in response to the violence of ethnic cleansing. Ceric called for "throw[ing] away European trash: alcohol, drugs, prostitution," while Karic oversaw efforts during the war to ban Serbian and Croatian music from Bosnian radio, increase Arabic-sounding pronunciation in the language, and change educational curricula to increasingly reflect Islamic concerns.[123] These efforts were met not only by popular resistance (evident daily in Sarajevo's cafés) but also by official antagonism. They helped set off an internal power struggle in the Bosnian government with those, like then Prime Minister Haris Silajdžić (himself the son of the chief imam at Sarajevo's main mosque), who were committed to an inclusive and secular notion of political community.

This struggle came to a head again in early 1995 when Bosnian television showed Izetbegović meeting with the Seventh Muslim Brigade in Zenica, whose insignia bear Islamic phrases in Arabic.[124] The members of Bosnia's collective presidency who were not members of the Party of Democratic Action (SDA) denounced this official endorsement and stressed that the army had to remain multinational, as did the army's commander.[125] Izetbegović's concessions to Islamic motifs in the military drew a sharp response from the father of a deceased Bosnian soldier, which began a public debate. In an open letter to the president, interestingly published in the nationalist weekly *Ljiljan*, Osman Tica asked,

> Why do you use the religious term *shehid* [Arabic word for martyr] for my son and other soldiers who have died? My son is not one, and I do not allow anyone to call him so. Why do you say a *fatiha* [Arabic word for prayer for the dead] for those who have been killed? When it comes to my son, remain silent. It is better not to say anything than to speak in a language which neither he nor I understand.[126]

Although Izetbegović was a regular defender in public of a multicultural Bosnia, these and other incidents called his commitment into question.[127] Whether they were revealing of his "true" beliefs or simply evidence of a politician's accommodation to the demands of differing constituencies is far from clear.[128] What is indisputable is that these are matters for public debate, a debate that illustrates that there is considerable opposition *within* Bosnia to these exclusivist tendencies. This contestation therefore highlights the domestic constituency with which international groups opposed to all forms of ethnic/nationalist exclusions could be allied.

That alliance has, however, been largely avoided by the very people who expressed Western concerns about increasing ethnic intolerance in Bosnia. As the next chapter demonstrates, the establishment of ethnically defined enclaves as the political structure for Bosnia has been the at least implicit goal of the international community's prescriptions for ending the war. Responding to the violence in a way that could contest even the possibility of fundamentalism thus requires more than the international community has offered Bosnia, for a negotiating strategy informed by ontopological assumptions could only exacerbate a conflict that employed the same logic.

Just as importantly, the international community's ethnic strategy overlooked the dimensions of the conflict explored in this chapter that problematized ontopological accounts and served poorly those Bosnians who pursued nonnationalist options in both their daily lives and their desires for the future. In a systematic struggle against heterogeneity, those representations of the conflict that have overlooked and underplayed the complex and contested nature of Bosnian life have been complicit in the violent installation of the nationalist imaginary they are allegedly opposed to.

Five
Responding to the Violence

An Alliance of Paramilitary and Peacemaker

In the spring of 1993, while the European Community and the United States struggled with a response to the war, there emerged in the American press a controversial proposition about the best option for Bosnia. John Mearsheimer, a well-known (neo)realist professor of international relations, argued in the *New York Times* that saving Bosnia required shrinking it.[1] While in this instance refraining from use of the term, Mearsheimer's argument advocated partition. It was an outcome strongly opposed by the Bosnian government, even though Mearsheimer declared he was operating from a pro-Bosnian position.

If one can speak in terms of "the international community," its diplomatic efforts to resolve the Bosnian war, culminating in the Dayton agreement, would appear to have been a repudiation of Mearsheimer's partitionist proposals. The officially propagated understanding of the Dayton agreement is that it calls for the restoration of a unified, multiethnic Bosnia, and most media narratives (even as they express doubts about its realization) have reiterated this notion of "the Dayton spirit." For instance, a quality newspaper in the United Kingdom declared that "the Bosnian peace agreement represents a brave attempt to assert fundamental Western values in the Balkans after a war in which combatants on all sides treated those values with contempt."[2]

For the proponents of partition, such claims manifest a naïveté insufficiently cognizant of the realities of bitter ethnic conflict. But was the product of international diplomacy a repudiation of proposals for the partition of Bosnia demanded by the neorealists? In its attempts to negotiate a settlement to the Bosnian war, did the international community operate with assumptions about ethnic conflict distinct from those embraced by the neorealists? To address these questions, this chapter makes an argument in four parts. First, it reviews the Mearsheimer argument in order to appreciate the assumptions on which it depends. Then, through a documentary review of the international community's peace proposals for Bosnia, it will be shown that the process that culminated in the Dayton agreement, which supposedly disavows partition in favor of unity, in actuality fostered partition albeit in the name of "multiethnicity." As a result, serious questions need to be asked about the conceptualization of "multiethnicity" invoked by the international community. Third, it will be argued that the common partitionist logic of both Mearsheimer's argument and the international community's diplomatic efforts is achieved through adherence to a contestable political anthropology about Bosnia that is governed by ontopological assumptions. Deployed by both the peacemakers and the paramilitaries in Bosnia, this anthropology gives rise to the nationalist imaginary in which there is a nexus between identity and territory. And finally, although the partitionist logic is styled as an unfortunate but necessary realism, it will be maintained that it embodies instead a dangerous idealism that is likely to produce the very outcomes it seeks to avoid.

Of course, international diplomacy is not the only, nor necessarily the most important, site in which nationalized conceptions of political community are installed for Bosnia. As Robert Hayden has well illustrated, the constitutions of the successor states to the former Yugoslavia performatively enact nationalist ideologies.[3] Manifesting the politics of the *coup de force* detailed in chapter 2, in which they are instruments in the violent founding of a community without foundations, the constitutions represent the disjuncture between the "prescriptive model of culture (culture-as-ideology) with what exists on the ground (culture-as-lived) but is not in accordance with the prescription."[4]

This is not to suggest a naive conception of "ideology" versus "reality," but instead, as Hayden observes, to draw attention to the double function of representational practices in the Bosnian war, for "extreme nationalism in the former Yugoslavia had not been only a matter of imagining allegedly 'primordial' communities, but rather of making existing heterogeneous ones unimaginable."[5] In this context, because the international community forswore a military response to the Bosnian war, international diplomacy functions as the principal site in which the international community exercised its responsibility.[6] To say as much is not to absolve those "on the ground" from their responsibility in fomenting the pathologies of ethnic cleansing. It is, rather, to ensure that international diplomacy does not likewise escape its responsibility for the situation to which it merely claims to react.

The argument here is that international diplomacy has been a conduit through which the tension between the objectified culture of nationalist projects and the lived experience of Bosnia has been resolved in favor of the nationalists. In different sites and variable ways it has played an important though not exclusive role in foreclosing the possibility of nonnationalist conceptions of political community in Bosnia. What the readings to follow demonstrate is the way in which a particular problematization constitutes an event as a problem, mandates specific political resolutions, and marginalizes alternatives. Bringing the deconstructive ethos to bear on such problematizations is indispensable to the consideration of other possibilities.

A Humanitarian Partition?

The primordialist imagination identified by Hayden is well illustrated in Mearsheimer's arguments. The context for Mearsheimer's original article was the Vance-Owen Peace Plan (discussed below), and the key proposal of Mearsheimer's position was that "ethnically homogeneous states must be created." Arguing that after "all the inter-communal slaughter" it stretched credulity to believe that "Vance-Owen's Bosnian state of 10 multi-ethnic, but semi-autonomous provinces" would be stable, Mearsheimer declared that "we should create instead a Bosnian state peopled almost exclusively by Muslims, a Croatian state for Croatians and a Serbian state made up mainly of Serbians." Enacting this homogeneous state-building proposal required

> drawing new borders and transferring populations. Croatians, Muslims and Serbians would have to concede territory and move people.... a new Muslim state must be created by concentrating Muslims now scattered across the region into central Bosnia. Remaining Bosnian territory should be given to Croatia and Serbia. Perhaps one million people—approximately 600,000 Muslims, 300,000 Serbs and 100,000 Croats—will have to move. Many others have already relocated.[7]

Mearsheimer's proposition invoked ontopological assumptions familiar to much political thought and central to many cartographic solutions previously proposed for other conflicts. Just as such assumptions govern Michael Walzer's account of Israeli nationalism to the detriment of Palestinians, and the logic that led the Bengal and Punjab Boundary Commission to divide India and create Pakistan by demarcating Muslim and non-Muslim "contiguous majority areas," so too Mearsheimer's discursive economy of settled identity rendered Bosnia for partition.[8] This discursive economy is implicated in the organization of an analytic space through which the disciplinary strategies of partitioning (where "each individual has his own place; and each place its individual") help bring into being a particular body politic.[9]

Although operating on a register unaware of these dimensions, Mearsheimer was not completely blind to the criticisms that his proposal would engender, though his main concern was with the charge that "altering borders is a bad precedent and that in many instances it rewards Serbian aggression." The ethics of forced population transfers went largely unremarked. This was so because, consistent with the pessimistic assumptions of his (neo)realist interpretive frame, the situation in the Balkans constituted a realm of necessity that had to be accommodated by any political options.[10]

Even though the ethics of partition were marginalized by Mearsheimer, a particular moral calculus was at work. One possible formulation of this would be to claim that partition as a solution to ethnic conflicts is "based purely on humanitarian grounds."[11] Another more likely formulation of this calculus would be to think in terms of the morality of realism, the position Mearsheimer identifies with. As is commonly recognized, realism rejects traditional morality as inappropriate to international affairs, and appeals instead to the idea of raison d'état. This gives rise to a curious paradox. In making the security of the state the superior value, in the service of which all sorts of policies can be justified, realism is instantiating an ethical criteria at the same time as it is rejecting the applicability of moral values. This means we can understand realism as involving a moral argument, albeit one that "amounts to a claim that the reasons for overriding the constraints of ordinary morality in emergency situations are themselves moral."[12]

This understanding aptly characterizes Mearsheimer's logic with regard to Bosnia, which runs as follows. In the exceptional context of the Yugoslav wars, the primary concern, and thus the highest value, is to establish defensible states so as to ensure stability. Given prior and unstated assumptions about identity and community, this involves the boundary drawing and population transfers of partition, which, although unseemly, are justifiable. However, the problematic nature of Mearsheimer's assumptions, as well as his poor grasp of the Bosnian war, exposes the unethical character of realism's morality.

Those problems notwithstanding, Mearsheimer's argument was subsequently reiterated.[13] Again, population transfer was integral to the scheme. However, he argued that although "populations would have to be moved in order to create homogenous states," this move would not occur until a peace agreement had been signed. Moreover, he proposed that the population transfer of one million people should take place under UN auspices, with the creation of a new "Balkan Population Exchange commission." Proposals such as these indicated an important element of the particular problematization at work in the argument. People in communities were constituted and marked as "populations" so that they could then be dealt with as a policy issue. Such representations, as Foucault observed, were one of the great innovations in the techniques of power implicated in state-building.[14]

The Mearsheimer partition plan depended, therefore, not on either the expressed positions of any or all the Bosnian communities but on the implications the authors drew from their own judgment about the reality of the situation, which they then projected back into their claims about actuality. This means that while they acknowledge one criticism of this aspect of their proposal — "some would contend that the population transfer required by partition entails needless injury to innocents" — the realm of necessity is again invoked to regulate options. The argument is underscored with the observation that "transfer is already occurring. Even Vance-Owen would produce its own population transfers, since minorities would doubtless be driven from areas designated for other groups. Transfer is a fact. The only question is whether it will be organized, as envisioned by partition, or left to the murderous methods of the ethnic cleansers." The authors do concede that "transferring hundreds of thousands of civilians from historic homes and countries" means that the partition plan "isn't morally pure." But its ethical limitations are subsumed by the observation that "it is the only plan that's realistic about what can be achieved in such a fraught area and idealistic about the principles at stake."[15] The disciplinary quality of their realism means that the problematic idealism of the principles (presumably raison d'état) is all too obvious.

Despite Mearsheimer's alleged fidelity to the facts on the ground, his argument for the partition of Bosnia persisted regardless of changed circumstances. In the aftermath of the Dayton agreement, and then again in the wake of the elections mandated by the agreement, Mearsheimer reiterated his position that anything short of complete tripartite partition was unworkable.[16]

Accordingly, the claim was that one year after the United States brokered the deal, it should now abandon the Dayton agreement and "move to organize a peaceful three-way partition of Bosnia." As before, this process would involve, notwithstanding the complex cartographic negotiations surrounding the agreement, a further redrawing of boundaries and additional population transfers. The aim would be to give the Muslims more territory and enclose more Muslims in a contiguous and defensible state. To achieve this, the three ethnic groups should trade more land in eastern and western Bosnia, and "America should also oversee the transfer of minorities trapped by partition boundaries. A registry should record abandoned property, to allow compensation for losses. Economic aid should be offered to help those transferred to start new lives." For the authors, all is again justified by the circumstances: "Bosnia will be divided one way or another. Only the final cost, in lives and property remains in doubt. The cost largely depends on whether the United States finally stops chasing the chimera of Bosnian unity and instead leads the process of partition."[17]

Having marshaled Bosnians into constituent populations, the Mearsheimer arguments then mark those populations with ethnic categorizations so as to naturalize partition. Invoking ethnicity as a brute social fact, the arguments contain no reflections on the meaning or worth of such social classifications. That task is taken up by Chaim Kaufmann in a contribution to *International Security* that links itself explicitly with the Mearsheimer propositions for partition and provides a fuller theorization of some of the assumptions on which they depend. However, this argument remains ignorant of the anthropological debates about the politicized nature of ethnicity discussed in the previous chapter, and thus unaware of how it is implicated in the ethnicization of the people it claims to merely describe.

According to Kaufmann, the civil wars that are flourishing around the world (of which Bosnia is one) can be divided into "ideological civil wars" and "ethnic conflicts." The difference between them revolves around the status of individual loyalties, with the former involving fluid loyalties and the latter being marked by "almost completely rigid" identifications.[18] This notion of rigidity is built into the very definition of ethnicity employed by Kaufmann. Citing Max Weber and Anthony Smith to claim that "an ethnic group (or nation) is commonly defined as a body of individuals who purportedly share cultural or racial characteristics, especially common ancestry or territorial origins, which distinguish them from members of other groups," Kaufmann argues that "opposing communities in ethnic civil conflicts hold irreconcilable visions of the identity, borders and citizenship of the state."[19] Although he tries to argue that the essay does "not take a position on the initial sources of ethnic identities" — while noting the literature that outlines constructivist, primordialist, and perennialist positions on ethnicity and nationalism — Kaufmann's caveat is flatly contradicted by the proposition to which it is a footnote:

"ethnic identities are fixed by birth."[20] Indeed, he maintains that ethnicity is the "hardest" of identity categories because it depends on "language, culture, and religion, which are hard to change, as well as parentage, which no one can change," and that it hardens further during violent conflict.[21]

Identifying this most fixed of categories, Kaufmann argues, can be achieved via "outward appearance, public or private records, and local social knowledge." For example, with respect to public records, Kaufmann maintains that "while it might not have been possible to predict the Yugoslav civil war thirty years in advance, one could have identified the members of each of the warring groups from the 1961 census, which identified the nationality of all but 1.8% of the population."[22] This remark, with its social scientific assumptions about the transparent nature of data, reveals some of the impoverished thinking evident in the argument, being totally oblivious to the general points about the politics of statistics, and the specific points about the genealogy of the Yugoslav census, discussed in chapter 4 and to be explored further in chapter 7.

But the problems with that assertion pale by comparison with the claim that physical characteristics are meaningful signposts for ethnicity. No examples are provided with respect to the former Yugoslavia, so turning his attention elsewhere Kaufmann declares that "in unprepared encounters ethnicity can often be gauged by outward appearance: Tutsis are generally tall and thin, while Hutus are relatively short and stocky; Russians are generally fairer than Kazakhs." In case the reader might imagine this was an ironic observation, Kaufmann cites in support of this a U.S. Army country study, which is paraphrased as follows (presumably to counter constructivist arguments): "Despite claims that the Hutu-Tutsi ethnic division was invented by the Belgians, 1969 census data showed significant physical differences: Tutsi males averaged 5 feet 9 inches and 126 pounds, Hutus 5 feet 5 inches and 131 pounds."[23] Leaving aside the dubious claim that an average of four inches and five pounds constitutes a significant difference, and deferring the disputable suggestion that even if there was a physical difference it could harbor any political significance, this astonishing remark exhibits a form of scientific racism long since discredited in anthropology and sociology.[24]

The crude essentialism and primitive rigidity of Kaufmann's conception of ethnicity set in train a logic that leads inexorably toward partition as the best and only solution to so-called ethnic conflict. If ethnicity is an exclusive and unchangeable dimension of identity, then communities understood in terms of ethnicity are necessarily opposed to those who are different. Because of this necessary antagonism and the way it is exacerbated in the course of conflict, opposing communities are inextricably drawn into a zero-sum security dilemma.

Of course, in terms of the performative constitution of identity that is a theme central to this book, an argument of this kind can be understood as a particular political production designed to bring into being and secure specific notions of identity. Indeed, the prevalence of the Kaufmann logic in many of the accounts of the Bosnian war and proposals for its resolution demonstrates well that point. But an attentiveness to the problematic of identity/difference, and the way in which political analyses and policy prescriptions constitute and materialize the categories they claim to merely describe, is absent from Kaufmann's (and others') analysis. In their view, the mechanical logic of these propositions reflects without question an external and unchanging reality.

In this context, Kaufmann confidently asserts that "solutions that aim at restoring multi-ethnic civil politics and at avoiding population transfers" simply cannot work.[25] Any proposal that involves the interaction of communities is bound to fail, and fail without question. As a result, only the total victory of one side, temporary suppression by external intervention, or partition stand as possible solutions. All others are impossible. Partition is what Kaufmann favors, for the safest way to overcome a security dilemma is "a well-defined demographic front that separates nearly homogenous regions."[26] Given this, "the international community must abandon attempts to restore war-torn multi-ethnic states. Instead, it must facilitate and protect population movements to create true national homelands."[27]

When Kaufmann's argument turns briefly to the specifics of the Bosnian situation, it, not surprisingly, follows closely that of Mearsheimer and his coauthors, although Kaufmann recognizes that the Dayton agreement strengthens territorial divisions of the kind he would favor, and pays only lip service to a unitary Bosnian state. The argument ends, like the others, with a defense of its position in terms of reality and realism. Noting (rightly) that "some observers attack separation and partition as immoral," Kaufmann maintains that "a humanitarian intervention to establish lasting safety for peoples endangered by ethnic civil wars" — the way in which he understands his proposal for partition and population transfers — is the only option currently feasible for a place like Bosnia. While intervention to counter ethnic hostility in the former Yugoslavia might have been possible in the 1980s, for Kaufmann it is "too late now."[28] Policies that seek to foster or restore nonethnic and nonnationalist policies are thus assuredly dismissed as unrealistic and impossible.

Of course, when it comes to unreal possibilities, few exceed the idea of the forcible transfer of up to a million people. Indeed, Kaufmann is forced to concede that the record of the international community's involvement in Bosnia might demonstrate that it "cannot muster the will even for much lesser enterprises, let alone *the campaigns of conquest* envisaged in this paper"[29] — which highlights the way in which this argument embodies two contradictory impulses.

The first, undertaken in the name of realism, is the authoritarian desire in which the various authors know best the interests of the people about whom they are writing, and feel uninhibited in therefore recommending upheavals over which those affected can have no say.[30] The partition proposals consciously override any consideration of what the Bosnian government argued and fought for, what any of the nonnationalist groups in Bosnia advocated, or what any of the hundreds of thousands of individuals who would be forced to move from their homes against their will might say or do.

The second impulse, a utopian moment, occurs when the cautions of realism that were previously endorsed are abandoned, and improbable and unlikely policy options are advocated. Thus, mass population transfer — which involves nothing less than the international community conducting and condoning ethnic cleansing — is recommended. At the same time, it is argued that the West should tell Serbia "that the cleansing of Kosovo will not be tolerated," with no reflection on how the latter can be credibly squared with the former.[31] Likewise, it is argued that the United States should, having expended vast amounts of diplomatic capital to broker the deal, abandon the Dayton agreement and begin again with boundary redrawing and population transfers so as to create a three-way partition.[32]

Now, the point is *not* that improbable and unlikely policy options cannot and should not be explored. They must, especially in a situation like that confronted in Bosnia. Only a proper consideration of all that might be conceivable is going to make a just resolution likely. What this consideration of the utopian impulse in the partition proposals illustrates, however, is that the acolytes of realism abandon all consistency and, counter to the assumptions that have informed their position, offer policy prescriptions that do not heed the limitations of a reality they claimed could not be circumvented. In other words, having dismissed all options bar their own as impossible, because the external world in Bosnia constitutes a realm of necessity full of unpalatable alternatives and unpleasant truths, they then overlook the parameters of their argument and regretfully offer as inescapable some of the most unrealistic proposals imaginable. It is thus not the improbable search for options that is a problem, but the reckless power play of the arguments for partition and the way they rule out other possibilities.

Kaufmann's article summarizes well the conceptual assumptions concerning identity that underpin Mearsheimer and his coauthors' problematization of Bosnia and the political option (partition) it mandates. Much like the dominant narratives examined in chapter 3, the assumptions' indebtedness to the governing codes of subjectivity in international relations — assuming pre-given agents with autonomous, intractable, and observable identities — allows the authors to portray a seamless, ethnically ordered world in which no other conceptions of identity have political import, and where group relations cannot be other than mutually exclusive and conflictual. However, the controversial and highly contestable nature of those assumptions means that the absolutist and sweeping implications they draw for Bosnia must be rendered debatable and subject to the deconstructive ethos.

Kaufmann's argument provides a useful springboard for a consideration of the international community's diplomatic and political responses to the conflict in Bosnia. According to Kaufmann, his argument is supported by a data analysis that allegedly supports the argument "that separation of groups is the key to ending ethnic civil wars." On this basis, he confidently asserts that "there is not a single case where non-ethnic civil politics were created or restored by reconstruction of ethnic identities, power-sharing coalitions, or state-building."[33]

The crucial question that has to be explored before that conclusion can be considered credible is whether in any of the applicable instances the international community tried to promote a nonethnic solution. In the case of Bosnia — as examples discussed in chapter 4 and examples that will be discussed in chapter 7 make clear — nonethnic and nonnationalist options were proposed and pursued by groups within Bosnia before, during, and after the war. That situation alone contradicts important elements of the argument advocating partition. But the central issue here is whether or not the international community has embraced and enacted a nonethnic or nonnationalist political strategy for the resolution of the Bosnian war. We cannot conclude that such solutions are impossible unless we can show that at least at one stage they were thought possible and effectively pursued.

Accordingly, the remainder of this chapter will closely examine the assumptions of the major peace plans proposed by the international community for Bosnia. Being preoccupied with the political presuppositions that informed the most important initiatives designed to resolve the Bosnian war, I am excluding a number of elements in the international community's response to the violence. By highlighting the diplomatic initiatives, this chapter pays little attention to the military options and their assumptions. The important questions surrounding the arms embargo, air strikes, sanctions policy and its enforcement, and the implications for UN peacekeeping operations (among other issues) are therefore not accorded any prominence, despite the fact that strategic plans for Bosnia have embodied their own virtual cartography.[34]

Negotiating Bosnia

The initiatives that the international community undertook in relation to Bosnia were part of a complex web of overlapping institutions with interwoven jurisdictions that require us to delve into a world of diplomatic and legal minutia. The purpose of this analysis is to explore the assumptions about identity made by the international community in its efforts to negotiate an end to the conflict. The focus is thus on the way in which through international diplomacy "Bosnia" was mapped as a particular place with specific people, so that it could be rendered as a problem requiring a particular solution.

The major proposals were made in the period between the European Community's first statements in June 1991 and the signing of the U.S.–brokered "General Framework Agreement for Peace in Bosnia and Herzegovina" (the Dayton accords) in Paris on 14 December 1995. For the purpose of this analysis, that period can be divided into two. The first covers those proposals made during the time (June 1991–February 1994) the EC and the United Nations were the principal sponsors of the peace process. The second (February 1994–November 1995) includes those formulated mainly through the intervention of the United States, Russia, and other leading players.[35]

From London to Geneva, via Lisbon

The peace process begins formally with a series of European Community declarations in mid-1991, but substantively when the EC Conference on Yugoslavia (ECCY) is established by way of statements on 27 August and 3 September 1991. Chaired by Lord Carrington, the ECCY held thirteen plenary sessions in Brussels between 12 September 1991 and 14 August 1992. At the eighth session, a draft convention was agreed to by five of the six republics of the former Yugoslavia. The ECCY also comprised a series of working groups, the most important of which held ten rounds of talks on constitutional arrangements for Bosnia in Sarajevo, London, Lisbon, and Brussels between 18–31 March 1992. At the fifth and sixth rounds of these talks, a statement of principles was agreed to by all parties, but later repudiated by the Bosnian government. An Arbitration Commission, the work of which was discussed in chapter 2, was part of this process.

The ECCY was followed by the UN–EC International Conference on the Former Yugoslavia (ICFY), which was established in August 1992 at the London Conference, where an important set of principles was produced.[36] Run by the cochairmen of its Steering Committee, Cyrus Vance (who was also the Special Representative for Yugoslavia of the UN Secretary-General) and David Owen (the EC's representative), the ICFY comprised six working groups, including one dealing specifically with Bosnia. Although the ICFY remained in operation throughout the entire period under consideration, its personnel changed, with Vance being replaced by Thorvold Stoltenberg on 3 May 1993, and Owen being replaced by Carl Bildt on 13 June 1995. During that time, its major products were the Vance-Owen Peace Plan of January 1993, the Union of Three Republics plan of September 1993, and the European Union Action Plan of November-December 1993.

The Carrington Plan, November 1991

The draft convention negotiated by the ECCY under Carrington's chairmanship provided for a constitutional structure whereby all the republics of the former Yugoslavia could have sovereignty and independence. This was set out in Chapter I, Article 1:

> The new relations between the Republics will be based on the following:
>
> a) sovereign and independent Republics with an international personality for those that wish it;
>
> b) a free association of the Republics with an international personality as envisaged in this Convention;
>
> c) a common state of equal Republics for those Republics which wish to remain a common state;
>
> d) comprehensive arrangements, including supervisory mechanisms for the protection of human rights and special status of certain groups and areas;
>
> e) European involvement, where appropriate;

f) in the framework of a general settlement, recognition of the in-dependence, within the existing borders, unless otherwise agreed, of those Republics wishing it.[37]

Coming after the declarations of independence by Croatia and Slovenia, though before their recognition by the EC, this arrange-ment was an attempt to preserve some form of sovereignty for a feder-ative body, yet accommodate those republics' impulse for self-deter-mination. Significantly, it contained within it a provision (paragraph d) for extending some form of self-determination, albeit without com-plete sovereignty, to "certain groups and areas." In Article 2 (b) of the convention, those groups and areas were designated as "national or ethnic groups." Having incorporated the various international legal instruments relevant to ethnic, national, and minority rights, the con-vention in Article 2 (b) (iii) then set out what those rights would mean for the various groups:

3. The Republic shall guarantee to persons belonging to a national or ethnic group the following rights:

- the principle of non-discrimination as set out in the legal in-struments mentioned in paragraph 2 of this Article;
- the right to be protected against any activity capable of threat-ening their existence;
- all cultural rights as set out in the instruments mentioned in paragraph 2 of this Article, in particular the right to identity, culture, religion, use of language and alphabet, both in public and in private, and education;
- protection of equal participation in public affairs, such as the exercise of political and economic freedoms, in the social sphere, in access to the media and in the field of education and cultural affairs generally;
- the right to decide to which national or ethnic group he or she wishes to belong, and to exercise any rights pertaining to this choice as an individual or in association with others. No dis-advantage shall arise from a person's choice to belong or not to belong to a national or ethnic group. This right shall partic-ularly apply in the case of marriage between persons of differ-ent national or ethnic groups.

Those persons of the same national or ethnic group living distant from others of the same origin, for example, in isolated villages, shall be granted self-administration, to the extent that it is practicable.

The above principles shall also apply in areas where members of the main national or ethnic group of a Republic are numerically in-ferior to one or more other national or ethnic groups in that area.

This extensive catalog of rights, which included the right to select the group to which one belonged, set out the beginnings of a principle of self-administration for those who were not in an area contiguous to the majority of their chosen group. Accommodating those demands — although they did not ultimately secure Milošević's agreement — meant that from the outset the international community's response to the crisis embodied the criteria and terms by which republics could be unraveled along ethnic and national lines. Although formal sovereignty was not proposed for the special autonomous areas, the measures ensured practical sovereignty.

The Statement of Principles, March 1992

Coming some weeks before widespread fighting broke out in Bosnia — being originally agreed to in Lisbon on 23 February 1992, and first published on 9 March 1992 — the "Statement of Principles for New Constitutional Arrangements for Bosnia and Herzegovina" was the first proposal to deal exclusively with the republic. Developed under the auspices of the ECCY Working Group on Bosnia and Herzegovina, a process then chaired (because of Portugal's EC presidency) by the Portuguese foreign minister José Cutiliero, the Statement of Principles left many difficult questions for future negotiations. But its key assumption and premise were that although Bosnia would be an independent state within its existing borders, it should be partitioned along ethnic lines into three nations. The three propositions of section A (titled "Independence") made this clear:

1. Bosnia and Herzegovina would be a state, composed of three constituent units, based on national principles and taking into account economic, geographic and other criteria.

2. Bosnia and Herzegovina would continue to have its existing borders and neither the government of Bosnia and Herzegovina nor the governments of the constituent units will encourage or support claims to any part of its territory by neighbouring states.

3. Sovereignty resides in the citizens of the Muslim, Serb and Croat nations and other nations and nationalities, who realise it through their civic participation in the constituent units and the central organs of the republic.[38]

The statement did not offer a final map agreed to by all parties. Instead, it declared in section E ("Definition of the Constituent Units") that:

A working group will be established in order to define the territory of the constituent units based on national principles and taking into account economic, geographical and other criteria. A map based on the national absolute or relative majority in each municipality will be the basis of work in the working group, and will be subject only to amendments, justified by the above-mentioned criteria.[39]

The significance of this provision was that a map that recorded the 1991 census figures and represented each municipality in Bosnia through its ethnic structure ("national absolute or relative majority") was to be the basis for the partition. The constituent units — often referred to as cantons — were to comprise those areas in which particular ethnic groups/national populations were in a majority.[40] This "mechanical division based on the crudest calculation of ethnic majorities" meant that the first peace proposal for Bosnia embodied, prior to the outbreak of open conflict, the very nexus between identity and territory on which the major protagonists also relied.[41] In terms already discussed in chapter 3, this meant that the intersection of census statistics and cartography was a site in which these techniques of power performed national subjectivities and materialized "Bosnia" in a form all too easily recognizable.

Although this statistical logic was designed to provide the clear dividing line between the constituent units and their populations favored by partitionists, the demographic circumstances of Bosnia undermined this intent. According to Mladen Klemenčić (in an analysis that equally relied on depoliticized notions of ethnicity), this proposal meant "that the Muslim unit would cover 43.7% of territory, on which 82.4% of the Muslim population of Bosnia-Herzegovina lived. The Serb unit would gain 43.8% of territory containing 50.1% of the total Serb population. The remaining 12.5% was proposed for the Croat unit, an area which contained 41.0% of total Croat population."[42] In other words, nearly 18 percent of the Muslim population, 50 percent of the Serb population, and 60 percent of the Croat population would after partition reside *outside* the constituent units designed for them.

The ethnic basis of the constituent units highlighted a profound tension within the Cutiliero Statement of Principles, a tension that was common to all subsequent peace initiatives. The statement professed a commitment to unitary notions of the Bosnian polity through its support for the independence and integrity of Bosnia. Yet the proposal for constituent units that together would comprise that supposedly unitary polity embodied — because of the exclusive and settled identities said to give rise to the constituent units — a separatist logic hostile to any notion of overarching authority. This was most evident in the idea that the constituent units could formalize connections with other republics of the former Yugoslavia. Although section A, paragraph 2, maintained that the governments of the constituent units would not "encourage or support claims to any part of its territory by neighbouring states," in section D, paragraph 2, the statement declared that "a constituent unit may establish and maintain relations and links with the other republics and with organizations in them provided that these relations and links are consistent with the independence and integrity of Bosnia and Herzegovina." Such a proposal attempted to marry two impulses that in the end would be mutually exclusive, especially given the widely recognized desire of the Bosnian Croat and Bosnian Serb leaderships to leave open the possibility of their territories being annexed by a Greater Croatia and Greater Serbia.

The ethnicization of Bosnia by the international community, in tandem with the parties to the conflict, was also reflected in other proposals of the Cutiliero principles. The working group assigned to draw the partition map was to "consist of three persons from each of the three parties represented in the talks on future constitutional arrangements for Bosnia and Herzegovina, together with three persons, including a chairman, nominated by the European Community."[43] Likewise, the civil service and the judiciary of Bosnia "would reflect proportionally the national composition of Bosnia and Herzegovina," while "the institutions (civil service, the judiciary, etc.) established by a constituent unit would reflect proportionally the national composition of the constituent unit."

These proposals revealed the conception of multiethnicity behind the negotiations: ethnic formulas ensured there was more than simply one ethnic group involved within the space bounded by international borders, even if the internal boundaries diminished the level of intercommunal contact. Partly as a result of this, whereas the Carrington plan was based on an elaborate series of provisions for the protection of minority rights, such provisos were less obvious in the statement. Section B ("General Principles") did emphasize a number of principles "generally practised among the democratic states of Western Europe" such as respect for human rights, and the section on the constituent units did note that "members of the nations who would be in a minority in a particular constituent unit would receive protection," but the emphasis was elsewhere.

Despite the shared logic between the statement and the major protagonists, and notwithstanding the agreement reached in Lisbon for it to be the basis for continuing negotiations, no party fully endorsed its outline. The Bosnian Serbs wanted greater independence for the constituent units and a larger share of territory. For the Bosnian Croats, although the political structures were acceptable, there were problems with the map.[44] Although the Bosnian government in principle opposed anything that embodied partition, to the surprise of many, it accepted the statement in Lisbon. Subsequently it became clear that its acceptance was the result of substantial pressure, and on more than one occasion it retracted its agreement. Finally, after more talks in Brussels on 30 March 1992, with Serbian paramilitaries by then having crossed the River Drina to begin the first ethnic cleansing campaigns, the Bosnian government rejected the statement.[45]

The London Principles, August 1992

From April 1992 onwards, the brutal strategies of ethnic cleansing, conducted overwhelmingly by Bosnian Serb forces, materialized a new map on the ground.[46] In this period the international community's response included the deployment of UNPROFOR to Bosnia and the imposition of economic sanctions against Serbia and Montenegro, but diplomatic negotiations, despite the formal existence of the ECCY process, were inactive. When the revelations concerning camps in which non-Serbs were interned increased the demand for a response, a new joint initiative between the EC and the United Nations established the formally titled International Conference on the Former Socialist Federal Republic of Yugoslavia (ICFY).[47]

With its first session held in London between 26–28 August 1992, this forum involved all parties, internal and external, to the conflict, and created a series of substantive working groups similar to the ECCY process. However, unlike the Lisbon negotiations earlier in the year, it did not produce a map or a negotiated settlement. Instead, it established a series of principles to serve as the basis for a negotiated settlement of the Yugoslav conflicts, and obtained agreement to a statement on Bosnia, both of which were intended to guide future cartographic considerations. The thirteen principles were as follows:

(i)   the imperative need that all parties and others concerned should cease fighting and the use of force, should respect agreed ceasefires and restrain those who commit or seek to promote breaches of them;

(ii) non-recognition of all advantages gained by force or fait accompli or of any legal consequences thereof;

(iii) the need for all parties to engage actively, directly or through intermediaries, in negotiations on the basis of these principles;

(iv) respect for the highest standards of individual rights and fundamental freedoms in a democratic society, as embodied in the International Covenants of the United Nations on Human Rights, the European Convention on Human Rights and its protocols and other instruments of the United Nations, the Conference on Security and Cooperation in Europe [CSCE] and the Council of Europe;

(v) implementation of constitutional guarantees of the human rights and fundamental freedoms of persons belonging to ethnic and national communities and minorities, the promotion of tolerance and the right to self-determination in accordance with the commitments entered into under the CSCE and in the EC Conference on Yugoslavia;

(vi) total condemnation of forcible expulsions, illegal detentions and attempts to change the ethnic composition of populations, and effective promotion of the closure of detention camps, and of the safe return to their homes of all persons displaced by the hostilities who wish this;

(vii) compliance by all persons with their obligations under international humanitarian law and in particular the Geneva conventions of 12 August 1949, and the personal responsibility of those who commit or order grave breaches of the Conventions;

(viii) the fundamental obligation to respect the independence, sovereignty and territorial integrity of all states in the region; and to respect the inviolability of all frontiers in accordance with the UN Charter, the CSCE Final Act and the Charter of Paris. Rejection of all efforts to acquire territory and change borders by force;

(ix) the requirement that a final settlement of all questions of succession to the former Socialist Federal Republic of Yugoslavia must be reached by consensus or by arbitration and the commitment of all parties to recognise each other mutually, to respect each others' status and rights under any such settlement and to share the duties and responsibilities of successor states;

(x) the obligations on all states and parties concerned to comply in full with all UN Security Council resolutions on the crisis in the former Socialist Federal Republic of Yugoslavia and to do their utmost to secure their implementation;

(xi) the vital need for humanitarian aid to be provided and, under appropriate protection and with the full cooperation of the local authorities, to reach the populations in need, with special consideration for the needs of children;

(xii) the obligation on all parties to cooperate wholeheartedly in the international monitoring, peacekeeping and arms control operations in the territory of the former Socialist Federal Republic of Yugoslavia and to contribute constructively to the suppression of violence throughout the area;

(xiii) the need to provide international guarantees to ensure the full implementation of all agreements reached within the framework of the International Conference.[48]

Unlike the overtly ethnic and separatist logic of the Cutiliero Statement of Principles, the London Principles asserted the priority of individual rights and the importance of sovereignty, independence, and territorial integrity. However, they also recognized the need for the constitutional protection of ethnic and national communities, along with the right to self-determination. Echoing elements of the Carrington plan of nearly a year earlier, the London Principles thus contained the conflicting imperatives of a unitary polity, on the one hand, and the recognition of forces that could undermine that unity, on the other. Nonetheless, with their clear condemnation of the practices of ethnic cleansing, the London Principles were not as accommodating of Bosnian Serb strategies and goals as the Lisbon agreement. This was underscored by the nine provisions for a political settlement contained in the "Statement on Bosnia" issued by the conference:

(a) a full and permanent cessation of hostilities and an end of all violence and repression, including the expulsion of populations;

(b) recognition of Bosnia and Herzegovina by all the former Yugoslav Republics;

(c) respect for the integrity of present frontiers, unless changed by mutual agreement;

(d) implementation of guarantees for the rights of persons belonging to all national communities and minorities in accordance with the UN Charter and CSCE provisions;

(e) just and adequate arrangements for people who have been forcibly expelled from their homes including the right to return and compensation for their losses;

(f) democratic and legal structures which properly protect the rights of all in Bosnia and Herzegovina, including national communities and minorities;

(g) assurances of non-intervention by outside military forces whether formed units or irregulars, except as provided for in relevant UN Security Council Resolutions;

(h) respect for all international Treaties and Agreements;

(i) restoration of trade and other links with neighbouring countries.[49]

This statement reemphasized the priority of Bosnia's sovereignty through the call for recognition and the demand for the respect of borders. Moreover, by insisting on "assurances of non-intervention by outside military forces whether formed units or irregulars," the statement acknowledged the external military threat Bosnia faced. Together, these provisions buttressed the unitary logic over and above the separatist possibilities of self-determination for ethnic and national groups.

Enacting the London Principles was the responsibility of the Steering Committee of the ICFY, under the cochairmanship of Cyrus Vance and David Owen. Beginning in early September 1992, they embarked on a series of meetings involving the six working groups, all of which were designed "to hold all the Yugoslav parties to the commitments made at the London session."[50] Although it was noted that the cochairmen "continued to give the highest priority of humanitarian issues," the Working Group on Bosnia and Herzegovina (chaired by Martti Ahtisaari) pursued negotiations on a constitutional settlement for the republic, which were to culminate in the Vance-Owen Peace Plan of January 1993.[51]

Ahtisaari reinvigorated the process that had ended after the rejection of the Cutiliero Statement of Principles by distributing papers to the parties and asking for written responses to a questionnaire on how they envisaged the organization of the republic. Although the London Principles were clear in the priority they accorded to the sovereignty and integrity of Bosnia, the thinking of the Working Group moved in directions that made that aim less attainable. As the November 1992 report on the ICFY process noted, "the parties have also submitted, on a no-distribution basis, their respective positions regarding the constituent units or regions into which they consider Bosnia and Herzegovina should be arranged."[52] Despite having made no mention of constituent units, the process of implementing the London Principles was taking the talks back to Lisbon.

A summary of the positions that emerged in these discussions was drawn up in a working paper by Ahtisaari on 4 October 1992. It identified five major constitutional options for Bosnia, and discussed the pros and cons of each. The five options were:

1. A largely centralised state with minor local functions assigned to a number (10–20) of communes whose boundaries would be determined on mostly other than ethnic lines. . . .

2. A centralised federal state but with significant functions (especially in fields of education and culture) carried by 4–10 "regions" whose boundaries would take into account ethnic and other considerations (likelihood that most would have a significant majority of one of the ethnic groups, and all would have significant minorities of the others) . . . .

3. A loose federal state of three primarily ethnically determined "constituent units" — consisting of areas that would not be geographically contiguous. . . .

4. A loose federation of three ethnically determined states with significant or possibly even total independence in the foreign relations and defence fields and basically merely cooperative arrangements in most economic ones. . . .

5. A Muslim state (possibly with boundaries drawn somewhat more generously than under the federation model), with the Serbs either becoming an integral part of Serbia/Yugoslavia or part of a federal unit of that state, and the Croats becoming a part of Croatia.[53]

The first option was the position of the Bosnian government, the second the "present apparent position of ICFY." The third option was that agreed to in Lisbon, and the working paper observed that the major problem with this proposal was that "without significant ethnic cleansing it will be impossible to draw boundaries that will give any coherence to three primarily ethnically based regions. (They will look like some of the Bantustans)." The fourth option — identified as the Bosnian Serb position — was also viewed as requiring "a great deal of ethnic cleansing . . . as a precondition." The fifth and final option, which was noted to be the "probable aim of the Serbs and Croats," had some powerful attractions. According to the ICFY paper, "it would seem to be the most stable of the structures, and the one toward which 3 and 4 would probably head — though then much more painfully and without leaving a viable Muslim state." Additionally, "it would reduce ethnic tensions to a minimum." However, four problems counted against it: "1. Would have to be preceded by a great deal of ethnic cleansing; 2. May be difficult to make the Muslim state (the only one in Europe) really viable. 3. It would violate the principle of the stability of boundaries. 4. It would seem to reward the Serb and Croat aggressions."

Vance and Owen's consideration of the constitutional options was based on the London Principles, especially those paragraphs concerned with reversing forced expulsions of populations and the inviolability

of borders.[54] They were also said to be thinking in terms of an important feature of Bosnian life, and the implications that flowed from it:

> The population of Bosnia and Herzegovina is inextricably inter-
> mingled. Thus there appears to be no viable way to create three ter-
> ritorially distinct States based on ethnic or confessional principles.
> Any plan to do so would involve incorporating a very large num-
> ber of members of the other ethnic/confessional groups, or consist
> of a number of separate enclaves of each ethnic/confessional group.
> Such a plan could achieve homogeneity and coherent boundaries
> only by a process of enforced population transfer—which has al-
> ready been condemned by the International Conference, as well as
> by the General Assembly (resolutions 771 (1992) and 779 (1992)).
> Consequently, the Co-Chairmen deemed it necessary to reject any
> model based on three separate, ethnic/confessionally based States.
> Furthermore, a confederation formed of three such states would be
> inherently unstable, for at least two would surely forge immediate
> and stronger connections with neighbouring States of the former
> Yugoslavia than they would with the other two units of Bosnia and
> Herzegovina.[55]

These reflections, along with the London Principles, might have
led the cochairmen to endorse option one, particularly as it was the only
one in which boundaries were determined "on mostly other than ethnic lines."[56] However, because this option (the Bosnian government
position) was not accepted by "at least two of the principal ethnic/
confessional groups," they opposed it and endorsed the view that it
"would not protect [Bosnian Croat and Bosnian Serb] interests in the
wake of the bloody civil strife that now sunders the country."[57]

As a result, Vance and Owen argued that "the only viable and
stable solution that does not acquiesce in already accomplished ethnic cleansing, and in further internationally unacceptable practices,
appears to be the establishment of a decentralized State."[58] This meant
a state in which the principal functions would be carried out by autonomous provinces. When it came to determining the nature of the
provinces, the cochairmen—though supposedly following the nonethnic nature of the London Principles, and having rejected arguments
for ethnic homogeneity—nonetheless reverted to ethnic considerations. They noted, for example, that "if the number of provinces were
too few, it would be difficult to realize ethnic homogeneity without
either violating the principle of geographic coherence or accepting
the results of ethnic cleansing."[59] Why "realiz[ing] ethnic homogeneity" should have been a factor at all given the previous reflections is
wholly unclear. Furthermore, in declaring how the boundaries of the

provinces would be determined, Vance and Owen returned to a formulation not dissimilar to the Cutiliero principles: "the boundaries
of the provinces should be drawn so as to constitute areas as geographically coherent as possible, taking into account ethnic, geographical ... historical, communications ... economic viability, and other relevant factors." Indeed, this consideration would have produced a
situation just like the Cutiliero principles. According to Vance and
Owen, "given the demographic composition of the country, it is likely
that many of the provinces (but not necessarily all) will have a considerable majority of one of the three major groups. Thus, a high percentage of each group would be living in a province in which it constitutes a numerical majority, although most of the provinces would
also have significant numerical minorities."[60] Although the constitutional parameters were different, that would have been a demographic
conclusion identical to the Cutiliero principles.

The ethnicization of Bosnia in the ICFY process embraced a number of other dimensions. One such dimension was adherence to the
anthropological assumptions of at least two of the parties to the conflict. As the report on the process stated,

> It is common ground among the parties that Bosnia and Herzego-
> vina is populated by three major "constituent peoples" or ethnic/
> confessional groups, namely the Muslims, the Serbs and the Croats,
> and also by a category of "others." Two of the parties contend that
> in designing a government for the country a predominant role must
> be given to these "constituent peoples." The other party considers
> that there should be no such overt recognition, although it admits
> that the political processes of the country have been and are likely
> to continue to be characterised by religio/ethnic factors.[61]

The second dimension, flowing from this, was to overlook the
wishes of one group (even though they were not just a group but the
legitimate government of Bosnia) and endorse the political ramifications of this anthropology. This meant that "the Constitution recognize[s] the existence of the groups in two ways: by providing that
certain posts or functions be assigned by rotation or by equitable balancing among the recognized groups ... and also by the conscious protection of group or minority rights."[62] In particular, the constitutional
structure was to incorporate an Upper House and a presidency (comprised of governors of the provinces), both of which—because the
provinces would have one ethnic group or another in the majority—
"will thus reflect roughly the ethnic composition of the country."[63]

At the same time, the ICFY proposals at times evinced some
doubts about the wisdom of the ethnicization of Bosnia. Paradoxically,

given the constitutional centrality of "three major 'ethnic' (national/
religious) groups," there was to be "no official ethnic identification
of citizens (e.g., on identity cards)." Despite the ethnic considerations
at play in the construction of the provinces, the proposed constitutional structure cautioned that "none of the provinces [are] to have a
name that specifically identifies it with one of the major ethnic groups."
And while there was to be "ethnic balancing and integration of the
military forces," there was to be "non-discriminatory composition of
the police."[64]

Similarly, Owen's public pronouncements often contradicted much
(if not all) of the essentialist identity assumptions prevalent in ICFY
thinking. When asked by *Foreign Affairs* in February 1993 whether
"given the hatred and the bloodshed of the past two years and the
historic ethnic enmities, is it realistic to hope these groups will lie
down together and live in peace," Owen replied:

> I think it's realistic because these people are of the same ethnic stock.
> I believe some political leaders in the Balkans are not authentically
> speaking for all their people. There are still very strong elements of
> moderation within Bosnia-Herzegovina. Many people there still
> see themselves as European and even now don't think of them-
> selves as Muslim, Croat or Serb, some deliberately and proudly call
> themselves just Bosnians. The sentiment is reflected in the degree
> of intermarriage. It's reflected in the fact that, even now, you can go
> to Sarajevo under bombardment and see Muslims, Serbs and Croats
> living together in the same streets and apartments. Throughout Yu-
> goslavia people are still all mixed in together and, in many cases,
> living peaceably.[65]

Nonetheless, clarity and consistency on the question of identity
were not among Owen's strong points. His support for a more complex picture of Bosnia was often undermined by statements on ethnicity that manifested some of the impoverished thinking evident in
the Kaufmann essay discussed above. Thus, when pondering whether
or not one could regard Izetbegović as a "fundamentalist," Owen re-
sorts to the idea that ethnicity can be physically observed: "There were
no outward and visible signs that he was a Muslim. He, his son and
his daughter dressed and acted as Europeans."[66]

Vance-Owen Peace Plan, January 1993

The ICFY process emerging from the London conference bore fruit
with the tabling of the Vance-Owen Peace Plan (VOPP) in Geneva in
January 1993, even though it was again only a basis for subsequent
negotiations rather than an agreed plan. Embodying all the consider-

ations discussed in the previous section, the plan itself, at least in the presentation of the constitutional framework, elided its reliance on ethnicity. Article 1 ("Constitutional Framework for Bosnia and Herzegovina") reads as follows:

Tripartite negotiations shall proceed on a continuous basis in Geneva, under the auspices of the International Conference in the Former Yugoslavia, in order to finalise a Constitution for Bosnia and Herzegovina in accordance with the following principles:

(1) Bosnia and Herzegovina shall be a decentralized State, the Constitution shall recognize three constituent peoples, as well as a group of others, with most governmental functions carried out by its provinces.

(2) The provinces shall not have any international legal personality and may not enter into agreements with foreign States or with international organisations.

(3) Full freedom of movement shall be allowed throughout Bosnia and Herzegovina, to be ensured in part by the maintenance of internationally controlled throughways.

(4) All matters of vital concern to any of the constituent peoples shall be regulated in the Constitution, which as to these points may be amended only by consensus of these constituent peoples; ordinary governmental business is not to be veto-able by any group.

(5) The provinces and the central Government shall have a democratically elected legislature and democratically chosen chief executives and an independent judiciary. The Presidency shall be composed of three elected representatives of each of the three constituent peoples. The initial elections are to be United Nations/European Community/Conference on Security and Cooperation in Europe supervised.

(6) A Constitutional Court, with a member from each group and a majority of non-Bosnian members initially appointed by the International Conference on the Former Yugoslavia, shall resolve disputes between the central Government and any province, and among organs of the former.

(7) Bosnia and Herzegovina is to be progressively demilitarized under United Nations/European Community supervision.

(8) The highest level of internationally recognized human rights shall be provided for in the Constitution, which shall also provide for the insurance of implementation through both domestic and international mechanisms.

(9) A number of international monitoring or control devices shall be provided for in the Constitution, to remain in place at least until the three constituent peoples by consensus agree to dispense with them.[67]

There were to be nine provinces plus a capital district for Sarajevo with special arrangements. Each community would have ended up as a majority in three provinces, with the Sarajevo district being a de facto fourth Muslim area. Klemenčić's analysis of the demographic consequences shows that the Bihać region with a 75-percent Muslim population would have been the most homogeneous, with Travnik, having a Croat plurality of 43.6 percent, being the least homogeneous. With ethnicity a central organizing criterion, the de facto homogeneity imagined by the VOPP was impossible in Bosnia in the absence of large-scale forced population transfers. The VOPP would have meant that nearly 43 percent of Bosnian Serbs, 44 percent of Muslims (30 percent if Sarajevo was regarded as "Muslim"), and 37 percent of Bosnian Croats remained *outside* their majority areas after the state was divided into provinces.[68]

For Vance and Owen, that outcome could have served as a vindication of their claims that the VOPP was designed to preserve a "sovereign, independent, multi-ethnic" Bosnia."[69] Impressed by the Sarajevan intellectuals who wanted to highlight the ethos of tolerance that stemmed from Bosnia's place at "the crossroads of civilizations, where the Muslim, Orthodox and Catholic religions mingled, home to Serbs, Croats, Bosnians, Jews and Gypsies," Owen saw the defense of this vision as his aim:

> Certainly it was that Bosnia-Herzegovina which inspired the London Declaration of Principles, enjoining Cyrus Vance and me to try to keep the citizens of this newly recognized country together in one state. Despite the cynics, in 1992 it was a task I genuinely believed to be desirable and achievable; and I still believe that had the Clinton administration supported the Vance-Owen Peace Plan, we would have been able to carry it out.[70]

This vision also informed, Owen argues, the logic behind the structure of at least seven provinces that emerged from the ICFY process. This number "was essential in order to have a significant mix of provinces so that the provincial map did not embody disguised partition, and so that the multi-ethnic nature of the country would be preserved."[71]

There is, however, an obvious tension between the identity assumptions of the ICFY process and Owen's public presentation of that logic. Given the ethnic ordering behind the construction of the provinces, the demographic consequences of the VOPP are testimony to the impossibility of division in Bosnia rather than to the implementation of a political ideal relentlessly pursued by Vance and Owen. For all that Owen argues that in the VOPP "we were careful not to label any provinces Serb, Croat or Muslim, contrary to the impression given by some newspapers and commentators, putting only numbers and place names on the map," there are a number of public instances in which the nexus between territory and identity that informed the VOPP was revealed. For example, in the *Foreign Affairs* interview—which the journal introduced with the remark that the VOPP meant Bosnia "would be divided into ten provinces, three majority Serb, three majority Croat, three majority Muslim and one mixed"—Owen countered the charge that he was rewarding "Serbian aggression" by arguing:

> The rural Bosnian Serbs sat on over 60% of the country before the war, and we are offering them three provinces covering 43%. I'm also careful not use the simplistic calculation "aggression" because this is both a civil war and a war of aggression. The Bosnian Serbs are fighting for territory in which they have lived for centuries. They have of course been aided and abetted by Serbs outside Bosnia-Herzegovina. And they have been substantially equipped militarily by Serbs outside Bosnia-Herzegovina. It is a very complex war in its origins.[72]

This response reflected assumptions about territory and identity remarkably similar to Radovan Karadžić's position. Moreover, it revealed the way in which Owen's frame of reference for the war—civil, with some international dimensions—underscored the importance of ethnicity. When the United States and Germany (the latter through a paper to its EC partners) argued in June 1992 that the international community should openly support the government of Bosnia against what they called "the terrorist wing" of the Serbian Democratic Party (SDS), Owen pronounced their position to be "unrealistic." As a result, the notion that successful negotiations would have to include all the parties, understood as "representatives of the three warring communities," came to the fore.[73] The equivalence of all sides manifested by this interpretation is reinforced by the care Owen shows for a cataloging of incidents during the war that could cast doubt on the Bosnian government's virtue.[74]

That multiethnicity was a principle not at the forefront of the international community's thinking on Bosnia can be demonstrated by the absence of any overt mention of it in the various peace plans. In consequence, Vance and Owen's claim that their ethnic provincialization of Bosnia was designed to defend a multiethnic society strongly suggests they were working with a notion of multiethnicity rather different from one that would contest de facto or de jure division along ethnic lines. Seemingly the sheer presence of more than one ethnic group within the external borders of the state, even if those groups were in their own spaces, was sufficient for the polity to qualify as multiethnic. However, as we shall see in the following chapter, the broader rubric of multiculturalism, and the different ways of conceptualizing cultural complexity, offer possibilities a good deal more subversive of identity politics than those that follow the international community's understanding. Indeed, a reflection on Owen's a posteriori assessment of the desirable political goals for the negotiations over Bosnia demonstrates that his notion of multiethnicity could accommodate a redrawing of boundaries in terms of ethnic and national criteria that would have been more divisive than that proposed by the VOPP.

During the second half of 1991, the first period of the Yugoslav conflicts, the Netherlands held the EC presidency. In a paper to other EC member states, the Dutch argued that the principle of self-determination could not be applied selectively; that is, it could not be applied to Croatia and Slovenia yet deemed inapplicable for minorities within those republics. This led them to conclude that the "voluntary redrawing of international borders [is] a possible solution." The Dutch paper continued:

> It is clear that this option would entail daunting problems. In the first place, it is impossible to draw Yugoslavia's internal borders in such a way that no national minorities would remain. Many minorities reside in relatively small pockets or even in isolated villages. On the other hand it cannot be denied that, if the aim is to reduce the number of national minorities in every republic, better borders than the present one could be devised.[75]

Although the paper stressed that this redrawing could not undermine the first Helsinki principle—whereby changes had to be "in accordance with international law, by peaceful means and by agreement" —it was a radical notion for the international community. Although the London Principles that constituted the mandate for Vance and Owen acknowledged the right of self-determination, they stressed the inviolability of all frontiers. Nonetheless, Owen argues it was incomprehensible that this notion was rejected by all other EC members. The reasons for that rejection, Owen notes, were that it would open up a Pandora's box, that "it was considered out of date to draw state borders along ethnic lines," and that nothing could obviate the fact that given the demographics of Yugoslavia there would always be minorities.[76]

This argument reveals two interesting features of early EC diplomacy in Yugoslavia. Firstly, Owen's admission that opponents of the Dutch argument considered it "out of date to draw state borders along ethnic lines" reveals the way in which assumptions about ethnicity are behind arguments couched in a variety of terms. Secondly, and unsurprisingly given the priority accorded ethnicity, the Dutch paper accepts (at least for argument's sake) that the aim "is to reduce the number of national minorities in every republic." Whose aim this might be is not stated. But Owen's commentary reveals whom the Dutch were willing to please when he writes that "it is true that there could not have been a total accommodation of Serb demands; but to rule out any discussion or opportunity for compromise in order to head off war was an extraordinary decision."[77]

Indeed, it is Owen's view that ignoring the Dutch argument was the biggest mistake in the war. He concludes *Balkan Odyssey* by declaring that

> the unwarranted insistence on ruling out changes to what had been internal administrative boundaries within a sovereign state was a fatal flaw in the attempted peacemaking in Yugoslavia. . . . Of course the world has to be aware of the dangers of drawing state borders along ethnic lines; but the world also has to recognize the dangers of ignoring ethnic and nationalist voices.[78]

In the face of this argument, Owen's much vaunted commitment to even a narrow understanding of multiethnicity pales.

The parties immediate to the conflict found much to disagree about in terms of the way the borders were drawn by the VOPP. Nonetheless, the Bosnian Croats readily accepted it, and the Bosnian government reluctantly signed it on 25 March 1993, thereby isolating the Bosnian Serbs, who rejected it via a referendum in May 1993 although Karadžić had originally but begrudgingly signed.[79] The United States, which had initially argued that the VOPP rewarded Serbian aggression, reversed its stance and called for a more accommodating position, effectively killing the proposal.[80] Not that the VOPP's demise was without cost for Bosnia. The political assumption of homogeneity in otherwise heterogeneous areas that marked the VOPP had disastrous implications for communal relationships, even though the VOPP was not implemented. Members of "majority" communities began to act violently toward those the VOPP marked as minorities, even when such distinctions could not be easily made on the ground.[81] As Kemal Kurspahic noted:

> The maps of a divided Bosnia-Hercegovina passed around at international conferences have become more of a continuing *cause* for the tragedy that has befallen us than a *solution*. When those maps were first introduced into the negotiation process in March 1992, in Lisbon, Serbian forces started an intensive campaign to "cleanse" the territory designated on the maps as "theirs." They embarked upon yet another campaign of killing, raping, imprisoning, and expelling all non-Serbs. When those maps were again reintroduced in January 1993, during the Vance-Owen negotiations in Geneva, incidents of the same type occurred in areas classified as supposedly Croatian — Gornji Vakuf, Busovaca, Vitez.[82]

The VOPP's official death gave birth to another proposal. In its place, the United States — in concert with Russia, Britain, and France — proposed the misnamed "Joint Action Plan," which established "safe havens" in six Bosnian areas and an international war crimes tribunal, while reinforcing their commitment to the delivery of humanitarian aid and the policing of a no-fly zone. Absent a political goal, "containment" was now the name of the international community's game.[83]

From Geneva to Paris, via Dayton, Ohio

The demise of the VOPP removed any drive from the ICFY process, and the United States' desire to be more flexible in meeting Serb demands meant that the negotiating process was given over to the combined initiative of Croatia and Serbia. The result was that the dismemberment of Bosnia became even more likely, and the position of Owen and Stoltenberg (Vance's replacement) even more uncomfortable.

When Owen and Stoltenberg resumed their efforts in June 1993 and met the parties in Geneva, the foundations for three peace plans "basically of the same family" were laid.[84] Although the not-so-covert ethnic principles of the VOPP meant division and possible de facto partition, the plans that followed — the Union of Three Republics (UTR), the European Union Action Plan (EUAP), and the Contact Group proposal — resulted in proposals for de jure partition that returned the process to the Cutiliero principles negotiated in Lisbon nearly eighteen months earlier. As Owen acknowledges, however much the change was downplayed we were now dealing with a three-part division. I was determined that what emerged should not be called the Owen-Stoltenberg map, a label which all the parties for different reasons were only too keen to slap on it: this was neither our map nor our plan and it was important that it should be seen to have come from the Serbs and the Croats.[85]

The Union of Three Republics Plan, September 1993

What had been agreed by the Serbs and Croats was a proposal in which any pretense of a unitary Bosnia was dispelled. Nine principles summarized their intent:

1. Bosnia and Herzegovina shall be a confederation, the constitution shall recognise three constituent peoples, as well as a group of others, with most governmental functions carried out by its republics.

2. The republics shall not enter into agreements with foreign states or with international organisations if it can damage the interests of other republics.

3. Full freedom of movement shall be allowed throughout Bosnia and Herzegovina to be ensured in part by the maintenance of internationally monitored throughways.

4. All matters of vital concern to any of the constituent peoples and their republics shall be regulated in the constitutions of the republics and tripartite constitutional agreement of confederation which as to these points may be amended only by consensus.

5. The republics shall have democratically elected legislatures and democratically chosen chief executives and an independent judiciary. The presidency of the confederation shall be composed of the three presidents of the republics. There shall be a confederal council of ministers composed of nine members, three from each of the republics. The chairman of the confederal council shall be prime minister. The confederal council shall include a foreign minister. The posts of prime minister and foreign minister shall rotate at agreed intervals among the three republics. The confederal parliament shall be indirectly elected by the legislature of the three republics. The initial elections are to be UN/EC/CSCE supervised.

6. A constitutional court, with a member from each republic, shall resolve disputes between the republics and the confederation, and among organs of the former. In the event that the constitutional court cannot settle disputes by consensus, they shall be re-

ferred for binding arbitration by a chamber of five drawn from judges of the International Court of Justice.

7. Bosnia and Herzegovina is to be progressively demilitarised under UN/EC supervision.

8. The highest level of internationally recognised human rights shall be provided for in the constitution, which shall also provide for ensuring implementation through both domestic and international mechanisms.

9. A number of international monitoring devices shall be provided for in the constitution, to remain in place at least until the three republics by consensus agree to dispense with them.[86]

As Owen's summary of the negotiation makes clear, "Karadzic said that Serbs could no longer accept the constitutional principles. Provinces were unacceptable. They were interested in a confederal solution with three republics — Republika Srpska, Herceg Bosna, and a Muslim Republic (Milosevic suggested Republika Bosna)."[87] It was the idea that a Bosnian Serb republic with contiguous territory, along with a similar Bosnian Croat unit, was now possible that drove these negotiations. Moreover, the positions of the Bosnian Croats and Bosnian Serbs were taken in tandem with the states of Croatia and Serbia, though Tudjman was supposedly more pliant.[88]

Flexible or not, the agenda of these negotiations was disclosed in a statement at the end of the meeting. Milošević and Tudjman declared jointly that "all speculations about a partition of Bosnia and Herzegovina between Croatia and Serbia are entirely unfounded."[89] Given that just such a scenario had been discussed between them from at least early 1991 onwards, the denial seemed to confirm the opposite.[90] Whatever the situation, a division of Bosnia into a Serb republic with 53 percent of the territory, a Muslim entity with at least 30 percent, and a Croat unit with 17 percent was the new framework for all talks. Once again, no amount of effort in drawing boundaries could avert a situation in which large numbers of "others" found themselves living in territory controlled by a different group. The Owen-Stoltenberg negotiations created a map in which 35 percent of Muslims and Serbs and 53 percent of Croats were "resident outside [their] titular republic."[91]

Owen and Stoltenberg were, however, supposedly operating still in terms of the London Principles, which explicitly rejected the rationale of this new position. Despite that, Owen suggested that the EC refrain from publicly articulating a new political goal. Such concerns, however, did not prevent Owen from deriding as "unrealistic" a Bosnian government position, which proposed that any federal arrangement should be based on equality for all citizens and equal rights for the constituent nations, and that the federal units "could not be divided exclusively along ethnic lines."[92] Although he and Stoltenberg might have been (as they claimed) steering the plans so as to address Bosnian concerns, no effort was being made to fundamentally alter the parameters of partition, as the London Principles required. The end result, after final negotiations aboard HMS *Invincible* in September 1993, was a plan for a Union of Three Republics in which Sarajevo became a UN–administered city, and a weak central administration appointed by the constituent republics could not disguise where the locus of identity and power lay. Two of the first three articles of its constitutional structure established the important elements:

Article 1

The Union of Republics of Bosnia and Herzegovina is composed of three Constituent Republics and encompasses three constituent peoples: the Muslims, Serbs and Croats, as well as a group of other peoples. The Union of Republics of Bosnia and Herzegovina will be a member state of the United Nations, and as a member state it shall apply for membership in other organisations of the United Nations system. . . .

Article 3

(a) Citizenship of Bosnia and Herzegovina shall be determined by a law adopted by the Union Parliament.

(b) Every person who on the entry into force of this Constitutional Agreement was entitled to be a citizen of the Republic of Bosnia and Herzegovina shall be entitled to be a citizen of a Constituent Republic as well as of the Union of Republics of Bosnia and Herzegovina.

(c) Dual citizenship shall be allowed.

(d) Decisions about citizenship shall be made by the designated organs of the Constituent Republics, subject to appeal to the competent courts.[93]

Advisers to the Bosnian government were under no illusions as to what all this meant, and argued that Article 1, which spoke of a "Union of Republics" rather than "United Republics," conferred in practice independence on the constituent elements. According to a signed memorandum of conversation with the ICFY's legal adviser, those advisers were told that Article 1 was designed to "establish a new state without explicitly using the word state," and that although their objections might have had merit, "there will be little understanding in the international community about these theological questions." The memorandum concludes: "Losing his temper, Szass makes plain that the purpose of the Owen-Stoltenberg plan is indeed to divide the Republic of Bosnia-Herzegovina into three independent states."[94]

Despite, or perhaps because of, this proposal, pressure on the Bosnian government to be more "realistic" was great, and included an August 1993 letter from the U.S. Secretary of State Warren Christopher to the Bosnian president urging his acceptance of ethnic partition.[95] In the end, the more significant part of the UTR plan was a side agreement between the Bosnian government and the Bosnian Serbs in which Izetbegović effectively conceded the future sovereignty and territorial integrity of Bosnia. In a declaration setting out this agreement, the parties concurred that

> after reaching a mutually acceptable resolution to the territorial delimitation of the three republics within the Union, and during the initial two year period of the Union's existence, there shall be a provision for a referendum to be held on a mutually agreed date within the Republics of the Union of the question of whether citizens of any particular republic agree to remain in the Union or the leave the Union.[96]

The way was therefore open for plebiscites that could lead to Republika Srpska and Herceg-Bosna being annexed by Serbia and Croatia respectively.

The European Union Action Plan, November 1993

The mutually acceptable resolution of territorial issues required by that side agreement was never accomplished, and although the Bosnian government accepted the UTR plan in principle, they declined to sign it. Dissatisfied with the less than one-third of the territory they had been allocated, they pursued an entity with 3 percent more territory. It was this circumstance that the European Union Action Plan (EUAP) of November 1993 addressed. It was not a new cartographic or constitutional exercise but, rather, a political push designed to get the territorial concessions the Bosnian government required before it could sign the UTR plan.[97] Indeed, the EUAP endorsed the idea of a Union of Republics of Bosnia and Herzegovina, and opposed the secessionist possibilities that flowed from the referenda proposed by the joint declaration of the Bosnian government and Bosnian Serbs.[98]

The thinking behind the EUAP, which was designed to be an element in the realization of common foreign and security policy for the EU, was prompted by Owen's consultations and reflections in October and November 1993. They began from the premise that "Bosnia and Herzegovina seems almost certain to split into two independent republics, and probably three." Arguing that this could happen either as part of a settlement or as the inevitable result of a settlement, Owen rather disingenuously claimed — given the consistent ethnic reasoning of the peace negotiations to this point — that "either way it will be decided by the parties, and there is no need for the international community to take a public stance on this. We have always said that we will accept whatever the parties agree to." Such an outcome might now be acceptable to a European constituency, he maintained, because "public opinion is already showing signs of becoming resigned to this as it sees the conflict more and more as a civil war."[99] Moreover, he argued that given the course of events and negotiations, the Muslims — whose nonethnic proposals were consistently rejected — were increasingly thinking in terms of an independent state of their own.[100]

With meetings in Geneva in late November and December 1993, followed by a conference in Brussels, the EU to little avail pressed the parties for agreement. What the EUAP did achieve, however, was the establishment of a calculus that would shape the diplomatic negotiations for the next two years. Because of its endorsement of the UTR plan with a slightly revised territorial split, the EUAP created the situation in which the Muslims (with one-third of the territory) and the Croats (with 17.5 percent) would together have 51 percent of Bosnia, leaving the Bosnian Serbs with 49 percent.[101]

The Washington Agreements, March 1994

The United States had remained largely on the negotiating sidelines during the second half of 1993, but following a policy review in early 1994, it became more engaged. The Clinton administration readied itself to increase pressure on the Bosnians to accept partition (something Owen thought they had already acceded to), an important part of which was the proposal for a Muslim-Croat federation of territories controlled by their communities in Bosnia, and a possible confederation between Bosnia and Croatia.[102]

From the European perspective, the American initiative contained within it some problems, not the least of which was the understanding of political identity in terms of which they operated. Although similarly ethnocentric — in the sense of being centered on ethnicity — differences were noted in a February 1994 report by Owen's private secretary. According to David Ludlow, one of the ICFY staff (Michael Steiner)

> is very concerned about the lack of objectivity and understanding of the background and history on the part of the Americans. He spent a long time trying to convince Oxman [an American negotiator] that there were three peoples in Bosnia, not just the Muslims and a collection of "minorities." US still sees its role as protector of the Muslims, and that the others must just follow along. Steiner is worried that the European voice will just not be heard.[103]

What the Washington Agreements of March 1994 achieved in establishing the federation was a return to the notion of cantonization via a two-republic solution.[104] Although at first somewhat different from the UTR plan's idea of three republics, the Washington Agreements were in effect very similar. They combined the Bosnian government-controlled territory with that of the Croat community, and left open the possibility for the Bosnian Serbs to constitute a second republic and join a union at a later stage. Articles 1 and 2 of the federation's constitution set out the key points:

Article 1

(1) Bosniacs and Croats, as constituent peoples (along with Others) and citizens of the Republic of Bosnia and Herzegovina, in the exercise of their sovereign rights, transform the internal structure of the territories with a majority of Bosniac and Croat population in the Republic of Bosnia and Herzegovina into a Federation, which is composed of federal units with equal rights and responsibilities.

(2) Decisions on the constitutional status of the territories of the Republic of Bosnia and Herzegovina with a majority of Serb population shall be made in the course of negotiations toward a peaceful settlement and at the ICFY.

Article 2

The Federation consists of federal units (Cantons). The methods and procedures for physically demarking the boundaries between the Cantons shall be established by Federation legislations. The Cantons shall be named solely after the cities which are the seats of the respective Cantonal governments or after regional geographic features.[105]

The first provision of the federation constitution marked a subtle but significant change in the political anthropology of the peace plans. Gone was the designation "Muslim"; in its place was the historical signifier *Bošnjak* (*Bosniac*—see chapter 7). This provision represented the international community's involvement in constitutional nationalism and authorized the exclusion of Bosnian Serbs, whether loyal to the Izetbegović government or not, from the official landscape of Bosnia. Bosniacs and Croats were thus accorded superior rights in the federation, with the unspecified but obvious connotation that Serbs would have to have their own entity in order to hold similar rights. Not surprisingly, this provision (which remains in force under the Dayton accords) drew the ire of the Serb Civic Council, which noted that the political exclusion of Serbs from the Bosnian Federation incorrectly assumed that Karadžić and the SDS leadership could represent them.[106]

The second provision, echoing the VOPP's stricture of avoiding ethnic names for the cantons, could not obscure the ethnic mathematics behind them, just as in the VOPP. With substantial powers and their own insignia, the cantons were to be demarcated according to the same 1991 population census that had been used in both the Cutiliero principles and the VOPP.[107] Even more significantly, this rationale—when combined with the elaborate mechanisms to ensure the institutions of power were balanced between the communities, including a provision that allowed the cantons of each community to establish a Council of Cantons for that community—meant that the "two-republic" appearance of the federation barely disguised its three-republic logic.[108] As a consequence, the international community should not have been surprised that this attempt to establish unity between the Bosnians and the Bosnian Croats in actuality confirmed and exacerbated the differences between them.

The process of defining the cantons culminated during talks in Vienna in early May 1994, with eight cantons plus Sarajevo as a capital district being established. The resultant map meant that 58 percent of Bosnia would be in federation territory, with the remaining 42 percent to be controlled by the Bosnian Serbs. With a population of more than 2.8 million, the federation's population was to comprise 52 percent Muslim, 24 percent Croat, and 17 percent Serb with the remaining 7 percent being "others."[109] That this in no way conformed with the strategic situation, whereby the army of the Bosnian Serbs controlled some 70 percent of Bosnia, was to prove something of an obstacle.

The Contact Group Plan, July 1994

In the wake of the military response to the February 1994 marketplace bombing in Sarajevo, and the Washington Agreements, the focus of diplomatic activity moved away from the ICFY and toward a Contact Group. Comprising representatives of the United States, Russia, Germany, Britain, and France, it was an ad hoc diplomatic arrangement that met for the first time on 26 April 1994 and gave the impression of EU and UN involvement.[110]

Operating initially in terms of the EUAP, the Contact Group process quickly became preoccupied with territorial issues at the expense of political structures. Although the ICFY staff involved in the process developed a constitutional structure based on a loose union, which was mostly derived from the UTR plan agreed to in principle aboard HMS *Invincible*, the position of the parties had changed in the intervening period. Much of that change was brought about by their reading of the political effects of the Washington Agreements. As a report by David Ludlow of Owen's staff notes, when presented with this revised constitutional package,

> the Croats made it clear that a two way arrangement between the Federation and the Serbs would be unacceptable to them. Any Union had to take into account the fact there were three constituent peoples. The Serbs were reluctant to discuss any type of Union arrangement at all. They argued that the establishment of the Bosniac-Croat Federation and the proposed confederation with Croatia ruled out any possibility of the Republika Srpska joining such a Union.[111]

In other words, contrary to its expressed intent, the three-republic logic of the Washington Agreements had strengthened the drive for total partition.

The doubts expressed by the Croats and the Serbs led to a situation where the Contact Group expressly decided to decouple the political and the territorial aspects of the negotiations, so as to concentrate on the latter. Although the ICFY staff argued strongly against Britain's forceful presentation of this position at a meeting in London on 16 June 1994, reiterating that their cochairmen believed strongly "neither side would accept a map without knowing what constitutional framework would accompany it," this was countered by the claim "that Krajisnik [a Bosnian Serb leader] had on a number of occasions said the constitution should be left to the end, as once the map was agreed, everything else would fall in to place."[112]

The Contact Group, having then decided in favor of the Bosnian Serbs' wishes to put aside the constitutional questions, received a message from the Bosnian Serbs that indicated that they "were ready to accept the map as it stood, but only if it was linked to a clear proposal on the constitution. This was seen as a wrecking move by the others, and would involve reversing the decision taken in Paris to leave discussion of the constitution aside." The resulting confusion highlighted a change in the Bosnian government's position but did not diminish the priority accorded to the map. It was "eventually agreed that a list of constitutional points could be established, which included a review process, but there had to be at least a loose constitutional union. However, there was no agreement to pass this to the parties officially."[113]

This "non-paper on constitutional policies" did find its way to the parties unofficially, and the response of Milošević (during a 21 September meeting with the Contact Group in Belgrade) highlighted the way in which the constitutional principles for a union countenanced partition at the same time as they claimed to oppose it.[114] Indeed, it seems that something of an inability to confront the partitionist consequences by some members of the Contact Group was behind the reluctance to enunciate fully the constitutional principles they envisaged.[115]

In the end, this political sleight of hand continued, and the Contact Group proceeded by offering in July 1994 a map for the parties to accept or reject as the basis for further negotiations. Organized around the 51:49 split of territory between two entities, the accompanying communiqué angered the Bosnian prime minister because it offered no commitment to protecting Bosnia's borders, made aggressor ___ ___tim equivalent by referring to "the two sides," and re-fer___ ___ian state delegation (which the Bosnians said also s___ ___ a "Bosniac/Croat delegation."[116]

___ ___s with the parties, the Contact Group ___ ___ on the table for acceptance. It ___ ___ tegy of, on the one hand, ___ ___l they accepted it, ___ force accept-___ the ___

to s___ ___

The Dayton accords o___ ___ ___is on 14 December 1995) were achieved ___ ___tegic balance during the summer of 1995. The Croatian military's capture of the Krajina areas, heavy NATO bombing of Bosnian Serb positions, and the retreat of the Bosnian Serb army brought about through the combined efforts of Bosnian and Croatian forces helped create the conditions for a resumption of negotiations.

The changed situation on the ground did not, however, produce any alteration to the political assumptions apparent in previous diplomatic rounds. Indeed, Owen argues that a close observer of the allied military intervention would have noticed that some of NATO's decisions (for example, Serb aircraft that counterattacked Croat and Muslim forces were not shot down as required by the no-fly zone policy, nor were the airfields from which they took off attacked) indicated a decision had been taken to ensure the outcome of the fighting did not stray from the basis of the Contact Group plan, the 51:49 territorial division.[118] Nonetheless, a memorandum prepared by the U.S. Ambassador to the United Nations, Madeleine Albright, in which she argued that the United States would have to sanction the trading of territory and the transfer of populations, marked an important confirmation of the long-term shift in American policy that produced an alignment with European proposals.[119]

Meeting in Geneva (8 September 1995) and New York (26 September 1995), the foreign ministers of Bosnia, Croatia, and Yugoslavia (the latter of whom was working on behalf of the Bosnian Serbs) agreed to six basic principles, the first two of which outlined the basis of the proposed resolution:

1. Bosnia and Herzegovina will continue its legal existence with its present borders and continuing international recognition.

2. Bosnia and Herzegovina will consist of two entities, the Federation of Bosnia and Herzegovina as established by the Washington Agreements, and the Republika Srpska (RS).

    2.1 The 51:49 parameter of the territorial proposal of the Contact Group is the basis for a settlement. This territorial proposal is open for adjustment by mutual agreement.

    2.2 Each entity will continue to exist under its present constitution (amended to accommodate these basic principles).

    2.3 Both entities will have the right to establish parallel special relationships with neighbouring countries, consistent with the sovereignty and territorial integrity of Bosnia and Herzegovina.

    2.4 The two entities will enter into reciprocal commitments (a) to hold complete elections under international auspices; (b) to adopt and adhere to normal international human rights stan-

dards and obligations, including the obligation to allow freedom of movement and enable displaced persons to repos-
sess their homes or receive just compensation; (c) to engage in
binding arbitration to resolve disputes between them.[120]

These principles provided the basis for the proximity talks held
at the Wright-Patterson Air Force Base between 1–21 November 1995,
which, although formally conducted by the Contact Group, were under the almost total control of the United States. The General Framework Agreement (GFA) produced by these talks consists of eleven
articles, which endorse the contents of eleven annexes, each of which
is an agreement between three parties: the Republic of Bosnia and
Herzegovina (the subject with international legal personality, comprising two entities), and each of the entities (the Federation of Bosnia
and Herzegovina and Republika Srpska).[121]

The Politics of the Enclave

Klemenčić (whose analysis concluded with the Washington Agreement maps of May 1994) argues that the international community's
peace proposals can be considered as comprising two forms. The first
includes the "division maps," in which the international boundaries
and integrity of Bosnia were maintained, but the country was internally reorganized so as to accommodate ethnic demands, such as in
the VOPP. The second are the "partition maps," which result more
or less in the dissolution of Bosnia, claims to the contrary notwithstanding, of which the UTR plan is the best example.[122]

However, Klemenčić's analysis misses an important dimension
that calls into question his categorization and suggests the partitionist logic is more common. By focusing solely on the mapping of the
proposals, he fails to pay sufficient attention to the divisive nature of
the constitutional proposals that accompany them. In this sense, given
that each of the initiatives involved devolutions of political power to
ethnic majorities and were accompanied by spatial arrangements to
match, they all embodied to some extent the logic of partition. It was
strongest in the Cutiliero principles, the UTR plan, and the EUAP and
the Contact Group proposals, all of which brought into being a form
of apartheid in southern Europe not long after it disappeared from
southern Africa.[123] While the logic of partition was absent from the
London Principles—as well as from the many UN Security Council
resolutions that began by "reaffirming the sovereignty, territorial integrity and political independence of Bosnia and Herzegovina"—
the VOPP was also nonetheless riven by a powerful tension between
its unitary claims and its ethnic provincial structure.

The political effects of the political anthropology that informed the international community's diplomacy with respect to Bosnia mean that the GFA is the logical product of a process that, from the Cutiliero Statement of Principles onwards, did not question its basic assumptions. Although the map that accompanied the GFA differed in terms of the actual territories assigned to the entities either side of the Inter-Entity Boundary Line, its adherence to the 51:49 parameter demonstrates the Dayton accords' indebtedness to the earlier talks. Furthermore, the constitutional arrangements (Annex 4) are nearly identical to those proposed before. Most importantly, although the acceptance of an autonomous Bosnian Serb unit has been on the cards since the UTR plan of 1993, the GFA is the first agreement to officially name and legitimize Republika Srpska.

Herein lies the single greatest paradox of the GFA, a paradox that has bedeviled the Bosnian peace process. On the one hand, the GFA — according to the preamble of the Constitution of Bosnia and Herzegovina — remains "committed to the sovereignty, territorial integrity, and political independence of Bosnia and Hercegovina in accordance with international law." To this end, Article 1 of the constitution declares that Bosnia and Herzegovina "shall continue its legal existence under international law as a state, with its internal structure modified and with its present internationally recognized borders. It shall remain a Member State of the United Nations and may apply for membership in organizations within the United Nations system and other international organizations."[124]

On the other hand, Bosnia now comprises two distinct entities each of which has its own ethnically divided political structures, controls citizenship, issues passports, and can "establish special parallel relationships with neighbouring states" (although this is supposed to be "consistent with the sovereignty and territorial integrity of Bosnia and Herzegovina").[125] Even more significantly, the standard international instrument of sovereignty — control over the legitimate use of force — rests not with Bosnia and Herzegovina but with the entities. Bosnia and Herzegovina has no integrated army or police force to secure its borders and territory. Indeed, the arrangements for the three-member shared presidency (one from each constituent nation) involve a Standing Committee on Military Matters that coordinates rather than commands military forces. It is comprised of a Serb member who is commander-in-chief of the Republika Srpska army, a Croat member who is commander-in-chief of the Croat Defence Council, and a Bosniac member who is commander-in-chief of the army of Bosnia and Herzegovina.[126]

Although the ICFY rejected the proposal (option five of Ahtisaari's October 1992 paper on constitutional alternatives) that most closely resembled the unvarnished call for the partition of Bosnia sounded by Mearsheimer, the logic of partition was never far removed from the international community's proposals. To be sure, Mearsheimer dispensed with the international community's fig leaf of sovereignty residing in a republic comprised of entities. However, although Mearsheimer cast his argument as a critique of the Dayton agreement and its supposed goal of a unitary state characterized by multiethnicity, the practical effect of the agreement has not been as antithetical to partition as he claimed.

The considerable affinities between Mearsheimer's proposals and the product of five years of international diplomacy have been made possible by a shared problematization of Bosnia. For Bosnia to be thought of as a problem requiring a solution, it has to be problematized in a particular way. Different problematizations mandate different political options. Rendered as a "civil war," Bosnia invites different strategies than those that might be involved if it were to be cast as "international aggression." What the above argument demonstrates is that both Mearsheimer and the international community have problematized Bosnia in terms of a nationalist imaginary — as a place where political identity is fixed in terms of ethnic exclusivity and requires territorial space to match. In other words, both Mearsheimer and the international community invoke and rely on a particular political anthropology of Bosnia to secure the "realistic" nature of their specific proposals.

This political anthropology is most evident in Mearsheimer's argument. Bosnia is a seamless, ethnically ordered world of Croats, Muslims, and Serbs, in which no other conceptions of identity have political import, and where group relations cannot be other than mutually exclusive and conflictual. Partition is thus the inevitable result. But if Bosnia is something other than a seamless, ethnically ordered world of Croats, Muslims, and Serbs, partition will be no more than one political option among others.

For the international community, Bosnia is more often than not a seamless, ethnically ordered world. This was indicated by the terminology of the peace plans, the openly articulated identity assumptions of the ICFY process and its negotiators, and the connection made between those identity assumptions and their spatial organization. Indeed, the nexus between territory and identity manifest, for example, in claims about land ownership having political significance helped resolve any ambivalence about the ethnicization of Bosnia. This was important, because a certain ambivalence about the priority accorded a political anthropology of ethnicity for Bosnia could be discerned from time to time in the peace process. The Carrington Plan of November 1991, for example, although it relied substantially on an unspecified ethnic rendering, nonetheless contained a provision that ensured an individual had

> the right to decide to which national or ethnic group he or she wishes to belong, and to exercise any rights pertaining to this choice as an individual or in association with others. No disadvantage shall arise from a person's choice to belong or not to belong to a national or ethnic group. This right shall particularly apply in the case of marriage between persons of different national or ethnic groups.[127]

Similarly, some ICFY proposals at times evinced some doubts about the wisdom of the ethnicization of Bosnia. Paradoxically, given the constitutional centrality of "three major 'ethnic' (national/religious) groups," there was to be "no official ethnic identification of citizens (e.g., on identity cards)." Despite the ethnic considerations at play in the construction of the VOPP provinces, the proposed constitutional structure cautioned that "none of the provinces [are] to have a name that specifically identifies it with one of the major ethnic groups." And while there was to be "ethnic balancing and integration of the military forces," there was to be "non-discriminatory composition of the police."[128] Furthermore, some of Owen's public pronouncements often contradicted much (if not all) of the essentialist identity assumptions prevalent in both ICFY thinking and some of his other statements.

Likewise, we should not underestimate, depending on one's understanding of the term, the multiethnic possibilities of at least some elements of the GFA. Had they been implemented fully so as to contest all forms of chauvinism, the Dayton accords' provisions for democratic elections (Annex 3), the defense of human rights (Annex 6), and refugee return and safety (Annex 7) could have embodied the much talked about spirit. But, as chapter 7 will demonstrate with respect to the electoral provisions, a good many of the procedures put in place to implement the GFA have served as obstacles to nonethnic and nonnationalist forces. When combined with a general absence of will to pursue multiethnic goals as a priority—an absence that has marked the entire peace process—the prospects for the Dayton agreement's overcoming its partitionist logic have been next to nothing.

In this context, the conventional wisdom that the Dayton agreement secures a unitary and multiethnic Bosnia functions to displace responsibility for the division of Bosnia from the international community to the local parties. The spurious surprise about reports that reveal, for example, that the Inter-Entity Boundary Line is functioning "more like a border than an administrative demarcation" helps make possible the view that "it is now up to Bosnian politicians to build the multi-ethnic democracy envisioned under Dayton."[129] While at one level undoubtedly true, such declarations fail to appreciate both the questionable nature of that interpretation and the obstacles to it that the GFA contains.

Such claims obscure the conclusion of that above analysis: that whenever a nonethnic or nonnationalist solution was proposed, it was either not supported or was rejected by the international community. After all, the very first international agreement was for ethnic cantonization and constituent republics, and the subsequent failure of the ICFY process to implement the London Principles ensured a speedy return to variations of that position. Moreover, as was noted earlier, Bosnian government suggestions that criteria other than ethnicity should predominate when establishing subnational units were more than once cast off as "unrealistic." Owen's insistence that he "tried to raise the profile of the multi-ethnic civic groups, decent people wanting to live together as before the war, but their voice, while championed by a few abroad, was drowned out by the propaganda of war," is both unsubstantiated by examples, and rings hollow given the potential power of his position in overcoming such disinformation.[130] Moreover, his reliance on a separatist political anthropology would have limited any such effort had it been tried.

None of this leads to the conclusion that the politics of partition was the sole prerogative of the international community. It is important to remember that the earliest moves in this direction came from elements within Croatia and Serbia. The first partition map appeared in the Croatian media in June 1991 and probably reflected the ongoing discussions with the Serbian leadership about the possible division of Bosnia. Shortly thereafter, following the strategy they initiated in Croatia, the Bosnian Serbs mapped their Serbian Autonomous Regions in Bosnia. There even appeared from sources hostile to the Bosnian government a "Muslim-drawn map" that used the 1991 census to carve out three cantons in the country.[131]

However, once the international community favored cantonization and opted for ethnicization through the Cutiliero Statement of Principles, an alliance of the Bosnian and Croatian communities put forward a scheme that sublimated (though did not eliminate) ethnic and national criteria, the effect of which would have been ethnic heterogeneity. This August 1992 plan, authorized by members of the Croatian Democratic Union (HDZ) and the Party for Democratic Action (SDA), was rejected by the leaderships of each community, in the latter's case probably because the Bosnian government's August 1992 plan proposed four cantons based on the functional regions of the four largest cities in the country.[132] By December of that year, the government had submitted to the ICFY a paper recommending thirteen regions in which the population contained not less than 20 percent minorities. Although four of these regions contained concentrations of 70 percent to 80 percent of one group, not one of them was "Muslim." Other than Tuzla (62 percent) none of the other regions were more than 54 percent "Muslim," thereby putting in doubt claims concerning the government's desire for ethnic homogeneity. Nor can it be suggested that the proposal would have ensured through pluralities "Muslim" control of a larger number of regions, for in at least four areas a combination of Croats and Serbs would have outnumbered and (depending on the constitutional arrangements and particular assumptions about electoral behavior) outvoted the larger group.[133]

But as the peace process became ever more relentless in its ethnicization of Bosnia, the likelihood — though never realized — that the government would end up endorsing plans for an at least de facto independent Muslim state increased. After the VOPP was tabled, the Bosnian journal *Ljiljan* published a map advocating ten cantons, six of which were Muslim. Although not official, it indicated that at least some elements of the leadership might have a fallback position that would have paralleled Serb and Croat thinking.[134] In July 1993, as a possible resolution to the concerns about the working draft of the UTR plan, the Bosnian government's advisers made a proposal that in its reliance on the traditional anthropology of the constituent peoples, meant it was not far from conventional thinking.[135] That situation was consummated by the September 1993 agreement — later disavowed — with the Bosnian Serbs that permitted the dissolution of the union if plebiscites in each republic so voted. As late as February 1994, the Council of Bosnia-Herzegovina Croats, which was opposed to the annexationist approach of their political leaders, put together a cantonization plan that defended the sovereignty and integrity of Bosnia by proposing three republics that were not based on ethnic principles.[136] But in the aftermath of the Dayton process, partition has become an option openly but cautiously debated in the Sarajevo media.[137]

All of this leads to the conclusion that while partition was not an invention of the international community, in favoring that political logic over other alternatives, the peace process was aligned with at least elements of one of the separatist parties. In effect, the international community has been allied with the political reasoning of the Bosnian Serb and/or Bosnian Croat leadership that favored the dismemberment of Bosnia, to the detriment of the Bosnian government's efforts to explore, even in its limited and sometimes uncertain way, nonethnic and nonnational options. As a result, the presuppositions of fixed identity — clearest in the idea of the Cutiliero principles that sovereignty was grounded in the citizens of ethnic nations — with a resultant spatialization of politics — in the form of ethnically produced cantons, constituent republics or entities — governed all options.

The political consequence of this political anthropology means that the Dayton agreement's adherence to "multiethnicity" is not antithetical to ethnic divisions. In consequence, Vance and Owen's claim that their ethnic provincialization of Bosnia was designed to defend a multiethnic society, and the public presentation of the Dayton agreement as being an instrument for the restoration of a multiethnic Bosnia strongly suggest that international diplomats have been working with a notion of multiethnicity rather different from one that would contest de facto or de jure division along ethnic lines. Seemingly the sheer presence of more than one ethnic group within the external borders of the state, even if those groups were in their own spaces, is sufficient for the polity to qualify as multiethnic.

In so far as we can pretend that Dayton and the other agreements intended a multiethnic Bosnia, it is an "enclave multiethnicity" they had in mind, where the aggregation of predominately homogeneous entities within a thin veneer of external unity substitutes for a more thorough complexity. This means that some conceptions of multiethnicity are consistent with partition. For it to be otherwise, we have to recognize that multiethnicity entails more than the mathematical antithesis of monoculturalism and homogeneity. As William Connolly has argued (using a broader category to contest the enclave formation), "multiculturalism...does not merely pose a challenge to national models of state politics and arboreal models of pluralism. *It also embodies within itself a quarrel between the national protection of diverse cultural minorities on the same territory and the pluralization of multiple possibilities of being within and across states.*"[138] With respect to Bosnia, the international community resolved that tension in favor of the former conception, and to the detriment of the latter.

The Dayton agreement thereby institutionalized a form of "metaracism" in which, in place of biological distinctions, "culture" is regarded as a naturalized property such that differences are inherently conflictual or threatening, and apartheid is legitimized as an "anti-racist" solution.[139] The contemporary prevalence of this political discourse — most obvious in the contentious debates about the impact of immigration on the identity of Britain, France, Germany, and the United States — demonstrates that the common political anthropology of both the peacemakers and the paramilitaries in the Bosnian war, with its nationalist nexus of territory and identity, is integral to the Western political imaginary. Although it has been said of the Dayton agreement that it embodies the Western values long abandoned in the Balkans, it represents rather the expected conclusion to a conflict shaped by those values. It is in line with the drive to "depluralize the nation" and counter to efforts that "denationalize pluralism."[140] In this context, the ethnic cleansing of Bosnia, rather than being outside of the European project, is at "the forefront of the construction of Europe."[141]

The central point of this argument is that things could have been different if the political anthropology of Bosnia — in which the conceptual landscape has been populated only by fixed ethnicity, three constituent peoples, and others — had been differently thought. The categories of identity politics were often a topic for diplomatic discussion. These moments include the November 1992 report by the ICFY cochairmen that made clear the assumptions they were working with (and how they had been contested in part by the Bosnian government), and the memorandum from Owen's staff during the negotiations for the Washington Agreements that made obvious the different approach of the Americans to the makeup of Bosnia. Moreover, the documents creating the Federation of Bosnia and Herzegovina, along with the Bosnian constitution in the GFA, spoke of "Bosniacs" rather than "Muslims," thereby indicating change was clearly possible. At those junctures, had the question of identity been thought of in terms of a necessary but political production that creates the grounds that are supposedly fixed and natural, then an appreciation of the political effects of particular representations could have been part of the process. The opening was there, but both the imagination and the commitment were sorely lacking.

Not that the deployment of different categories or names would have been sufficient. What was required, in Connolly's terms, was to initiate strategies that would have resulted in the pluralization of possibilities of being on the same territory. In the first instance, an attentiveness to and support for the local forces that contested the nationalist imaginary would have been necessary. Consistent with this, in the realm of international diplomacy, would have been the implementation of one of the agreed resolutions. If the mandate of the London Principles had been scrupulously followed, nonethnic and nonnational options could have been formulated. While the political difficulties of implementing such options cannot be underestimated (though in contrast to options like forced population transfers, neither should they be overestimated), it is often forgotten that *all* parties to the conflict agreed to those principles. Although the fact that they followed the international community's first encouragement in Lisbon of ethnic division no doubt weakened them, holding the parties to their August 1992 commitments was far from impossible.

Equally, all this leads to the conclusion that the arguments of Mearsheimer, Kaufmann, and others about what is and is not possible are fundamentally flawed. Because they depend on a contestable political anthropology, which resulted in the absence of a comprehensive and sustained effort by the international community to pursue nonethnic and nonnational options, it is impossible to credibly conclude that such initiatives could not in principle succeed. While the complete details of the Mearsheimer position were rejected during the ICFY process, and the Dayton agreement's multiethnic and unitary facade appears to contradict them, the practical effects of the international community's pursuing a logic akin to that of Mearsheimer has meant that partition is far from being a distant and future possibility.

The international community's logic is testimony to diplomacy's failings rather than the realist's virtue. Indeed, the conclusion to be drawn from this analysis is that proposals for the ethnicization of Bosnia and its partition constitute a dangerous idealism, rather than the sober realism they style themselves as. Because each of the proposals for division acknowledged that they could not realize the homogeneity they sought (for there was always going to a substantial percentage of each group outside of its area), they endangered the heterogeneous remainder they could never expunge. In effect, the proposals for division created new "ethnic minorities" at the same time as they legitimized strategies for their eradication. In seeking to ameliorate violence, proposals for partition have thus ended up encouraging it. Combined with the authoritarian impulse behind the proposals—population transfer would be forced, without reference to what those affected wanted—these arguments demonstrate the urgent need for modes of thought and strategies for action that do not seek a violent relationship to difference. Although thought and action are coeval and inseparable, chapter 6 outlines primarily what is involved in such thought, while chapter 7 deals principally with what this would mean for action. Together the remaining chapters call into question Mearsheimer's faith that it is because of Bosnia one should be a realist, and suggest instead that, for Bosnia's sake, it is to be regretted that the international diplomats were not attuned to a deconstructive ethos.[142] Only then would the violence enabled by the international community's problematization of Bosnia as an intractable ethnic problem requiring partition have been exposed.

Six

Deconstruction and the Promise of Democracy

Beyond Partition and the Politics of the Enclave

The norm of territorial and cultural alignment, with its nexus between sovereignty and identity, is central to international relations' construction of the world as comprising sovereign states in an anarchic realm. It is also the norm (identified here as "ontopology") that informed both the nationalists of the former Yugoslavia and the negotiators of the international community. Although it is no more than a form of "nostalgia for the politics of place,"[1] it is a nostalgia that in Bosnia animated ethnic cleansing, and continues to function powerfully because it constitutes a cartography of autonomous moral agents who can bear the burden of responsibility and act accordingly.

This moral geography enabled the international community's robust response to the Gulf War. But the response to the Bosnian war demonstrated the power of this formulation, albeit in reverse. Much effort was expended to deal with a conundrum: if the violence of Bosnia did not threaten a vital national interest such that it warranted the commitment of the military, but it nonetheless demanded some sort of reaction, what would be the rationale for action?

The absence of "political will" (which is the signifier for the mobilization of a response) to match the carnage witnessed by the international public demonstrated that the traditional grounds by which a response was authorized were either ineffective or inoperative. Previously, the will to oppose aggression per se has been effective as a rallying cry because it entails an affirmative aim, the restoration of sovereignty. In pursuit of an equally positive goal, efforts to garner support for measures to oppose ethnic cleansing have more often than not either tried to rely on its shock value, with a subsequent demand that humanitarian initiatives be put in place, or have attempted to indirectly render some other sovereign territory as the issue by making reference to the potential for "regional instability" and "containment."

In the case of Bosnia, abhorrence of aggression has proved insufficient as a basis to bring about an effective response because restoration of sovereignty, revisiting the status quo ante, could not be the goal. Since the dissolution of Yugoslavia in 1991, there has been no going back. The absence of such conventional grounds—combined with the seeming inability of humanitarian concerns to muster the requisite support to deal with the political dynamics of the conflict rather than just its symptoms—means alternative rationales for action have been required. A deterritorialization of responsibility is needed.

The fatal predicament for Bosnia has been the absence of such alternative grounds in the discourse of the international community. An important reason for silence is that the affirmative political goal around which opposition to aggression and its ontopological presuppositions could have been arrayed is for the most part considered ineligible. The most obvious political goal required acceptance of the very possibility that is being so actively contested in the cultural terrain of America and other Western nations: multiculturalism. A reflection on the idea of *balkanization* will make this clear.

During the Persian Gulf War of 1990–91, the argument was made by Charles Krauthammer (and supported by commentators such as George Will) that the cultural contestation afoot in America—associated with the issues of multiculturalism, proliferating identities, changes in the educational curricula, "political correctness," postmodern discourses, and so on—was fragmenting the unity of society and "the American idea" to such an extent that the resultant "balkanization" poses "a threat that no outside agent in this post-Soviet world could match." While Krauthammer's argument declared that "America will survive...Saddam Hussein," it left the impression (in a manner reminiscent of Norman Podhoretz's arguments in the late 1970s) that this new catalog of so-called internal subversives might weaken the country's vigilance toward the demons of the future.[2] In a similar vein, William Lind—whose discourse of danger bears a resemblance to the "clash of civilizations" argument of the Bosnian Serb leader Radovan Karadžić, quoted in chapter 3—has declared that "culture" must be the basis for a new conservative foreign policy agenda, for Western culture is under the most "explicit assault" since "the last Turkish siege of Vienna in 1683." Those perpetrating this threat are identified as " 'politically correct' radicals" at home and "other cultures" abroad. The identity of the latter group is not much of a secret, because Lind opines that if the necessary vigilance (in the form of a "domestic revival" necessitated by large-scale immigration) is not summoned, "the twenty-first century could find once again Islam at the gates of Vienna, as immigrants or terrorists if not as armies."[3]

In other instances where there has not been so specific a link made between internal and external threats to America, *balkanization* has nonetheless been employed to try and regulate domestic debates. Understanding the term to mean the way in which differences are raised into "cultural ramparts" and a social field is split "into sects, groups, little nodes of power," Robert Hughes, for example, has observed in his polemic against certain forms of multiculturalism in America that "on the dismembered corpse of Yugoslavia, whose 'cultural differences' (or, to put it more plainly, archaic religious and racial lunacies) have been set free by the death of Communism, we see what that stale figure of speech once meant and now means again."[4]

This preoccupation with fragmentation depends on the fictive notion of a prior time of unfragmented community that is itself produced by a discourse of coherence. It is a concern, moreover, not restricted to the United States. Although some of its intensity plays out differently elsewhere, other countries that sought to minimize their involvement in anything other than a humanitarian action in Bosnia host domestic arguments that are not dissimilar. For example, the contentious debates about the impact of immigration on the identity of Britain and France (among others) are testament to the way in which claims about a "core culture" being the essence of a sovereign nation predominate in contemporary politics. According to Verena Stolcke, Europe as a whole is witness to the power of a new rhetoric of inclusion and exclusion that can be identified as "cultural fundamentalism." Unlike racism, it organizes peoples not hierarchically, but segregates them spatially, with each culture in its place, everyone with their own right to difference securely demarcated and defended.[5] Although this suggests a break between race and culture, the racial has always been imbricated with the cultural.[6]

What the cultural fundamentalism of Europe and the balkanization fears of America reveal is that the opposition to multiculturalism is enabled by the belief that there can and should be a necessary alignment between territory and identity, state and nation. Within the United States, this logic plays itself out in the way multiculturalism is perceived as a threat to the unity of America, a tearing asunder of the collective ideal that founds the nation (such that Hughes speaks of "fraying" while Arthur Schlesinger worries about "disuniting").[7] Of course, it is this very logic—as chapters 3 and 5 made clear—that provided both the basis for the Bosnian war, its representation, and the international community's diplomatic response. It is this very logic that unites the rationalization of the deputy commander of Serbian nationalist forces, General Milan Gvero ("We say everybody has to live on his own territory, Muslims on Muslim territory, Serbs on Serbian")[8] with the political prescriptions of John Mearsheimer ("we should create . . . a Bosnian state peopled almost exclusively by Muslims, a Croatian state for Croatians and a Serbian state made up mainly of Serbians").[9] And it is this logic that permits Henry Kissinger to dismiss partition as a problem for Bosnia with the observation that "it is important to understand that Bosnia has never been a nation: there is no specifically Bosnian cultural identity."[10]

There are obvious differences in the intensity of feeling associated with the logic of alignment between territory and identity in Europe and the United States when compared to the former Yugoslavia. It would be imprudent to suggest that political struggles in the former will in any way resemble the disaster of the latter (Hughes's allusions notwithstanding), or that adherents to the argument wish it were so. But it is equally difficult to avoid recognizing the analogous assumptions between the two debates. That is because each is animated by the powerful idea that community involves the desire for presence, a desire that is nostalgic for the time when (it is alleged) community was closely knit, homogeneous, and harmonious.[11] Each embodies, therefore, a phenomenology of coherence as well as a particular political anthropology.

This affinity in political logic can be further suggested by considering the way those who are concerned about balkanization and thus opposed to multiculturalism in the United States and Europe view the former Yugoslavia in the same light. That is, they argue that a commitment to the monoculturalism of ontopological assumptions — even if those concerns are fudged by expressing them in terms of what has been called the "multiethnicity of the enclave" — is essential to counter the balkanization of the Balkans. However, this position holds only so long as one equates multiculturalism with balkanization; that is, only so long as multiculturalism is thought of in ontopological terms.

Multiculturalism is a concept that derives much of its appeal (as well as the angst it attracts) from being situated in an antagonistic relationship with "national" or "state" identities. But being so positioned, it has sometimes resulted in a corporatist appropriation of the concept to serve the interests of global market strategies.[12] Even worse, multiculturalism has been implicated in the logic of the allegedly new cultural racism, with its valorization of "hybridity" recalling nineteenth-century racialists, its celebration of difference in the form of "culturalism" instantiating determinate borders of identity consistent with apartheid politics, and its critical potential constrained (as will be discussed below) by a disenabling reliance on "tolerance."[13] When multiculturalism relies on the logic of individualism (that established individual differences are the basis for respect) or the inward focus of authenticity (that monologically derived characteristics are the basis for identity), it is ripe for an extended critical analysis.[14] Such a critical stance, however, is not derived from a fear of domestic balkanization but from an appreciation for the way in which the assumptions that structure such positions rely on notions of the autonomous generation of settled identities, thereby occluding the social and contingent process through which identities are constituted in relationship to difference.

It was these dimensions that the international community's politics of the enclave overlooked with respect to Bosnia. Reclaiming multiculturalism for a radical critique of the norm of ontopology involves a return to William Connolly's formulation of the issue. There the crucial distinction is between a notion of multiculturalism that pluralizes the possibilities of being on the same territory, and that which suppresses those possibilities through the proliferation of territorially distinct enclaves.[15] This distinction helps establish a radicalized notion of multiculturalism, with its attendant deconstructive ethos, as the condition of possibility for the exercise of our responsibility to the other.

Following this, a non-ontopological view of multiculturalism—something that, as chapter 7 will argue, is more prevalent in Bosnia than normally acknowledged—exposes a cruel paradox flowing from the line of argumentation that links multiculturalism to balkanization at home and abroad. To reject a notion of multiculturalism that problematizes the politics of the enclave and the logic of partition is to hasten the balkanization of the region, because balkanization stems from the desire for a bounded community and the nostalgia for a politics of place rather than a problematization of identity politics. Perhaps because they suspect this is so, those who argue in ontopological terms—such as Mearsheimer and the international negotiators—defend their position by maintaining that anything else is no longer possible in Bosnia.[16] As chapter 4 demonstrated, and chapter 7 will argue, that claim is easily contestable, whether made in the past, present, or future tense.

In these terms, it can be suggested that the international community shied away from making multiculturalism the affirmative political goal for Bosnia for two reasons. In the first place, to mount the case for political assistance to communities throughout the former Yugoslavia that embodied that ethos would require resolving in favor of plurality one of the most hotly contested cultural controversies in the United States and other Western nations. If one endorsed plural and nonnationalist conceptions of political community abroad, the same priorities would have to at least be widely accepted at home. But even more importantly, this failure stems from lack of conceptual resources to think of the question of community in other than an essentializing, nostalgic manner.

Overcoming this lack requires thinking through a set of radically different onto-political assumptions about subjectivity, laying the groundwork for which requires a detailed excursus into the realm of continental philosophy. Given the long-established and widely held traditions of political thought and international practice about community and identity against which one has to contend, being in a position to articulate a counter position requires a sustained argument about the way we apprehend ethics, identity, and politics. Specifically, because those who have made the case for partition employ ontopological assumptions, and because those assumptions constitute the governing codes of subjectivity in international relations, contesting the politics of the enclave means disturbing that problematic of subjectivity and its attendant approaches.

It is in this context, where the norm of ontopology has curtailed an effective and progressive response to the Bosnian war, that this chapter seeks to offer the thought behind a deconstructive rereading of the relationship between violence and the political that can expand the political possibilities. Taking up the points argued in chapter 2, which made clear the way in which the founding moment (along with the many subsequent moments of refounding) of a sovereign presence such as the state involves an interpretive and performative force, or *coup de force*, the *"primitive conceptual phantasm* of community, the nation-State, sovereignty, borders, native soil and blood" that drives ethnic-nationalist conflict can be revealed as a mystical artifice.[17] Which is not to say that the ontopological narrative can be easily dismissed. It is to say that its grounds for authority and legitimation are performatively constructed through its constative declaration. Were those grounds natural, the outpouring of violence evident in places such as Bosnia would not be necessary for its security. The tragic irony is that the greater the violence, the less certain the cause. As Derrida has declared, "deconstruction is the case."[18] But in unpacking ethnic-nationalist conflict in this manner, what affirmative position for Bosnia is produced by a deconstructive argument?

Developing a response to that challenge is the goal of this and the next chapter. This chapter begins by considering the important role of ethics and politics in the thought of Emmanuel Lévinas and Jacques Derrida, for it is in their work we find the most sustained provocations to prevailing understandings of subjectivity and responsibility essential to a refiguration of community.[19] After considering the politicized conceptions of democracy and multiculturalism to which this argument gives rise, chapter 7 will illustrate these concerns by bringing the argument to bear on the question of democratic practices past, present, and future in Bosnia.

Ethics after the End of Philosophy

The *end of philosophy*—the problematic term that signifies, among other developments, the Heideggerian critique of metaphysics and its many offspring—appears to pose something of a hurdle for thinking through the ethical challenges of our era.[20] Not the least of these obstacles is the view that in the wake of the Heideggerian critique, the ground for moral theory has been removed, because the *ethos* of moral philosophy cannot remain once the *logos* of metaphysics has gone.[21] At the same time, and equally in the wake of Heidegger, are a range of concerns—the German *Historikerstreit*, the wartime writings of Paul de Man, various attempts at Holocaust revisionism, along with Heidegger's own Nazi affiliations—that many take to be proof of the dangers that postmetaphysical thinking portends.

In this contemporary milieu, a 1934 essay by Emmanuel Lévinas ("Reflections on the Philosophy of Hitlerism") has been republished with a preface offering a different account of danger. In that short note, Lévinas argued that the origins of National Socialism's "bloody barbarism" were not to be found in an aberration of reasoning or an accident of ideology but rather in "the essential possibility of *elemental Evil* into which we can be led by logic and against which Western philosophy had not sufficiently insured itself."[22] Moreover, the possibility of evil as a product of reason, something against which Western philosophy had no guard, was "inscribed within the ontology of a being concerned with being." As such, this possibility remains a risk: it "still threatens the subject correlative with being as gathering together and as dominating," even though this subject (the subject of liberalism and humanism) is "the famous subject of transcendental idealism that before all else wishes to be free and thinks itself free."[23]

In this statement, Lévinas offered the core of a thought developed over the past six decades, a thought with the potential to chart an ethical course for subjects implicated in deconstruction but who want to resist destruction.[24] Lévinas's philosophy — that of ethics as first philosophy — is "dominated by the presentiment and the memory of the Nazi horror,"[25] and from under the shadow of Auschwitz seeks to install a disposition that will prevent its repetition.[26] Yet this summons is not answered by the admonition to return to the dominant moral-philosophical discourse of modernity with its traditional concept of responsibility, where ethics is most often understood in terms of the moral codes and commands pertaining to autonomous agents (whether they be individuals or states).[27] For Lévinas, being beholden by reason to elements of that tradition was the basis upon which the Holocaust (among other related atrocities) was possible.[28] Instead, Lévinas argues that in order to confront evil, it is the totalities of that moral-philosophical discourse that must be contested, for "political totalitarianism rests on an ontological totalitarianism."[29]

The critique of "ontological totalitarianism" puts Lévinas in tension with the legacies of (Greek) philosophy, at least in so far as Lévinas understands that philosophy to have been dominated by a way of thinking in which truth is equivalent to presence: "By this I mean an intelligibility that considers truth to be that which is present or co-present, that which can be gathered or synchronized into a totality that we would call the world or *cosmos*."[30] That which is Other is thereby reduced to the Same. This transformation is considered by Lévinas to be an "alchemy that is performed with the philosopher's stone of the knowing ego," a being concerned with being.[31] "Political totalitarianism" originates in this privilege granted to presence because it disenables and resists an understanding of that which cannot be thematized, the "otherwise than Being."[32] In this context, anti-Semitism — as one of the bases for the Nazi horror — is more than "the hostility felt by a majority towards a minority, nor only xenophobia, nor any ordinary racism." Instead, it can be understood as "a repugnance felt for the unknown within the psyche of the Other, for the mystery of its interiority or . . . a repugnance felt for the pure proximity of the other man, for sociality itself."[33]

However, there is for Lévinas another tradition of thought that takes us in this otherwise direction: the Hebraic (as opposed to Hellenic) tradition.[34] Although Lévinas does not discount the Greek tradition's capacity to understand the interhuman realm as presence, he argues that this realm "can also be considered from another perspective — the ethical or biblical perspective that transcends the Greek language of intelligibility—as a theme of justice and concern for the other as other, as a theme of love and desire, which carries us beyond the infinite being of the world as presence."[35] Lévinas cannot, therefore, be understood as being bound by an either/or logic through which one tradition is rejected in favor of another. Instead, he argues that "the interhuman is thus an interface: a double axis where what is 'of the world' qua *phenomenological intelligibility* is juxtaposed with what is 'not of the world' qua *ethical responsibility*."[36]

This double axis of presence and absence, identity and alterity, "essence and essence's other" stands as "the ultimate relationship in Being," the "irreducible structure upon which all the other structures rest."[37] It is that which constitutes, or reterritorializes, the space— the "null-site," a non-place of a place—of responsibility, subjectivity, and ethics in the location deterritorialized by Heidegger (and others).[38]

Responsibility, Subjectivity, Ethics

Lévinas's thought radically refigures our understanding of responsibility, subjectivity, and ethics, for the meaning of each is implicated in the other: "responsibility [is] the essential, primary and fundamental structure of subjectivity. For I describe subjectivity in ethical terms. Ethics . . . does not supplement a preceding existential base; the very node of the subjective is knotted in ethics understood as responsibility."[39] Of these concepts, responsibility is perhaps the most important because, for Lévinas, being is a radically interdependent condition, a condition made possible only because of my responsibility to the Other:

> Responsibility for the Other, for the naked face of the first individual to come along. A responsibility that goes beyond what I may or may not have done to the Other or whatever acts I may or may not have committed, as if I were devoted to the other man before being devoted to myself. Or more exactly, as if I had to answer for the other's death even before being. A guiltless responsibility, whereby I am none the less open to an accusation of which no alibi, spatial or temporal, could clear me. It is as if the Other established a relationship or a relationship were established whose whole intensity consists in not presupposing the idea of community.[40]

This responsibility is unlike that associated with the autonomous moral agents of traditional conceptions. It is "a responsibility without limits, and so necessarily excessive, incalculable, before memory . . . a responsibility before the very concept of responsibility."[41] It is a responsibility that is pre-original, anarchic, and devolved from an "infrastructural alterity,"[42] and thus reworks our understanding of both subjectivity and ethics.

Responsibility understood as such refigures subjectivity because the very origin of the subject is to be found in its subjection to the Other, a subjection that precedes consciousness, identity, and freedom; does not therefore originate in a vow or decision; and — ergo — cannot be made possible by a command or imperative.[43] In other words, subjects are constituted by their relationship with the Other. Their being is called into question by the prior existence of the Other, which has an unremitting and even accusative hold on the subject. Moreover, and this is what rearticulates ethics, this relationship with the Other means that one's being has to be affirmed in terms of *a right to be* in relation to the Other:

> One has to respond to one's right to be, not by referring to some abstract and anonymous law, or judicial entity, but because of one's fear for the Other. My being-in-the-world or my "place in the sun," my being at home, have these not also been the usurpation of spaces belonging to the other man whom I have already oppressed or starved, or driven out into a third world; are they not acts of repulsing, excluding, exiling, stripping, killing?[44]

Having decentered subjectivity by making it an effect of the relationship with the Other, Lévinas's thought recasts ethics in terms of a primary responsibility that stakes our being upon the assertion of our right to be. As Lévinas declares, "We name this calling into question of my spontaneity by the presence of the Other ethics."[45] In turn, the recasting of ethics reinforces the decentering of subjectivity:

> Ethical subjectivity dispenses with the idealizing subjectivity of ontology, which reduces everything to itself. The ethical "I" is subjectivity precisely insofar as it kneels before the other, sacrificing its own liberty to the more primordial call of the other. The heteronomy of our response to the human other, or to God as the absolutely other, precedes the autonomy of our subjective freedom. As soon as I acknowledge that it is "I" who am responsible, I accept that my freedom is anteceded by an obligation to the other. Ethics redefines subjectivity as this heteronomous responsibility, in contrast to autonomous freedom.[46]

Lévinas's philosophy of ethics as first philosophy is clearly in accord with the demise of universality as signaled by "the end of philosophy," especially as his enterprise has been animated by a concern for the political consequences of Being, ontology, and totality. At the same time, and partly because its truly radical nature goes beyond the confines of either/or logic, it can be argued that there remains an important moment of generality in Lévinas's thought. It is to be found — paradoxically — in "the very particularity" of the obligation to the Other.[47] We are all in that circumstance, and it is thus a form of transcendence. Not the transcendence of an ahistorical ego or principle, but transcendence in the sense that alterity, being's other, is a necessity structured by *différance* rather than ontology, which effects a transcendence without presence.[48] As Lévinas observes, "The fundamental experience which objective experience itself presupposes is the experience of the Other."[49]

The ethical transcendence of alterity that marks the moment of generality in Lévinas's thought also fundamentally problematizes liberal humanism, an oft-considered alternate ground for ethics. In the prefatory note to "The Philosophy of Hitlerism," Lévinas posed a radical question: "We must ask ourselves if liberalism is all we need to achieve an authentic dignity for the human subject. Does this subject arrive at the human condition prior to assuming responsibility for the other man in the act of election that raises him up to this height?"[50] The answer could only be "no." In *Otherwise than Being or Beyond Essence*, Lévinas wondered "if anything in the world is less conditioned than man, in whom the ultimate security a foundation would offer is absent. Is there then anything less unjustified than the contestation of the human condition?"[51] But this concern for justification abounds only if one requires sovereign grounds in advance of the Other. If that hope, driven by the perceived security such a foundation would offer, is expunged — and expunged it need be, otherwise *ressentiment* derived from the elusiveness of a foundation will thrive — the human condition will be understood as stemming from the relationship of alterity, and will be seen as without warrant prior to the responsibility the relationship with the Other entails. Accordingly, subjectivity is "imposed as an absolute" not through any interior value, but because it "is sacred in its alterity with respect to which, in an unexceptionable responsibility, I posit myself deposed of my sovereignty. Paradoxically it is qua *alienus* — foreigner and other — that man is not alienated."[52]

Liberalism is thus insufficient for human dignity because the election that justifies man "comes from a god — or God — who beholds him in the *face* of the other man, his neighbor, the original 'site' of the Revelation."[53] Similarly, humanism is insufficient, and "modern antihumanism . . . is true over and beyond the reasons it gives itself." What Lévinas finds laudable in antihumanism is that it "abandoned the idea of person, goal and origin of itself, in which the ego is still a thing because it is still a being." As such, antihumanism does not eradicate the human but "clears the place for subjectivity positing itself in abnegation, in sacrifice, in a substitution which precedes the will." It would therefore be a grave error to conclude in haste that Lévinas's antihumanism is either inhuman or inhumane. To the contrary. Lévinas declares that "humanism has to be denounced only *because it is not sufficiently human,*"[54] because it is insufficiently attuned to alterity. If one understood "humanism" to mean a "humanism of the Other," then there would be no greater humanist than Lévinas.[55]

The Politics of Responsibility

Lévinas's thought is appealing for rethinking the question of responsibility, especially with respect to situations like the Bosnian war, because it maintains that there is no circumstance under which we could declare that it was not our concern. As Lévinas notes, people can (and obviously do) conduct their relationship to the Other in terms of exploitation, oppression, and violence. But no matter how allergic to the other is the self, "the relation to the other, as a relation of responsibility, cannot be totally suppressed, even when it takes the form of politics or warfare." In consequence, no self can ever opt out of a relationship with the other: "it is impossible to free myself by saying, 'It's not my concern.' There is no choice, for it is always and inescapably my concern. This is a unique 'no choice,' one that is not slavery."[56]

This unique lack of choice comes about because in Lévinas's thought ethics has been transformed from something independent of subjectivity—that is, from a set of rules and regulations adopted by pregiven, autonomous agents—to something insinuated within and integral to that subjectivity. Accordingly, ethics can be understood as something not ancillary to the existence of a subject; instead, ethics can be appreciated for its indispensability to the very being of the subject. This argument leads us to the recognition that "we" are always already ethically situated, so making judgments about conduct depends less on what sort of rules are invoked as regulations, and more on how the interdependencies of our relations with others are appreciated. To repeat one of Lévinas's key points, "Ethics redefines subjectivity as this heteronomous responsibility, in contrast to autonomous freedom."[57]

Suggestive though it is for the domain of international relations—where the bulk of the work on ethics can be located within a conventional perspective on responsibility[58]—Lévinas's formulation of responsibility, subjectivity, and ethics nonetheless possesses some problems when it comes to the implications of this thought for politics.

What requires particular attention is the means by which the elemental and omnipresent status of responsibility, which is founded in the one-to-one or face-to-face relationship, can function in circumstances marked by a multiplicity of others. Although the reading of Lévinas here agrees that "the ethical exigency to be responsible to the other undermines the ontological primacy of the meaning of being," and embraces the idea that this demand "unsettles the natural and political positions we have taken up in the world and predisposes us to a meaning that is other than being, that is otherwise than being,"[59] how those disturbances are negotiated so as to foster the maximum responsibility in a world populated by others in struggle remains to be argued. To examine what is a problem of considerable import given the context of this essay, I want to consider Lévinas's discussion of "the third person," the distinction he makes between the ethical and the moral, and — of particular importance in a consideration of the politics of international action — the role of the state in Lévinas's thought.

Lévinas's philosophy, although clearly nonindividualist and antihumanist in its rendering of subjectivity, is nonetheless located within the logic of an individual, one-to-one relationship with the Other. Which is not to say that it is asocial. Aside from the fact that the basic premise of the one-to-one relationship is the interdependent character of subjectivity, Lévinas clearly recognizes that the world does not simply comprise one-to-one relationships. "In the real world there are many others," he writes.[60] But can Lévinas's articulation of ethics as first philosophy, and of responsibility as the primary structure of subjectivity, be expanded from the one-to-one to the one-and-the-many? And if so, how is this expansion achieved? While some have argued it cannot, Lévinas's discussions of "the third person," the state, and morality indicate that transference is considered within his thought.[61] The question is, then, whether the means by which that transference is possible fulfill the radical promise of Lévinas's argument.

If ethics is "a responsible, non-totalizing relation with the Other," then politics for Lévinas is "conceived of as a relation to the third party (*le tiers*), to all others, to the plurality of beings that make up the community."[62] There is thus a distinction derived from the existence of the third party in Lévinas's thought concerning others, which contrasts the Other as neighbor, the participant in the one-to-one relationship, with all others, those with whom my neighbor is the third party.[63] Additionally, the neighbor appears to exercise the primary demand of responsibility, and then serves as the basis for my relationship with all others: "My relationship with the other as neighbor gives meaning to my relations with all the others."[64]

Lévinas recognizes that the (inevitable) entry of the third party poses a dilemma: "The responsibility for the other is an immediacy antecedent to questions, it is proximity. It is troubled and becomes a problem when a third party enters."[65] The concern arises because the third party dissolves the uniqueness of the one-to-one relationship, not just because it presses the numerical claim that the world comprises many others, but because it establishes that "the third party is simultaneously other than the other, and makes me one among others."[66] However, as Alphonso Lingis observes, "to find that the one before whom and for whom I am responsible is responsible in his turn before and for another is not to find his order put on me relativized or cancelled."[67]

Nonetheless, the entry of the third party does raise questions that potentially put in doubt the generality of responsibility to the Other. As Lévinas remarks, "when others enter, each of them external to myself, problems arise. Who is closest to me? Who is the Other?"[68] These questions suggest the need for a calculation as to the nature of responsibility. Because there are always three people in the world, Lévinas says, "this means that we are obliged to ask who the other is, to try to define the undefinable, to compare the incomparable, in an effort to juridically hold different positions together."[69]

It appears, particularly when Lévinas asks, "Who is closest?" that this calculation of the order of responsibility has a spatial dimension. Yet in his discussion of the concept of *proximity*, the term that deals with this issue of closeness, the spatial implications of the concept are sometimes denied. Proximity, argues Lévinas, is "not an 'experience of proximity,' not a cognition which a subject has of an object. Nor is it the representation of the spatial environment, nor even the 'objective' fact of this spatial environment observable by a third party or deducible by me."[70] Lévinas also maintains that "the proximity of beings of flesh and blood is not their presence 'in flesh and bone.' "[71] In formulations of this kind, it seems that proximity is the condition of possibility for the interhuman relationship of the one-to-one, the basis upon which one cannot escape the transcendental demand of particular responsibility. Proximity is understood to be the relationship with the other, which "cannot be reduced to any modality of distance or geometrical contiguity, nor to the simple 'representation' of a neighbor; it is already an assignation, and extremely urgent assignation — an obligation, anachronously prior to any commitment."[72]

In these terms, proximity could also signify the closeness of culture, the priority of time over space. But on other occasions the spatial dimension is there, notably when the third party enters: "In proximity a subject is implicated in a way not reducible to *the spatial sense which proximity takes on* when the third party troubles it by demanding justice."[73] Indeed, the major problem with the entry of the third party is that the disturbance of responsibility in the one-to-one relationship it creates requires justice. As Lévinas argues, "if there were only two people in the world, there would be no need for law courts because I would always be responsible for and before, the other."[74] The justice that is required is, according to Lévinas, a justice of laws, and courts, and institutions, which means that as soon as the third party enters, "the ethical relationship with the other becomes political and enters into a totalizing discourse of ontology."[75]

Moreover, the spatial dimension that is foregrounded by the third party's disturbance and the resultant need for justice is associated with the state: "Who is closest to me? Who is the Other? . . . We must investigate carefully. Legal justice is required. There is need for a state."[76] Equally, in *Otherwise than Being*, Lévinas writes that "a problem is posited by proximity itself, which, as the immediate itself, is without problems. The extraordinary commitment of the other to the third party calls for control, a search for justice, society and the State."[77] Indeed, Lévinas has an approving view of the state, regarding it as "the highest achievement in the lives of western peoples,"[78] something perhaps attributable to his contestable interpretation of the legitimacy of the State of Israel.[79]

This view needs to be contrasted with Lévinas's belief, cited above, that not even in politics or warfare can the relationship with the other, the relationship of primary responsibility and the demand it imposes, be eradicated. Lévinas's faith in the state as the sovereign domain in which freedom can be exercised has the capacity to overlook the restrictions on the freedom of others the state's security requires. This potential was, disturbingly, most evident in an interview Lévinas gave on the topic of the massacre of Palestinians in the Sabra and Chatila refugee camps, which occurred during the 1982 Israeli invasion of Lebanon, after Israeli forces knowingly let Lebanese Christian soldiers into the camps to pursue suspected "Arab infiltrators." Although Lévinas spoke of those events as a "catastrophe" and as events "which we would rather hadn't happened," and although he sees profound need for the "honor of responsibility," he concludes that there is a "lack of guilt."[80] The following exchange ensued:

> [Q.] Emmanuel Lévinas, you are the philosopher of the "other." Isn't history, isn't politics the very site of the encounter with the "other," and for the Israeli, isn't the "other" above all the Palestinian?

[A.] My definition of the other is completely different. The other is the neighbour, who is not necessarily kin, but who can be. And in that sense, if you're for the other, you're for the neighbour. But if your neighbour attacks another neighbour or treats him unjustly, what can you do? Then alterity takes on another character, in alterity we can find an enemy, or at least then we are faced with the problem of knowing who is right and who is wrong, who is just and who is unjust. There are people who are wrong.[81]

In this answer the notion of the Other is restricted to the neighbor in such a way as to keep the Palestinians outside of the reach of those to whom the "I" is responsible. Although Lévinas elsewhere argues that "justice remains justice only, *in* a society where there is no distinction between those close and those far off,"[82] it seems that the border *between* societies, the state border that is enabled by the transformation of alterity into enmity (and especially those borders that separate Israel from its neighbors), permits the responsibility for the Other as neighbor to be diminished. Indeed, while Lévinas argued in the 1982 interview that he rejected the idea that responsibility had limits — "my *self*, I repeat, is never absolved from responsibility towards the Other" — in *Otherwise than Being* he remarked almost in passing that "my responsibility *for all* can and has to manifest itself also in limiting itself."[83]

This potential limiting of responsibility, which takes place on the passage from ethics to politics, can also be identified in the transition from ethics to morality. For Lévinas, the distinction between the ethical and the moral is one that is important to maintain, even though they are intimately intertwined. Ethics does not decree rules for society; it is morality that governs society. But it is ethics — as "the extreme sensitivity of one subjectivity to another," the heteronomous responsibility of our subjectivity — that governs morality: "The norm that must continue to inspire and direct the moral order is the ethical norm of the interhuman."[84]

Notwithstanding the interrelated nature of the norm of the interhuman and the rules of governance, in the shift to morality Lévinas argues that ethics "hardens its skin as soon as we move into the political world or the impersonal 'third' — the world of government, institutions, tribunals, prisons, schools, committees, and so on."[85] This "hardening of the skin" is a manifestation of the way in which Lévinas understands politics to involve "a totalizing discourse of ontology,"[86] a discourse most evident in arguments enunciated by and for the state. Nonetheless, in his discussion of the shift from ethics to morality, Lévinas exhibits a less sanguine attitude to the state than noted above:

> If the moral-political order totally relinquishes its ethical founda-
> tion, it must accept all forms of society, including the fascist or to-
> talitarian, for it can no longer evaluate or discriminate between them.
> The state is usually better than anarchy—but not always. In some
> instances—fascism or totalitarianism, for example—the political
> order of the state may have to be challenged in the name of our eth-
> ical responsibility to the other. That is why ethics must remain the
> first philosophy.[87]

Even though Lévinas's limited reservations about the state are here restricted to the nature of (domestic) political order, the idea that "the state may have to be challenged in the name of our ethical responsibility to the other" at least allows for the possibility of extending political action in terms of the ethical relation beyond the bounds suggested by Lévinas's previous reflections on the third party and the state. There is no doubt, however, that to fulfill the promise of Lévinas's ethics with respect to international politics, this possibility for challenge has to be carried a good deal further. Moreover, I would argue, this possibility for challenge has to be pursued in order to maintain fidelity with Lévinas's conviction that neither politics nor warfare can obliterate the relationship of the self to the other as a relation of responsibility. Indeed, this endeavor might be thought of in terms of making Lévinas's thought more "Lévinasian," for pursuing this possibility of challenge flows from the recognition that "injustice—not to mention racism, nationalism, and imperialism—begins when one loses sight of the transcendence of the Other and forgets that the State, with its institutions, is informed by the proximity of my relation to the Other."[88]

Supplementing Lévinas

Augmenting Lévinas's thought so that when it comes to the question of politics and the state it is more "Lévinasian" is a twofold process. It involves the retention of those aspects that suggested how an ethical attitude could be fashioned in a manner consistent with (and perhaps enabled by) the questioning of the metaphysics of presence, especially the idea that heteronomous responsibility is our raison d'être that cannot be escaped. And it involves a ceaseless effort of folding the ethical relation into the social effects of the ontologies of politics that harden skin and feign presence, so that the relationship with the Other that makes those effects possible, the state among them, is never elided.[89] In particular, this means that the heteronomous responsibility that is our raison d'être must be made to intervene in the claims to autonomous freedom associated with raison d'état. This possibility can be thought, I want to argue, if we turn to Derrida.

The affinities between "Lévinasian ethics" and deconstructive thought are considerable. Most notably, alterity incites ethics and responsibility for each, as both depend on the recognition of a structural condition of alterity prior to subjectivity and thought. As Derrida argues—in defense of the proposition that deconstructive thought entails an affirmation—"deconstruction is, in itself, a positive response to an alterity which necessarily calls, summons or motivates it. Deconstruction is therefore vocation—a response to a call. . . . The other precedes philosophy and necessarily invokes and provokes the subject before any genuine questioning can begin. It is in this rapport with the other that affirmation expresses itself."[90] As such, "Deconstruction is not an enclosure in nothingness, but an openness towards the other."[91]

The unconditional affirmation of deconstructive thought has enabled Simon Critchley to argue that the question of ethics and deconstruction is not one of deriving an ethics from deconstruction but of recognizing that deconstruction has a basic ethicality, that it takes place ethically, because of its orientation to the call of the other. But, for Critchley, deconstruction alone "fails to navigate the treacherous passage from ethics to politics,"[92] and requires the supplement of Lévinas's unconditional responsibility to traverse this passage. The Lévinasian fortification is effective because "for Lévinas *ethics is ethical for the sake of politics*—that is, for the sake of a new conception of the organization of political space." In consequence, Critchley's argument (although it is not specifically intended as a critique of Derrida) is that "politics provides the continual horizon of Lévinasian ethics, and that the problem of politics is that of delineating a form of political life that will repeatedly interrupt all attempts at totalization."[93]

That this is the problem of politics certainly brooks no disagreement from the argument being made here. However, the discussion above of Lévinas's reflections on politics and the state suggested that while his critique of "ontological totalitarianism" unsettled "political totalitarianism" *within* states, it did not carry through either to the dangers of "political totalitarianism" that inhere in the strategies necessary to secure (even liberal-democratic) states nor to the question of "political totalitarianism" *between* states. Thus, while Critchley supplements Derrida with Lévinas in pursuit of the political goal this argument shares, I would suggest that in order to establish the grounds for "a form of political life that will repeatedly interrupt all attempts at totalization," his argument requires a resupplementation in the form of Derridean deconstructive thought.

This move connects to Derrida's provocative and suggestive statement—which was left in chapter 2 inviting this response—that deconstructive thought can be considered "a stroke of luck for politics, for all historical progress."[94] Part of the reason for this is that deconstructive thought can be regarded as the "at least necessary condition for identifying and combatting the totalitarian risk."[95] To see how this is so, recall that the containers of politics are indispensably deconstructible because their foundations of authority are "mystical." At the same time, remember that such structures exist and exercise power because the interpretive and performative *coup de force* that brings them into being occludes the mystery within that unfounded process. Consider also that the greatest acts of violence in history have been made possible by the apparent naturalness of their practices, by the appearance that those carrying them out are doing no more than following commands necessitated by the order of things, and how that order has often been understood in terms of the survival of a (supposedly pregiven) state, a people, or a culture. Then it is possible to appreciate that only if we examine, through strategies of deconstructive thought (among others), the *coup de force* that encloses this logic in a timeless quality can we resist such violence.

With regard to Bosnia (and other such conflicts), although it sounds outrageous, deconstructive thought is at least the necessary condition for thinking about a solution that does not come from either the victory of one side over the other, or an acceptance of the logic of partition. Only if we can think of politics organized in terms of ethnicity and nationalism as being enabled by the unfounded questions of history violently deployed in the present for contemporary political goals, and resist its presentation as a natural outgrowth of ancient animosities, can we exercise our responsibility toward the other, and do other than wait for the carnage to subside. Indeed, even more outrageously, we can say that without deconstructive thought there might be no questions of ethics, politics, or responsibility. Were there in fact secure foundations, privileged epistemological grounds, and unquestionable ontological bases "somehow removed from the strife, investments, and contamination regularly associated with them,"[96] then social action would be no more than the automatic operation of a knowledge, and ethics and politics would be no more than technology.[97]

To say, however, that without deconstructive thought there would not be politics is not to argue that deconstructive thought gives us a politics. Nor is it to diminish the importance of the question of the impasse Critchley identifies within deconstruction when it comes to the question of politics. While agreeing that deconstruction's understanding of the social as forever without closure was "a crucial step in the subversion of dominant conceptions of society and the development of new political strategies," Critchley identified the political problem within deconstruction in these terms: "how is one to account for the move from undecidability to the political *decision* to combat that domination?"[98]

Undecidability is one of the Derridean concepts that most attracts criticism. Often (mis)understood as licensing an anarchical irresponsibility, it is taken to be the very negation of politics, understood in terms of the decision, and a concomitant denial of responsibility. However, as Derrida makes clear, he has "never proposed a kind of 'all or nothing' choice between pure realization of self-presence and complete freeplay or undecidability."[99] Indeed, the very notion of undecidability is the condition of possibility for a decision. If the realm of thought was preordained such that there were no options, no competing alternatives, and no difficult choices to make, there would be no need for a decision. Instead, the very existence of a decision is itself a manifestation of undecidability, so that we can comprehend undecidability "as an opening of the field of decision and decidability." As Derrida argues, "even if a decision seems to take only a second and not to be preceded by any deliberation, it is structured by this *experience and experiment of the undecidable*."[100] It is for this reason Derrida has talked in terms of undecidability rather than indeterminacy: the former signifies the context of the decision, a context in which there is "always a *determinate* oscillation between possibilities," whereas the latter suggests a relativism or indeterminism absent from deconstructive thought.[101] Moreover, just as deconstructive thought is necessary for politics, undecidability is a prerequisite for responsibility. Were there no decisions to be made, were all choices eradicated by the preordination of one and only one path, responsibility—the ability to respond to differing criteria and concerns—would be absent. Rather than being its abnegation, the possibility of decision ensured by undecidability is the necessary precondition for the existence and exercise of responsibility. Which leads Derrida to state: "There can be no moral or political responsibility without this trial and this passage by way of the undecidable."[102]

The Politics of the Decision

The theme of undecidability gives us the context of the decision, but in and of itself undecidability does not provide an account of the decision that would satisfy the concern raised by Critchley. "Decisions have to be taken. But how? And in virtue of what? How does one make a decision in an undecidable terrain?"[103] These questions point to the nub of the problem, for sure, but they are issues that do not go unnoticed in Derrida's work. They are of particular concern for Derrida in "Force of Law."

In that essay, subsequent to making the case for the intrinsic deconstructibility of the law and noting how this is good news for politics and historical progress, Derrida argues that the law's deconstructibility is made possible by the *un* deconstructibility of justice. Justice is outside and beyond the law: "Justice is the experience of the impossible."[104] Justice is not a principle, or a foundation, or a guiding tradition. Justice is infinite, and — in a favorable comparison to Lévinas's notion of justice — "the heteronomic relation to others, to the faces of otherness that govern me, whose infinity I cannot thematize and whose hostage I remain."[105] In these terms, justice is like the pre-original, anarchic relation to the other, and akin to the undecidable. It represents the domain of the impossible and the unrepresentable that lies outside and beyond the limit of the possible and the representable. But it cannot be understood as "utopian," at least insofar as that means the opposite of "realistic." It is not indeterminate. It is undecidable. It is that which marks the limit of the possible; indeed, it is that which brings the domain of the possible into being and gives it the ongoing chance for transformation and refiguration, that which is one of the conditions of possibility for ethics and politics.

In this context, justice enables the law, but the law is that which "is never exercised without a decision that *cuts,* that divides."[106] The law works from the unrepresentable and seeks to represent; it takes from the impossible and conceives the possible; it is embedded in the undecidable but nevertheless decides. Nonetheless, "the undecidable remains caught, lodged, at least as a ghost — but an essential ghost — in every decision, in every event of decision. Its ghostliness deconstructs from within any assurance of presence, any certitude or any supposed criteriology that would assure us of the justice of the decision, in truth of the very event of a decision."[107]

The undecidable within the decision does not, however, prevent the decision nor avoid its urgency. As Derrida observes, "a just decision is always required *immediately*, 'right away.'" This necessary haste has unavoidable consequences because the pursuit of "infinite information and the unlimited knowledge of conditions, rules or hypothetical imperatives that could justify it" are unavailable in the crush of time. Nor can the crush of time be avoided, even by unlimited time, "because the moment of *decision, as such,* always remains a finite moment of urgency and precipitation." The decision is always "structurally finite," it "always marks the interruption of the juridico- or ethico- or politico-cognitive deliberation that precedes it, that *must* precede it." This is why, invoking Kierkegaard, Derrida declares that "the instant of decision is a madness."[108]

The finite nature of the decision may be a "madness" in the way it renders possible the impossible, the infinite character of justice, but Derrida argues for the necessity of this madness. Most importantly, although Derrida's argument concerning the decision has, to this point, been concerned with an account of the *procedure* by which a decision is possible, it is with respect to the necessity of the decision that Derrida begins to formulate an account of the decision that bears upon the *content* of the decision. In so doing, Derrida's argument addresses more directly — more directly, I would argue, than is acknowledged by Critchley — the concern that for politics (at least for a progressive politics) one must provide an account of the decision to combat domination.

That undecidability resides within the decision, Derrida argues, "that justice exceeds law and calculation, that the unpresentable exceeds the determinable *cannot* and *should not* serve as alibi for staying out of juridico-political battles, within an institution or a state, or between institutions or states and others."[109] Indeed, "incalculable justice *requires* us to calculate." From where do these insistences come? What is behind, what is animating, these imperatives? It is both the character of infinite justice as a heteronomic relationship to the other, a relationship that because of its undecidability multiplies responsibility, and the fact that "left to itself, the incalculable and giving (*donatrice*) idea of justice is always very close to the bad, even to the worst, for it can always be reappropriated by the most perverse calculation."[110] The necessity of calculating the incalculable thus responds to a duty, a duty that inhabits the instant of madness and compels the decision to avoid "the bad," the "perverse calculation," even "the worst." This is the duty that also dwells with deconstructive thought and makes it the starting point, the "at least necessary condition," for the organization of resistance to totalitarianism in all its forms. And it is a duty that responds to practical political concerns when we recognize that Derrida names the bad, the perverse, and the worst as those violences "we recognize all too well without yet having thought them through, the crimes of xenophobia, racism, anti-Semitism, religious or nationalist fanaticism."[111]

Furthermore, the duty within the decision, the obligation that recognizes the necessity of negotiating the possibilities provided by the impossibilities of justice, is not content with simply avoiding, containing, combating, or negating the worst violence—though it could certainly begin with those strategies. Instead, this responsibility, which is the responsibility of responsibility, commissions a "utopian" strategy. Not a strategy that is beyond all bounds of possibility so as to be considered "unrealistic," but one which in respecting the necessity of calculation takes the possibility summoned by the calculation as far as possible, "*must* take it as far as possible, beyond the place we find ourselves and beyond the already identifiable zones of morality or politics or law, beyond the distinction between national and international, public and private, and so on."[112] As Derrida declares, "The condition of possibility of this thing called responsibility is a certain *experience and experiment of the possibility of the impossible: the testing of the aporia* from which one may invent the only *possible invention, the impossible invention*."[113] This leads Derrida to enunciate a proposition that many, not the least of whom are his Habermasian critics, could hardly have expected: "Nothing seems to me *less* outdated than the classical emancipatory ideal. We cannot attempt to disqualify it today, whether crudely or with sophistication, at least not without treating it too lightly and forming the worst complicities."[114]

Residing within—and not far below the surface—of Derrida's account of the experience of the undecidable as the context for the decision is the duty of deconstructive thought, the responsibility for the other, and the opposition to totalitarianism it entails. The Lévinasian supplement that Critchley argues deconstruction requires with respect to politics thus draws out that which is already present. It is, though, perhaps an element that needs to be drawn out, for Derrida has been candid about, and often criticized for, his political hesitancy. In answer to a question about the potential for translating the "theoretical radicality of deconstruction" into a "radical political praxis," Derrida confessed (his term) "that I have never succeeded in directly relating deconstruction to *existing* political codes and programmes."[115] This "failure" is derived not from any apolitical sentiment within deconstructive thought but from the "fundamentally metaphysical" nature of the political codes within which both the right and the left presently operate. The problem for politics that this disjuncture creates is, according to Derrida, that one has "to gesture in opposite directions at the same time: on the one hand to preserve a distance and suspicion with regard to the official political codes governing reality; on the other, to intervene here and now in a practical and *engagé* manner whenever the necessity arises." This, Derrida laments, results in a "dual allegiance" and "perpetual uneasiness" whereby the logic of an argument structured in terms of "on the one hand" and "on the other hand" may mean that political action, which follows from a decision between the competing hands, is in the end insufficient to the intellectual promise of deconstructive thought.[116] But in *The Other Heading*, Derrida's reflection on the question and politics of European identity, the difficulty of simultaneously gesturing in different directions is posed in an affirmative political manner.

The title of Derrida's essay calls attention to the sense of (Lévinasian) responsibility that motivates it, the necessary recognition "that there is another heading ... the *heading of the other*, before which we must respond, and which we must *remember, of which* we must *remind ourselves*, the heading of the other being perhaps the first condition of an identity or identification that is not an ego-centrism destructive of oneself and the other."[117] These differing headings have given rise to paradoxes within European identity (the way in which "European" has been made possible by the "non-European"), and continue to pose dilemmas for the prospect of European identity. Moreover, these paradoxes and dilemmas are understandable in terms of a "double injunction":

> *on the one hand*, European cultural identity cannot be dispersed (and when I say "cannot," this should also be taken as "must not" — and this double state of affairs is at the heart of the difficulty). It cannot and must not be dispersed into a myriad of provinces, into a multiplicity of self-enclosed idioms or petty little nationalisms, each one jealous and untranslatable. It cannot and must not renounce places of great circulation or heavy traffic, the great avenues or thoroughfares of translation and communication, and thus, of mediatization. But, *on the other hand*, it cannot and must not accept the capital of a centralizing authority that, by means of trans-European cultural mechanisms ... be they state-run or not, would control and standardize.[118]

"Neither monopoly nor dispersion," that is the condition for European identity Derrida identifies as the consequence of the double injunction. With neither of the two available options being desirable, one confronts an aporia, an undecidable and ungrounded political space, where no path is "clear and given," where no "certain knowledge opens up the way in advance," where no "decision is already made." Moreover, one confronts an aporia that even if "we must not hide it from ourselves," embodies a political hesitation: "I will even venture to say that ethics, politics, and responsibility, *if there are any*, will only ever have begun with the experience and experiment of aporia." But — and here we must recall the ghost of undecidability within each and every decision — were there no aporia, there could be no politics, for in the absence of the aporia every decision would have been preordained, such that "irresponsibly, and in good conscience, one simply applies or implements a program."[119]

How then does one remain faithful to the double injunction yet traverse the aporia? Derrida takes a step forward, a step of increasing specificity, by articulating the double injunction in terms related to the question of gesturing in different directions drawn from the political issue at hand, European identity:

> if it is necessary to make sure that a centralizing hegemony (the capital) not be reconstituted, it is also necessary, for all that, not to multiply the borders, i.e., the movements [*marches*] and margins [*marges*]. It is necessary not to cultivate for their own sake minority differences, untranslatable idiolects, national antagonisms, or the chauvinisms of idiom. Responsibility seems to consist today in renouncing neither of these two contradictory imperatives. One must therefore try to *invent* new gestures, discourses, politico-institutional practices that inscribe the alliance of these two imperatives, of these two promises or contracts: the capital and the a-capital, the other of the capital.[120]

Increasing though the specificity may be, it remains not very specific. As Derrida observes, it "is not easy" to imagine of what such inventions might consist. Indeed, "it is even impossible to conceive of a responsibility that consists in being responsible *for* two laws, or that consists in responding *to* two contradictory injunctions." Of course, says Derrida. Without question. "No doubt." But then — and here we return again to the relationship of the decision and undecidability, the law and infinite justice — "there is no responsibility that is not the experience and experiment of the impossible."[121] And although Derrida remains faithful to "the perpetual uneasiness" inherent in the "dual allegiance" that these impossible political inventions must respect, he ventures that there are duties dictated by responding to the demands of the other heard within the call of European memory.

With an increasing specificity, he argues that these duties include:

welcoming foreigners in order not only to integrate them but to recognize and accept their alterity;

criticizing...a totalitarian dogmatism [fascism] that...destroyed democracy and the European heritage;

criticizing also "a religion of capital that institutes its [fascism's totalitarian] dogmatism under new guises, which we must also learn to identify;

cultivating the virtue of such *critique, of the critical idea, the critical tradition*, but also submitting it, beyond critique and questioning, to a deconstructive genealogy that thinks and exceeds it without yet compromising it;

assuming the idea of European democracy, but not as an idea that is given or functions as a regulative ideal, but as something "that remains to be thought and *to come*...not something that is certain to happen tomorrow, not the democracy (national or international, state or trans-state) of the *future*, but a democracy that must have the structure of a promise;

respecting differences, idioms, minorities, singularities, but also the universality of formal law, the desire for translation, agreement and univocity, the law of the majority, opposition to racism, nationalism, and xenophobia;

tolerating and respecting all that is not placed under the authority of reason...[which] may in fact also try to remain faithful to the ideal of the Enlightenment...while yet acknowledging its limits, in order to work on the Enlightenment of this time, this time that is ours—*today*.

Above all else, maintaining fidelity to the other heading and the heading of the other "surely calls for responsibility, for the responsibility to think, speak, and act in compliance with this *double contradictory imperative*—a contradiction that must not be only an apparent or illusory antimony...but must be effective and, *with experience, through experiment*, interminable."[122] Significantly, Lévinas has also argued for a politics that respects a double injunction. When asked, "Is not ethical obligation to the other a purely negative ideal, impossible to realize in our everyday being-in-the-world," which is governed by "ontological drives and practices"; "Is ethics practicable in human society as we know it? Or is it merely an invitation to apolitical acquiescence?" Lévinas's response was that of course we inhabit an ontological world of technological mastery and political self-preservation. Indeed, without these political and technological structures of organization we would not be able to feed mankind. This is the greatest paradox of human existence: we must use the ontological *for the sake of the other*, to ensure the survival of the other we must resort to the technico-political systems of means and ends.[123]

In Pursuit of Democracy

In pursuing Derrida on the question of the decision, a pursuit that ends up in the supplementing of Derridean deconstruction with Lévinasian ethics, Critchley was concerned to ground political decisions in something other than the "madness" of a decision, and worried that there could be a "refusal of politics in Derrida's work" because the emphasis on undecidability as the condition of responsibility contained an implicit rejection of politics as "the field of antagonism, decision, dissension, and struggle," the "domain of questioning."[124] Yet from the above discussion, I would argue that Derrida's account of the procedure of the decision also contains within it an account of the duty, obligation, and responsibility of the decision within deconstructive thought. Moreover, the undecidable and infinite character of justice that fosters that duty is precisely what guarantees that the domain of politics bears the characteristics of contestation rightly prized by Critchley. Were everything to be within the purview of the decidable, and devoid of the undecidable, then — as Derrida constantly reminds us — there would be no ethics, politics, or responsibility, only a program, technology, and its irresponsible application. Of course, for many (though Critchley is clearly *not* among them), the certainties of the program are synonymous with the desires of politics. But if we seek to encourage recognition of the radical interdependence of being that flows from our responsibility to the other, then the provocations that succor give rise to *a different figuration of politics*, one in which *its purpose is the struggle for — or on behalf of — alterity, and not a struggle to efface, erase, or eradicate alterity.* Such a principle — one that is ethically transcendent if not classically universal — is a powerful starting point for rethinking the question of responsibility vis-à-vis "ethnic" and "nationalist" conflicts. It offers also an important connection between the onto-political fundaments of deconstructive thought (as argued in chapter 2) and transgressive understanding of multiculturalism.

But the concern about politics in Derrida articulated by Critchley is not about politics per se, nor about the possibilities of political analysis, but about the prospects for a progressive, radical politics, one that will demand — and thus do more than simply permit — the decision to resist domination, exploitation, oppression, and all other conditions that seek to contain or eliminate alterity. Yet, again, I would argue that the above discussion demonstrates that not only does Derridean deconstruction address the question of politics, especially when Lévinasian ethics draws out its political qualities, but it does so in an affirmative antitotalitarian manner that gives its politics a particular quality, which is what Critchley and others like him most want (and rightly so, in my view). We may still be dissatisfied with the prospect that Derrida's account cannot *rule out forever* perverse calculations and unjust laws. But to aspire to such a guarantee would be to wish for the demise of politics, for it would install a new technology, even if it was a technology that began life with the markings of progressivism and radicalism. Such dissatisfaction, then, is not with a Derridean politics but with the necessities of politics per se, necessities that can be contested and negotiated but not escaped or transcended.

It is in this context that the limits of the Lévinasian supplement proposed by Critchley as necessary for deconstruction become evident. While it is the case that Lévinas's thought is antagonistic to all totalizing forms of politics, recognizing the way that ontological totalitarianism gives rise to political totalitarianism, I argued above that the limit of its critical potential is exposed by the question of the state. In this regard, insofar as Derridean deconstruction requires the Lévinasian supplement, that supplement itself needs to be supplemented, and supplemented with recognition of the manner in which deconstruction's affirmation of alterity deterritorializes responsibility, and pluralizes the possibilities for ethics and politics over and beyond (yet still including) the state.[125]

Developing this argument involves an elaboration of Derrida's concept of a democracy as a promise, as something "to come," and an effort to situate this notion in relation to the conventional literature on democracy in international relations. The latter is where we go next.

Post–Cold War Conflict and the Failure of Democracy

The end of the Cold War has directed attention to the question of democracy. This concern has been manifested in a number of prominent ways: the idea that liberal democracy, even if it is only partially and imperfectly implemented, is the sole remaining universal ideology of our time; the notion that the success of democracy could create a more pacific world, since democracies do not fight each other;

and the contention that democracy should be the centerpiece of foreign and security policy.[126]

These intertwined notions of democratic triumph, democratic pacificism, and democratic importance are open to a number of objections.[127] Most interestingly, however, the reinvigorated focus on democracy, with its optimistic overtones, comes at the same time as continuing despair about the operation of democracy in those polities where it has been long established. Not that this sentiment forecloses all other concerns; after all, much of the debate concerning the desirability of full-scale European integration has been marked by lamentation over the "democratic deficit" that would result.

Above all else, and perhaps because of these contradictory attitudes, the fascination with democracy in recent times stems from the way in which political developments in the former Soviet bloc appear to the West as "the reinvention of democracy." "We" who are jaded with scandal-prone, crisis-ridden, and bureaucratized democracy marvel at "their" eager and vital embrace of "our" ideals. Yet our fascination is also a morbid one. "We" came to expect that communism would naturally be replaced by democracy — for what sentiment could be more natural than democracy? — but were shocked by the fact that what we witnessed instead was a parade of often violent chauvinisms.[128]

However, because our gaze to the East has been driven by the thought that what we are witnessing is the reinvention of democracy, we have read these emergent forms of conflict (such as in Bosnia) — which we have labeled "ethnic" and "nationalist" — as impediments to democracy, obstacles on the (inevitable) path to greater liberalism. What we have been less able to confront is the possibility that the collapse of communism has been followed by the failure of democracy, and that, at least as conventionally thought, democracy has been insufficient in the face of new forms of conflict. Even worse, we have not stopped long to contemplate that democracy could be one of the facilitators if not causes of these conflicts.

Nowhere has this ambiguous legacy of democracy been more evident than in Bosnia-Herzegovina. Even before the conflict in that territory burgeoned into full-scale community war, political transformation in the wake of the collapse of communism put in place the differences the violence later sought to confirm. As two observers have noted, "Democracy in Bosnia-Herzegovina had meant the transition from multiculturalism to ethnic-based politics. The elections of 1990 brought clear victories to the Serb, Croat, and Muslim parties, and the defeat of the Social Democrats, Reformists, Liberals and other parties organised around political issues rather than identity."[129]

What these reflections highlight is the need to rethink the relationship between democracy and conflict; indeed, to rethink what we mean by democracy and how it stands in relation to the identity politics at the root of much of the conflict in the post–Cold War world. To do that, this section of the chapter will consider the predominant assumptions concerning democracy prevalent in much of the literature, and then articulate what is involved in an alternative and radicalized conception of democracy. This conception stems from a consideration of the ethos of the Enlightenment, democracy as the neglected political form of that ethos, and the specific affinities between the Enlightenment ethos, democracy, and deconstructive thought. After thinking through the democratic political possibilities enabled by deconstructive thought, the chapter concludes with some reflections on how this ethos gives rise to important, general principles that could be materialized in the context of the Bosnian war and its aftermath.

The Conventional Assumptions and the Neglected History

The most central and the most common assumption in writings on democracy is an instrumental and institutional sense of politics. Democracy is defined as comprising a select range of rules and governing regulations involving periodic elections, universal franchise, and limits on executive power.[130] Concomitant with this focus is a limited rendering of the relationship between democracy and violence, especially evident in the literature on democratic pacificism.[131]

Such assumptions are sorely tested in a world marked by increasing interdependence where the territorial basis for accountability demanded by conventional models is being undermined by the pluralization of power centers characteristic of heightened globalization, and where the constitutive role of violence in the international order is becoming more apparent.[132] A number of recent proposals have thus taken as their project the need to recast the spatial boundaries within which accountability operates. David Held has written of the need to develop a "federal model of democracy" — in which there are regional parliaments, transnational referenda, and procedures to democratize the institutions of international governance — as well as a sharper appreciation for the multiplicity of sites of power in contemporary society.[133] Paul Hirst, focusing equally on the need to break the nexus between democracy and the nation-state, has argued for the idea of "associative democracy" as a supplement to liberal democracy, in which the decentralization of state authority, a cooperative economic structure, and the organization of social life into voluntary associations would be encouraged.[134]

While each of these proposals has much to recommend it, there remains an often unacknowledged limit to the argument that curtails the prospect for radical democracy. This limit, enabled by the concern of each to concentrate on a range of institutional reforms that could be legislated, comes via the sentiment that a better democratic structure could be designed and achieved. While there is little doubt that, at face value, this is the case, the issue is whether the design and construction of an improved institutional structure are sufficient for the democratic reforms desired. That is, can the democratic spirit be institutionally conceived and implemented such that it is then secured, or does it require something more, something that might include such institutional reforms, yet goes beyond them, by fostering a different sense of democracy and politics? A consideration of the emergence of democracy, via the work of Claude Lefort, will provide some indispensable pointers in this regard.

As Lefort has argued, by contrasting the political logic of democracy to the political structures of the ancien régime, we see that the key feature of the latter is that power was embodied in the sovereign in accordance with a "theological-political logic."[135] With the collapse of church authority, however, the transcendental guarantee disappears, and the radical singularity of democracy can be made evident. The uniqueness of democracy lies in the fact that the locus of power becomes an *empty place*: popular sovereignty is a ground for authority, but it is a "ground" that is not permanently "grounded," as no person, group, or other authority can permanently appropriate the place of power. As Lefort declares, "democracy is instituted and sustained by the *dissolution of the markers of certainty*. It inaugurates a history in which people experience a fundamental indeterminacy as to the basis of power, law, and knowledge, and as to the basis of relations between *self* and *other*, at every level of social life."[136] In consequence, democracy implies a new form of the social, one that is devoid of inherent meaning or purpose:

The reference to an empty place...implies a reference to a society without any positive determination, which cannot be represented by the figure of a community. It is because the division of power does not, in a modern democracy, refer to an *outside* that can be assigned to the Gods, the city or holy ground; because it does not refer to an *inside* that can be assigned to the substance of the community. Or, to put it another way, it is because there is no materialization of the *Other*—which would allow power to function as a mediator, no matter how it were defined—that there is no materialization of the *One*—which would allow power to function as an incarnation.... It should be added that, once it has lost its double reference to the *Other* and to the *One*, power can no longer condense the principle of Law and the principle of Knowledge within itself. It therefore appears to be limited.[137]

Lefort's reading of democracy thus highlights the radical indeterminacy, akin to deconstructive thought, that is at democracy's heart and is its most politically original feature. The consequence of this indeterminacy is that democracy is marked by a double phenomenon: "a power which is henceforth involved in a constant search for a basis because law and knowledge are no longer embodied in the person or persons who exercise it, and a society which accepts conflicting opinions and debates over rights because the markers which once allowed people to situate themselves in relation to one another in a determinate manner have disappeared."[138] In this context, democracy recognizes that its main danger lies not in the power of violence but the violence of power. With its necessary refusal of a self-referential legitimacy or an absolutism in the name of one or other social agent, democratic power has to remain in an antagonistic relationship to itself.[139]

The Ethos of Democracy

This reading of democracy thus refigures the conventional understanding of what is meant by that term, and its relationship to conflict. Democracy is not a substance, a fixed set of values, a particular kind of community, or a strict institutional form. To be sure, some values, communities, and institutional forms — given certain historical experiences — are more attuned to democracy than others. But what makes democracy democratic, and what marks democracy as a singular political form, is a particular attitude or spirit, an ethos, that constantly has to be fostered. And what distinguishes that ethos is its antagonistic character and the culture of problematization to which it gives rise. This ethos is not antithetical to all established forms, but it stands in particular relation to them: "The key to a culture of democratisation is that it embodies a productive ambiguity at its very centre, never allowing one side or the other to achieve final victory: its role as a mode of governance is balanced and countered by its logic as a cultural medium of denaturalisation of settled identities and conventions."[140] Conflict of a kind is therefore essential for democracy to be democratic. As Connolly notes, the balance between the elements of democratization is not always even, and disturbance more often than not has to be favored over settlement: "In a world where the paradox of politics is perpetually susceptible to forgetfulness, there is a perpetual case to be made on behalf of renewing democratic energies of denaturalisation."[141]

This rendering of democracy highlights some surprising intersections. First, it demonstrates that at the core of modernity and the Enlightenment there is an indeterminacy with regard to foundations for action and being. In the wake of Christendom's demise, the feigned certainty of the transcendental guarantee, although never actually a guarantee in the truest sense, has been absent and without a logical successor. In this sense, nihilism is not something endorsed by specific theoretical projects but rather the condition of modern life that all theoretical projects seek to counter.[142] Second, reason, which is normally figured as the Enlightenment answer to the problem of the demise of certain foundations, is itself a principle that cannot rationally ground its own privilege, and is thus subject to the same sort of indeterminacy it seeks to overcome. Third, democracy as an ethos of disturbance is the political form that is both attuned to and derived from these conditions of indeterminacy in the modern era. All these propositions require further exploration. But they point to an interesting conclusion. It is that deconstruction, the form of critical thought that both is enabled by and responds to the challenges and dangers of indeterminacy, and is considered by many to be antithetical if not hostile to the Enlightenment, reason, and democracy, is in actuality that which is among those closest to these goals.

Such an understanding of the Enlightenment ethos — which follows on from the discussion concerning Foucault's critical ontology in the first chapter — has been occluded by the argument that reason operates as a new principle of grounding that can secure the void left by the demise of the transcendental guarantee. This is an argument, moreover, that continues to be readily translated into political terms. Eric Hobsbawm, writing about the violence of the twentieth century, has declared that only "the old rationalism of the Enlightenment" stands between us and "an accelerated descent into darkness."[143] However, upon closer reflection, the continued reiteration of reason's foundational status involves what Derrida would call a *coup de force*, a violence without ground, which seeks to give reason that status by its own performance, rather than by uncovering what is already there. That is because — as argued in chapter 2 — reason cannot ground the authority of reason. We can maintain that such is the case, even faithfully declare that it could not be otherwise. But what reason can we give that would secure the notion that reason grounds the authority of reason? Our inability to answer that question in purely rationalist terms suggests the authority of reason itself depends on an interpretive *coup de force* not unlike that involved in the founding of a state or law.[144]

For Derrida, as for Foucault, their differences notwithstanding, this questioning of reason is carried out in the spirit of the Enlightenment. This duty in the name of the Enlightenment is equally one that is concerned with the ethos of the Enlightenment, rather than any particular period in history or definable table of values. This probing of the limits, which thinks beyond the limits of established practice but does not render it impossible, operates with a commitment to both the singular and the general.

What is crucial, then, to the ethos of the Enlightenment is to think and act in terms of the double contradictory imperative articulated by Derrida (and discussed above). This double imperative — contradictory in appearance only if one succumbs to the blackmail of the Enlightenment — embodies the spirit of Foucault's "limit-attitude" and involves thinking the limit yet going beyond it, maintaining a commitment to reason by questioning its operation and that which escapes it, and resisting the inside/outside demarcation while exposing how the outside inhabits and helps constitute the inside. In short, the double imperative resists in its operation the reduction of our thought and action to the positions of either/or, for/against, by foregrounding the necessary interdependence of (supposed) opposites upon one another, and the traces of each that mark the other. The double imperative, that which distinguishes the ethos of the Enlightenment, thus affirms "the necessity of contamination."[145]

Above all else, this double imperative refigures our understanding of the relationship between the universal and the particular and, indeed, the manner in which that relationship is in the first place conceivable. Thought tagged as deconstructive has long been (mis)interpreted as inhabiting only one side of the double imperative. It has been argued, in asides too numerous to mention, that poststructuralist critiques favor the particular and thereby denigrate the universal, inviting in consequence a host of illiberal outcomes, and that by questioning in a critical spirit all that is involved in the positing of the universal, a dangerous and licentious relativism is celebrated. Such observations are, literally, half-baked, for they fail to heed the other side of the double imperative. In this context, the notion of the universal and the particular remains, but these terms come to represent something other than antinomies existing autonomously in a relationship of contradiction. Instead, they exist in a relationship of radical interdependence and are each contaminated by the trace of the other.

This situation can be best examined by reflecting on the emergent forms of conflict that are said to mark the post–Cold War world. What we have seen in so-called ethnic and nationalist struggles appears to be the political demise of universalism and its practical substitution by particularism. That is because each of these struggles operates not in terms of the aspirations of a "universal subject" (such as a class) or a "universal history" (such as class struggle), but in terms of a particular subject (a specific ethnic or national group) and a particular history (the aspirations of that group).

However, even in these terms, the apparent political demise of universalism cannot be said to have produced the theoretical dissolution of universalism. It has, instead, led to its reconfiguration along lines best exposed by the operation of the double imperative. The universalism of today is one enabled by the assertion of particularism, it is a "universality that is the very result of particularism."[146] That is because the right of national self-determination involves the declaration of a universal principle, albeit a universal principle that derives its force from the plurality of particular groups seeking self-determination because of their heterogeneous singularity, rather than a universal subject confident of its homogeneity and global applicability. As Rodolphe Gasché, writing in terms of how best to comprehend a thought as philosophically radical as Derrida's, states: "Paradoxically, even the most radical singularity must, in order for it to be recognized for what it is, have an addressable identity, guaranteed by a set of universal rules that, by the same token, inscribe its singularity within a communal history, tradition, and problematics."[147] However, the particular or singular does not exist and cannot be known as such. As with the radical interdependence of the decision and the undecidable, the possible and the impossible, the particular and the universal might only be conceivable in relation to one another. It might be said that the universal can only be witnessed in moments of particularity, and the particular can only be rendered through a universal concept. The claims of "ethnic" or "national" particularism would themselves then be regarded as a form of limited universalism.

However, to adopt even a greatly reworked concept of the universal in the context of an argument animated by Derrida's thought is to invite a problem, although not because a deconstructive approach is hostile to something other than the particular. Rather, the concept of the universal, even when problematized and reworked, calls forth foundational elements of philosophical traditions that Derrida's thought has sought to disclose, disturb, and dislodge. Indeed, the possibility of deconstructive thought flows from the deconstruction of the ideality that gives rise to the concept of the universal in all its forms.

Acknowledging this, while retaining a sense of the nonparticular that gives meaning to the particular, involves the notion of "iterability." For Derrida, the structure of iteration accounts for the performative constitution of general meanings through processes of repetition without having to invoke a prior ideality. This recalls the discussion (in chapter 2) of the manner in which performativity draws attention to "the reiterative and citational practice by which discourse produces the effects that it names."[148] The structure of iteration thereby produces the ideality of "the universal" by constituting the possibility of the relation between the universal and the particular. This relation might provide a foundation, but it is a foundation founded on the mystical foundations of authority. This can be disclosed by deconstructive thought because the repetition of iterability is always linked to alterity. Because "there is ideality only through and by repetition . . . repetition brings with it an alterity that forbids the unity of the foundation it was supposed to insure."[149] In this sense, the claims of "ethnic" or "national" particularism, and the practices they generate, would be regarded as iterations that helped effect the ideality of universalism.

Deconstruction and the Necessary Impossibility of Democracy

The iterability of "universalism" and "particularism" has important consequences for our both our understanding of democracy and the political possibilities that might be pursued in Bosnia. The political crisis of "universalism" that flows from the iteration of particularisms has highlighted the contingent grounds upon which the past claims to global preeminence of specific subjects were constructed. This shift from a concern with the being of a subject to the circumstances of its constitution retains the appearance, as Ernesto Laclau observes, of a certain sense of transcendentality.[150] This sense, although it is effected by reiterative practices, establishes the conditions of possibility for democracy.

The notion of a universal subject, because it is enabled by a suppression of all forms of particularism is, in general, antidemocratic. While there is no surety that the questioning of universalism will automatically result in democratic outcomes, without it such outcomes are not conceivable. As Laclau and Chantal Mouffe have observed:

> The critique of the category of unified subject, and the recognition of the discursive dispersion within which every subject position is constituted, therefore involves something more than the enuncia-

tion of a general theoretical position: they are the *sine qua non* for thinking the multiplicity out of which antagonisms emerge in societies in which the democratic revolution has crossed a certain threshold. This gives us a theoretical terrain on the basis of which the notion of *radical and plural democracy* . . . finds the first conditions under which it can be apprehended.[151]

Democracy, the political form enabled by and responding to the dissolution of the markers of certainty, requires a plurality of political actors and forces capable of taking the place of each other in power.[152] The democratic opportunity enabled by the demise of universalism, even if (and perhaps because) universalism's trace remains, follows therefore from the *identification of the ethos of democracy as a radical questioning of limits and the identification of the ethos of the Enlightenment as democratic.* In other words, the Enlightenment, democracy, and deconstructive political criticism (now understood as the attitude that appreciates the interdependence of modernity and countermodernity, rather than a misleading "postmodernity") are not related by homology but by the particular affinities of the ethos of each.[153]

The sort of democracy envisaged by this argument—where the emphasis is on the ethos of democracy rather than (though not necessarily excluding) the institutions or procedures of democracy—should be distinguished "from its current concept and from its determined predicates today."[154] Its principal characteristic is that it has "the structure of a promise," as something that is not certain to happen but remains to be thought and "to come."[155] This notion of a "democracy *to come*" is very different, however, from the idea of a future democracy, a utopian project that cannot be witnessed. A democracy *to come* exists and operates in the present as "a pledged injunction that orders one to summon the very thing that will never present itself in the form of full presence." A democracy *to come* is the contemporaneous operation in the political of the double imperative. As an ethos, it moves through the iteration of the universal and the particular, the impossible and the possible, the incalculable and the calculable, thereby opening and keeping open "this gap between the infinite promise (always untenable at least for the reason that it calls for the infinite respect of the singularity *and* infinite alterity of the other as much as for the respect of the countable, calculable, subjectal equality between anonymous singularities) and the determined, necessary, but also necessarily inadequate forms of what has to be measured against this promise."[156] Democracy's structure as a promise, therefore, keeps the horizon of impossibility firmly in view so that a plurality of possibilities can be conceived, thereby rendering as contingent whatever is put in place as possible. Democracy's structure as a promise, as something *to come*, does not diminish either the necessity or the urgency of action enabled by a decision.[157] Instead, it seeks to secure—knowing that complete and final security is neither possible nor desirable, for that would mean an end to the double imperative and the paradox of politics—the conditions of a just decision, one that has traversed the terrain of the undecidable. Thus, deconstructive thought is necessary for politics, especially a democratic politics, and undecidability is a prerequisite for responsibility.

The structure of the decision in relationship to the undecidable is thus not only a further instance of the double imperative but also one way in which the ethos of democracy follows the structure of a promise, as something ever present yet still *to come*. In this context (and by way of explanation for the subhead of this section), democracy is not something that can be fully realized, and certainly not fully and successfully institutionalized. It is, insofar as it remains honest to the ethos of democracy, necessarily impossible. Which is not the same as saying it cannot be possible, or that it is totally utopian, the antithesis of "realistic." It is to say that the central element of democracy should remain the ethos, one that embodies the temporality, oscillation, critique, disturbance, denaturalization, problematization—the "ad infinitum" of nomadic movements.[158] For while that ethos is not hostile to the creation and establishment of institutional arrangements that might coexist with its spirit—especially those that respond to the globalization of economics and politics, the "virtualization of space and time"—coexistence cannot become an accommodation that fully captures the ethos thereby making those arrangements beyond its purview.[159] Were such capture achievable, it would paradoxically be at the moment of realization that the ethos of democracy had been extinguished. Stasis, for the ethos of democracy, is death; antagonism and conflict are its lifeblood.[160]

That said, the discussion of democracy to this point—as ethos, the double imperative, a promise, something *to come*, that which involves both the decision and the undecidable—could be read as privileging process and procedure over content and outcome. To an extent that is both correct and desirable; after all, if the content and the outcome were preordained, we would not have democracy, let alone ethics, politics, and responsibility. Nonetheless, is it possible to say more than that? Having deployed Derrida to this stage, we might respond with the observation that the normative status of his political concerns is not much in doubt, for Derrida names the bad, the perverse, and the worst as those violences "we recognize all too well

without yet having thought them through, the crimes of xenophobia, racism, anti-Semitism, religious or nationalist fanaticism."[161] For
those who share his progressive sentiments, that might be personally satisfying, but it does not address the question of whether the
logic of the argument concerning the ethos of democracy goes beyond the procedure of the decision to ensure a particular political outcome. In other words, and to put it in its strongest terms, is there
something in the logic of the argument that indemnifies us against
totalitarianism? The immediate answer to that is, "No, but . . ."

It is, in the first instance "no" because once a transcendental guarantee has been dissipated, the *possibility* of totalitarianism cannot be
denied. That is because totalitarianism is a political form hostile to
democracy's status as an empty place, and seeks to reoccupy that place
as a social power proclaiming the unity, totality, and naturalness of
its essence. In other words, with the demise of a hegemonic political
form (such as Christendom) and the emergence of a nonhegemonic
political form (democracy), competition from alternative hegemonic
political forms (totalitarianism) can only be expected. As Lefort notes,
in "extreme situations, representations which can supply an index of
social unity and identity become invested with a fantastic power, and
the totalitarian adventure is underway."[162] This is arguably the situation in a number of Eastern European countries today, even, given
some variation in the extent of totalitarianism, in those that might be
considered formally democratic. With the collapse of communism, even
democrats have sought political refuge, not in an adherence to the
democratic ethos but in the figure of the nation.

However (in the second instance, and focusing on the "but" of
the above answer), to say that the *possibility* of totalitarianism *cannot
be insured against,* that we cannot *guarantee* a progressive political outcome, is not a point that detracts from the logic of the argument concerning the ethos of democracy. Once certitude is gone and contingency is apparent, there is a range of possibilities. But even if we
accept that totalitarianism *can* and *might* be one of those possibilities,
the highlighting of the constructed character of any social resolution
means that the costs and containments of totalitarianism will be apparent to the democratic ethos and subject to engagement. Thus, while
political indeterminacy can be hijacked by fundamentalist strategies
and movements (as was the case in Bosnia with nationalists and their
international allies), it is also what allows for the disturbances and
denaturalizations of the ethos of democracy. In this context, the ethos
of democracy involves more than a particular process or set of procedures, no matter how important they are. The ethos of democracy

fosters pluralization, and as such its insistent questioning expands the field of freedom by multiplying the lines of possible political connection in the social.[163] Its strategies are thus not devoid of content, nor are they shy of political preferences, although those preferences are more enabling than prescriptive, for "enabling" is consistent with the democratic ethos whereas "prescriptive" veers toward totalitarianism.

Moreover, the ethos of democracy is animated by the constant desire and urgent need for emancipation. Those critical of deconstruction have long made great play of the point that whatever its (negatively conceived) critical potential, it has been absent the emancipatory ideal necessary to transform its insights into practice. Yet in recent writings Derrida has drawn attention to the emancipatory ideal at the heart of deconstructive thought, declaring that "nothing seems to me less outdated than the classical emancipatory ideal. We cannot attempt to disqualify it today, whether crudely or with sophistication, at least not without treating it too lightly and forming the worst complicities."[164] This is, for Derrida, a natural step for deconstructive thought because it is a project "impossible and unthinkable in a pre-Marxist space." Indeed, Derrida maintains that "deconstruction has never had any sense or interest, in my view at least, except as a radicalization, which is to say also *in the tradition* of a certain Marxism, in a certain *spirit of Marxism*."[165] That unrenounceable spirit of a certain Marxism

> is not only the critical idea or questioning stance (a consistent deconstruction must insist on them even as it also learns that this is not the last or first word). It is even more a certain emancipatory and *messianic* affirmation, a certain experience of the promise that one can try to liberate from any dogmatics and even from any metaphysico-religious determination, from any *messianism*. And a promise must promise to be kept, that is, not to remain "spiritual" or "abstract," but to produce events, new effective forms of action, practice, organization, and so forth.[166]

The structure of democracy as a promise must, therefore, given the centrality of an emancipatory ideal, be a promise that is kept so that it brings new possibilities into being. The urgency of emancipation thereby operates "in the name of a new Enlightenment for the century to come," and rather than "renouncing an ideal of democracy and emancipation," tries to "think it and put it to work otherwise."[167] Accordingly, the emancipatory ideal so conceived differs from its traditional formulation, where the object was "the *global* emancipation of humanity" in the name of a universal subject enacting a

universal history. Although global emancipation of a universal subject might have once been the promise of progressive politics, its totalizing aspiration is now — especially in a world characterized by the
deepening politicization of new domains of social life — depoliticizing and disenabling, for no particular subject or history can embrace
the many aspirations and struggles that currently abound. Thus, one
should speak in terms of "emancipations" rather than the now fundamentalist idea of "Emancipation."[168]

These political possibilities of deconstructive thought might even
be summarized in terms of a general principle for the ethos of democracy, albeit a principle that derives its legitimacy from the transcendentality of particularism. This principle would declare that we should
actively nourish and nurture antagonism, conflict, plurality, and multiplicity, not at the expense of security or identity — for this is not an
either/or option — but in terms of security's and identity's contamination by and indebtedness to its other(s). This is the reverse of what
the international community effectively prescribed for Bosnia.

This cultivation of what Connolly has called "the fugitive fund
of difference" does *not*, however, endorse as sufficient an ethic of tolerance.[169] Tolerance — along with the associated positions of liberalism and pluralism — underplays the agonistic interdependence of
competing positions and accepts as established and separate that
which is always implicated in the other and in the process of being
made.[170] As Connolly argues with respect to liberalism,

> Liberalism remains a philosophy of tolerance among culturally es-
> tablished identities more than one of attentiveness to how these
> identities are established and the ways in which new possibilities
> of identity are propelled into being. In other words, liberalism is at-
> tentive to "difference" as already defined, heterodox identities in
> an existing network of social relations, but tone-deaf to "*différance*"
> as that which resides within an existing network *but has not yet re-
> ceived stable definition within it.* As a result of this thinness in the ap-
> preciation of difference, dominant forms of liberalism remain unat-
> tuned to the crucial role new *enactments* or *performances* play, first in
> generating new claims to identity, and second in *retroactively* crys-
> tallizing violence in previous patterns of being.[171]

Tolerance does not, therefore, allow either for an appreciation of
the constitution of difference or for distinctions and discriminations
between various modes of difference. In addition, particularly as it is
argued in the context of multiculturalism, tolerance conceals a strategy
of power that reinstalls the dominant identity supposedly in question.
Like pity, tolerance is an attitude that always emanates from those

who are dominant and in a position to tolerate. Tolerance, though better than intolerance, still involves an acceptance of difference by those in a position to accept, and an acceptance that positions the other in "our" sphere of influence within limits that "we" set. It involves, therefore, a relationship with those constituted in the process as subjugated. As Ghassan Hage argues, "multicultural tolerance should be understood as a mode of spatial management of cultural difference while reproducing the structuring of those differences around a dominant culture."[172] This is clearest when the discourse of cultural difference transmutes into a discourse of "national minorities" who then require protection from the majority.[173] In this context, multicultural tolerance, much like the ontopological rendering of multiculturalism discussed at the outset of this chapter, is largely a different mode of racism, albeit with a more humane face.

In contrast, the principle being articulated here goes beyond the narrow and static confines of tolerance and maintains that the active affirmation of alterity *must* involve the desire to actively oppose and resist — perhaps, depending on the circumstances, even violently — those forces that efface, erase, or suppress alterity. That which is to be opposed is not simply that which causes disturbance or irritation. There will always be an agonistic and sometimes antagonistic relationship between the numerous identities and settlements that variously contain difference. That which is to be opposed is that which, in dealing with difference, moves from disturbance to oppression, from irritation to repression, and, most obviously, from contestation to eradication.

But how do we know when that threshold, if it is an identifiable limit, has been crossed? How do we know when the agonism of democracy has been transfigured into the violence of totalitarianism? Certain historical examples come quickly to mind, and in those cases it is not difficult to think of the distinctions that can and must be made. Their horrors notwithstanding, those historical examples are the easy cases. The difficult cases are those where the contrasts are not so clear, the struggle for justice not so clear-cut. How, then, do we discriminate in the name of the principle and ethos of democracy?

At this point it is necessary to say that we have reached the juncture at which it is no longer possible to speak in the abstract. Which is not to say that we have arrived at the moment where the political possibilities of deconstructive thought are exhausted. To the contrary, this is where they really begin, and where they distinguish themselves most clearly from more conventional approaches. For it is at this point that the implication of appreciating how the universal is effected by the structure of iteration becomes most evident.

With classical notions of the universal, where the universal is the regulative ideal that conditions and directs all that is particular, the relationship between the universal and the particular is one-dimensional and one-way. The universal is that which is repeated and invoked in the moment of the particular. But given the notion of iterability through which the ideality of the universal is produced, the universal is only universal insofar as it is an effect of reiterative and citational practices. The relationship, therefore, is not one involving the *application* of universal principles to specific cases. It is one in which the particular is a *materialization* of those practices that effect the universal, and the universal is an effect that appears as the *exemplification* of the many particulars.

In a more conventional analysis, this would be the point at which one could no longer speak in the abstract because the issue would be one of implementing the universal, of establishing a case in which the applicability of the universal could be judged. Should there be a disjuncture between the two, the result would be solely a discussion of the difficulties of implementing the universal. In contrast, in terms of the principle and ethos of political criticism (particularly deconstructive thought), this is the point at which we can no longer speak in the abstract because it is *no longer sufficient* to do so. That is, we can no longer speak in the abstract, not because we now face the issue of simply applying the universal, but because we could not have enunciated the universal other than through the structure of iteration that produces and names the particular.

Democracy, Deconstruction, and Bosnia

That said, because we are not looking for a contained and limited case study of the universal but, rather, an embodiment of the ethos of democracy and the ethos of deconstruction, the limited space remaining can in no way do justice to this task. Of course, within the logic of the double imperative, any limit on space would be too much of a limit given the infinite character of justice and the necessarily ceaseless pursuit of an emancipatory ideal. Justice, democracy, and emancipation are not conditions to be achieved but ambitions to be strived for; they are promises the impossibility of which ensures their possibility; they are ideals that to remain practical must always be still *to come*. The agonistic space created by the moving poles of the double imperative is the necessary condition for ethics, politics, and responsibility.

Nonetheless, by turning to some features of the conflict in Bosnia and highlighting some themes, we can see how within the ambit of political criticism things can at least be thought differentially if not practiced differently.

The distinctive character of these themes is derived in part from a contrast with the dominant way of understanding the Bosnian war and the international proposals for its resolution, as examined in chapters 3 and 5. Against the ontopological rendering of the war, with its contestable political anthropology, the ethos of political criticism and its deconstructive interventions give rise to two guidelines that can enable political possibilities consistent with this argument:

> A variety of political strategies which *on the one hand* requires the constant pluralization of centers of power, sources of knowledge, loci of identification, and the spaces of community, while *on the other hand* recognizes that each deterritorialization necessitates and results in a reterritorialization, that in turn has to be disturbed (and so on).

> An emancipatory ideal of multiculturalism, which *on the one hand* affirms cultural diversity without situating it, while *on the other hand* recognizes that multiculturalism can itself succumb to an enclave mentality that suppresses cultural interdependence and plurality.

These guidelines direct us toward an appreciation of the role geographic (especially geopolitical) imaginaries have in shaping our political possibilities. The moral cartography enabled by the norm of ontopology has territorialized responsibility and bounded the possibility of ethical space in which encounters with alterity occur. Pursuing the deconstructive ethos involves recognizing the arbitrary yet powerfully sedimented nature of such limits, developing political modes and strategies through which our responsibility to the other can be democratically if imperfectly realized, and articulating conceptions of community that refuse the violent exclusions and limitations of identity politics.

Seven
Bosnia and the Practice of Democracy

The Incomplete Victory of Chauvinism

Different problematizations produce different "Bosnias," and those different "Bosnias" are rendered as different problems to be addressed by different political options. Within some of the most common representations, "Bosnia" is ethnicized as an intractable civil war such that a new politics of apartheid is required. Within the frame of this argument, the Bosnian war reveals the performative nature of identity such that a deconstructive politics is warranted. Through a process of iteration and reiteration—whether in the context of the strategies of violence, "external" representations of the conflict, or in terms of the assumptions that shaped international diplomacy—a nationalist imaginary has been installed as the regulative ideal for politics in Bosnia. As Homi Bhabha has observed, this naturalization of the nexus of territory and identity requires a great deal of work and necessitates the worst violence: "the hideous extremity of Serbian nationalism [and those who shared its logic] proves that the very idea of a pure, 'ethnically cleansed' national identity can only be achieved through the death, literal and figurative, of the complex interweavings of history, and the culturally contingent borderlines of modern nationhood."[1] This violence results in the effacement (but not erasure) of our inescapable responsibility to the other.

Even by those who would wish otherwise, the literal and figurative death of complex histories and hybrid identities has been reluctantly pronounced in Bosnia. Thus, Robert Hayden has concluded that "the multiethnic Bosnia that was once actual, and for that reason prescriptive from the point of view of the international community, no longer exists and thus can no longer be prescriptive."[2] Conventional readings of the situation seem to lead inexorably to this conclusion, and the evidence amassed in its favor appears hard to question. With ethnic partition in place, nationalist parties victorious, populations increasingly homogenized, and ethnic cleansing still in operation, there seems little alternative to unhappy resignation about the lost possibilities.

But as successful as they might appear in Bosnia, the military nationalists and their political allies have not triumphed completely: important elements of heterogeneity persist in both thought and practice. That ethnic cleansing (albeit in different modes and a little less violently) is still under way suggests that the nationalist project has not reached its fulfillment. That project, as Hayden argues, "has not only been a matter of imagining allegedly 'primordial' communities, but rather of making existing heterogenous ones unimaginable."[3] Its persistence thus testifies to the ineradicable existence of heterogeneity. Not that the nationalist project could ever be perfectly installed, for the eradication of all difference — given the contingent status of identity, the relational character of difference, and the processual nature of society — is an impossibility. In practice this means that although hundreds of thousands have been expelled from their homes, tens of thousands of "others" remain in "alien" territory.[4] While nationalist formulations have seemingly colonized political discourse, nonstate groups still pursue civic alternatives. Where individuals are supposed to embody hatred toward the other, many express publicly the desire for coexistence and reintegration. An unhappy resignation at this juncture would, therefore, prevent the reclamation of these and other possibilities.

The purpose of this chapter is to draw attention to those dimensions that escape both nationalist triumphalism and secular pessimism, and to demonstrate how — in terms of the previous chapter's argument concerning the ethos of democracy, the pursuit of justice, and the importance of strategies of pluralization to the radicalization of multiculturalism — they have been pursued in the past, are being articulated still, and can be fostered further. To begin that process, however, requires reflection on "the multiethnic Bosnia that existed" and the manner in which it can still aid judgments about the political possibilities.

To make that case I want to draw extensively on the ethnographic account provided in Tone Bringa's superlative study *Being Muslim the Bosnian Way.*[5] As a form of knowledge often overlooked within international relations, Bringa's anthropology confronts us with the complexities of identity in the former Yugoslavia so often wished away. Most importantly, it demonstrates the lived experience of a nonterritorial multiculturalism in Bosnia, one that denaturalizes ontopological assumptions common to Western political thought.

This is not to suggest that *multiculturalism* was necessarily a term prominent in Bosnian discourse. Its use by some Bosnian representatives during the war, as a means of mobilizing support in "the West" (a rhetorical strategy that might in retrospect be regarded as unintentionally perverse, given the overriding concern with discourses of coherence in Europe and the United States), cannot automatically be taken as embodying the identity assumptions being articulated here. Indeed, Bringa is careful to note that just as Bosnia was not a historically naturalized tribal war waiting to happen, neither should it be viewed as "the ideal example of a harmonious and tolerant multicultural society, where people did not classify each other in terms of 'Serb,' 'Muslim,' or 'Croat.'"[6] The absence of the term, however, does not mean that the contingent and hybrid senses of identity, foregrounded by the revaluation of multiculturalism through the argument in the previous two chapters, are alien to Bosnia. To the contrary, Bringa's account demonstrates their centrality to the identity marked as Bosnian/Muslim. That pluralized notions can be signified by singular terms that do not require the prefix *multi-* that "we" employ says more about "our" own discourses of identity than those of "others."

Moreover, based on fieldwork in the central Bosnian village of "Dolina" (fictitiously named), Bringa's study shows that sentiments aligned with the radicalized sense of multiculturalism were evident even in rural areas beyond the oft-cited urban locations of Sarajevo and Tuzla. But it does so in a way that shows how these notions of what this argument is calling *multiculturalism* are not reducible to simplistic historical narratives that effect a retroactive writing of Bosnia's essential past so as to support a nationalist future. Instead, Bringa's account manifests the aporetic relations of identity/difference, analogous to Derrida's notion of *différance*, that helped constitute Bosnia and allow for the possibility of its already existing reconstitution.[7]

The *Différance* of Bosnia

In the Ottoman empire, especially through the *millet* system, there existed a communal form that embodied the idea of multiculturalism as the pluralization of the possibilities of being on the same territory. One important element of the empire's organization was that Muslims were under the direct jurisdiction of the imperial administration, while non-Muslims were in communities (*millets*) with spiritual heads. This meant that membership of a "nation" was determined by religious affiliation rather than shared language, common territory, history, or ethnicity. Most importantly, all these communities shared the same territory within the imperial system—individual *millets* did not have separate, demarcated territories, even though they did have distinct administrative structures and discrete cultural universes. *Millets* were thus deterritorialized collective cultural identities based in the first instance on religious identification, albeit with implicit hierarchical notions.[8]

The significance of the *millet* system for Bosnia lies not in claiming that this is *the* origin or source of a radicalized multiculturalism, but in recognizing the legacy of deterritorialized identities it gave rise to. The *millet* system meant that different communities not only shared the same territory, they shared the same economic life and, despite religious differences and their disparate cosmologies, also shared many aspects of social life at the most prosaic of levels.[9] Bringa stresses that for modern Bosnia, *différance* was lived and negotiated on a daily basis:

> To most Bosnians (and particularly to the post–World War II generations) difference in ethnoreligious affiliation was one of the many differences between people, like the differences between men and women, villager and city dweller. It was acknowledged and often joked about but it never precluded friendship. Indeed, for these Bosnians being Bosnian (*bosnanac*) meant growing up in a multicultural and multireligious environment, an environment where cultural pluralism was intrinsic to the social order. Dealing with cultural difference was part of people's most immediate experience of social life outside the confines of their home, and it was therefore an essential part of their identity. In the village mutual acknowledgement of cultural diversity and coexistence was an intrinsic quality of life and people's everyday experience, and therefore an important element in the process of individual identity formation.[10]

One had in the *millet* system and its legacies, therefore, a community of similarities and differences, experienced simultaneously on shared territory, which sometimes witnessed violent conflicts but which more often than not managed a productive existence. It thus embodied a mode of being that could not be easily understood in dichotomous terms as separate or mixed, or some straightforward combination of the two. That it was both of these at the same time (symbolized strikingly when it occasionally involved the shared celebration of religious days and combined use of sacred sites) meant it is more accurately understood in terms of the aporetic relations of identity/difference than any essentialist or reductionist notion.[11]

The logic of the *millet* system thus manifested what I have previously called "radical interdependence." This was ever more the case because the similarities and differences were not determined prior to their interaction. They were produced by their mutual interaction, and produced in such a way as to remain in flux. This is evident in the fact that, although contemporary analysts see ethnoreligious identity being a hard and fast category, Bringa notes that "fluid confessional definitions are widely reported in Bosnia far into the twentieth century. Ethnographic data show a nondoctrinal attitude toward religion by Bosnians of all three confessions."[12] Indeed, perhaps the central theme to Bringa's study is the way in which being Muslim involves a "Muslim being" that has a complex and sometimes ambivalent relationship with Islam, such that a number of the cultural practices of the Muslim community were regarded by their religious instructors as non-Islamic.[13]

This ambiguity in the Muslim-Islam identity has been played out in the changing political categorizations in Bosnia. As noted in chapters 3 and 4, relying unproblematically on census data to map the Bosnian populations obscures the genealogy of identity and its flux. The question of national identity, save for its mention on servicemen's JNA identity card, went officially unrepresented in daily life. But every ten years it was prompted by the census, though considering the shifts in census categorizations, national identity for "Muslims" was at best fluid.[14]

Before the war (1992–) "Muslim" was not a national category with territorial meaning, even for villagers in rural areas. According to Bringa, in the community where she worked, people employed nonnational terms as their primary and most important symbols. Catholics were thus "Catholic" and not "Croat," and in areas to the north people were often "Orthodox" rather than "Serb."[15] These designations came from and manifested the diverse array of group identities in the former Yugoslavia, understandings that differed considerably from the Western taxonomy of ethnic groups and nations. As Bringa observes, the Yugoslav situation was one in which there was no automatic overlap between nation, state, and citizenship of the kind that there is in a place like the United States, cultural pluralism notwithstanding. Accordingly, the "western European conceptualization" of "nation" and "ethnic group" was inappropriate, overlooked the "local conceptualization," and thereby distorted understanding. As Bringa concludes, "terms used officially and increasingly by non-Bosnian commentators such as nations and ethnic groups were not used locally before the war."[16]

The terms *Muslim, Catholic,* and *Orthodox* referred to the idea of *nacija*. Although translated as "ethnoreligious group or nation," it signifies first and foremost a religious community that does not have a necessary relationship to nationality and territory. A *nacija* could have a relationship to a national group, but that could be a national group that was one of two types. The first is a *nardnost*, and is the closest to what in the West would be an "ethnic group." But *nardonosti* only exist in relation to the second type, a larger *narod*, a "nation" or "people." Moreover, although membership in a *narod* might have meant having a particular *nacionalnost* ("nationality"), *nacionalnost* did not confer citizenship. Citizenship and nationality in the West are more often than not synonymous, but for the former Yugoslavia citizenship was additional to nationality. A Yugoslav citizen could be a person of different nationalities, for there was no corresponding Yugoslav nation. The significance of this is twofold. The various articulations that are possible between *nacija*, *narod*, *nacionalnost*, and Yugoslav citizenship mean that one's state, residence, or place of birth is not a determinant of identity. In consequence, the territorial dimension to identity is sublimated, and the scope for self-ascription and self-identification is enlarged to the point of being decisive.[17]

The scope for alternate articulations can be illustrated by considering the changing census categories in which "Muslims" could be located. In 1948 the census permitted one to be a "Muslim of undeclared nationality," a member of a *nacija* without a corresponding *narod*. Alternatively, one could choose the *narod* to which one belonged, so that "Muslim-Serb" and "Muslim-Croat" were possible. By 1953, those who did not want to be undeclared, or declared in relation to a *narod* could designate themselves "Yugoslavs of undeclared nationality," a form of nationalism twice removed. In 1961 a new option was in place—*Muslimani u smislu narodnosti*, meaning "Muslims in the sense of *narodnost*." This marked one step on the ladder to a more clearly defined articulation, which culminated in 1971 with the political recognition of "Muslim" as a *narod*.[18] All this meant that at different times the same people would have slotted into different categories, depending on their judgments about which was more appropriate or beneficial.[19]

Although the nationalization of "Muslim" was officially in place by the early 1970s, with Muslims becoming the sixth of the *Jugoslovenski narodi* ("nations of Yugoslavia"), Bringa's ethnography demonstrates its problematic acceptance outside national political discourse. Moreover, a certain ambiguity about the relationship between the "Muslim" nation, religion, and territory was maintained. Partly because Yugoslavia's leadership wanted to keep some distance between Bosnian Muslims, Islam, and the Bosnian republic, the conferring of *narod* status was made via the ethnonym *Musliman* rather than, say, *Bošnjak*. Although that ethnonym would at first glance seem to confirm the religious affiliation, it reflected instead another distinction. As a means of preventing the conflation of "Bosnian" and "Muslim" — a conflation that the West had no hesitation in making during the war — a contrast was drawn between *Musliman* and *musliman*. *Muslimani* were "the subjects of the secular, areligious, Yugoslav Bosnian-Hercegovinian republic, while the *muslimani* were the subjects of the Islamic community and its bureaucratized organization, the Islamic Association."[20] The category *Muslimani* could thus embrace those Bosnians outside of Islam, while Muslims beyond Bosnia could be *muslimani*. A large measure of undecidability was therefore structured into Bosnian/Muslim identity.

That undecidability was further exacerbated in relation to the nexus between Bosnian/Muslim identity and the territory of Bosnia. In terms of the political structure of Yugoslavia, the six nations of the federal republic each had a national home in one of the republics, the constitution of which reflected this axis — except Bosnians/Muslims. The constitution of the republic of Bosnia Herzegovina (as proclaimed in 1974 and amended in 1990) declared its territory was home to the *narodi* of the republic (Serbs, Croats, and Muslims) as well as members of other nations and nationalities living within it. This not only provided a second territorial home to Serbs and Croats, it meant there was no such exclusive home (as in the case of Serbia and Croatia) for Bosnians/Muslims.[21]

Bringa argues that in the context of the war, Bosnians/Muslims might have been better served had they embraced the territorialization of identity that nationalism espoused and promoted the notion of an exclusive *Bošnjak* or *Bosanac* identity.[22] Although both translate as "Bosnian," *Bošnjak* proclaims a historically rooted and culturally distinctive sense of self, while *Bosanac* persists with a regional conception that could accommodate all *nacije*, *narodi*, and *narodnosti*. However, the former term, used by the Ottomans and the Hapsburgs, was not as decisive as some of its proponents no doubt hoped. Indeed, *Bošnjak* furthered the undecidability of Bosnian/Muslim identity because it had at times referred both to residents of the Bosnian province and to Muslims. It was thought to be better suited than *Bosanac* to the political climate of the time, because *Bosanac* did not resolve the competing conceptions of identity and relied instead on a geographical sense. Nonetheless, both terms were the subject of an intense public debate in Bosnia from 1990 onwards.

In the context of the rise of nationalism in Serbia and Croatia, Bosnian/Muslim intellectuals revived the idea of *Bošnjaętvo* ("Bosnianness" or "Bosnianhood," *Bošnjaštvo*) and promoted the category *Bošnjak*. Although the latter term dates as far back as 1166, the notion of *Bošnjaštvo* did not develop until the end of the nineteenth century as an alternative to Serbian and Croatian nationalism then on the rise. By the early part of the twentieth century, Muslims, including those outside Bosnia such as the Sandžak Muslims, referred to themselves as *Bošnjak* and to their language as *Bošnjčaki*.[23]

This popular debate was evidence of the search for a formulation of identity that could endow a unique and distinctive sense of community so that a mode of belonging to Bosnia could be articulated, and the expansionist claims of Serbia and Croatia could be better resisted. Without a historical narrative of "Bosnianness" to match the claims of a naturalized Serbian and Croatian sense of self, supporters of the Serbian and Croatian nationalist projects dismissed Bosnian/Muslim identity as "invented" and therefore "unnatural." In those terms, it was argued, Bosnians/Muslims were "in reality" ethnically Serb and/or Croat, and therefore not only had no territorial claims of their own but should embrace one or the other of the nationalist enterprises.[24] In this context, it is not surprising that by 1994, the idea of *Bošnjak* (Bosniac) as signifying a Muslim national sense with territorial dimensions had gained currency, albeit to varying degrees, with the Bosnian political leadership, the international community — who had it written into the constitution of the Bosnian Federation — and the Sarajevo media.[25]

The conflation of "Bosnian" and "Muslim" thus seemed complete by the end of the war. As Bringa laments,

> the Bosnians have apparently been organized into tidy, culturally and ethnically homogenous categories, and the Muslims seem finally to have become a neat ethno-national category its neighbours and the international community can deal with and understand. They have been forced by the war and the logic of the creation of nation-states to search for their origins and establish a "legitimate" and continuous national history.[26]

While many of the outcomes of the Bosnian war can be read in these terms, there are also, given the extent and nature of the violence, a perhaps surprising number of developments that manifest the desire to exceed the categorization deemed necessary. That such impulses persist is perhaps less surprising if one considers the different register on which Bosnians/Muslims conceptualized identity.

According to Bringa, the ambivalent relationship of Bosnians/Muslims to ethnonationalist discourse stems from the fact that for them "a myth of origins was neither a part of, nor necessary to, knowing one's identity":

> This is where the nation-aspiring, ethnically-focused Serbs and Croats differed from the Bosnian Muslims. Among the latter, shared collective identity was not perceived through the idiom of shared blood and a myth of common origins, which is so often invoked in discourses on ethnic or national identity by other European peoples.... [The Muslims] referred to their identity in an idiom which de-emphasized descent ("ethnicity") and focused instead on a shared environment, cultural practices, a shared sentiment, and common experiences.[27]

The collective identity of Bosnians/Muslims (which included many Serbs and Croats) was thus capable of being contested by ethnonationalist Serbs and Croats because it was articulated in "a different idiom," one that could not be accommodated by the prevailing political categories. It was an idiom in which the ontopological assumptions of West European discourse — academic and political — played no significant role. This meant that instead of subscribing to the conventional view that a secure identity requires the abjection or sublimation of heterogeneous sources, "the Bosnians emphasized and added their heterogeneous sources of identity to one another, so that an overarching Bosnian homogeneous identity was never ideologically and institutionally constructed to supersede this." Bosnians/Muslims therefore operated within a frame that refused a dichotomous and exclusive rendering of identity/difference:

> Although "Bosnian" was a unifying identity in the sense that it straddled ethnoreligious communities, it did not subsume these differences. Indeed, at its core was the tension between two opposing needs: on the one hand belonging to distinct but parallel ethnoreligious communities, and the need to communicate separateness, and on the other the awareness of sharing the same territory, social environment, and sets of cultural codes, and therefore of being interdependent and basically the same.[28]

"Bosnia" can therefore be thought of as signifying an articulation of identity that embodies many of the onto-political assumptions of deconstructive thought. In a manner akin to the double contradictory imperative, "Bosnia" is testament to the constitution of an identity that was realized in a community without essence. It is an identity enabled not by closure but by the aporias abundant in a context of radical interdependence. It is an identity that operated in terms of the care for the complex relationship of identity/difference many want to advocate. In this context, if we wish to enable deterritorialized conceptions of identity in a globalizing world, Bosnia might contain a number of instructive reflections.

It would be in some ways perverse, however, if we romanticized the aporetic and differential nature of Bosnian identity. All identities are inherently deconstructible, but as the Bosnian war so savagely illustrated, Bosnia's was perhaps more susceptible to deconstruction than most. That susceptibility, however, stems not from any inherent weakness of nonethnic, nonnationalist, non-ontopological politics. It stems from a particular conjunction of circumstances in which the investments in ethnonationalist politics by actors both internal and external to the situation were too great to overcome easily. When ontopological assumptions abound in West European and North American politics, when they flourish in academic analyses and media accounts of foreign conflicts, when they inhabit the political imagination of those asked to find a resolution to wars understood in those terms, and when they form the basis of nationalist projects backed by military force in the regions of concern, alternatives are always going to struggle. Investments in different assumptions, however, could produce different outcomes.

Moreover, even when those investments are not as great as they might be, alternatives do not disappear, and the desire for them is not diminished, even by a war as horrific as that we have witnessed in Bosnia. Drawing attention to Bosnian identity, therefore, is not to engage in nostalgia for the politics of multiculturalism. It is to appreciate how even in the face of overwhelming odds, the logic of nationalism and the nation-state cannot eradicate the heterogeneous condition that problematizes it. This is evident in a commentary published in the Sarajevo daily paper *Oslobodjenje* in January 1996, which argued that the fragile balance between integration and antagonism was complicated by the lack of a political concept that could accommodate the complexities of Bosnia's identities in the future. The main struggle, it argued, was between the aspiration for an ethnically pure national state by Bosnia's neighbors, and the promotion of the "the civic concept" by those within the country (such as the Bosniacs, Croat Nation Council [HNV], and Serb Civic Council [SGV]).[29]

The purpose of this argument, then, is to identify how our responsibility to the other can be materialized in specific circumstances and where, in the realm of policy and tactics, alternative investments informed by nonnationalist assumptions could have been made. It is, in short, to see how the proponents of "the civic concept" could have been — and can still be — aided in their efforts to overcome the extreme nationalists. Given the violent relation to the other national-ism empowered in numerous sites, a diagnosis of where and how ontopological assumptions operated in relation to Bosnia, and where and how they could have been contested, might have wider implica-tions. The final section of this book considers in practical terms, there-fore, those strategies that aided closure of the political options in on-topological terms, and those strategies that might have problematized closure and might still foster new openings.

Fostering Democracy

As the previous chapter argued, the political possibilities enabled by deconstructive thought can be thought of as giving rise to a general principle (albeit in terms of the iteration of a particular generality) for the ethos of democracy. This principle would declare that we should actively nourish and nurture antagonism, conflict, plurality, and multi-plicity, not at the expense of security or identity but in terms of secu-rity's and identity's contamination by and indebtedness to its other(s).

This does not mean that *deconstruction* itself constitutes the polit-ical concept that would resolve the dilemmas of Bosnia. It means, rather, that deconstructive thought can help identify and energize the political ethos through which the development of a political life ade-quate to the complexities of Bosnia might be possible. Of course, how the principle derived from deconstructive thought is materialized de-pends on the circumstances in which it needs to work. In the context of Bosnia, and in contrast to the logic of nationalism and the power of ontopological politics that seem to govern that domain, this prin-ciple animates a political goal: the need for strategies of pluraliza-tion in the service of a radicalized ideal of multiculturalism, where multiculturalism is understood in terms of the aporetic and differen-tial nature of Bosnian identity detailed above.

This political goal and the ethos that enables it can be thought in relation to any number of specific issues relevant to the Bosnian war and its aftermath. In so doing, the discussion is moving from the realm of the undecidable and the many problematizations of "Bosnia" to the domain of the decision that responds to the problem of Bosnia ren-dered by a particular problematization. This does not mean we leave behind the onto-political concerns of the argument. To the contrary, we have to recognize the way every decision requires the passage through the undecidable, and how every account of problem-solving practices depends on a prior problematization. Shifting to the regis-ter of policy, therefore, is a means of demonstrating how the mad-ness of the decision and the urgency of the response embody specific resolutions of the undecidable and particular problematizations. It is only in this context that the question of what is at stake in the otherwise prosaic moments of a political operation becomes clearer.

Moreover, only then can we appreciate to the full extent necessary how the pluralization of sovereignty and space is insufficient as a progressive project unless accompanied by the deconstruction of identity. What follows, although far from an exhaustive account of all important moments or possibilities, are some important themes about the war, its aftermath, and its representation that helped foreclose nonnationalist options but can be problematized in relation to the principle and goal articulated above.

The failure of political organization to match the cultural plurality of Bosnia during the implosion of the former Yugoslavia prior to the violence, and the resultant success of ethnic and nationalist chauvinisms in occupying the empty place of power, aided and abetted by the international community.

The Bosnian elections of 1990 mark for some the beginning of the end of Bosnian identity and its hybridity.[30] The first elections in the aftermath of communism, they brought nationalist parties to power, with some 75 percent of the population voting for either the Croatian Democratic Union (HDZ), the Party for Democratic Action (SDA), or the Serbian Democratic Party (SDS). Thus, these parties followed the pattern of every winning bloc in the former Yugoslavia: unless a political group could articulate its programs in terms of a nationalism contra communism, it lost badly.[31] Amid the nationally charged climate of a collapsing Yugoslavia, and the ambivalence within the SDA as to its political goal for Bosnia, Izetbegović's status as a political dissident from the communist era who had never been a party member might help explain why the electorate abandoned the more overtly secular and multiethnic parties (which had polled the best in preelection surveys) for the SDA.[32] Although nonnationalist alternatives failed electorally at this point, there was no necessary correlation between electoral success and a popular mandate for exclusive ethnic nationalism. In part this was recognized by the parties themselves, who formed before the election a coalition organized around their common anticommunist position, something that persisted afterwards despite their overwhelming success.

The contested nature of ethnic nationalization in Bosnia can also be witnessed in the context of a proposed change in the broadcasting laws. Draft legislation that would have divided the republic's radio and television broadcasters into ethnic components (with one service each for Serbs, Croats, and Muslims) was introduced to the Bosnian parliament in 1991. It was supported enthusiastically by Serbian and Croatian nationalists, and originally had the blessing of the SDA. However, once the SDA concluded this would be a forerunner to the ethnic partition of the republic, it withdrew its support. The impetus for that change of heart by the SDA came from the trenchant opposition of journalists (regardless of their identity), who were supported by nine out of ten viewers in their opposition to ethnic structures.[33] This example demonstrates that there was a substantial body of sentiment within Bosnia against division that, given a chance to be expressed, could be mobilized in opposition to exclusivist policies.

The regrettable fact is that at almost every juncture, the international community's initiatives have been allied with nationalist logics and thus worked against a radicalized multicultural ethos. Of course, to speak in terms of "the international community" is to overlook the significant differences between "its" members and constitute an agent of dubious unity. Nonetheless, for the argument here, especially given the dominance of a shared political anthropology concerning Bosnia, the commonalities of the imagined community of international society are more important than the tactical differences. This was argued in chapter 5 concerning international diplomacy; it is being extended here to cover the post-Dayton context in Bosnia.

In particular, the 1996 elections in Bosnia provided for by the Dayton agreement contributed greatly to the entrenchment of ethnonational divisions in postwar politics. Although the elections were supposed to be conducted once there was freedom of assembly, expression, and movement throughout Bosnia, they were held at the insistence of the international community before efforts directed toward reintegration could have been successful. Indeed, by mid-September 1996 only two hundred thousand of nearly two million refugees had returned to Bosnia (and they more often than not returned to areas in which they had not lived in 1991), while some ninety thousand people had been "ethnically cleansed" in the months *after* the Dayton accord was signed.[34]

Some of the specific electoral procedures put in place by the international community explicitly allowed for abuse by nationalists. The large number of deaths and the massive population displacement caused by the war (the UN High Commission for Refugees estimated that 60 percent of Bosnia's people were forced from their homes, with more than 1.3 million [30 percent] being dispersed among sixty-three countries worldwide) made constructing a viable electoral register difficult. As a result, the criteria by which a person could register stated that a "citizen who no longer lives in the municipality in which he or she resided in 1991 shall, as a general rule, be expected to vote, in person or by absentee ballot, in that municipality." Exceptions to that rule were permitted if citizens applied (on a P2 form) to cast his or her ballot elsewhere.[35]

As the International Crisis Group observed, this turned Dayton's electoral procedures into "an ethnic cleanser's charter." The possibility that people could vote other than where they resided in 1991 meant they could vote either where they, after ethnic cleansing, resided in mid-1996, or where, after more ethnic cleansing, they intended to reside. This provision allowed for nationalist projects carried out by ethnic cleansing to be furthered by bureaucratic pressure on refugees. For example, the SDS-controlled Commission for Refugees and Displaced Persons required displaced Bosnian Serbs wanting humanitarian assistance to present a certificate that was only obtainable after they had completed a P2 form indicating their intention to vote in a district other than where they lived in 1991. In the absence of such a certificate they would be denied food, clothing, and shelter. This official pressure extended to radio broadcasts declaring that Serbs who planned to vote in their prewar places of residence were "directly attacking the Serbian nation." The coercion paid off, and three-quarters of Serb refugees registered to vote in places the regime desired. As one observer remarked, this meant that on the state radio of Republika Srpska "announcers can now boast that the outcome they engineered was really an expression of the people's will." One broadcast, handily overlooking the tens of thousands who had not succumbed to the pressure, declared that "none of the [Serb] refugees expressed a wish to vote in the Muslim-Croat entity, proving once again that living together is impossible."[36] Similar abuses by HDZ authorities were also recorded.[37]

These pressures meant that refugees who intended to return to the integrated areas from which they were expelled were denied the opportunity to do so. Despite the violence of their expulsions, many who could freely exercise choice expressed the desire to return.[38] Nonetheless, although the international organization monitoring the elections—the Organization for Cooperation and Security in Europe (OSCE)—identified these abuses early on as a threat to the goal of multiculturalism, in the face of considerable pressure from member states, such as the United States, it did not consider them sufficient to cancel the national elections. They did, however, postpone the municipal elections so as to minimize the fraud. Those elections—subsequently postponed another two times—were scheduled for September 1997. Although the abuses of the P2 forms were supposed to be overcome, the Agreement on Local Elections reached by the OSCE and the authorities of Bosnia on 1 December 1996 only perpetuated the problem. Under the terms of this accord, voters could register in a municipality of intended future residence if they provided evidence of some connection with that municipality, such as an invitation from "blood relatives" or an employment offer. In response to the original voter registration abuses, OSCE demanded no more than an apology from the SDS. Instead of resorting to face-saving measures lacking in substance, the OSCE could have more profitably negotiated different registration regulations. But the new provisions have not diminished the opportunities for abuse, even though they have exhausted the opportunity to denationalize the electoral register.[39]

Other elements of the period prior to the 1996 elections demonstrated the extent to which the international community in effect appeased nationalist sentiment. No political parties other than the HDZ, SDA, and SDS were permitted representation on the OSCE-organized Provisional Election Commission, thereby marginalizing overtly multicultural groups such as the Party for Bosnia, the Social Democrats, and Liberals, among others. The nationalists' control meant that favorable regulations could be enacted by the Election Commission. For example, it decided that to register a party in one of the Bosnian entities required ten thousand signatures from supporters. This was twice the number (and had to come from half the territory) that was required in 1990, thereby making it difficult for minority groups to establish themselves. Ironically, nationalist parties had tried to establish the larger threshold in 1990 and failed, which meant that the OSCE-authorized regulations were more exclusionary than had been the case in Bosnia before the war.[40]

Perhaps the most startling policy of the international community, however, was its funding of political parties regardless of their policies. "Free speech" was the criterion for the distribution of more than US$5 million in aid, and no effort was made to distinguish between those who supported the professed multiethnic goal of Dayton and those who did not. In this context, that nationalists who, like the SDS, advocated further division received money was problematic enough. But the OSCE went further and gave nearly a quarter of a million dollars to the Serb Unity Party. Their leader is the militia leader Željko Raznatović, or "Arkan," who was named by the United States as a war criminal because his ethnic cleansing operations in Bosnia were infamous for their brutality.[41] This funding demonstrates in this context the inability of liberal principles such as "free speech" to account for our responsibility to the other. Discriminatory funding in

favor of multicultural political forces, and withholding it from others, would have been one concrete manifestation of the ethos of
democracy. Ensuring that those complicit in ethnic cleansing are not
given access to aid funds would be another.[42]

The conduct of the 1996 election campaign was rife with problems. Violence against opposition candidates such as Haris Silajdžić
in Bosnian/Muslim-controlled federation territory replicated the intimidation of those outside the ruling circles in both Croat-controlled
federation territory and Republika Srpska.[43] Come election day, the
logistics designed by both local and international authorities to enable displaced voters to cross the Inter-Entity Boundary Line (IEBL)
and vote in their former homes were often poorly arranged and barely
advertised. As a result, substantially fewer than expected traveled
(13,500 from the federation into Republika Srpska, with only 1,200
going in the opposite direction). In contrast, the logistics employed
by the Federal Republic of Yugoslavia to transport from Serbia to
Srpska some 37,000 displaced persons, who originally lived in the
federation, so they could vote in areas they had never previously seen,
worked flawlessly. In the end, the elections were certified by the international community as democratic, free, and fair despite a turnout
of 103.9 percent (thereby suggesting widespread fraud), all of which
only served to legitimize the nationalists.[44]

Yet the nationalist veil is not totally drawn. It is probable that some
of the support for the nationalists was tactical. As one refugee voter
planning to vote for Izetbegović's party declared, "we don't want a
Muslim country, but we need to vote SDA to get a state. . . . Later on
maybe we can have different parties, but now it has to be the SDA or
we will be stateless, like the Kurds."[45] The election also threw up
some surprises that contravened the identity-territory nexus, most
obviously the fact that the SDA easily polled the second highest
number of votes in the poll for the National Assembly of Republika
Srpska, winning fourteen of the eighty-three seats (17 percent).[46] That
such a result was possible given the nationalist political parameters
the Dayton agreement established for Bosnia was more than a little
remarkable. The political institutions for which people voted in 1996
were carefully structured in ethnic terms. For the country as a whole,
there is a House of Representatives with forty-two members, comprising two-thirds from the federation and one-third from the Serbian entity. All procedures of this body require an attentiveness to
the ethnic composition of the votes, so that a majority should comprise at least one-third of the votes from members from the territory
of each entity. Then there is a House of Peoples, with fifteen ap-

pointed delegates to be appointed by the lower house in line with the two-thirds to one-third division. The ministry, the constitutional court, and the presidency are all similarly structured.[47]

However, the SDA's success in Republika Srpska demonstrates the bind introduced by Dayton's ethnicization of politics and territorial link. Citizens could vote only for presidential candidates from "their" entity. Therefore, although those Bosnians/Muslims who broached division to vote in their 1991 places of residence that are now in Republika Srpska could vote for the SDA in the parliamentary poll, they could *not* vote for a non-Serb member of the presidency. This meant that not only could their votes be cast for Serb candidates, they could not be cast for Bosnian/Muslim candidates. This created a double irony: the lack of movement across the IEBL on election day, usually cited as evidence of the failure of reintegration, meant that the chairmanship of the presidency was denied to those who wanted to further division. Had reintegration been further advanced, the political process and structure established by the Dayton agreement would have most likely ensured that the same (SDS) leaders who had wanted the dismemberment of Bosnia occupied the most powerful position in postwar Bosnia.[48]

In this context, the international community's structural solutions for Bosnia produced the very ethnicization of politics they later criticized, furthered the nationalist project they ostensibly wanted to contest, and provided no space for the nonnationalist formations they professed to support. Through the violence of conceptual determination, the international community legitimized, replicated, and extended the violence of ethnic cleansing. Prior to Dayton, a recognition of this could have changed the course of diplomacy. After Dayton, at the very least, a differently organized electoral procedure and institutional array could have produced different outcomes.

The way in which many external academic and political analyses of the conflict in Bosnia have themselves embodied the hegemony of ethnic-nationalist explanations.

As the exegesis of the academic, media, and political narratives in chapter 3 made clear, ontopological assumptions shaped the vast majority of representations of the conflict. They in turn mapped "Bosnia" as a particular place with specific people, so that it could be rendered as a problem requiring a particular solution. A more sophisticated appreciation of the way these narratives were themselves instruments of "foreign policy," whereby they functioned to stabilize notions of "our" identity in relation to "theirs," would have created the space for alternative representations able to accommodate the issues discussed in chapter 4, and the different political effects that they would have produced.

The limited political imagination of the international community that, bound by an outmoded conception of the national interest as the impetus for responsibility, enunciated no affirmative political goal for Bosnia and effaced any responsibility by emphasizing the process of negotiations and minor strategic initiatives in the military realm as the means for enacting responsibility.

As chapters 3 and 5 demonstrated, the ontopological representations of the conflict had specific consequences for how the international community conceived of its responsibility. Because it struggled to make sense of the fighting in terms of "the national interest," it resorted to a depoliticized notion of "humanitarianism" to position itself in relation to what was seen as an intractable situation. In this context, Gulf War–like military interventions were ruled out, and negotiations emphasized. When military action was contemplated and deployed, it was in terms of highly specific air strikes, weapons exclusion areas, and no-fly zones. None of these were comprehensively implemented, and none of them were tied to a political goal other than to support the process of negotiations, regardless of what was being negotiated.

This is *not* to suggest that large-scale military intervention should have been undertaken. The point is that because of the starting assumptions of the debate ("the national interest" in relation to an intractable conflict), the advisability or otherwise of military intervention became the site for questioning the international community's responsibility. As a result, logistical questions about such interventions displaced any notion of responsibility, and the negotiating process and the minor military action undertaken became substitutes for action that would have more adequately addressed the dynamics of the conflict in terms of an affirmative political goal.

The manner in which the international efforts at resolution, by reducing all combatants to equivalent ethnic factions and proposing settlements on the basis of cultural and territorial separation, have been equally dominated by the ethnic-nationalist exclusions they are seeking to ameliorate.

The reading of international diplomacy's proposals for the resolutions of the conflict in chapter 5 showed how an indebtedness to a contested political anthropology meant that the international community became entangled in an alliance of political logic with those they allegedly opposed. The ontopological mapping of Bosnia that was central to the five years of negotiations (and began before the fighting proper in Bosnia) supported the limited political imagination of the international community, which was organized in terms of the national interest, and enabled responsibility to be further effaced. An appreciation of the politics of identity central to international action would have been the first necessary step in enacting proposals that were less amenable to nationalist desires.

This problem afflicted even those international instruments that were used to press Bosnia's case for assistance. As the argument in chapter 4 made clear, the Genocide Convention on which many opposed to the ethnicization of the conflict relied for support was itself prone to nationalist understandings of the political. Unable to accommodate the notion of groups with hybrid or mutable identities, and thus powerless to address the threats to multicultural polities, the Genocide Convention requires amendment if it is to meet the challenge of a war on identity like that witnessed in Bosnia.

The continuing failure of the international community after the signing of the Dayton agreement to act in terms of nonnationalist logics.

Given the long-established pattern whereby the international community has acted in terms of the same nationalist imaginary as those who have sought to divide and partition Bosnia, it is perhaps not surprising that in the wake of the Dayton agreement — as the complicity of NATO's Implementation Force (IFOR) in the Serbian exodus from Sarajevo (detailed in chapter 4), and the conduct of the 1996 elections demonstrated — this alliance has continued. It is evident in a number of other important areas, each of which highlights moments at which alternative assumptions could have enabled different policies with potentially more progressive outcomes.

Under Annex 7 of the Dayton agreement "all refugees and displaced persons have the right freely to return to their homes of origin." The parties to the agreement (the Republic of Bosnia and Herzegovina, its two entities, Croatia, and the Federal Republic of Yugoslavia, along with the five member states of the Contact Group and the EU representative who acted as witnesses) are pledged to ensure that not only is this possible, but that they "shall take all necessary steps to prevent activities within their territories which would hinder or impede the safe and voluntary return of refugees and displaced persons."[49] In practice, the obverse of this pledge has been the norm. On virtually every occasion in which groups have attempted to cross the IEBL either to visit their former homes or to repair those homes now located in the Zone of Separation on either side of the IEBL—events that have more often than not involved Bosnians/Muslims encountering authorities in Republika Srpska, though clashes between Muslims and Croats within the federation have also been noted—those returning have been, if permitted to proceed, violently harassed.[50] On many of these occasions, IFOR has stepped in to *prevent* the refugees' movement, either physically, or by insisting that permission from Bosnian Serb authorities be first obtained. And if it has not prevented the movement, it has retreated from fulfilling its obligations to secure the movement as detailed in the Dayton agreement. This negligence produced a potential spiral of conflict, as the return of refugees to a town like Jusici illustrated well.[51]

Although the international community's (in)actions have created such dilemmas, it effaces its own responsibility by constantly criticizing *all* sides in Bosnia (except itself) for their "provocative" actions in events such as those implicated in the return to Jusici. The moral equivalency that once marked the international community's attitude to the war in terms of "three warring factions" has now found its postwar, noncombatant equivalent: "all the parties" are equally responsible for any instance of postwar hostility. But as so often has been the case, those responsible are nationalist leaderships pursuing a project with dubious levels of popular support, while gaining sustenance from the international community's inability to discriminate in the nonnationalists favor.[52] In this context, the journey of Vlakjo and Stefanka Subotic and five others—Bosnian Serbs who decided to return from four years in Republika Srpska to be welcomed by their non-Serb neighbors in Breza, to the northwest of Sarajevo—is beyond the imagination of those in power.[53] It is the exception that demonstrates the violence of ontopological representations, and the exception that demands official efforts to foster more of the same.

The refugee, of course, is a figure whose very existence problematizes nationalist communities with their ontopological assumptions. In Giorgio Agamben's felicitous formulation, "because the refugee destroys the old trinity of state-nation-territory, the refugee, an apparently marginal figure, deserves to be, on the contrary, considered as the central figure of our political history."[54] Perhaps because of the radical possibilities raised by the refugee, the international community's efforts involve a homogeneous notion of "home" to which the displaced person can be repatriated. This effacement of the refugee's deterritorialized existence is most evident in relation to Bosnia, where the idea of "home" has come to mean a place in which there is a common ethnic majority rather than the space where the affected individuals once lived. Thus, Germany, one of the Contact Group members to have witnessed the Dayton agreement, began forcible repatriation of some of the three hundred thousand Bosnians from Munich, on the grounds that they can return to "Muslim" areas in the federation regardless of whether they ever resided there. In its desire to expel the Bosnian difference from its own contested national community, Germany is contributing by this repatriation to the construction of a newly homogeneous national community in Bosnia, all in the name of the Dayton agreement, human rights, and multiculturalism.[55] In moments like these, the way in which ontopological assumptions have colonized the international imagination and furthered a particular problematization of Bosnia could not be clearer. As a result, these moments manifest opportunities for an alternative praxis informed by different assumptions. Hospitality rather than repatriation would be one materialization of the ethos this argument represents.[56]

The choices and outcomes in circumstances such as these, however, are rarely clear-cut. The fact that an unpublished UNHCR report concluded that virtually no Bosnian refugees had returned to areas outside their group's control, regardless of where they called "home," led some to conclude that UNHCR had decided that only those who wanted to go to areas of their ethnic majority should be given assistance.[57] Yet when UNHCR aided those who wished to return to their former residences, the bureaucratic hurdles they had to negotiate meant their efforts were easily hijacked. For example, refugees expelled from eastern Bosnia who wished to visit their old homes were required to apply to the United Nations for a permit. The United Nations, in turn, had to seek the authority of Republika Srpska officials. On one such occasion, which represents a single instance of a larger policy, the Srpska authorities simply matched the UN–supplied names of the ninety-six people who had applied to visit to the ninety-six homes they wished to visit, and then blew up those homes so as to make a visit futile and reintegration difficult. As the spokesperson for UN-HCR lamented, "what is so discouraging is that our effort to bring people back together was used to cement ethnic cleansing."[58] While there are accounts of IFOR reports concerning Bosnian/Muslim police setting fire to Bosnian Serb houses in the northwest of the country, they are both few and far between, and represent less extensive and less systematic activity.[59] Subsequent Bosnian Serb detonations brought the number of houses destroyed in the final months of 1996 to over two hundred, and evidence from one site revealed that the blasts had been professionally arranged with materials obtained from the Yugoslav National Army.[60]

The overall reluctance of the international community to act in ways contrary to the nationalists is best manifested by the reluctance to arrest individuals indicted as war criminals. Although Operation Tango, the British army's move against two indicted suspects in Prijedor, foreshadowed other possibilities, the record to that point was dismal. Most notable in this regard, of course, was the way in which both Radovan Karadžić and Ratko Mladić were able to pass by or through IFOR/SFOR checkpoints without interference let alone arrest. Similarly, although the whereabouts of others have been well known for some time, for all the talk about the importance of bringing people to account for their actions, civilian representatives of the international community did no more than write letters in protest to those harboring them, while most military representatives went out of their way to avoid encounters and interpret their mandate for arrest in the most restrictive fashion possible.[61]

The continuation of ethnic cleansing by nationalists of all stripes, though to varying degrees.
In this climate of international noninterference and inaction, ethnic cleansing continued apace despite the signing of the Dayton agreement and the certification of the September 1996 election. Although contained by the presence of international forces in the country, so that the worst excesses of 1992 are not yet being revisited, ethnic cleansing still operates as a means of constituting the most homogeneous national space possible. But as in the earlier periods of the conflict, not all ethnic cleansing is equal. Instances occur in the name of all nationalist projects, but some are more extensive and organized than others.

According to a report by Human Rights Watch (HRW), the worst cases of ethnic cleansing redux are found in Republika Srpska.[62] In response, HRW urged the international community to make public all information on these abuses (which had until the report been the subject only of confidential IFOR documents), to become more proactive in countering such abuses, and to reintroduce sanctions if the Srpska authorities did not disband such programs. Although HRW's focus was on Republika Srpska, similar officially organized expulsions are being carried out by authorities in Mostar, as well as in other territories controlled by the HDZ's Croatian nationalists.[63] But the situation in Bosnian/Muslim political spaces is generally more complex.

On the one hand, the small but not insignificant number of Serbs returning to their homes in Bosnian/Muslim territory have encountered few if any official barriers and have been welcomed by their neighbors, even when they have returned to live among Muslim refugees from Srebrenica who had been subject to some of the worst violence.[64] On the other hand, there has been intimidation by Bosnian/Muslim refugees from Srebrenica of those Serbs remaining in the suburbs of Sarajevo.[65] Indeed, the clash between the housing demands of Srebrenica's refugees who have been (temporarily, it is said) placed in the apartments of those Serbs who left Sarajevo under pressure from their own leadership but now want to return is proving to be one of the biggest tests of the Bosnian government's multicultural resolve.[66]

Wartime property laws instituted by the Bosnian government, though more enlightened than those in Republika Srpska, have been used to appropriate large numbers of apartments from one community for another. A May 1992 decree permitted municipalities to seize all apartments vacated after 30 April 1991 unless the occupants were the victims of an ethnic cleansing campaign. Then in December 1995, the Sarajevo government quietly decreed that residents who had left the city for whatever reason had a mere seven days to reclaim their residence if they were in Bosnia, and fourteen days if they were outside the country. Those who have subsequently returned and found their residences occupied have had no success in presenting their case to the authorities, and these developments have prompted stern rebukes from the government's supporters.[67]

Other contradictory impulses are evident in areas of Bosnian/Muslim authority. The SDA embraced a form of pluralism when it appointed Izetbegović's opponent in the 1996 presidential race, Haris Silajdžić, as one of the cochairmen of Bosnia's Council of Ministers. Yet there have been reports that institutions such as the army are purging their ranks of loyal non-Muslims. Although the 5th Corps based at Bihac remains solidly multiethnic, the SDA sought to exercise greater control over its affairs by adding the commanding general (along with other military figures) to the party's ruling council.[68]

Even seemingly marginal events have become contested in this politicized environment. While Christmas in Sarajevo still witnessed multireligious observances, there were signals from the authorities that the symbol of Father Christmas (or Grandfather Frost, as he became in the former Yugoslavia) was "foreign" to Bosnian/Muslim culture and to be frowned upon. All this led one resident to observe that "in its heart, Sarajevo is still a multi-ethnic city, but no thanks to the government. . . . Now it's because of the people who are resisting the government."[69] That there is still popular capacity for resistance in the name of multiculturalism, however, is something to be recognized and supported. The sometimes contradictory and often less than emphatic official line on nationalism provides the probability that this resistance could be exploited, although given the increasingly evident frustration with the Dayton process among Bosnia's political leadership, time may not favor such an effort.[70]

Following on from these themes, which have dealt with moments in the foreclosing of alternatives, we can also highlight the following as political strategies that could still be adopted in furtherance of the ethos of democracy. If pursued these would contribute to the deconstruction of settled identities, the pluralization of sovereignties and space, and the enactment of new political communities.

The multiplication of sources of knowledge and analysis, both within the media of the former Yugoslavia as well as the institutions of the West, such that nonsovereign and nonstate perspectives are given greater legitimacy.

The proliferation of information is not in and of itself progressive: with regard to Bosnia it has often "bred casuistry and indifference."[71] What is required for critical interventions in established modes of thought is the pluralization of knowledge so that attitudes that disturb established categories can be circulated. In this regard, independent media in the former Yugoslavia have existed throughout the war and played a vital role. Magazines and papers like *ARKZin* in Zagreb and *Vreme* in Belgrade, and radio stations like Radio ZID in Sarajevo and B-92 in Belgrade maintained and furthered nonnationalist perspectives.

Likewise, the establishment and use of Internet facilities, such as the ZaMir network linking sites in the former Yugoslavia with the rest of Europe, and the work of numerous groups in cyberspace, such as the feminist movement Electronic Witches, have enabled the mutual dissemination of information and the coordination of humanitarian and peace initiatives among many nonstate coalitions. The power of this media should not be overestimated: ZaMir hosts on average no more than two thousand users at any one time. But neither should the impact of such strategic interactions be underestimated. The "Sarajevo-Live, Sarajevo On-Line" event of March-April 1995 provided the impetus for renewed coverage of the city's situation in the mainstream media. These efforts have received some funding from sources such as the U.S. National Endowment for Democracy and the Soros Foundation, but their regular appeals for more assistance demonstrate that this funding is insufficient and should be greatly supplemented.[72]

The benefits to be derived from assistance to independent media can be contrasted with the international community's efforts in Bosnia. Although not without their problems, the state-run media operating in the Bosniac-controlled territory of the federation entity were the most free of all the authorities in the region.[73] Despite this, and the concomitant need to extend medial pluralization to Croat-controlled federation territory and Republika Srpska, the international community organized a radio network (the Swiss-financed FERN, or Free Election Radio Network) and television system (the Office of the High Representative's $11-million TV-IN), which were based in and concentrated on Bosniac territory.[74] Because of technical problems and obstacles placed in its path by the Bosnian government, TV-IN went to air less than a week before polling day, making it a spectacular failure.

Money would have been better spent on supporting those indigenous efforts at alternative media, some of which were occurring even in Republika Srpska. Although pluralism in the Srpska media is of a narrower range than elsewhere, as in the case of the former army officer Milovan Stankovic's paper *Alternativa*, it exists nonetheless. It is being furthered by initiatives such as funding for a paper (*Ogledalo*) produced jointly by federation and Srpska journalists, and the promotion of the independent Sarajevo journal *Dani* in the Srpska city of Banja Luka.[75]

Use of these and other such sources by the international media would also have an impact on the circulation of nonnationalist perspectives. Although stories about events and issues that problematize ontopological perspectives can be often found in the international media (many of them are the basis for this account), they often fail to disturb the overall narrativization of Bosnia that comes from the international media's focus on the formal aspects of international relations. Greater use of independent media in the regions would help disturb that narrativization further by drawing attention to the many important dimensions of politics in Bosnia (such as the Helsinki Citizen's Assembly [hCa] initiatives discussed below) that otherwise escape notice.

The encouragement of meticulous genealogies and different histories to draw attention both to the complex character of identity in the region, and the novelty of policies designed to put in place the territorialized ethnic exclusivism that diminished the space for those identities.

Reading micronarratives in a manner that disturbs the spatial imaginaries of essentializing macronarratives and opens up the prospect of ethical encounters and an appreciation of our inescapable responsibility to the other is an important strategy of politicization. Such new narratives of subjugated knowledges need to be produced and circulated so as to demonstrate the manifestly political nature of ontopological accounts, and the exclusions they depend on. In its own way, hopefully, this book is a contribution to that enterprise. Likewise, further instances of the knowledge embodied in ethnographies such as Bringa's *Being Muslim the Bosnian Way,* the analyses that make up *WarReport,* and some of the reportage that takes place on the Internet need to be encouraged. Support needs to be given for what Foucault calls those diverse inquiries that make up the "patient labor giving form to our impatience for liberty."[76]

To this end, the documentary sources being collected by bodies such as the International Criminal Tribunal for the Former Yugoslavia constitute a potential to be exploited. Indeed, the greatest contribution of the war crimes trials may come from the construction of an archive and the furtherance of historical memory they aid, rather than from the trial and punishment of certain individuals they seek.[77] Although the inability of the international community to enforce compliance with the arrest warrants and indictments of The Hague tribunal is to be deplored, the conduct of the Rule 61 proceedings against Karadžić and Mladić legitimized non-ontopological accounts. By working with notions of individual responsibility stemming from military and political command, the tribunal is diminishing the notion of inevitable and intractable communal conflict. Similarly, the convictions of Drazen Erdemovic — who pleaded guilty to the murder of Bosnians/Muslims at Srebrenica — and Dusan Tadic ensured that revisionist accounts of genocidal activity were more difficult to make, and helped problematize further ethnic renderings of the fighting.[78] However, without sufficient funding from the international community for The Hague tribunal and the collection of evidence, this effort will be severely hampered.[79]

Support in both principle and substance for the peace initiatives and proposals of local communities and NGOs overlooked by international diplomacy.

Given that the international community's political anthropology mandated the ethnic division of Bosnia to such an extent that it seemed natural, it is important to recall that those implicated in the conflict but beyond the orbit of high diplomacy put forward alternative plans. From the beginning of the fighting, activists in the region, in conjunction with supporters around Europe, met to advocate political strategies different from those being commonly discussed. At the Conference for a Balkan Peace (held parallel to the official London Conference in August 1992), the Citizens and Municipal Peace Conference organized in Ohrid, Macedonia, in November 1992, and the Verona Forum in Vienna during June 1993 (among others), plans for a different form of civil intervention were discussed.

Emphasizing the need to counteract ethnic division, and wanting to think beyond the limited notion of military means, proposals centered around the idea of an internationally guaranteed protectorate — similar to the UN Transitional Authority in Cambodia — to secure the space for democratic politics.[80] As Anthony Borden wrote, what was required was a new conception of "emancipatory intervention" that had as its first task the mobilization of "a vision of civil and democratic politics in the region."[81]

That vision, as has been stressed here in a number of places, was not absent from the region but required support through creative alliances with those in the region and beyond. It was, moreover, a vision that went well beyond its superficial similarity with the UN's adhoc, ill-conceived, and inadequately implemented notion of "safe havens." The details of what it would have entailed, or whether it was feasible, though interesting and important, are not the primary issue. Rather, the crucial point is that these proposals were formulated, and more often than not overlooked, yet with the necessary support could in principle have produced an outcome markedly different from the efforts of international diplomacy. In line with the ethos of democracy, they constitute an important alternative that did not attract the necessary consideration, even though they remain the policy of hCa.[82]

Other political arrangements that might be pursued include local autonomies or "special functional transnational zones" as supplements.[83] Of course, pursuing these in the contest of new forms of UN trusteeship could sanction a return to colonialism if not accompanied by a progressive political goal and a central role for indigenous political authorities who adhere to that goal.[84] The situation of Mostar exhibits well the promise and problems of these schemes. While its transnational status as a city secured by European Union administration offered the promise of nonnationalist possibilities, the reliance on ethnic political formulas (such as the division of the city into ethnic districts for the June 1996 local elections) and a reluctance to support its professed goals with international military support have meant that despite the best intentions of individual EU administrators in Mostar (such as Hans Koschnick), ethnic cleansing has persisted and policies for reintegration have been thwarted.[85]

The development of proposals for political space legitimized by their resistance to exclusivism and enabled by the multiplication of sources of sovereignty.

The alternative peace proposals were often conceived under the umbrella of the work of the Helsinki Citizens Assembly, and dependent on the notion of "civil society."[86] Indeed, "civil society" has become perhaps the buzzword for progressive politics and the rearticulation of nationalist space in Bosnia, and is the most common signifier for nonnationalist perspectives and programs. Of course, "civil society" is an inherently contestable notion in anthropology and political theory.[87] Moreover, experience in the former Yugoslavia demonstrates that "civil society" is not inherently progressive: in Croatia and Slovenia it has hosted varying degrees of nationalist sentiment and has been the modus operandi of a "new globalized professional middle class" more concerned with the political assumptions and parameters of their foreign funders than the requirements of local communities.[88] So although as the signifier of the nonstate realm of politics it marks an important potential break with nationalism, that break requires constant attention for it to be kept open in order to foment the space for alternatives and alternative spaces.

Nonetheless, in Bosnia the idea of initiatives for "civil society" highlights the pursuit of nonnationalist options and draws the connections between the nongovernmental organizations whose work in specific sites contributes to an overcoming of ethnic divisions and nationalist spaces. Thus, the initiatives of the hCa offices in Sarajevo and Tuzla, which include a network of women journalists establishing an independent newspaper; the work of the Forum of Tuzla Citizens, Circle 99 in Sarajevo, the Belgrade Circle, and the Antiwar Campaign in Zagreb, with their transnational civic dialogue and Citizen's Alternative Parliament; the Bijeljina-based Helsinki Committee for Human Rights in Republika Srpska; the legal advocacy for refugees conducted by Job 22 in Bosnia; the economic reconstruction initiatives of the Tuzla Agency for Local Development Initiatives (TALDI); and the intellectual connections of the World University Service's "Academic Lifeline for Bosnia and Herzegovina," among many others perhaps unknown, are part and parcel of these developments.[89] They all disclose what Michael Shapiro calls a "post-liberal political imaginary." The discourses of this imaginary "delineate spaces of difference and register rifts and disjunctures, aspects of dissociation engendered by forces emanating from the operations of power, surveillance and exchange." Temporally, post-liberal discourses "are occupied with the present forces of social and political containment and the counter-forces of resistance."[90]

Although a good number of these initiatives are sustained through networks with others beyond Bosnia, many if not all have been organized and run by Bosnians. They are also being formed all the time. For example, Muslim, Serb, and Croat refugee associations in seventeen towns, which represent those who wish to return home regardless of nationalist opposition, have established "The Coalition for Return" in order to reject "the ideology of ethnic separation."[91] These examples not only demonstrate the local possibilities that can be fostered through investments of various kinds, they show that the problems of imposing external assumptions through a new professional NGO class can be avoided.

Importantly, "civil society" initiatives that problematize do not have to involve the establishment of groups or movements. They can be the effects of isolated policies and practices. For example, individual IFOR units have sometimes had the ambition (in line with the Dayton agreement but in contrast to normal IFOR practice) to literally breach ethnic division by removing nationalist paramilitaries from roadblocks that have barred passage across the IEBL.[92] Notable in this regard have been the efforts of one U.S. colonel, Gregory Fontenot, based in the Posavina region of northern Bosnia. By clearing an area of mines, providing sewage pipes, building access roads, and maintaining a military presence for oversight and traffic control, his troops have helped create a vast market on what is known as Route Arizona. Located in the federation borderlands abutting the Zone of Separation, it has proved to be an economic magnet for the reintegration of communities from the federation and Republika Srpska. As a result, it has attracted the overt hostility of Srpska authorities, who want to prevent any such example, and the bureaucratic concern of Bosnian officials who want the taxes the market avoids.[93] One of its supreme ironies is that many of the people it brings together are from Brčko, site of some of the worst ethnic cleansing in 1992, and a town still divided by those who maintain that reintegration is impossible.

Another positive project has been the UNHCR program to establish inter-entity bus routes in Bosnia, allowing a few individuals the chance to travel on protected transport between towns and cities in disputed areas. Whether this project has involved routes connecting districts of Sarajevo divided by the IEBL, such as Ilidza and Lukavica, or more distant towns, such as Banja Luka-Zenica, Republika Srpska authorities have routinely harassed the effort. Their opposition has ranged from local police halting a bus because it failed to meet un-specified safety standards, to acts of minor violence directed against the vehicles, to complete bans for the service. To counteract this op-position, UNHCR has effectively "transnationalized" the endeavor by bringing in Danish drivers and buses with foreign registrations.[94] The bus lines that operate in these terms thus constitute an extrater-ritorial space that helps to rearticulate community in Bosnia.

Whether, in the end, the pursuit of nonnational options (perhaps more often than not best pursued by nonstate organizations) results in antistate political arrangements is open to serious question. As Slavoj Žižek has noted, critical social movements have regularly condemned the state as the source of the problem rather than the solution. But it is possible to see Bosnia as the utopia of state abolition realized, al-beit one in which that realization stems from the way in which new states are being installed by nationalist communities and their allies. In response to this, argues Žižek, it is

> necessary to draw what at first glance seems a paradoxical, yet cru-cial conclusion: today the concept of utopia has made an about-face turn—utopian energy is no longer directed towards a stateless com-munity, but towards a state without nation, a state which would no longer be founded on an ethnic community and its territory, there-fore simultaneously towards a state without territory, towards a purely artificial structure of principles and authority which will have severed the umbilical chords of ethnic origin, indigenousness and rootedness.[95]

If what results from that is a state, it is a very different state from that assumed by the state-centric discourses of comparative politics and international relations. It might be a "state *of* minorities inhabited by a general ethos flowing from multiple cultural sources . . . where most constituencies recognize the contestable character of the beliefs most fundamental to their identities, using such reciprocal recognition to bridge multiple lines of difference."[96] What this conclusion points to, however, is that for a progressive outcome the pluralization of space is insufficient unless matched by a deconstruction of identity. Given the enthusiasm among more progressive thinkers for propos-als such as a "Europe of the regions," the dismemberment of Bosnia into plural entities might be read as a step in that direction. But be-cause its new spatial arrangements are made in terms of naturalized identities, Bosnia's partition should be appreciated as regressive. What is required, therefore, is an effort "to think of 'community' through a space which does not structure essentialized identities," as part of an overall attentiveness to the "geographies of resistance."[97]

Even more than that, what is required is space hospitable to what Derrida calls "a new International," in which a particular bond can be realized:

> There is today an aspiration towards a bond between singularities [not "political subjects" nor even "human beings"] all over the world. This bond not only extends beyond nations and states, such as they are composed today or such as they are in the process of decomposition, but extends beyond the very concepts of nation or state. For example, if I feel in solidarity with this particular Algerian who is caught between F.I.S. and the Algerian state, or this particular Croat, Serbian or Bosnian, or this particular South African, this particular Russian or Ukrainian, or whoever — it's not a feeling of one citizen towards another, it's not a feeling peculiar to a citizen of the world, as if we were all potentially or imaginary citizens of a great state. No, what binds me to these people is something different than membership of a world nation-state or of an international community extending indefinitely what one still calls today "the nation-state." What binds me to them — and this is the point; there is a bond, but this bond cannot be contained within traditional concepts of community, obligation or responsibility — is a protest against citizenship, a protest against membership of a political configuration as such. This bond is, for example, *a form of political solidarity opposed to the political* qua *a politics tied to the nation-state*.[98]

The bond of which Derrida speaks is akin to that identified by Alphonso Lingis when he asks, "Is there not a growing conviction, clearer today among innumerable people, that the dying of people with whom we have nothing in common — no racial kinship, no language, no religion, no economic interests — concerns us?"[99] It is a political bond, enabled not by the absence or irrelevance of the nation/state but by its continuing power and our agonistic relationship with it. It is a political bond, therefore, that recognizes that we are connected by the practices of government, but that we struggle with the strategies of governmentality that try to contain our freedom.[100] In this sense, the issues discussed in this chapter do not constitute a "utopian" response. Rather than proposing an avoidance of or escape from the deleterious consequences of the international community's problematizations of "Bosnia," they demand a contestation of and intervention in the political forms bequeathed to Bosnia, and they highlight the various ways and plural sites in which this disturbance can be effected and new options enacted.

The construction of new rationales for international responsibility — new general principles enabled and iterated by the crises of particularities — such as a "radicalized humanitarianism" that is not dependent on a limited humanism, and the development of new strategies for intervention that encourage nonmilitary and nonstate actors.

This theme effectively summarizes the thrust of the above argument. Moreover, it isolates the key to the enactment of the above strategies. What is highlighted and proposed depends on having the will to do something in specific circumstances where rationales such as "the national interest" and "humanitarianism" are insufficient. In the end it comes down to having and fostering a deeper appreciation of our preexisting responsibility to the other. And it comes down to the recognition that our inescapable responsibility can be enacted in political terms through deconstructive strategies that allow for the emergence of the (often already present) political ethos that struggles with chauvinistic and exclusivist practices.

The Distinctive Contribution of Deconstructive Thought

Deconstructive thought cannot claim sole authorship or exclusive rights for a number of the specific proposals mentioned above, nor can it be thought of as a concept that serves as a solution. In the first instance this is because of the promotion and pursuit over the past five years of many of these initiatives by nonethnic, social democratic forces in the former Yugoslavia, though it can be argued that with their critiques of essentialist and exclusivist policies such forces have embodied the ethos of democracy. Nonetheless, it is also possible to arrive at similar conclusions with respect to some of these points from a variety of starting points. Nor can deconstructive thought provide an unconditional assurance that the pursuit and implementation of any or all of these suggestions would have brought an end to the fighting in Bosnia, ensured a just solution, and prevented hostilities in the future.

But to say as much is not to devalue the political possibilities enabled by deconstructive thought. While no theoretical project can ever guarantee a specific outcome in the realm of politics (for were such guarantees available, the realm would no longer be politics), it can be safely said that with respect to Bosnia the international community's response, informed as it is by theorizations concerning territory and identity drawn from a broadly defined realist discourse, has furthered the violence and would not be difficult to improve upon. The fact that a range of political options informed by deconstructive thought might *possibly* better address the conflict is something strongly in its favor. For us to be able to say that options informed by deconstructive thought might *probably* better address the conflict would require the additional step of ensuring a substantial investment of social resources—meaning those funds of economic, political, and social capital held by those immediately party to the conflict, as well as by those more distant in whom a sense of responsibility could be cultivated—in the enactment of the ethos.

However, while no one option above can be considered the exclusive property of deconstructive thought, the *combined effect* of the options above (along with the others yet to be thought) and the ethos of deconstruction does enact something not captured by other positions. The distinctive contribution of deconstructive thought's possibilities is twofold. In the first instance is its recognition that what others see as contradictions comprising obstacles to a just politics are the "contradictions"—better understood as agonistic interdependencies—necessary for a politics, and as such they have to be contested and negotiated rather than transcended and escaped. Although many liberals might advocate any of the above proposals in terms of tolerance, the indebtedness of liberalism's tolerance to already established differences—as argued in chapter 6—means that the way in which the proposals above either play into the hands of putatively natural differences (i.e., those that support national imaginaries) or contest them cannot be addressed by such a perspective.

In this context, we can refigure the relationship between identity, democracy, and violence in Bosnia. The political implosion of the former Yugoslavia involved the dissolution of the markers of certainty. Although that condition is concomitant with the idea of democracy as an empty place of power, that empty place was quickly colonized by a definable social agency organized in terms of an identity politics founded on exclusive notions of ethnicity and nationalism. As such, the institution of formal democracy helped established the conditions of possibility of violence, especially when it was sanctioned by the international community. But rather than concluding that this outcome condemns democracy in favor of an entirely other political arrangement, we should call for the cultivation of the ethos of democracy that, paradoxically, necessitates the encouragement of one form of conflict (that which contests, disturbs, and denaturalizes exclusive forms of identity) while resisting that form of conflict that effaces, suppresses, and seeks to erase plural and hybrid identities.

Likewise, the disposition of negotiating rather than escaping antinomies applies to issues such as sovereignty in the Bosnian war. While *on the one hand* we need to foreground the way in which a certain relationship between sovereignty and identity results in violence, and recognize the inadvisability of the West's insistence on sovereignty in the form of a unitary Yugoslavia as the basis of its initial response to the conflict, *on the other hand* we also need to recognize that a grave injustice has been perpetuated by a failure to support the sovereignty of Bosnia and ensure the legitimacy of the Izetbegović government as much more than one of the three "factions" in the conflict, and that new proposals for a just settlement will involve the rearticulation of sovereignty. An issue such as the war in Bosnia thus involves much more than one-sided gestures of acceptance or rejection, whether they be demands that one has either democracy or totalitarianism, that one be either for or against a principle such as sovereignty, or that one is either in favor of or opposed to tactics such as the use of force. The argument here is that only the ethos of deconstructive thought can appreciate the contradictions, paradoxes, and silences of political problems in a complex world, and enable flexible strategies that are neither merely pragmatic nor purely ad hoc by fostering and negotiating their agonistic interdependencies.

The second distinctive political contribution of deconstructive thought, and perhaps its most important, is its recognition that in order to enact the promise of democracy, justice, and multiculturalism, all political proposals have to be *preceded* by the qualification of a "perhaps" and *followed* by an insistent and persistent questioning. With this all-important temporal dimension, deconstructive thought calls for an ongoing political process of critique and invention that is never satisfied that a lasting solution can or has been reached. As Derrida observes, "once again, here as elsewhere, wherever deconstruction is at stake, it would be a matter of linking an *affirmation* (in particular a political one), *if there is any*, to the experience of the impossible, which can only be a radical experience of the *perhaps*."[101] There is no political hesitation in either the notion of a political affirmation "if there is any" or the "perhaps." Likewise, there is no uncertainty in the idea that even preferred proposals made in deconstruction's name have to be subject after their implementation to an unrequited questioning. As Laclau states, "a society is democratic, not insofar as it postulates the validity of a certain type of social organization and of certain values vis-à-vis others, but insofar as it refuses to give its own organization and its own values the status of a *fundamentum inconcussum*."[102] It is deconstructive thought's political strength that it does not see weakness in questioning nor quietism in the "perhaps." It is politics' gain that deconstructive thought affirms each, for they are the necessary prerequisites for politics to be politics rather than a predetermined technology or an undemocratic program hostile to the ethos of the Enlightenment. It would be to Bosnia's advantage if those who were host to this ethos in its political field were aided and supported by all possible means. And it would be to "our" advantage if such support was refracted back into American and European articulations of the political.

Note on Sources

In writing about events and issues as contested as Bosnia, it is important to foreground the contestability of one's position. At the same time, it is also important to acknowledge the extensive array of evidence, much of it corroborated by the least prejudicial of authorities, on which one's position rests.[1] In the age of the Internet, in addition to the extensive material contained in the notes, this means noting a series of electronic addresses that access the sites from which important information has been obtained.

Central to the research for this book has been the material provided by E-mail in BosNet digests and news bulletins. BosNet, unlike the Internet bulletin board news groups, is not a forum for open discussion by individuals but a moderated information provider that mostly circulates material published elsewhere. As BosNet's World Wide Web site makes clear, its moderators self-consciously support particular principles, most notably "equal rights for all citizens of B&H," and seek to promote particular concepts, such as "democracy, political awareness, education, tolerance and understanding amongst various groups and individuals of B&H nationality (in and out of the country)"; all of which "promotes freedom to analyze, discuss, criticize events/issues from B&H political, economical, social, and other aspects of life."

The value of BosNet is that daily postings consist of either full articles or news briefs compiled from numerous sources, including reports by European and U.S. news agencies, ONASA (Oslobodjenje's news agency in Sarajevo), the Open Media Research Institute, quality newspapers in Europe and the United States, and various governmental and nongovernmental reports. A Bosnian language service (or Serbo-Croat language service, depending on your view about the politicization of language in the Balkans) is available, though I have been restricted to sources in English or translated into English.[2] The citations for approximately two-thirds of these materials in the notes came via BosNet; the remaining one-third were accessed directly. To save space, only the original citation is provided in the notes. To ensure accuracy, an extensive sample of the former was cross-checked with directly accessed hard copy, and found to contain no editing or errors. The spirit of BosNet is opposed to national separatism and in favor of a unified Bosnia, but its distribution of information critical of the authorities in Bosnia means its nonpartisan value can be appreciated and its services gratefully acknowledged. More information about BosNet can be obtained from its World Wide Web site, which was found at the address http://www.bosnet.org at the time of the writing of this book.

Of the many other relevant sites, the following have provided information for this research. World Wide Web addresses were valid at the time of the writing of this book.

Beserkistan (the world news service of Pacific Interactive Media Corporation):
http://www.linder.com/berserk/bosbgc.html

Coalition for International Justice's War Criminals Watch:
http://www.wcw.org

Human Rights Watch/Helsinki Watch:
http://www.hrw.org

Institute for War and Peace Reporting (publishers of *WarReport*): http://www.demon.co.uk/iwpr/

International Court of Justice:
http://www.law.cornell.edu/icj/

International Crisis Group Bosnia Project: http://www.intl-crisis-group.org/projects/balkans.html

NATO in Bosnia: http://www.nato.int/ifor/i-other.htm

Office of the High Representative in Bosnia:
http://www.ohr.int

Open Media Research Institute (the source for the *OMRI Daily Digest*, renamed the *RFE/RL Newsline* in 1997):
http://www.omri.cz (for material until March 1997);
http://www.rferl.org/ (for current material)

Organization for Security and Cooperation in Europe
Mission in Bosnia: http://www.oscebih.org/

United Nations Commission of Experts on the Former
Yugoslavia: http://www.cij.org/cij/commission.html

United Nations International Criminal Tribunal for the
Former Yugoslavia: http://www.un.org/icty

Notes

Preface

1. Peter Maas, *Love Thy Neighbour: A Story of War* (London: Papermac, 1996), 185. Turajlić was shot in January 1993 by Bosnian Serb forces at a checkpoint near Sarajevo airport while in a UN armored vehicle.

2. Michel Foucault, *The Use of Pleasure*, vol. 2 of *The History of Sexuality*, trans. Robert Hurley (New York: Vintage Books, 1985), 10.

3. Ibid., 11.

4. "Polemics, Politics, and Problematizations: An Interview with Michel Foucault," in *The Foucault Reader*, ed. Paul Rabinow (New York: Pantheon Books, 1984), 389.

5. Michel Foucault, *Discipline and Punish: The Birth of the Prison*, trans. Alan Sheridan (New York: Vintage Books, 1979), 141–43, 170–94.

1. Ethics, Politics, and Responsibility

1. These accounts come from encounters during a visit to Bosnia in July and August 1996.

2. Similar sentiments were expressed by another survivor of the massacre, Murad Bektic. Like Ziad, Bektic believed that he could return to Srebrenica: "It is our land. We will not be separated from our land.... We lived together [with the Serbs] before and we can again as long as all the war criminals are handed over. Living together is possible." Quoted in "Srebrenica's New Serbs Stake Their Claim," *The Guardian*, 11 July 1996.

3. See Michael Ignatieff, "Introduction: Virtue by Proxy," in *International Perspectives on the Yugoslav Conflict*, ed. Alex Danchev and Thomas Halverson (Houndmills: Macmillan, 1996), xi–xiv. There have been many overly idealized renderings of Bosnia designed to mobilize the opposition to nationalism. For examples, see (despite its admirable aims), Salman Rushdie, "Bosnia on My Mind," *Index on Censorship* 23 (May/June 1994): 16–20. But the argument of this book will be that Ignatieff's claim that European intervention was "narcissistic" and designed to "save ourselves" focuses on the wrong object of desire. As chapters 5 and 6 will demonstrate, "we" intervened not to save the ideal of multiculturalism abroad; instead, "we" intervened to shore up the nationalist imaginary so as to contain the ideal of multiculturalism at home.

4. Allen Feldman, "On Cultural Anesthesia: From Desert Storm to Rodney King," *American Ethnologist* 21 (May 1994): 404–18; and McKenzie Wark, "Fresh Maimed Babies: The Uses of Innocence," *Transition* 65 (spring 1995): 36–47.

5. Michel Foucault, "Politics and Ethics: An Interview," in *The Foucault Reader*, ed. Paul Rabinow (New York: Pantheon, 1984), 377. For an extended discussion of this, along with the problems associated with the representation of "postmodernism" it contests, see the epilogue to my *Writing Security: United States Foreign Policy and the Politics of Identity*, rev. ed. (Minneapolis: University of Minnesota Press, 1998).

6. Michel Foucault, "What Is Enlightenment?" in *The Foucault Reader*, ed. Rabinow, 39.

7. Susan Sontag, *Against Interpretation and Other Essays* (New York: Octagon Books, 1986), 14.

8. John Gerard Ruggie, "Territoriality and Beyond: Problematizing Modernity in International Relations," *International Organization* 47 (1993): 145–46.

9. Jacques Derrida, "Like the Sound of the Sea Deep within a Shell: Paul de Man's War," trans. Peggy Kamuf, in *Responses: On Paul de Man's Wartime Journalism*, ed. Werner Hamacher, Neil Hertz, and Thomas Keenan (Lincoln: University of Nebraska Press, 1989), 132. For an impressive critique of Derrida's article, see David Carroll, "The Temptation of Fascism and the Question of Literature: Justice, Sorrow, and Political Error (An Open Letter to Jacques Derrida)," *Cultural Critique* 15 (1990): 39–81.

10. Rodolphe Gasché, "Edges of Understanding," in *Responses*, ed. Hamacher et al., 208.

11. Jürgen Habermas, "Work and Weltanschauung: The Heidegger Controversy from a German Perspective," *Critical Inquiry* 15 (1989): 433.

12. Gerald Graff, "Looking Past the De Man Case," in *Responses*, ed. Hamacher et al., 248.

13. David Lehman, *Signs of the Times: Deconstruction and the Fall of Paul de Man* (New York: Poseidon Press, 1991), 67, 84–85, 106–7.

14. The comparison was made by Jon Wiener, *Professors, Politics and Pop* (New York: Verso, 1991), 3. Critical responses can be found in Gasché, "Edges of Understanding," 209; and J. Hillis Miller, "An Open Letter to Professor Jon Wiener," in *Responses*, ed. Hamacher et al., 335.

15. Stephen Krasner, "The Accomplishments of International Political Economy," in *International Theory: Positivism and Beyond*, ed. Steve Smith, Ken Booth, and Maryisa Zalewski (Cambridge: Cambridge University Press, 1996), 124.

16. Ibid., 125. This is a common line of argument hardly confined to international relations. For example, see the conclusion in Terry Eagleton, *The Illusions of Postmodernism* (Oxford: Basil Blackwell, 1997).

17. Ibid.

18. Quoted in Rabia Ali and Lawrence Lifschultz, ed., introduction to *Why Bosnia? Writings on the Balkan War* (Stony Creek, Conn: Pamphleteer's Press, 1993), xix.

19. In BosNews (electronic bulletin board), 1 February 1995.

20. Quoted in Ali and Lifschultz, introduction to *Why Bosnia?* xxi.

21. For the exhibition catalogs, see, for example, *Genocid Nad Bošnkacima 1992–1995 / Genozid An Den Bosniaken 1992–1995 / Genocide upon the Bosniaks 1992–1995* (Tuzla and Wuppertal: Galerija Portreta Tuzla and Verlag Bosnanska Riječ—Das Bosnische Wort, 1996); and *Slike Rata Brčko 1992–1993* (Muslimanska Društva I Institucije Općine Brčko, n.d.). On the evening of 14 July 1996, Bosnian TV broadcast a lengthy account of the International Congress for the Documentation of Genocide in Bosnia and Herzegovina convened in Bonn, Germany, from 31 August to 4 September 1995.

(That broadcast was also notable for the prominence given to Haris Silajdžić, speaking to the conference as prime minister, even though he was at the time of transmission an opposition candidate in the September 1996 elections.) For a report on that conference, see "The Bonn Declaration on Genocide in Bosnia and Herzegovina, September 4th, 1995," in BosNet (Digest 391) (electronic bulletin board), 8 September 1995. For a historical account of previous genocides that is widely available in Bosnia, see Vladimir Dedijer and Autun Miletić, *Genocid Nad Muslimanima 1941–1945* (Sarajevo: Svjetlost, 1990).

22. Quoted in Christopher Hitchens, "Why Bosnia Matters," in *Why Bosnia?* ed. Ali and Lifschultz, 8–9.

23. T. D. Allman, "Serbia's Blood War," in *Why Bosnia?* ed. Ali and Lifschultz, 62. This representation is endorsed by those arguing that the media coverage of the war has been biased against the Serbs. See, for example, Carl G. Jacobsen, "Yugoslavia's Wars of Secession and Succession: Media Manipulation, Historical Amnesia, and Subjective Morality," *Mediterranean Quarterly* 5 (summer 1994): 24–41. For an argument that emphasizes the way in which this understanding obscures Serbia's complicity with the Nazis and collaboration in the Holocaust, see Philip J. Cohen, *Serbia's Secret War: Propaganda and the Deceit of History* (College Station: Texas A&M University Press, 1996).

24. David Solomon, "Holocaust Memory Haunts Serbs," *YugoFax* 1 (6 September 1991): 3.

25. Quoted in Robert Block, "The Madness of General Mladic," *New York Review of Books*, 5 October 1995, 8.

26. "Pro-Nazi Legacy Lingers of Croatia," *New York Times*, 31 October 1993; and "Nationalism Turns Rancid in Croatia," *New York Times*, 13 November 1993.

27. *OMRI Daily Digest* 26 (6 February 1996); *OMRI Daily Digest* 64 (29 March 1996); and *OMRI Daily Digest* 117 (17 June 1996).

28. *OMRI Daily Digest* 81 (24 April 1996), in BosNet (Digest 138), 24 April 1996.

29. For just two examples from the many available, see "Separating History from Myth: An Interview with Ivo Banac," in *Why Bosnia?* ed. Ali and Lifschultz; and "Bosnia Won't See Peace without a War," *Guardian Weekly*, 11 December 1994.

30. Slavenka Drakulić, *The Balkan Express: Fragments from the Other Side of the War* (New York: W. W. Norton and Company, 1993), 3.

31. Ibid., 143–46.

32. For a discussion of the meaning of "prosaics," see my "Political Prosaics, Transversal Politics, and the Anarchical World," in *Challenging Boundaries: Global Flows, Territorial Identities*, ed. Michael J. Shapiro and Hayward Alker (Minneapolis: University of Minnesota Press, 1996), especially 19–24.

33. I take this to be suggested, for example, by arguments such as Molly Cochran's account of so-called postmodern ethics, which concludes with the observation that all "the postmoderns" can do is offer critiques and warnings to "those engaged in the task of finding an ethical theory of international relations with content." Molly Cochran, "Postmodernism, Ethics, and International Political Theory," *Review of International Studies* 21 (1995): 250. For the idea that ethical theory in international relations usually involves the articulation of codes, norms, and rules, see Chris Brown, "Review Article: Theories of International Justice," *British Journal of Political Science* 27 (1997): 273–97.

34. Mervyn Frost, *Ethics and International Relations: A Constitutive Theory* (Cambridge: Cambridge University Press, 1996), 209; emphasis in the original.

35. This observation is akin to the argument made in Bonnie Honig, *Political Theory and the Displacement of Politics* (Ithaca, N.Y.: Cornell University Press, 1993).

36. For an overview of these perspectives in international relations, see *Traditions of International Ethics*, ed. Terry Nardin and David R. Mapel (Cambridge: Cambridge University Press, 1992).

37. For an introduction to the way in which the problematization of community puts responsibility into doubt, see Daniel Warner, "An Ethic of Responsibility in International Relations and the Limits of Responsibility/Community," *Alternatives* 18 (1993): 431–52.

38. Frost, *Ethics and International Relations*, ch. 4.

39. Ibid., 210. Presumably the United States is mistakenly absent from this list.

2. Violence and the Political

1. "Conference on Yugoslavia Arbitration Commission: Opinions on Questions Arising from the Dissolution of Yugoslavia," *International Legal Materials* 31 (1992): 1494. The commission, comprising five presidents from European constitutional courts, was established by the European Community on 27 August 1991 as part of the peace conference chaired by Lord Carrington. Headed by French jurist M. Robert Badinter, it is sometimes referred to as the Badinter Commission. Maurizio Ragazzi, "Introductory Note," ibid., 1488–89. A legal critique of the commission's work can be found in Hurst Hannum, "Self-Determination, Yugoslav, and Europe: Old Wine in New Bottles?" *Transnational Law and Contemporary Problems* 3 (spring 1993): 57–69.

2. "Conference on Yugoslavia Arbitration Commission," 1495.

3. Quoted in Marc Weller, "The International Response to the Dissolution of the Socialist Federal Republic of Yugoslavia," *American Journal of International Law* 86 (July 1992): 588 n.

4. Ibid., 586–88. For the conclusions about the recognition of the various republics, see "Conference on Yugoslavia Arbitration Commission," 1501–17.

5. Ragazzi, "Introductory Note," 1490.

6. "Conference on Yugoslavia Arbitration Commission," 1496–97.

7. Quoted in Weller, "The International Response to the Dissolution of the Socialist Federal Republic of Yugoslavia," 578.

8. "Conference on Yugoslavia Arbitration Commission," 1495. For legal discussions of this concept, see the articles in "Symposium: State Succession in the Former Soviet Union and in Eastern Europe," *Virginia Journal of International Law* 33 (winter 1993).

9. Quoted in Weller, "The International Response to the Dissolution of the Socialist Federal Republic of Yugoslavia," 595.

10. "Conference on Yugoslavia Arbitration Commission," 1519.

11. Ibid., 1523.

12. "Documents Regarding the Conflict in Yugoslavia," *International Legal Materials* 31 (1992): 1473.

13. Quoted in International Court of Justice, "Case Concerning Application of the Convention on the Prevention and Punishment of the Crime of Genocide (Bosnia and Herzegovina v. Yugoslavia [Serbia and Montenegro]), Request for the Indication of Provisional Measures, Order of 8 April 1993," in Francis A. Boyle, *The Bosnian People Charge Genocide: Proceedings at the International Court of Justice Concerning Bosnia v. Serbia on the Prevention and Punishment of the Crime of Genocide* (Amherst Mass.: Alethia Press, 1996), paragraphs 16 and 17, 166.

14. See Samuel Weber, "Piece Work," *Strategies* 9/10 (1996): 1–17.

15. In the context of the former Yugoslavia, this rendering is evident in James Gow, "Deconstructing Yugoslavia," *Survival* 23 (July/August 1991): 291–311; and William Ney,

"Two Trips to Sarajevo," *The New Combat* (autumn 1994): especially 62–63. Interestingly, Ney's views were not shared by the Sarajevan professor of philosophy with whom he talks during the siege.

16. These reflections on political conditions are paralleled by Derrida's remarks on the way in which thinkers such as Nietzsche, Heidegger, and Benjamin are associated both with destructive accounts of the history of the West at the end of the nineteenth century and affirmative accounts of the future. For Derrida this is not a contradiction but, rather, a testament to "the question of originary affirmation" in such thought: "However negative, however destructive one's account of the history of the West may have become at this time, something is calling thought from the future; it is this call which makes both the passage via destruction, and an affirmation with this destruction, absolutely necessary. . . . However important their thought is, they are symptoms of, spokesmen for something which is taking place in the world, at least in the West, which causes affirmation to be carried through by a devastating upheaval. . . . So, my question is the following: why is it that this re-affirmation can have a future only through the seism of a destruction? But that is hardly a question; rather, it is the experience of *what is taking place,* of the revolution which bears us along." "Nietzsche and the Machine: Interview with Jacques Derrida by Richard Beardsworth," *Journal of Nietzsche Studies* 7 (spring 1994): 23–24.

17. This linkage is clearly expressed in the preface to *Genocide after Emotion: The Postemotional Balkan War,* ed. Stjepan G. Meštrović (New York: Routledge, 1996).

18. Jacques Derrida, "The Time Is Out of Joint," trans. Peggy Kamuf, in *Deconstruction Is/In America: A New Sense of the Political,* ed. Anselm Haverkamp (New York: New York University Press, 1995), 25.

19. Ibid., 15.

20. Jacques Derrida, "Afterword: Toward an Ethic of Discussion," in Derrida, *Limited Inc* (Evanston Ill.: Northwestern University Press, 1988), 136.

21. Jacques Derrida, *Specters of Marx: The State of the Debt, the Work of Mourning, and the New International,* trans. Peggy Kamuf (New York: Routledge, 1994), 74.

22. Jacques Derrida, "Like the Sound of the Sea Deep within a Shell: Paul de Man's War," trans. Peggy Kamuf, in *Responses: On Paul de Man's Wartime Journalism,* ed. Werner Hamacher, Neil Hertz, and Thomas Keenan (Lincoln: University of Nebraska Press, 1989), 155.

23. William E. Connolly, "The Irony of Interpretation," in *The Politics of Irony: Essays in Self-Betrayal,* ed. Daniel W. Conway and John E. Seery (New York: St. Martins, 1992), 119.

24. Ibid., 145. In a subsequent articulation, Connolly speaks of this in terms of "positive ontopolitical interpretation." One reason for the emphasis on "positive" is that Connolly argues deconstruction, while "a related strategy of disturbance and detachment" that is "first and foremost an ethical project," nonetheless "refuses to pursue the trial of affirmative possibility very far, out of a desire to minimize its implication in ontological assumptions it could never vindicate without drawing upon some of the same media it has just rendered ambiguous." Part of the impetus behind this book is to explicate more fully the manner in which deconstruction's affirmations are better developed than is commonly recognized, especially by readings markedly less sensitive than Connolly's. See William E. Connolly, *The Ethos of Pluralization* (Minneapolis: University of Minnesota Press, 1995), 36.

25. Connolly, "The Irony of Interpretation," 147.

26. Richard Kearney, "Dialogue with Jacques Derrida," in Kearney, *Dialogues with Contemporary Continental Thinkers: The Phenomenological Heritage* (Manchester: Manchester University Press, 1984), 117–18.

27. Jacques Derrida, "Some Statements and Truisms about Neologisms, Newisms, Postisms, Parasitisms, and Other Small Seismisms," trans. Anne Tomiche, in *The States of "Theory": History, Art and Critical Discourse* (Stanford: Stanford University Press, 1990), 85.

28. Derrida, "The Time Is Out of Joint," 17.

29. This necessarily involves — as has the consideration of deconstructive thought to this point — the difficult task of condensing and foreshortening many of the complex themes in Derrida's writing. In addition to engaging relevant texts of Derrida's not considered here, Richard Beardsworth has demonstrated how considerations of the political are integral to much of Derrida's thought even when it is not marked overtly as political. See Richard Beardsworth, *Derrida and the Political* (London: Routledge, 1996).

30. Judith Butler, *Bodies That Matter: On the Discursive Limits of "Sex"* (New York: Routledge, 1993), 2. In my *Writing Security* (rev. ed. [Minneapolis: University of Minnesota Press, 1998]), the performative constitution of identity was the central theme, articulated there in terms of foreign policy and the state. Butler's earlier book (*Gender Trouble: Feminism and the Subversion of Identity* [New York: Routledge, 1990]) was influential in my thinking, and her refinements of the argument in *Bodies That Matter* are significant for the way the performative constitution of identity bears on the subjects of international relations. However, to align Butler with Derrida is not to suggest that their respective concepts of performance and the *coup de force* are identical. Nonetheless, Butler's reading of performativity through Austin and Derrida highlights the obvious affinity. Derrida's arguments in this regard were first articulated in "Signature, Event, Context," which is reprinted along with responses to the controversy it sparked in Derrida, *Limited Inc.* Butler's debts are evident in her "For a Careful Reading," in Seyla Benhabib, Judith Butler, Drucilla Cornell, and Nancy Fraser, *Feminist Contentions: A Philosophical Exchange* (New York: Routledge, 1995), 133–36; and *Excitable Speech: A Politics of the Performative* (New York: Routledge, 1997).

31. Some of the debate surrounding the various notions of constructivism increasingly prominent in the study of international relations is considered in the epilogue to the revised edition of my *Writing Security*.

32. Butler, *Bodies That Matter*, 4–12.

33. Ernesto Laclau and Chantal Mouffe, *Hegemony and Socialist Strategy: Towards a Radical Democratic Politics*, trans. Winston Moore and Paul Cammack (London: Verso, 1985), 108. This is the third occasion on which I have included this formulation as a vital predicate in my arguments. It is repeated here because the difficulty in conveying the importance of this move and its effects is one of the most common sources of critiques for arguments such as this. I would be a rich person if I had had a contribution in any currency from respondents each time they said something along the lines of "yes, but what about the external reality/material conditions/real world"! For those earlier uses, see my *Writing Security*, 6; and *Politics without Principle: Sovereignty, Ethics, and the Narratives of the Gulf War* (Boulder: Lynne Rienner, 1993), 9.

34. Butler, *Bodies That Matter*, 9, 12; emphasis in the original.

35. In addition to my *Writing Security*, see Cynthia Weber, *Simulating Sovereignty: Intervention, the State and Symbolic Exchange* (Cambridge: Cambridge University Press, 1994); Weber, "Performative States" (paper presented to the International Political Theory Group, Keele University, 2 April 1997); Roxanne Lynne Doty, *Imperial Encounters: The Politics of Representation in North-South Relations* (Minneapolis: University of Minnesota Press, 1996); G. M. Dillon and Jerry Everard, "Stat(e)ing Australia: Squid Jigging and the Masque of State," *Alternatives* 17 (summer 1992): 281–312; and François Debrix, "Deploying Vision, Simulating Action: The United Nations and Its Visualization

Strategies in a New World Order," *Alternatives* 21 (January-March 1996): 67–92. In one way or another we are all indebted to Richard Ashley's work; see, especially, Ashley, "Untying the Sovereign State: A Double Reading of the Anarchy Problematique," *Millennium: Journal of International Studies* 17 (1988): 227–62.

36. Jacques Derrida, "Force of Law: The 'Mystical Foundation of Authority,'" in *Deconstruction and the Possibility of Justice*, ed. Drucilla Cornell, Michael Rosenfeld, and David Gray Carlson (New York: Routledge, 1992).

37. Jacques Derrida, "Declarations of Independence," trans. Tom Keenan and Tom Pepper, *New Political Science* 15 (1976): 10. A similar reading of this, along with a good explication of the performative, can be found in Bonnie Honig, *Political Theory and the Displacement of Politics* (Ithaca, N.Y.: Cornell University Press, 1993), ch. 4.

38. Jacques Derrida, "The Laws of Reflection: Nelson Mandela, in Admiration," in *For Nelson Mandela*, ed. Jacques Derrida and Mustapha Tlili (New York: Seaver Books, 1987), 18.

39. Renata Salecl, "The Crisis of Identity and the Struggle for New Hegemony in the Former Yugoslavia," in *The Making of Political Identities*, ed. Ernesto Laclau (London and New York: Verso, 1994), 213.

40. For a good discussion of the symbolic politics of genocide, see Bette Denich, "Dismembering Yugoslavia: Nationalist Ideologies and the Symbolic Revival of Genocide," *American Ethnologist* 21 (May 1994): 367–90.

41. Derrida, "Force of Law," 14.

42. Ibid.

43. Ibid., 13–14.

44. Ibid., 35.

45. Ibid., 19.

46. Ibid., 14.

47. This point is overlooked by those who blithely offer rationalism as a counter to barbarism. For a clear example, see Eric Hobsbawm, "Barbarism: A User's Guide," *New Left Review* 206 (July/August 1994): 44–54.

48. Martin Heidegger, "The Principle of Reason," in Heidegger, *The Principle of Reason*, trans. Reginald Lilly (Bloomington and Indianapolis: Indiana University Press, 1991), 120–21.

49. Ibid., 129.

50. Jacques Derrida, "The Principle of Reason: The University in the Eyes of Its Pupils," trans. Catherine Porter and Edward P. Morris, *Diacritics* (fall 1983): 7–8.

51. Ibid., 9.

52. Ibid.

53. Ibid., 18–19.

54. Derrida, "Force of Law," 14.

55. Ibid., 14.

56. Ibid., 19.

3. Ontopology

1. Discussion from the forum on refugees, University of Tuzla, 2 August 1996.

2. This phrase comes from the memorial to the victims of the massacre in the old town of Tuzla. The massacre has also been memorialized in a book titled *Ubistvo Svitanja: Civilne Žrtve Rata u Tuzli* (Tuzla: Godine, 1996).

3. In so doing, I want to expand on thoughts that I first articulated in relation to the Gulf War of 1990–91 in my *Politics without Principle: Sovereignty, Ethics, and the*

Narratives of the Gulf War (Boulder: Lynne Rienner, 1993), especially chapter 1. White's major works are *Metahistory: The Historical Imagination in Nineteenth-Century Europe* (Baltimore: Johns Hopkins University Press, 1973), *Tropics of Discourse: Essays in Cultural Criticism* (Baltimore: Johns Hopkins University Press, 1978), and *The Content of the Form: Narrative Discourse and Historical Representation* (Baltimore: Johns Hopkins University Press, 1987). The concern with narrative in history is, of course, not restricted to White's work. For an account of others prior to White who shared this focus, see David Carr, *Time, Narrative, and History* (Bloomington: Indiana University Press, 1986), 7–8.

4. Peter Novick, *That Noble Dream: The "Objectivity Question" and the American Historical Profession* (Cambridge: Cambridge University Press, 1988), 606–12. These quotes are at 606–7.

5. For White's reflections on his position, see Ewa Domanska, "Interview/Hayden White," *Diacritics* 24 (spring 1994): 91–100. The recent poststructuralist drift in White is noted by Wulf Kansteiner, "Hayden White's Critique of the Writing of History," *History and Theory* 32 (1993): especially 285–86.

6. White, "The Historical Text as Literary Artifact," in *Tropics of Discourse*, 81.

7. White, "The Value of Narrativity in the Representation of Reality," in *The Content of the Form*, 1.

8. Ibid., 24.

9. Ibid., 4–5, 16.

10. Ibid., 2.

11. The number of story structures White's argument explicitly deals with is limited to four: romance, tragedy, comedy, and satire. Each of these plots mandates a respective mode of argument (formist, mechanicist, organicist, contextualist), ideology (anarchist, radical, conservative, liberal), and dominant trope (metaphor, metonymy, synecdoche, irony). However, White stresses that this does not exhaust the modes of emplotment; it only highlights those useful for classifying particular historical works. See White, *Metahistory*, introduction, especially 7. In deploying White in this argument I am less interested in the relevance of these specific story structures and their entailments for political accounts (though, as we shall see, tragedy often comes to the fore) than the general argument about narratives and their emplotment.

12. White, "The Fictions of Factual Representation," in *Tropics of Discourse*, 121.

13. White, "The Historical Text as Literary Artifact," 82.

14. White, "The Question of Narrative in Contemporary Historical Theory," in *The Content of the Form*, 44.

15. Domanska, "Interview/Hayden White," 97.

16. White, "The Value of Narrativity in the Representation of Reality," 20.

17. Ibid., 24.

18. White, "The Politics of Historical Interpretation," in *The Content of the Form*, 75.

19. White, "The Value of Narrativity in the Representation of Reality," 20.

20. Alex Callinicos, *Theories and Narratives: Reflections on the Philosophy of History* (Oxford: Polity Press, 1995), 66.

21. Saul Friedlander, introduction to *Probing the Limits of Representation: Nazism and the "Final Solution,"* ed. Saul Friedlander (Cambridge: Harvard University Press, 1992), 1.

22. Ibid., 20.

23. Quoted in Carlo Ginzburg, "Just One Witness," in Friedlander, ed., *Probing the Limits of Representation*, 86. For a full discussion of these points, see Pierre Vidal-Naquet, *Assassins of Memory: Essays on the Denial of the Holocaust* (New York: Columbia University Press, 1993).

24. Friedlander, introduction to *Probing the Limits of Representation*, 20; emphasis added.

25. Christopher R. Browning, "German Memory, Judicial Interrogation, and Historical Reconstruction: Writing Perpetrator History from Postwar Testimony," in Friedlander, ed., *Probing the Limits of Representation*, 339 n. This line of argument, echoing that of Krasner and Ruggie discussed in chapter 1, is associated with deconstruction and de Man in Deborah Lipstadt, *Denying the Holocaust: The Growing Assault on Truth and Memory* (London: Penguin, 1993), 17–19, 29. As with Krasner's and Ruggie's position, it is short on philosophical acuity.

26. White, "The Politics of Historical Interpretation," in *The Content of the Form*, 76.

27. Ibid.

28. Ibid.

29. Ibid., 77–78.

30. Browning, "German Memory, Judicial Interrogation, and Historical Reconstruction," 32. Significantly, White's point would prevent the very historical inquiry Browning undertakes — reconstructing the murderous activities of a police unit that is absent from any documentary account of the Holocaust. See also Martin Jay, "Of Plots, Witnesses, and Judgements," in Friedlander, ed., *Probing the Limits of Representation*.

31. White, "The Historical Text as Literary Artifact," 84. This suggests the intersubjective constraints of audience and professional community indicated by Jay, "Of Plots, Witnesses, and Judgements," 105.

32. Hayden White, "Historical Emplotment and the Problem of Truth," in Friedlander, ed., *Probing the Limits of Representation*, 40.

33. White, "The Question of Narrative in Contemporary Historical Theory," 45.

34. Perry Anderson, "On Emplotment: Two Kinds of Ruin," in Friedlander, ed., *Probing the Limits of Representation*, 64–65.

35. Callinicos, *Theories and Narratives*, 76.

36. Ibid., 78.

37. White, "Historicism, History, and the Figurative Imagination," in *Tropics of Discourse*, 110.

38. Jay, "Of Plots, Witnesses, and Judgements," 98–99. This is also the case in contexts less textually concerned than history. In archaeology, for example, the material record used to construct cultural sequences needs to be appreciated for the way in which it is embedded in narratives prior to its emplotment by archaeologists. See Ian Hodder, "The Narrative and Rhetoric of Material Culture Sequences," *World Archeology* 25 (1993): 268–82.

39. As Michael André Bernstein has noted, the term *Holocaust* has its own genealogy that makes it problematic for some. *Holocaust* is derived from the Greek *holokauston* and was used in the sense of "totally consumed by fire." It has been deployed to refer to sacrifice by fire, such that in its English usage in the sixteenth and seventeenth centuries, it invoked this sense of religious burnt offering, and sacrifice more generally. In contrast, the Hebrew terms *shoah* (meaning "wasteland" or "destruction") and *churban* ("destruction") have sometimes been used because they imply a historical turning point, but reject the notion of sacrifice. In the end, *Holocaust* in the sense we now know it, to signify the Nazi genocide, did not become common until 1957–59. Michael André Bernstein, *Foregone Conclusions: Against Apocalyptic History* (Berkeley: University of California Press, 1994), 132 n.

40. Jay, "Of Plots, Witnesses, and Judgements," 104. For an argument that similarly contests White's desire to avoid the politics of representation when it comes to the Holocaust, see Hans Kellner, " 'Never Again' Is Now," *History and Theory* 33 (1994): 127–44.

41. James E. Young, *Writing and Rewriting the Holocaust: Narrative and the Consequences of Interpretation* (Bloomington: Indiana University Press, 1988), 4–5.

42. The notion of micro- and macronarratives is suggested by the account of first- and second-order narratives in Jay, "Of Plots, Witnesses, and Judgements," 103–4. It resonates also with Arjun Appadurai's reflections on ethnography in a deterritorialized and globalizing world, where macronarratives legitimize the security strategies that micronarratives contest. See Arjun Appadurai, *Modernity at Large: Cultural Dimensions of Globalization* (Minneapolis: University of Minnesota Press, 1996), especially chapter 3. However, in this chapter, my focus is on the narratives that secure identities; the resistances are mostly dealt with in chapters 4 and 7.

43. White, *Metahistory*, 432–33.

44. Ibid., 26.

45. White, "The Politics of Historical Interpretation," 74. This critique is the central argument in Ginzburg, "Just One Witness."

46. Amos Funkenstein, "History, Counterhistory, and Narrative," in Friedlander, ed., *Probing the Limits of Representation*, 79; emphasis added.

47. Ibid., 80.

48. Ibid., 69.

49. Ibid., 80–81.

50. Jay, "Of Plots, Witnesses, and Judgements," 104.

51. Ibid.

52. There are, of course, any number of actors that could be considered at this point, but the focus will be on two key protagonists, thereby excluding a discussion of Bosnian Croat representative practices. This should not be read as embodying either an attribution or an absolution of responsibility. This concern makes the representation of "Bosnia" in this argument an issue to be examined. Because the mapping of Bosnia as a place populated by the coherent and settled identities of "Serbs," "Croats," and "Muslims" is being contested, it would in one sense be desirable to offer and use (except when quoting from others) an alternative set of representations. Despite this, in a number of places the book reluctantly persists — even as it wants to problematize them — with national categorizations. This is not entirely satisfactory but testifies to the way language cannot easily accommodate hybridity, and to the power of the national imaginary in Bosnia, for even though the contingent character of such terms is easily identified, alternative summary representations are more difficult to imagine.

53. Karadžić's remarks, which were made immediately after the fall of Srebrenica, come from an interview to the Spanish weekly *El Pais*, in BosNet (Digest 337) (electronic bulletin board), 16 July 1995.

54. International Court of Justice, Public sitting, Friday 2 April 1993, Verbatim record, in Francis A. Boyle, *The Bosnian People Charge Genocide: Proceedings at the International Court of Justice Concerning Bosnia v. Serbia on the Prevention and Punishment of the Crime of Genocide* (Amherst, Mass.: Alethia Press, 1996), 124–25. This position was rejected by all but two of the justices, one of whom was appointed by Yugoslavia to sit on the court for this case. Nonetheless, Yugoslavia persisted with this argument in later hearings in an (unsuccessful) attempt to have the International Court of Justice dismiss Bosnia's application. Details of this important case will be discussed in chapter 4. However, in its consideration of whether the "grave breaches" provisions of the Geneva Convention applied to Dusan Tadic, the International Criminal Tribunal for the Former Yugoslavia (ICTY) determined in its verdict (albeit with the presiding judge in dissent) that although the Bosnian Serb army was highly dependent on the Serbian army and both pursued complementary strategic goals, the JNA's official declaration on 19 May

1992 of its withdrawal from Bosnia made the conflict an "internal" rather than "international" affair. Details of the reasoning behind this contested conclusion are available on the ICTY's World Wide Web site (see the Note on Sources). The ICTY's verdict depended on intricate concerns about how to judge an agent's responsibility, and run contrary to the amassed political evidence of the illusory nature of the withdrawal and subsequent Serbian military involvement in Bosnia, some of which is discussed in the next chapter.

55. "Peace Pact—Hint of War," *New York Times,* 22 November 1995.

56. Quoted in "Exuding Confidence, Serbian Nationalists Act as If War for Bosnia Is Won," *New York Times,* 23 May 1993.

57. Quoted in "Bosnia: From Appeasement to Genocide," *Sydney Morning Herald,* 3 December 1994.

58. Views reported in "In Dream of 'Greater Serbia,' the Serbs Find Suffering and Decay," *New York Times,* 17 September 1995.

59. "Serbs Invoke Past," *New York Times,* 8 September 1995.

60. "Serbian General Who Calls the Shots," *New York Times,* 17 April 1994.

61. "Through the Serbian Mind's Eye," *New York Times,* 10 April 1994.

62. "Karadzic Welcomes Serbian Patriarch," *OMRI Daily Digest* 80 (24 April 1995).

63. "Greek Volunteers Fight with Bosnian Serbs," *OMRI Daily Digest* 108 (5 June 1995); "Greek Volunteers Fought alongside Bosnian Serbs," *OMRI Daily Digest* 136 (14 July 1995).

64. "Belgrade Meeting Backs Peace Plan," *New York Times,* 15 May 1993.

65. "Bosnia Enclave Looks Ahead Wearily," *New York Times,* 24 December 1995.

66. Quoted in "In Dream of 'Greater Serbia,' the Serbs Find Suffering and Decay."

67. Quoted in "NATO Show of Force May Strengthen Serb Leader's Support," *Los Angeles Times,* 27 May 1995.

68. Monitoring Summary of World Broadcasts, BBC Monitoring Service, 12 July 1995, BosNet (Digest 336), 14 July 1995.

69. Quoted in Thomas Harrison, "A Question of International Solidarity," in *Why Bosnia? Writings on the Balkan War,* ed. Rabia Ali and Lawrence Lifschultz (Stony Creek, Conn.: Pamphleteer's Press, 1993), 181–82.

70. Quoted in Laura Silber and Alan Little, *The Death of Yugoslavia,* rev. ed. (London: Penguin Books, 1996), 208.

71. "Bosnians Open Old Prayer Book," *BosNews* (electronic bulletin board), 19 April 1995.

72. "Izetbegović Speech on the Day of Bosnian Independence," *BosNews,* 2 March 1995.

73. David Rieff, "We Hate You," *The New Yorker,* 4 September 1995, 43.

74. "Boutros-Ghali Hints There May Be More Air Strikes," *New York Times,* 27 May 1995; "57 Killed during the Week Ending June 19th," press release, Embassy of the Republic of Bosnia and Herzegovina, Washington, D.C., 23 June 1995; and "Crisis in Srebrenica; Bosnia Calls for Air Strikes," press release, Embassy of the Republic of Bosnia and Herzegovina, Washington, D.C., 9 July 1995.

75. This was the objection raised by the Bosnian delegation at the Budapest meeting of the Conference on Security and Cooperation in Europe, 4–5 December 1994. Quoted in "Whatever You Do, Don't Mention the War—in '94," *Sydney Morning Herald,* 10 December 1994.

76. "Application of the Republic of Bosnia and Herzegovina, 20 March 1993," in Boyle, *The Bosnian People Charge Genocide,* 4.

77. International Court of Justice, Public sitting, Thursday 1 April 1993, Verbatim record, in Boyle, *The Bosnian People Charge Genocide,* 106.

78. Ibid., 97.

79. Noel Malcolm, " 'The Whole Lot of Them Are Serbs,' " *The Spectator* 10 June 1995, 18. The Owen quote is from David Rieff, "On Your Knees with the Dying," in *Why Bosnia?* ed. Ali and Lifschultz, 21.

80. Rasim Hurem, "Open Letter to Mr Thorvald Stoltenberg," 29 June 1995, in Bos-Net (Digest 329), 9 July 1995. This invocation of a distinct and settled Bosnian/Muslim identity as the basis for mobilization is not uncommon. In an argument designed to counter the notion that American involvement in Bosnia would lead to another Vietnam, one columnist wrote that "in Bosnia, unlike Vietnam, nationalism works for us as well as against us. Our ally isn't some puppet government with a dubious claim to popular allegiance; it is an ethnically and religiously distinct group whose security and identity are deeply at stake." "TRB from Washington: Who Lost Bosnia?" *New Republic,* 29 May 1995.

81. "Sarajevo Postcard: Il Postino," *New Republic,* 25 March 1996.

82. The first three quotes are from Robert J. Donia and John V. A. Fine, *Bosnia and Hercegovina: A Tradition Betrayed* (London: Hurst and Company, 1994), 7–8; the fourth from Ali and Lifschultz, introduction to *Why Bosnia?* xiii.

83. Anthony Borden, *The Bosnians: A War on Identity* (London: Institute for War and Peace Reporting, 1993), 2. The focus here will be on U.S. politicians and arguments. This is in part because of the argument of Susan Woodward, who identifies a contrast between the American versus European framing of the conflict. See Susan Woodward, *Balkan Tragedy: Chaos and Dissolution after the Cold War* (Washington, D.C.: Brookings Institution, 1995), 7. Woodward maintains that the notion of civil/ethnic war was common in Europe and Canada but less so in the United States. While agreeing with her reading of the European situation, the argument here, by concerning itself primarily with American spokespeople, argues that the notion of civil/ethnic war, and its attendant assumptions, was at least as common in official American circles. For an account of American discourse that emphasizes the clash between positions that invoked historical analogies of the Holocaust and those that emphasized Vietnam, see Gearóid Ó Tuathail, *Critical Geopolitics: The Politics of Writing Global Space* (Minneapolis: University of Minnesota Press, 1996), chapter 6.

84. "An 'American Renewal': Transcript of the Address by President Clinton," *New York Times,* January 21, 1993.

85. Quoted in "Bosnia Reconsidered," *New York Times,* 8 April 1993. The remarks were made on 28 March 1993 on CBS News *Face the Nation.*

86. Marshall Harris, introduction to Boyle, *The Bosnian People Charge Genocide,* xv–xvi. Harris worked in the office that was asked for these data, and later resigned from the State Department in protest against U.S. policy. The counterargument to Christopher was made by the Deputy Assistant Secretary of State for Human Rights and Humanitarian Affairs, James K. Bishop. See "U.S. Memo Reveals Dispute on Bosnia," *New York Times,* 25 June 1993.

87. "U.S. Goal on Bosnia: Keeping the War within Borders," *New York Times,* 19 May 1993.

88. Harris, introduction to Boyle, *The Bosnian People Charge Genocide,* xi.

89. "Excerpts from Clinton News Conference: 'The U.S. Should Lead' on Bosnia," *New York Times,* 24 April 1993.

90. Ibid.

91. Harris, "Introduction," in Boyle, *The Bosnian People Charge Genocide,* xiii.

92. The genocide representation was endorsed by the all-party congressional Commission on Security and Cooperation in Europe. See, for example, the report of their April 1995 hearings in "Hearing of the CSCE," BosNews, 5 April 1995.

93. Harris, introduction to Boyle, *The Bosnian People Charge Genocide*, xix. Harris attended this luncheon and attributes the statement to Tim Wirth.

94. "Backing Away Again, Christopher Says Bosnia Is Not a Vital Interest," *New York Times*, 4 June 1993.

95. "U.S. Rejects Plea to Act in Bosnia," *New York Times*, 25 January 1994.

96. "Perry Calls Time on Bosnia Drift," *Manchester Guardian Weekly*, 11 December 1994.

97. Quoted in Michael Sells, "Religion, History, and Genocide in Bosnia-Herzegovina," in *Religion and Justice in the War over Bosnia*, ed. G. Scott Davis (New York: Routledge, 1996), 23.

98. Quoted in Chandler Rosenberger, "More to Bosnia than 'Ethnic Hatreds,'" *Wall Street Journal*, 25 September 1995.

99. "Clinton's Address to American Nation on Bosnia Mission," *New York Times*, 28 November 1995.

100. "The Silent Opposition," *New York Times*, 27 November 1995.

101. "US Analysts Oppose Plan for Bosnian 'Safe Havens,'" *International Herald Tribune*, 10 June 1993.

102. Yahaya M. Sadowski, "Bosnia's Muslims: A Fundamentalist Threat?" *Brookings Review* 13 (January 1995): 10. On this "Islamophobia" and its questionable grounding in the writings of Bosnian president Izetbegović, see John Kelsay, "Bosnia and the Muslim Critique of Modernity," in *Religion and Justice in the War over Bosnia*, ed. Davis.

103. A good overview of the arms issue can be found in "Hypocrisy in Action: What's the Real Iran-Bosnia Scandal?" *The New Yorker*, 13 May 1996. For accounts of Iranian forces in Bosnia, see "NATO Swoops on Bosnian 'Terror Camp,'" *The Guardian*, 17 February 1996; and "Secrets and Lies in Bosnia," *The Guardian*, 13 June 1996.

104. Quoted in "How the CIA Intercepted SAS Signals," *The Guardian*, 29 January 1996. An account of the ethnic and historical prejudices evident in briefing memoranda provided for British forces in Bosnia can be found in Francis Wheen, "Portillo's Balkan Blind Spot," *The Guardian*, 28 May 1997.

105. UNPROFOR strategic maps were sometimes titled *Warring Faction Update*. See Timothy Garton Ash, "Bosnia in Our Future," *New York Review of Books*, 21 December 1995.

106. "London Briefing—January 19, 1995," Bosnia Hercegovina Information Centre, London, in BosNews, 19 January 1995.

107. "UN Commanders in Bosnia to Rely upon Technology," *New York Times*, 15 February 1994.

108. Quoted in Christopher Hitchens, "Minority Report," *The Nation*, 12–19 June 1995. Hitchens was reviewing and quoting from Norman Cigar, *Genocide in Bosnia: The Policy of "Ethnic Cleansing"* (College Station: Texas A&M University Press, 1995).

109. "Hostages to a Brutal Past," *US News and World Report*, 15 February 1993.

110. For articles from the print media in Australia, Britain, and the United States containing these and other representations, see "Old Tribal Rivalries in Eastern Europe Pose Threat of Infection," *New York Times*, 13 October 1991; "Serbs Savour Ancient Hatreds," *Manchester Guardian Weekly*, 27 December 1992; "Europe's New Tribalism Could Infect Us All," *Manchester Guardian Weekly*, 7 February 1993; "Meddling in the Balkans: A Peril of the Ages," *New York Times*, 11 April 1993; "As Ethnic Wars Multiply, U.S. Strives for a Policy," *New York Times*, 7 February 1993; "Balkan War Has Left the West Powerless—and New Threats Loom," *Sydney Morning Herald*, 28 November 1994; and "Seeds of Balkan Imbroglio Planted in Centuries Past," *Canberra Times*, 20 June 1995.

111. "Editorial: Peace in Bosnia," *New York Times*, 22 November 1995.

112. "No Movement in Bid to Restart Bosnia Talks," *Chicago Tribune*, 28 January 1995.

113. A. M. Rosenthal, "Why Only Bosnia?" *New York Times*, 30 May 1995.

114. William Safire, "Break the Siege," *New York Times*, 15 June 1995. See Samuel P. Huntington, "The Clash of Civilizations," *Foreign Affairs* 72 (summer 1993): 22–49.

115. Gearóid Ó Tuathail, "An Anti-Geopolitical Eye: Maggie O'Kane in Bosnia, 1992–93," *Gender, Place and Culture* 3 (1996): 171–85.

116. In an analysis of news coverage of Bosnia and Rwanda in American print media — which itself begins with the observation that both countries "have been embroiled in brutal civil wars" (21) — Myers, Klak, and Koehl paint a less-ethnicized picture of Bosnian reporting than is suggested here, a conclusion I would argue is colored by their comparison with the limitations of the Rwanda reporting they rightly stress. See Garth Myers, Thomas Klak, and Timothy Koehl, "The Inscription of Difference: News Coverage of the Conflicts in Rwanda and Bosnia," *Political Geography* 15 (1996): 21–46.

117. Francis Wheen, "Winner in a War of Words," *The Guardian*, 2 August 1995.

118. Bogdan Denitch, *Ethnic Nationalism: The Tragic Death of Yugoslavia*, rev. ed. (Minneapolis: University of Minnesota Press, 1996), 17.

119. Ibid.

120. Ibid., 32–33. For more on this contested debate, see Ivo Goldstein, "The Use of History: Croatian Historiography and Politics," *Helsinki Monitor* 5 (1994): 85–97.

121. For an argument that highlights this feature with respect to Yugoslavia, see Ivo Banac, "Historiography of the Countries of Eastern Europe: Yugoslavia," *American Historical Review* 97 (October 1992): 1084–1104.

122. Those single-authored monographs include Christopher Bennett, *Yugoslavia's Bloody Collapse* (London: Hurst and Co., 1995); Lenard J. Cohen, *Broken Bonds: Yugoslavia's Disintegration and Balkan Politics in Transition*, 2d ed. (Boulder: Westview, 1995); Mihailo Crnobrnja, *Yugoslav Drama*, 2d ed. (London: I. B. Tauris, 1996); Denitch, *Ethnic Nationalism*; Paul Mojzes, *Yugoslavian Inferno* (New York: Continuum, 1994); Edgar O'Ballance, *Civil War in Bosnia* (London: Macmillan, 1995); Sabrina Petra Ramet, *Balkan Babel: The Disintegration of Yugoslavia from the Death of Tito to Ethnic War*, 2d ed. (Boulder: Westview Press, 1996); Silber and Little, *The Death of Yugoslavia*; and John Zametica, *The Yugoslav Conflict* (London: Institute of International Strategic Studies, 1992).

123. For an example, see White, "The Value of Narrativity in the Representation of Reality," 6–10.

124. Ibid., 16.

125. David Owen, *Balkan Odyssey* (London: Victor Gollancz, 1995), 46.

126. White, "The Value of Narrativity in the Representation of Reality," 20.

127. Mojzes, *Yugoslavian Inferno*, 87–91; Woodward, *Balkan Tragedy*, 7–8.

128. While *Broken Bonds* makes no mention of Serbian Autonomous Regions in Bosnia, it does note in passing (142) that the SDS in Croatia proposed a Krajina state encompassing Serb areas in Croatia and Bosnia.

129. John (as he was then) Zametica, "Squeezed Off Map," *Manchester Guardian Weekly*, 23 May 1993.

130. See, for example, the report "Karadzic Wants 64% of Bosnia," *OMRI Daily Digest* 165 (24 August 1995). The meaning, let alone political significance, of "legal possession," "ownership," or "registration" in prewar Bosnia is a complex affair. As a republic within a socialist state that possessed a unique system of social ownership, rendering these issues in terms common to capitalist property relations is a questionable

move, albeit with clear political consequences. For a discussion of the Yugoslav situation, see Branko Horvat, *The Yugoslav Economic System* (White Plains, N.Y.: International Arts and Sciences Press, 1976).

The Zametica argument is contested by a map produced in Sarajevo, which maintains (using the same contestable categories) that 53 percent of Bosnia was "state owned," with only 28 percent "privately owned." See *Zemljišna Karta Sa Nacionalnom Strukturom Republike Bosne I Hercegovine* (Sarajevo: JP Geodetski Zavod BiH, 1992).

131. In this link between the condition of global cultures and the conflict in the Balkans, Denitch shares affinities with the dubious perspective of Stjepan Mestrović's *The Balkanization of the West: The Confluence of Postmodernism and Postcommunism* (New York: Routledge, 1994).

132. Ramet, *Balkan Babel*, 153–56. The comparative point is made by Andras Riedlmayer in a newspaper report: see "For Refugees, A Lament for Loss and Vigil for Peace—Bosnians Here Saw Religious Tolerance before Balkan War, Say Nationalism, Not Religion Ignited War," *Washington Post*, 9 December 1995. For an account that emphasizes the religious dimensions of the Bosnian war, see Michael Sells, *The Bridge Betrayed: Religion and Genocide in Bosnia* (Berkeley: University of California Press, 1996).

133. This phrasing of equivalence marked a change from the first edition, which declared more boldly that "if our book has a single core thesis, it's this: that under Milošević's stewardship, the Serbs were, from the beginning of Yugoslavia's disintegration, the key secessionists." Laura Silber and Allan Little, *The Death of Yugoslavia* (London: BBC Books, 1995), xxiv.

134. Timothy Mitchell, "The Object of Development: America's Egypt," in *Power of Development*, ed. Jonathan Crush (New York: Routledge, 1995), 130.

135. See Bennett, *Yugoslavia's Bloody Collapse*, xiv; Cohen, *Broken Bonds*, 25; Crnobrnja, *The Yugoslav Drama*, 16; Denitch, *Ethnic Nationalism*, title page; Mojzes, *Yugoslavian Inferno*, x; O'Ballance, *Civil War in Bosnia*; Ramet, *Balkan Babel*, xxvii; Silber and Little, *The Death of Yugoslavia*, vi; Woodward, *Balkan Tragedy*, map 1; Zametica, *The Yugoslav Conflict*, 2.

136. J. B. Harley, "Maps, Knowledge, and Power," in *The Iconography of Landscape: Essays on the Symbolic Representation, Design, and Use of Past Environments*, ed. Denis Cosgrove and Stephen Daniels (Cambridge: Cambridge University Press, 1988), 278.

137. Ibid., 287.

138. See Benedict Anderson, *Imagined Communities: Reflections on the Origin and Spread of Nationalism*, rev. ed. (London: Verso, 1991), 170–78; and Jacqueline Urla, "Cultural Politics in an Age of Statistics: Numbers, Nations, and the Making of Basque Identity," *American Ethnologist* 20 (November 1993): 824–25.

139. Michel Foucault, *The History of Sexuality*, vol. 1, trans. Robert Hurley (New York: Pantheon, 1978), 25.

140. Urla, "Cultural Politics in an Age of Statistics," 820.

141. Anderson, *Imagined Communities*, 174. Anderson discusses the census at 164–70.

142. Woodward, *Balkan Tragedy*, 429 n; Anthony Borden, *The Bosnians: A War on Identity* (London: Institute for War and Peace Reporting, 1993), 4–5. Silber and Little, *The Death of Yugoslavia*, 229, argue that the nationalization of "Muslim" is not complete until the 1974 constitution. For reflections on the problematic character of "Bosnian/Muslim" in contemporary discourse, see Woodward, *Balkan Tragedy*, 298–302; and Norman Fairclough, " 'Mainly Muslim': Discourse and Barbarism in Bosnia," *Discourse and Society* 5 (1994): 431–32.

143. See Bennett, *Yugoslavia's Bloody Collapse*, 180; Cohen, *Broken Bonds*, 139, 241; Crnobrnja, *The Yugoslav Drama*, 22; Denitch, *Ethnic Nationalism*, 28–29; Mojzes, *Yugosla-*

vian Inferno, 33; O'Ballance, *Civil War in Bosnia*, vii; Ramet, *Balkan Babel*, 1, 186, 244; Silber and Little, *The Death of Yugoslavia*, 231; Woodward, *Balkan Tragedy*, 32–35; Zametica, *The Yugoslav Conflict*, 36.

144. For example, Mojzes, *Yugoslavian Inferno*, x; Woodward, *Balkan Tragedy*, 226–27.

145. Ramet, *Balkan Babel*, chs. 1–3; Silber and Little, *The Death of Yugoslavia*, chs. 1–11; and Woodward, *Balkan Tragedy*, ch. 3.

146. Bennett, *Yugoslavia's Bloody Collapse*, chs. 2–5; Cohen, *Broken Bonds*, ch. 1; Crnobrnja, *The Yugoslav Drama*, chs. 1–4; Denitch, *Ethnic Nationalism*, ch. 1; Mojzes, *Yugoslavian Inferno*, chs. 2–3.

147. Jacques Derrida, *Specters of Marx: The State of the Debt, the Work of Mourning, and the New International*, trans. Peggy Kamuf (New York: Routledge, 1994), 82.

148. Ibid., 82.

149. Cornelia Sorabji, "Ethnic War in Bosnia?" *Radical Philosophy* 63 (spring 1993): 33.

150. Bernstein, *Foregone Conclusions*, 9.

4. Violence and Identity in Bosnia

1. In her account of being subject to these strategies in Croatia, Slavenka Drakulić writes of the way they worked to produce her own identity as "Croatian," a concept that prior to 1991 had no particular meaning: "Along with millions of other Croats, I was pinned to the wall of nationhood — not only by outside pressure from Serbia and the Federal Army but by national homogenization within Croatia itself." Drakulić, *The Balkan Express: Fragments from the Other Side of the War* (New York: W. W. Norton and Company, 1993), 51. Similar logics were replicated in other sites. For example, one can consider the way in which historical and nationalist icons were deployed to secure power by the Serbian intelligentsia as Yugoslav communism unraveled, a process most obvious in the 1986 memorandum of the Serbian Academy of Arts and Sciences. See "Memorandum de l'Academie Serbe des Sciences et des Arts, Belgrade, Septembre 1986," *Dialogue* 2/3 (September 1992): 3–27. For other examples, see Branka Magas, *The Destruction of Yugoslavia: Tracking the Break-Up 1980–92* (New York: Verso, 1993), especially chapter 3.

2. Jacques Derrida, *Specters of Marx: The State of the Debt, the Work of Mourning, and the New International*, trans. Peggy Kamuf (New York: Routledge, 1994), 74.

3. Benedict Anderson, *Imagined Communities*, rev. ed. (London: Verso, 1991), xiv.

4. Some public commentary has, however, been even more direct. Writing in a British journal of opinion, the historian Paul Johnson declared that "the problems of the Balkans are infinitely complex and ultimately insoluble because they are rooted in the nature of the inhabitants themselves. . . . Short of exterminating them, there is really nothing to be done." Paul Johnson, "Don't Count Balkan Raindrops, Look Out for the Eastern Typhoon," *The Spectator*, 22 May 1993, 20, quoted in Kenneth Anderson, "Illiberal Tolerance: An Essay on the Fall of Yugoslavia and the Rise of Multiculturalism in the United States," *Virginia Journal of International Law* 33 (winter 1993): 387 n.

5. These orientations are akin to the notions of foreshadowing, backshadowing, and sideshadowing in historical narratives explored in Michael André Bernstein, *Foregone Conclusions: Against Apocalyptic History* (Berkeley: University of California Press, 1994). Foreshadowing is where the present is valued "as the harbinger of an already determined future," backshadowing is "a kind of retroactive foreshadowing in which the shared knowledge of the outcome of a series of events by narrator and listener is used to judge the participants in those events as though they too should have known

what was to come," and sideshadowing—which contests the previous two—involves "a gesturing to the side, to a present dense with multiple, and mutually exclusive, possibilities for what is to come." Ibid., 1–2, 16. Bernstein developed these notions in tandem with Gary Saul Morson, *Narrative and Freedom: The Shadows of Time* (New Haven: Yale University Press, 1994). It would be my contention that ontopological narratives exhibited the tendencies of foreshadowing and backshadowing, while the counternarratives in this chapter are moments of sideshadowing.

6. Allen Feldman, *Formations of Violence* (Chicago: University of Chicago Press, 1991), 18–19. Feldman's argument, and others like it, is reviewed in Christian Krohn-Hansen, "The Anthropology and Ethnography of Political Violence," *Journal of Peace Research* 34 (1997): 233–40. Relevant themes are developed in *Violence, Identity, and Self-Determination,* ed. Samuel Weber and Hent de Vries (Stanford: Stanford University Press, 1997), but the book appeared to late to be considered in detail here.

7. Feldman, *Formations of Violence,* 2.

8. Derrida, *Specters of Marx,* 74–75.

9. Feldman, *Formations of Violence,* 2, 7.

10. Ann Norton, *Reflections on Political Identity* (Baltimore: Johns Hopkins University Press, 1988), 145.

11. Jacques Derrida, "Force of Law: The 'Mystical Foundation of Authority,' " in *Deconstruction and the Possibility of Justice,* ed. Drucilla Cornell, Michael Rosenfeld, and David Gray Carlson (New York: Routledge, 1992), 32.

12. Richard Beardsworth, *Derrida and the Political* (London: Routledge, 1996), xiv.

13. Ghassan Hage, "The Spatial Imaginary of National Practices: Dwelling-Domesticating/Being-Exterminating," *Environment and Planning D: Society and Space* 14 (1996): 463–85.

14. Marcus Banks, *Ethnicity: Anthropological Constructions* (London: Routledge, 1996), 182–83.

15. Ibid., 183. For the intersection of social science and journalistic accounts of post–Cold War conflicts as "civil/ethnic," see the front-page story "As Ethnic Wars Multiply, U.S. Strives for a Policy," *New York Times,* 7 February 1993; and the headline story (based on a SIPRI report) "The End of War—and Peace," *The Independent,* 14 June 1996.

16. John Comaroff, "Humanity, Ethnicity, Nationality," *Theory and Society* 20 (October 1991): 665; Banks, *Ethnicity,* 39–43. For a critique of primordialism, see J. D. Eller and R. M. Coughlan, "The Poverty of Primordialism: The Demystification of Ethnic Attachments," *Ethnic and Racial Studies* 16 (April 1993): 183–202; and Arjun Appadurai, *Modernity at Large: Cultural Dimensions of Globalization* (Minneapolis: University of Minnesota Press, 1996), chapter 7.

17. Comaroff, "Humanity, Ethnicity, Nationality," 666; Banks, *Ethnicity,* 39.

18. Milton J. Esman, *Ethnic Politics* (Ithaca, N.Y.: Cornell University Press, 1994), 14.

19. Ibid., 23, 47, 14, 1.

20. Ibid., 14, 10, 13, 47.

21. Banks, *Ethnicity,* 129–30. Two of Anthony Smith's key works are *The Ethnic Origins of Nations* (Oxford: Basil Blackwell, 1986); and *National Identity* (London: Penguin, 1991). The importance of Smith's theorization for mainstream international relations can be seen in his contribution to a defining collection on "ethnic war." See Anthony D. Smith, "The Ethnic Sources of Nationalism," in *Ethnic Conflict and International Security,* ed. Michael Brown (Princeton, N.J.: Princeton University Press, 1993). In what is fast becoming established practice in the security studies literature

dealing with "ethnic" conflict, a footnote to Smith substitutes for any consideration of the argument's most fundamental category. This lack of consideration for ethnicity as a concept—regardless of the claims being made about the causes or types of ethnic conflict—is widely evident. See Steven Van Evera, "Hypotheses on Nationalism and War," *International Security* 18 (spring 1994): 5–39; Stuart Kaufman, "An 'International' Theory of Inter-Ethnic War," *Review of International Studies* 22 (1996): 149–71; and David A. Lake and Donald Rothchild, "Containing Fear: The Origins and Management of Ethnic Conflict," *International Security*, 21 (fall 1996): 41–75.

22. Bogdan Denitch, *Ethnic Nationalism: The Tragic Death of Yugoslavia* (Minneapolis: University of Minnesota Press, 1994), 141. The concern with ascription rather than acquisition is shared by Esman, *Ethnic Politics*, 16. In the context of Bosnia, a good critique of this tendency can be found in Rob Nixon, "Of Balkans and Bantustans," *Transition* 60 (1993): 4–26.

23. For example, V. P. Gagnon's account is instrumentalist in that it argues conflict is pursued along ethnic cleavages by elites, but it is primordialist to the extent that it does not attempt to theorize "ethnicity" as a politically significant identity. V. P. Gagnon, "Ethnic Nationalism and International Conflict," *International Security* 19 (winter 1994/95): 130–66. In his review of the way ethnic cleansing has been used by the British media, Banks highlights the "mixed strands of primordialism and instrumentalism in journalistic discourse on ethnicity." He concludes, however, that "the term has tended to provide its own explanation by resting on largely primordialist understandings of ethnicity." Banks, *Ethnicity*, 170, 171.

24. Barry Posen, "The Security Dilemma and Ethnic War," in *Ethnic Conflict and International Security*, ed. Brown, 111–14.

25. "WWII Hell Relived," *Los Angeles Times*, 6 February 1995.

26. "Bosnian War Strains NATO Relations," *Manchester Guardian Weekly*, 4 December 1994.

27. See, respectively, "In Dream of 'Greater Serbia,' the Serbs Find Suffering and Decay," *New York Times*, 17 September 1995; "Message from Serbia," *Time* (n.d.), in BosNet (electronic bulletin board) (Digest 330), 10 July 1995; "A Step along a Treacherous Road," *The Independent*, 27 September 1995; "Tough Talker Heads Bosnia," *The Guardian*, 23 January 1996; and "Serb Mayor Tries to Stem Exodus," *The Independent*, 14 March 1996.

28. David Owen, *Balkan Odyssey* (London: Victor Gollancz, 1995), 1–3, 29, 242, 334.

29. Maria Todorova, "The Balkans: From Discovery to Invention," *Slavic Review* 53 (summer 1994): 453–82.

30. The quote is from "Krajina Serbs Put Trust in the UN for Protection," *The Independent*, 6 September 1995. For the latter point, manifested especially in scholarship from northern republics in the former Yugoslavia dealing with the southern republics, see Milica Bakić-Hayden and Robert M. Hayden, "Orientalist Variations on the Theme 'Balkans': Symbolic Geography in Recent Yugoslav Cultural Politics," *Slavic Review* 51 (spring 1992): 1–15; and Milica Bakić-Hayden, "Nesting Orientalisms: The Case of the Former Yugoslavia," *Slavic Review* 54 (winter 1995): 917–31.

31. Larry Wolff, *Inventing Eastern Europe: The Map of Civilization on the Mind of the Enlightenment* (Stanford: Stanford University Press, 1994).

32. This discussion is drawn from Kathryn A. Manzo, *Creating Boundaries: The Politics of Race and Nation* (Boulder: Lynne Rienner, 1996), 18–23. Smith makes the argument about ethnic nations in *National Identity*, 11.

33. This is the central theme of Manzo's *Creating Boundaries*. As she argues, the concept of "ethnicity" has helped make this obfuscation possible, because it functions as "a code for racialized differences among people presumed to be of the same race"

(19). The interweaving of ethnicity, nationalism, and race is also a central concern of Banks's *Ethnicity.*

34. Banks, *Ethnicity,* 42.

35. Katherine Verdery, "Ethnicity, Nationalism, and State-Making," in *The Anthropology of Ethnicity: Beyond "Ethnic Groups and Boundaries,"* ed. Hans Vermeulen and Cora Grovers (Amsterdam: Het Spinhuis, 1994).

36. Comaroff, "Humanity, Ethnicity, Nationality," 668–69.

37. For instance, the *Concise Oxford English Dictionary* (Oxford: Clarendon Press, 1990) — after including in its definition of *ethnicity* the usual ambiguous formulations like "having a common national or cultural tradition," "denoting origin by birth or descent rather than nationality," and "relating to race or culture" — suggests the term also refers to "(clothes etc.) resembling those of a non-European exotic people" and means "pagan, heathen."

38. John Comaroff, "Of Totemism and Ethnicity: Consciousness, Practice and the Signs of Inequality," *Ethnos* 52 (1987): 302–3. For an account of the former Yugoslavia that adheres to a similar understanding of ethnicity, see Bette Denich, "Unmaking Multi-Ethnicity in Yugoslavia: Metamorphosis Observed," *Anthropology of East Europe Review* 11 (1993): 43–53.

39. Verdery, "Ethnicity, Nationalism, and State-Making," 44.

40. Katherine Verdery, "Whither 'Nation' and 'Nationalism'?" *Daedalus* 122 (summer 1993): 37.

41. Bernstein, *Foregone Conclusions,* 82–83.

42. Mensur Camo, "A Peacenik's Guide to 'The Other Bosnia,'" *WarReport* 21 (August/September 1993): 16–17.

43. "Besieged Muslims Place Their Dignity over Life," *New York Times,* 7 March 1993.

44. "A Public Trial in Bosnia's Sniper Season," *Manchester Guardian Weekly,* 21 March 1993, 10.

45. "In Tuzla Everyone Is a Prisoner," *Manchester Guardian Weekly,* 28 March 1993.

46. "The Tearing Apart of Yugoslavia: Place by Place, Family by Family," *New York Times,* 9 May 1993.

47. "Banja Luka's Muslim Leaders Say Church 'Failed to React,'" *Ecumenical News International,* 5 February 1996; and "Muslims Find Rare Sanctuary in Tiny Serb Schindler's Ark," *The Guardian,* 14 February 1996.

48. "Images of Future Peace Elude Bosnia's War-Weary Young," *The Guardian,* 23 November 1995.

49. "Teenagers Robbed of Their Dreams," *The Guardian,* 17 August 1996.

50. Davorka Zmijarevic, "Blood Boundaries," *YugoFax* 4 (28 September 1991): 4.

51. Anderson, "Illiberal Tolerance," 398.

52. "The World of Radovan Karadzic," *U.S. News and World Report,* 24 July 1995.

53. Tihomir Loza, "A People with Tolerance, A City without Laws," *WarReport* 21 (August/September 1993): 11.

54. See, respectively, "Sarajevo Recovers Faint Trace of a Normal Existence," *New York Times,* 28 January 1995; "Serbs from Sarajevo to Belgrade," BosNews, 29 March 1995; and "Sarajevans Rally for Peace," BosNet (Digest 498), 12 December 1995.

55. *New York Times,* 28 July 1995.

56. For a succinct rendition of this interpretation, see the interview with Vlado Azinovic of Sarajevo's Radio ZID, conducted in Zagreb on 14 February 1995 by Jo van der Spek, originally published in Croatian in *ARKzin* 32, and translated and posted by van der Spek in BosNews, 24 February 1995.

57. Ruza Maksimovic, quoted in "Sarajevans Rally for Peace," BosNet (Digest 498), 12 December 1995.

58. Chuck Sudetic, "The Long Road Ahead," *WarReport* 43 (July 1996): 8–9.

59. Quoted in Kemal Kurspahic, "Serbian Sincerity, and Ours," *New York Times*, 7 May 1993.

60. "Exiles Yearn for City Lights," *The Guardian*, 16 October 1995.

61. "Serb Trippers Find Joy and Tears in Sarajevo," *The Guardian*, 30 January 1996. Similar attitudes are reported in "Many Bosnian Serbs Questioning the War," *New York Times*, 18 January 1996; and "Across a Balkan Bridge, Hate and Suspicion Linger," *New York Times*, 2 March 1996.

62. A similar situation existed in Croatia when hostilities broke out, though its significance has gone largely unremarked. Only about a quarter (some 200,000) of the Serbs in Croatia lived in the Serb-majority areas that declared autonomy and were to receive assistance from the Belgrade authorities. Nearly three-quarters of Croatia's Serbs lived in Croat-majority areas, thereby demonstrating the mixed nature of the society and the problematic nature of the nationalist argument. Laura Silber and Alan Little, *The Death of Yugoslavia* (London: Penguin, 1995), 167 n.

63. Quoted in "Bosnian Federal Police Enter Vogosca," *OMRI Daily Digest* 39 (23 February 1996).

64. Senad Avdic, "Planning the Siege of Sarajevo," *Oslobodjenje* (weekly edition) 5–12 January 1995. An edited translation (by Bernard Meares) was posted in BosNews, 20 January 1995. Avdic was editor of *Slobodna Bosna*, and much of this information was published in a 21 November 1991 article titled "Sarajevo in the Chetnik's Sights." As Avdic laments, not many in Sarajevo believed what they read.

65. Official efforts to prevent reintegration have been evident throughout Bosnia. See, for example, the story recounted by American officers of the way their attempts to promote interaction between Serb and Muslim villages, desired by the residents of each, were thwarted by Pale: "U.S. Troops Seek to Aid Push Toward Reconciliation in Balkans," *New York Times*, 28 March 1996.

66. The restricted atmosphere in which the plebiscite returned a large vote against Serbs coming under "Muslim" control is reported in "Sarajevo Serbs Vent Rage with Futile Vote," *The Independent*, 13 December 1995; "20,000 Bosnian Serbs May Have Left Sarajevo," *OMRI Special Report: Pursuing Balkan Peace* 1: 4 (30 January 1996); "Night Brings Terror and Arson to Sarajevo Suburb," *New York Times*, 17 March 1996; "Arson and Looting in Grbavica," *OMRI Daily Digest* 55 (18 March 1996).

67. "Serb Children Being Kidnapped to Make Parents Leave; SGV," BosNet (Digest 92), 11 March 1996.

68. See "20,000 Serbs May Have Left Sarajevo."

69. "New Signals to Sarajevo Serbs," *OMRI Daily Digest* 246 (20 December 1995); "Sarajevo Serbs Staying Put?" *OMRI Daily Digest* 2/37 (21 February 1996); "Serb Mayor Tries to Stem Exodus," *The Independent*, 14 March 1996; and "Sarajevo Serbs Seek to Curb Exodus," *OMRI Daily Digest* 54 (15 March 1995).

70. "Izetbegovic Condemns Muslim Violence," *OMRI Daily Digest* 55 (18 March 1996).

71. See "Arson and Looting in Grbavica"; and "Serbs Murder under Noses of NATO Force," *The Guardian*, 9 March 1996.

72. See the report from the Balkan Institute, posted in BosNet (Digest 82), 29 February 1996.

73. It should be noted, however, that the new federation police force that slowly took charge in these areas was a "multiethnic" body (a contingent of ninety in Ilijas,

for example, included twenty-five Serbs and fifteen Croats), and in Grbavica was welcomed by those one thousand to two thousand Serbs who resisted Pale's intimidation. See "Bosnian Federal Police Enter Ilijas"; and "Bosnian Federal Police Enter Grbavica," *OMRI Daily Digest* 56 (19 March 1996). The International Police Task Force acknowledges that many federation police have little sympathy for Serbs who remained, and that Serb complaints—usually involving refugees coming to their homes and demanding housing—have often been ignored. "Knock at the Door Strikes Fear into the Serbs Who Refuse to Leave," *The Guardian*, 6 June 1996.

74. The best overview of this is "Serbs in Sarajevo Suburbs: Trial for Reintegration," *OMRI Special Report: Pursuing Balkan Peace* 1: 18 (7 May 1996).

75. Human Rights Watch, *Non-compliance with the Dayton Accords: Ongoing Ethnically-Motivated Expulsions and Harassment in Bosnia*, Research Report 8 (12 D), August 1996.

76. Quoted in *Genocide: Conceptual and Historical Dimensions*, ed. George J. Andreopoulos (Philadelphia: University of Pennsylvania Press, 1994), appendix I, 230.

77. Leo Kuper, "Theoretical Issues Relating to Genocide," in *Genocide*, ed. Andreopoulos, 32.

78. Frank Chalk, "Redefining Genocide," in *Genocide*, ed. Andreopoulos, 48.

79. In addition to the Andreopoulos collection, see Irving Louis Horowitz, *Taking Lives: Genocide and State Power*, 3d ed. (New Brunswick, N.J.: Transaction Books, 1982); Leo Kuper, *The Prevention of Genocide* (New Haven, Conn.: Yale University Press, 1985); Frank Chalk and Kurt Jonassohn, *The History and Sociology of Genocide: Analyses and Case Studies* (New Haven, Conn.: Yale University Press, 1990); and Eric Markusen and David Kopf, *The Holocaust and Strategic Bombing: Genocide and Total War in the Twentieth Century* (Boulder, Colo.: Westview Press, 1994).

80. "American Policy 'Borders on Complicity in Genocide,'" *Manchester Guardian Weekly*, 22 August 1993.

81. The author, Richard Johnson, was still employed by the State Department at the time he wrote the paper for the National War College. "State Dept. Official Says U.S. Ignores Genocide in Bosnia," *New York Times*, 4 February 1994. For an NGO perspective, see the resolution from the American Jewish Congress, in BosNet (Digest 357), 2 August 1995.

82. Daryl G. Press, "What's Happening in Bosnia Is Terrible, but It's Not Genocide," *Baltimore Sun*, 26 September 1993.

83. George Kenney, "The Bosnia Calculation: How Many Have Died?" *New York Times Magazine*, 23 April 1995. Kenney has seemingly been transformed from a critic of U.S. policy for its failure to respond to genocide to an accomplice in revisionist attempts to claim the charge of genocide was fabricated. This latter position is evident through his promotion of the claim that the infamous pictures of emaciated Bosnians/Muslims detained behind barbed wire in Serbian camps were invented by the journalists who reported them. This controversy is reported in "A Shot That's Still Ringing," *The Guardian*, 12 March 1997. One of the journalists present when the camp was revealed in August 1992, Ed Vulliamy, has rejected the charges in "I Stand by My Story," *The Observer*, 2 February 1997. For an eyewitness account of the camps—which has a portion of one of the photographs in question on its cover—see Rezak Hukanović, *The Tenth Circle of Hell: A Memoir of Life in the Death Camps of Bosnia* (London: Little, Brown and Company, 1997).

84. The remark by Warren Christopher (quoted in chapter 3), where he denied that the conflict in Bosnia was genocide because the Jews in Germany had not themselves committed genocide, embodies this view. Echoes of it can also be found in sug-

gestions for reworking the convention definition. See Israel Charney, "Toward a Generic Definition of Genocide," 75; and Helen Fein, "Genocide, Terror, Life Integrity, and War Crimes," 97, both in *Genocide*, ed. Andreopoulos. Similarly, negotiations for a permanent international criminal tribunal have seen proposals to embellish the definition of genocide with terms ("substantial," "systematic," or "widespread") that increase thresholds so as to limit responsibility. See the posting by Jordan Paust in Tribunal Watch (electronic bulletin board), 23 May 1996.

85. "CIA Says 'Most Ethnic Cleansing' Done by Serbs," *New York Times*, 9 March 1995. Released nearly a year after it was prepared, the question of why such conclusions were not forthcoming earlier needs to be raised. For an analysis of this, see Charles Lane and Thom Shanker, "Bosnia: What the CIA Didn't Tell Us," *New York Review of Books*, 9 May 1996. For accounts of Bosnian offenses, mostly against Bosnian Croats, see "The Brutalized Become the Brutal," *New York Times*, 11 October 1993; "In War in Bosnia, the Only Winner Is Despair," *New York Times*, 15 November 1993. In recognition of this, but in marked contrast to other authorities, the Bosnian government has arrested and handed over those members of its armed forces indicted by The Hague tribunal. See the Reuters report in Tribunal Watch, 2 May 1995. Details of Bosnian Croat crimes, often in coordinated campaigns with "the Chetniks," were detailed in a Croatian journal. See Antum Masle's report (trans. Daniel Margetich) from *Globus* (259) 24 November 1995, in BosNet (Digest 505), 19 December 1995.

86. Helsinki Watch, *War Crimes in Bosnia-Hercegovina*, 2 vols. (New York: Human Rights Watch, 1992/93); *Final Report of the Commission of Experts Established Pursuant to Security Council Resolution 780 (1992)*; "UN Report Slams Serbian Atrocities," *OMRI Daily Digest* 122 (23 June 1995); and "Amnesty International Report Singles Out Serbs," *OMRI Daily Digest* 131 (7 July 1995). An overview of the UN Commission of Experts is contained in M. Cherif Bassiouni, "The United Nations Commission of Experts Established Pursuant to Security Council Resolution 780 (1992)," *American Journal of International Law* 88 (October 1994): 785–805. On Mazowiecki, see David Warszawski, "UN Envoy Condemns International Duplicity," *WarReport* 16 (November/December 1992). In addition to the numerous reports from quality newspapers cited throughout this book, three series by investigative journalists warrant particular mention: the dispatches of Roy Gutman in 1992–93; Maggie O'Kane and Ed Vulliamy's accounts in *The Guardian*, and David Rhode's Pulitzer Prize–winning stories for the *Christian Science Monitor*. Gutman's writing is collected in *Witness to Genocide* (New York: Macmillan, 1993). Maggie O'Kane's reports are discussed in Gearóid Ó Tuathail, "An Anti-Geopolitical Eye: Maggie O'Kane in Bosnia, 1992–93," *Gender, Place and Culture* 3 (1996): 171–85; while Vulliamy's work produced a series titled "Bosnia: The Secret War," published in various issues of *The Guardian* in 1995–96. Three that deal with ethnic cleansing include "Horror Hidden beneath Ice and Lies," *The Guardian*, 19 February 1996; "Butcher of the Drina Bridge," *The Guardian*, 11 March 1996; and "Hard Truths Swept under Red Carpets," *The Guardian*, 22 June 1996. David Rhodes's five reports on the Srebrenica massacre, which detail the evidence and establish that forces from Serbia proper were involved, were published between 18 August and 16 November 1995, and form the basis of his *End Game: The Betrayal and Fall of Srebrenica* (New York: Farrar, Straus and Giroux, 1997).

87. See Branko Madunic and Zeljko Zetelja, "Interview with Tadeusz Mazowiecki," *Globus* (250) 22 September 1995, in BosNet (Digest 469), 16 November 1995.

88. The International Tribunal for Crimes in the Former Yugoslavia, *Indictment against Radovan Karadzic and Ratko Mladic (24 July 1995)*.

89. "Application of the Republic of Bosnia and Herzegovina, 20 March 1993," 77–80; and "Request for the Indication of Provisional Measures of Protection Submitted

by the Government of the Republic of Bosnia and Herzegovina, 20 March 1993," 81–87, both in Francis A. Boyle, *The Bosnian People Charge Genocide: Proceedings at the International Court of Justice Concerning Bosnia v. Serbia on the Prevention and Punishment of the Crime of Genocide* (Amherst, Mass.: Alethia Press, 1996). The Yugoslav counsel's remarks are recorded in "ICJ Public Sitting, Friday 2 April 1993, Verbatim Record," in ibid., 140.

90. ICJ Public Sitting, Thursday 1 April 1993, Verbatim Record, in Boyle, *The Bosnian People Charge Genocide,* 106.

91. "Request for the Indication of Provisional Measures of Protection Submitted by the Government of the Republic of Bosnia and Herzegovina, 27 July 1993," in Boyle, *The Bosnian People Charge Genocide,* 226–27. A year later, the 31 July 1994 edition of the Belgrade paper *Politika* carried a statement by Milošević, this time attempting to secure Bosnian Serb support for the Contact Group peace plan, with similar remarks. Quoted in Owen, *Balkan Odyssey,* 296; emphasis added. The Yugoslav Commission evidence was raised by Bosnia's counsel, and regarded as tainted by the majority of ICJ judges. See ICJ Public Sitting, Wednesday 25 August 1993, No. 2, Verbatim Record, in Boyle, *The Bosnian People Charge Genocide,* 283; and "Separate Opinion of Judge Weeramantry," *I.C.J. Reports 1993,* 52; and "Separate Opinion of Judge Shahabuddeen," *I.C.J. Reports 1993,* 41.

92. No substantive action has been taken subsequent to the ICJ's second order for provisional measures in September 1993. Yugoslavia has not filed a counter-memorial contesting the merits of Bosnia's application, preferring instead to make a number of preliminary objections challenging the admissibility of the application and the jurisdiction of the court. These objections were rejected in a July 1996 ruling by the court. Details are available on the International Court of Justice's World Wide Web site (for details, see the Note on Sources to this book). It has been suggested that Bosnia was required to drop the case as a precondition for the establishment of diplomatic relations with the Federal Republic of Yugoslavia agreed in Paris on 3 October 1996. Senad Pecanin, "Coming to Terms," *WarReport* 46 (October 1996): 30.

93. Alison Wiebalck, "Genocide in Bosnia and Herzegovina? Exploring the Parameters of Interim Measures of Protection at the ICJ," *Comparative and International Law Journal of Southern Africa* 28 (1995): 86.

94. International Court of Justice, "Case Concerning Application of the Convention on the Prevention and Punishment of the Crime of Genocide (Bosnia and Herzegovina v. Yugoslavia [Serbia and Montenegro]), Request for the Indication of Provisional Measures, Order of 8 April 1993," paragraphs 52A–52B, in Boyle, *The Bosnian People Charge Genocide,* 177–78.

95. "Declaration of Judge Tarassov," in Boyle, *The Bosnian People Charge Genocide,* 179.

96. ICJ, "Order of 8 April 1993," paragraph 44, in Boyle, *The Bosnian People Charge Genocide,* 175.

97. On 27 July 1993 Bosnia asked for ten additional measures, including an order requiring Yugoslavia to cease military support for the fighting in Bosnia; that all efforts to "partition, dismember, annex or incorporate" Bosnia's territory be ended and declared illegal; that Bosnia should have unhindered access to all means necessary for the defense against genocide; and that the UN forces should do all in their power to secure humanitarian supplies. Wiebalck, "Genocide in Bosnia and Herzegovina," 97–98.

98. "Application of the Convention on the Prevention and Punishment of the Crime of Genocide, Provisional Measures, Order of 13 September 1993," *I.C.J. Reports 1993,* 26, 27 (paragraphs 48, 52).

99. Ibid., 25 (paragraphs 45, 46).

100. In accepting the Bosnian government's information and corroborating evidence, Judge Elihu Lauterpacht argued that the court was following "the doctrine of judicial notice" whereby "tribunals may not and do not close their eyes to facts that stare them in the face." After pointedly remarking that Yugoslavia neither rebutted Bosnia's documented claims nor denied "that atrocities of the character and on the scale described have occurred," Lauterpacht concluded that "what matters for present purposes is the general *concordance* of evidence." This was a consideration the court had entertained in earlier decisions, and given that "in this case, the evidence all points conclusively in one direction," it was once again apposite. "Separate Opinion of Judge Lauterpacht," *I.C.J. Reports 1993,* 101 (paragraph 40), 102 (paragraph 43). This majority position was explicitly endorsed by two other judges: see the "Separate Opinion of Judge Shahabuddeen," *I.C.J. Reports 1993,* 39; and "Separate Opinion of Judge Weeramantry," *I.C.J. Reports 1993,* 51. The minority position was argued in "Dissenting Opinion of Judge Kreca," *I.C.J. Reports 1993,* 136, 138.

101. These are mentioned in "Serb Leader Continues to Deliver Assistance to Bosnian Serbs," *New York Times,* 11 June 1995; "Milosevic Role Cited as Contradicting Peacemaking Pledge," *Washington Post,* 5 July 1995; "Despite Promises Serbs Are Rebuilding Army in Bosnia," *New York Times,* 18 November 1995. Further corroboration and documentary evidence of the links can be found in "'Only Passivity Is Dishonourable,'" *The Guardian,* 12 January 1996; and "Serbian Lies World Chose to Believe," *The Guardian,* 29 February 1996. Such evidence was overlooked by the ICTY when in the Tadic verdict it based its determination on the "internal" character of the Bosnian war on the alleged withdrawal of Yugoslav Army (JNA) forces from Bosnia in May 1992.

102. *Final Report of the Commission of Experts Established Pursuant to Security Council Resolution 780 (1992),* paragraph 97. It is also being questioned by those scholars who argue that in the modern world of bureaucracy and structural constraints, intentionality is difficult to even conceptualize. See Chalk, "Redefining Genocide," 53–56.

103. "Serb Chief Painted as Warmonger by Ex-Aide," *New York Times,* 16 December 1995. After publication of *The Last Days of the Socialist Federation of the Republic of Yugoslavia,* both Jović and the head of the publishing house that issued the book were sacked from their jobs.

104. Avdic, "Planning the Siege of Sarajevo." Both Jović's thesis and the U.S. intelligence reports are confirmed in "America's Big Strategic Lie," *The Guardian,* 20 May 1996. The argument about the Bosnian Serb army is found in David Rieff, "Arrest Them: The Cast against the Serb War Criminals," *Washington Post,* 8 September 1996.

105. "The President's Secret Henchmen," *The Guardian,* 3 February 1997; and "War Veterans Turn on Yugoslav Army," *The Guardian,* 8 February 1997.

106. "Separate Opinion of Judge Lauterpacht," 111 (paragraph 70). This argument was revisited in the July 1996 court decision.

107. Ibid., 113. The quote is from paragraph 78; the other reflections are from paragraphs 74–79.

108. Ibid., 124–25 (paragraph 118). This tension was seized upon and extended by Judge Milenko Kreca in his dissent, where he argued that "the people" of Bosnia "does not refer to an actual homogenous national, ethnic or religious entity, for the phrase 'People of Bosnia and Herzegovina' used by the Applicant, in fact, covers three ethnic communities." As such, Kreca contended, to accept any of the applicant's argument would be to stretch the Genocide Convention so that it covered new groups. A possible extension of the convention to new groups is the subject of an emerging consensus among scholars of genocide and human rights advocates. See Chalk, "Redefining Genocide," 49–53.

109. *Final Report of the Commission of Experts Established Pursuant to Security Council Resolution 780 (1992)*, paragraph 96.

110. Ibid. Interestingly, Radovan Karadžić has conceded that "the Serb side" engaged in killings and purges, but—in an attempt to avoid the obvious legal implications—maintains that they were not the result of a policy. "Karadzic 'Regrets' but Still Rejects Serb Atrocities," *The Guardian*, 28 May 1997.

111. Ivica Buljan, "Dirty Cleansing," *Feral Tribune*, 7 August 1995.

112. These practices are outlined in "Bosnia's Serbs: 'Ethnic Cleansing' Redux," *New York Times*, 17 February 1994; and "For Serb Evictions, A New Phase," *Boston Globe*, 22 June 1994.

113. An account of forced labor brigades can be found in "Human Rights: Civilians Forced to Work on the Frontline," BosNews (Digest 213), 16 March 1995. Based on a report issued by Anti-Slavery International (ASI) in London, it notes that although all sides have used forced labor, "impartial observers agree that the most systematic violations are occurring in the Serb-held areas of northern Bosnia." According to ASI, the anecdotal evidence suggesting similar abuses by Croat and Bosnian forces indicates that "where it does happen, it is a result of decisions by individual commanders. It cannot be seen as an institutionalised practice." Accounts of Serbian authorities rounding up "Serbian" refugees can be found in "Krajina Refugees in Serbia Press-Ganged," *OMRI Daily Digest* 117 (16 June 1995); and "Belgrade Press-Gangs Refugees for Distant Wars," *The Independent*, 20 June 1995. A journalist on the independent Belgrade magazine *Vreme* reported this campaign, which affected some three thousand men of military age, in BosNet (Digest 315), 23 June 1995. This operation revealed two important things: (1) the absence of nationalist fervor among Serbian refugees, who clearly had little desire to fight for the territory from which they had been displaced; and (2) the continuing military and police links between Serbia and its surrogate republics in Bosnia and Croatia.

114. "Muslim and Croat Refugees Detail Atrocities," *New York Times*, 13 October 1995; and "2 Officials Report New Mass Killings by Bosnian Serbs," *New York Times*, 20 October 1995.

115. This event raises a host of disturbing questions about the nature of the violence perpetrated and the response of both the Bosnian government and the international community. In addition to the references in note 86, a comprehensive overview can be found in "Days of Slaughter: The Killing of Srebrenica," *New York Times*, 29 October 1995; and Jan Willem Honig and Norbert Both, *Srebrenica: Record of a War Crime* (London: Penguin Books, 1996). For Serbia's account, see "Belgrade Blames Bosnian Muslims for Srebrenica Massacre," *OMRI Daily Digest* 245 (19 December 1995). This is contradicted by all the available evidence, including that obtained from exhuming mass graves. See, for example, "Possible Mass Grave in Bosnia Raises Hope of Tracing Killers," *New York Times*, 17 March 1996; and the account of the forensic anthropology team in *Record: Newsletter of Physicians for Human Rights* 10 (January 1997). The *New York Times* article also discloses the discovery of documentary evidence left behind by Serbian and Bosnian Serb forces, including "what appear to be billing records from the local garbage company to the Bosnian Serb authorities reporting on the number of bodies collected and buried day by day." Transcripts of intelligence intercepts revealing Bosnian Serb army plans before and during the massacre, as well as Serbia's involvement in the planning of the operation, are quoted at length in a report by Roy Gutman, "How Troop-Hostage Talks Led to Slaughter of Srebrenica," *Newsday*, 29 May 1996. The most damning evidence of the massacre comes from the conviction (after he pleaded guilty) of Drazen Erdemovic at the ICTY. Erdemovic, in fact a Bosnian

Croat who served in the Bosnian Serb army, admitted that he was part of one firing squad that had killed some twelve hundred people. See the Reuters report in Tribunal Watch, 31 May 1996. As some of the testimony in the ICTY revealed, officers of the Bosnian Serb army forced the bus drivers who brought the Bosnian Muslims to the firing squads to kill a prisoner, thereby implicating them in the crime and making confessions unlikely. See "Two Views of Bosnian Firing Squad," *Washington Post*, 6 July 1996.

116. An account of Muslims having crosses carved into their cheeks and necks was broadcast by National Public Radio, *Morning Edition* (Baltimore, 7 March 1994); and can be found in testimony to the ICTY, which was reported by Reuters in Tribunal Watch, 15 May 1996. The symbolic impact on the victim as well as the perpetrator is suggested by Jule Peteet, "Male Gender and Rituals of Resistance in the Palestinian *Intifada*: A Cultural Politics of Violence," *American Ethnologist* 21 (February 1994): 31–49. The gender dimensions are discussed in Adam Jones, "Gender and Ethnic Conflict in Ex-Yugoslavia," *Ethnic and Racial Studies* 17 (January 1994): 115–34. The systematic nature of rape as a weapon of war in Bosnia is discussed in *Final Report of the Commission of Experts Established Pursuant to Security Council Resolution 780 (1992)*, paragraphs 102–9, 232–53; *Mass Rape: The War against Women in Bosnia-Herzegovina*, ed. Alexandra Stiglmayer (Lincoln: University of Nebraska Press, 1994); Cheryl Bernard, "Rape as Terror: The Case of Bosnia," *Terrorism and Political Violence* 6 (spring 1994): 29–43; and Beverly Allen, *Rape Warfare: The Hidden Genocide in Bosnia-Herzegovina and Croatia* (Minneapolis: University of Minnesota Press, 1996). The sexual violence perpetrated by men against men has not often been reported, but accounts can be found in "Thousands of Men Raped in Bosnia. A Taboo on War Reporting," abridged translation from *Le Nouveau Quotidien*, 10–12 March 1995, in BosNews (Digest 211), 13 March 1995; and a Reuters report in Tribunal Watch, 3 July 1996. The ICTY hearing covered in the latter report was the first time the tribunal had addressed the issue of rape as a weapon of war. These developments have important implications for international law. See Theodore Meron, "Rape as a Crime under International Humanitarian Law," *American Journal of International Law* 87 (July 1993): 424–28; and Catherine N. Niarchos, "Women, War, and Rape: Challenges Facing the International Tribunal for the Former Yugoslavia," *Human Rights Quarterly* 17 (1995): 649–90. Some of the evidence for the ICTY's hearings on rape is coming from pornographic videos distributed in the Netherlands, which allegedly show rapes being committed by Bosnian Serb forces. See "Hague Tribunal Will Use Video-Records of Raping," in BosNet (Digest 44), 30 January 1996.

117. The deliberate nature of much of this violence is manifested in the statement of Zvornik's mayor in the wake of the "cleansing" of forty thousand Muslims from the town. Kissing a cross on a cliff overlooking the town, he declared that his first act would be to build a church: "The Turks destroyed the Serbian church that was here when they arrived in Zvornik in 1463. Now we are rebuilding the church and reclaiming this as Serbian land forever and ever." That reclamation involved the demolition of both an Ottoman tower and the mosque. "In a Town 'Cleansed' of Muslims, Serb Church Will Crown the Deed," *New York Times*, 7 March 1994. As with other aspects of ethnic cleansing, while overall responsibility lies predominantly with the leadership of Bosnian Serb forces, no side has been entirely free of guilt. The ordered nature of Bosnian Croat (HVO) violence against Bosnian Muslim sites is documented in Matej Vipotnik, "Searching for Bosnia's Lost Cultural Treasures," *Beserkistan*, 1996. However, there is no evidence of a deliberate or official strategy on the part of the Bosnian army. A UN report on the 1993 conflict in central Bosnia confirms this: "In every area where Muslims lived before the war and which is today controlled by [Croat] forces, no mosques remain intact. On the other hand in the overwhelming majority of areas un-

der [Bosnian] control the Catholic churches and monasteries still stand." Quoted in "Croats, Bosnians: An Uneasy Alliance Turns Tense," *Boston Globe*, 21 September 1995. Indeed, one account suggests that during the Bosnian-Croatian fighting of 1993 there is only a single instance of cultural destruction by elements within the Bosnian army (involving the Franciscan monastery at Guca Gora), and that was contrary to specific instructions from the government to protect such sites. See Azra Begic, "The Fate of Moveable Heritage in Sarajevo and Central Bosnia: An Insider's Observations," trans. Marian Wenzel, *Museum Management and Curatorship* 14 (March 1995): 80–83. According to Begic, in support of the thesis that the violence directed against Sarajevo and elsewhere was planned in advance, many Serbian Orthodox collections and treasures were removed from Bosnia and sent to Belgrade some months before the fighting began. For a report on the fate of libraries, see Andreas Riedlmayer, "Erasing the Past: The Destruction of Libraries and Archives in Bosnia-Herzegovina," *Middle East Studies Association Bulletin* 29 (July 1995): 7–11. Official overviews can be found in the five volumes commissioned by the Council of Europe, *Information Report on the Destruction by War of the Cultural Heritage in Croatia and Bosnia-Herzegovina* (Strasbourg: Council of Europe, Parliamentary Assembly, 2 February 1993–12 April 1994); as well as the *Final Report of the Commission of Experts Established Pursuant to Security Council Resolution 780 (1992)*, paragraphs 285–301, where the commission concludes that the damage to historic sites in Dubrovnik and Mostar (the only examples they considered in detail) could not be justified by military necessity.

118. As one Sarajevan woman, who had adopted Islamic dress and practices despite the objections of her "Muslim" parents, observed, "To be honest, I don't think I would have ever bothered about our culture or the Koran if it weren't for the war." One of her friends noted, "At first you try to find answers. Why? Why does one group of people want to exterminate another? Then you realize that someone is forcing you to belong to a group — or a 'nation,' as it were, in the former Yugoslavia — to which you have very loose ties, if any. And one day you really do belong to it." "A Sarajevan Face of Islam," *OMRI Special Report: Pursuing Balkan Peace* 1: 39 (1 October 1996).

119. These debates are discussed in "Ethnic Rift Divides Sarajevo's Defenders," *New York Times*, 26 September 1993; "Partition in Fact, Bosnia Sees Even Its Dreams Die," *New York Times*, 3 October 1993; and "In War for Bosnia, the Only Winner Is Despair," *New York Times*, 15 November 1993.

120. "The Bosnian Dream of a Multi-ethnic Future Is Dying," *Manchester Guardian Weekly*, 9 October 1994.

121. "Serb Defeats Expose Discord in Sarajevo," *Glasgow Herald*, 12 September 1995.

122. "Surreal Attempt at Democracy," *Canberra Times*, 22 October 1994.

123. Ibid.; and "The Bosnian Dream of a Multi-ethnic Future Is Dying."

124. "Nationalism Divides Bosnian Leadership," *Manchester Guardian Weekly*, 12 February 1995.

125. See the articles and commentary from *Oslobodjenje*, 31 January 1995, in Bos-News, 2–3 February 1995. A year later, elements of the debate were still running, along with demands that the Bosnian army could not be Muslim. See the summary of reports from *Oslobodjenje*'s weekly magazine *Svijet* (8 February 1996), in BosNet (Digest 62), 11 February 1996. One article in that issue noted that almost one-fifth of the Bosnian army was non-Muslim at war's end. See "Serbian General in Bosnian Army to Be Sacked," *OMRI Daily Digest* 33 (15 February 1996). How "Muslim" the other four-fifths are is debatable. One report from the trenches included the portrait of "young Edo" who "swigs on a bottle of Croatian beer in one hand, and clasps his army-issue pocket edition of the Koran in the other: 'See — a real Bosnian Muslim!' he laughs." "Time

Wars," *The Guardian Weekend*, 16 September 1995. The "real" Muslims are likely to be members of the seventh or ninth Muslim brigades. The former's location in Zenica was not coincidental, given that this town hosted a group of the two hundred Islamic volunteers that came to fight in Bosnia. Their attempts to impose strict religious practices alienated the local population. The Bosnian army reportedly had to intervene and restrain this militia after they massacred thirty-five Bosnian Croat civilians at Uzdal. This was "the first time Muslim forces had engaged in anything resembling 'ethnic cleansing' that their enemies had been practicing for more than a year." Yahaya M. Sadowski, "Bosnia's Muslims: A Fundamentalist Threat?" *Brookings Review* 13 (January 1995). For life in the ninth brigade, see "Islamic Warriors Shun the Peace to Fight Their Holy War," *The Guardian*, 6 January 1996.

126. "Bosnian President Accused of Using Islam 'For Political and Military Gains,'" BosNews (Digest 112), 27 March 1996. This debate is reviewed in Gojko Beric, "The State Religion," *WarReport* 40 (April 1996): 34–35.

127. Speaking at an SDA conference in early 1994, Izetbegović was reported as decrying the practice of symbolizing communal coexistence by tying together national flags: "Don't do this. Tying flags together is a romantic folly devoid of meaning." Quoted in "Surreal Attempt at Democracy."

128. One constituency to whom these statements might have been directed was Iran, the only country to have backed Bosnia from the beginning, to which Bosnia had sent some troops for training, and from which came $500,000 in campaign finance. See "Bosnians Send Troops to Iran for Training," *New York Times*, 4 March 1996; and "Bosnian's Muslim Ruling Party Confirms Receiving Funds from Iran," *OMRI Daily Digest* 3 (6 January 1997). Not that Iran was ideologically pure in these matters, given the secret sale of oil rigs from Iran to Serbia in 1995 despite the UN embargo against Belgrade. "U.S. Scrambles to Block Oil Rigs from Reaching Serbia," *New York Times*, 8 April 1995.

5. Responding to the Violence

1. John J. Mearsheimer, "Shrink Bosnia to Save It," *New York Times*, 31 March 1993.

2. "Dayton Deal Holds Seeds of Own Destruction," *The Independent*, 23 November 1995. See also "U.S. Report Says Chances Poor for Bosnia to Hold Together," *New York Times*, 17 May 1996, in Tribunal Watch (electronic bulletin board), 18 May 1996. Richard Holbrooke, the chief U.S. negotiator at Dayton, affirms the contradictory position that partition was not the intention of Dayton but is a danger flowing from it. See "Letters to the Editor: Richard Holbrooke on Bosnia," *Foreign Affairs* 76 (1997): 170–72.

3. Robert Hayden, "Imagined Communities and Real Victims: Self-Determination and Ethnic Cleansing in Yugoslavia," *American Ethnologist* 23 (1996): 783–801.

4. Ibid., 784.

5. Ibid., 783.

6. As Owen argued, "it was clear to me by the end of August 1992 that there was no will in any of the major Western nations to take up arms against Serbian expansionism. So it had to be dealt with primarily by negotiation." "Text of the Interview with Lord David Owen on the Future of the Balkans Published by *Foreign Affairs*, Spring 1993," IN 16/2/93: "Foreign Affairs" Interview, *Balkan Odyssey* CD-ROM, Academic Edition v1.1 (London: The Electric Company, 1995). The premise that the Serbs had to be dealt with rather than defeated was the basis of British policy, and originally a source of tension with the Americans. See "Tragic Cost of Allies' Hidden Hostility," *The Guardian*, 21 May 1996.

7. Mearsheimer, "Shrink Bosnia to Save It."

8. See respectively Michael J. Shapiro, *Violent Cartographies: Mapping Cultures of War* (Minneapolis: University of Minnesota Press, 1997), 190–94; and Sunil Khilnani, *The Idea of India* (London: Hamish Hamilton, 1997). The partition of India was proffered as the best analogy for Bosnia by Ronald Steel, "A Realistic Entity: Greater Sarajevo," *New York Times,* 26 July 1995.

9. Michel Foucault, *Discipline and Punish: The Birth of the Prison,* trans. Alan Sheridan (New York: Vintage Books, 1979), 143. Cf. Radha Kumar, "The Troubled History of Partition," *Foreign Affairs* 76 (1997): 22–34.

10. Mearsheimer, "Shrink Bosnia to Save It." The entailments of Mearsheimer's (neo)realism are clearly set out in John J. Mearsheimer, "The False Promise of International Institutions," *International Security* 19 (winter 1994/95): especially 9–14, 47–49.

11. See Chaim Kaufmann, "Possible and Impossible Solutions to Ethnic Civil Wars," *International Security* 20 (spring 1996): 137 n.

12. Terry Nardin, "Ethical Traditions in International Affairs," in *Traditions of International Ethics,* ed. Terry Nardin and David R. Mapel (Cambridge: Cambridge University Press, 1992), 15.

13. John J. Mearsheimer and Robert A. Pape, "The Answer: A Partition Plan for Bosnia," *The New Republic,* 14 June 1993.

14. Michel Foucault, *The History of Sexuality,* vol. 1, trans. Robert Hurley (New York: Vintage Books, 1978), 25.

15. Mearsheimer and Pape, "The Answer."

16. John J. Mearsheimer and Stephen Van Evera, "When Peace Means War," *The New Republic,* 18 December 1995; John Mearsheimer and Stephen Van Evera, "Partition Is the Inevitable Solution for Bosnia," *International Herald Tribune,* 25 September 1996.

17. Mearsheimer and Van Evera, "Partition Is the Inevitable Solution for Bosnia." The penchant for partition has been common in American opinion-making circles, being propagated by the likes of George Will, Lawrence Eagleburger, Henry Kissinger, and others. See George Will, "Morality and Map-Making," *Washington Post,* 7 September 1995; transcript from ABC News, *This Week with David Brinkley,* 3 September 1995, in BosNet (Digest 389), 6 September 1995; Henry Kissinger, "America in the Eye of the Hurricane," *Washington Post,* 8 September 1996; Michael O'Hanlon, "Bosnia: Better Left Partitioned," *Washington Post,* 10 April 1997.

18. Kaufmann, "Possible and Impossible Solutions to Ethnic Civil Wars," 138.

19. Ibid., 138 n.

20. Ibid., 140 n, 140.

21. Ibid., 141.

22. Ibid., 145.

23. Ibid., 146 n. In another article, while retaining the notion that fixed ethnicity is central to understanding the Bosnian war, Kaufmann states that the religious communities of Catholic Croats, Orthodox Serbs, and Muslims are "ethnically indistinguishable." Although this would seem to undermine much of his prior argument, he shores it up by declaring that religious conflicts follow the pattern of interethnic conflicts. Chaim Kaufmann, "Intervention in Ethnic and Ideological Civil Wars: Why One Can Be Done and the Other Can't," *Security Studies* 6 (autumn 1996): 66 n.

24. For the discrediting of scientific racism, see the "AAPA Statement on Biological Aspects of Race," *American Journal of Physical Anthropology* 101 (December 1996): 569–70.

25. Kaufmann, "Possible and Impossible Solutions to Ethnic Civil Wars," 139.

26. Ibid., 149.

27. Ibid., 137.

28. Ibid., 174.

29. Ibid., 175; emphasis added.

30. The only concession offered comes when Kaufmann declares that "once the conquest is complete, all enemy ethnics in custody must be moved across the separation line" (while "friendly ethnics" are to be resettled). He then notes that "rules for marginal cases [those who do not fit the friend/enemy distinction], such as mixed families, will have to be decided in consultation with the client." Kaufmann, "Intervention in Ethnic and Ideological Civil Wars," 96 n. I use the notion of "authoritarian" advisedly, but do not wish to imply anything about the character or personal politics of the individuals who have authored the argument I am criticizing. My charge is that the logic of proposals for partition is authoritarian. In this sense, I am — partly because of the larger issue of the tendencies embodied in a (neo)realist ontology — following both the argument and caution of Richard Ashley, who suggests that elements of neorealism's ontology reflected what Morgenthau called "the totalitarian state of mind." Richard K. Ashley, "The Poverty of Neorealism," *International Organization* 38 (spring 1984): 257–58.

31. Mearsheimer and Pape, "The Answer."

32. Mearsheimer and Van Evera, "Partition Is the Inevitable Solution for Bosnia."

33. Kaufmann, "Possible and Impossible Solutions to Ethnic Civil Wars," 161.

34. These issues are covered in a number of overviews. See, for example, Sabrina P. Ramet, "The Yugoslav Crisis and the West: Avoiding 'Vietnam' and Blundering into 'Abyssinia,' " *East European Politics and Societies* 8 (winter 1991): 189–219; Stuart Kaufmann, "The Irresistible Force and the Imperceptible Object: The Yugoslav Breakup and Western Policy," *Security Studies* 4 (winter 1994–95): 281–329; David Rieff, *Slaughterhouse: Bosnia and the Failure of the West* (New York: Simon and Schuster, 1995); and James Gow, *Triumph of the Lack of Will* (London: Hurst & Co., 1997). On the military virtuality of Bosnia, see James Der Derian, "Global Swarming, Virtual Security, and Bosnia," *Washington Quarterly* 19 (summer 1996): 45–56.

35. The overview of the peace process that follows is taken from Paul C. Szasz, "Introductory Note: Documents regarding the Conflict in Yugoslavia, September 25, 1991–November 16, 1992," *International Legal Materials* 31 (1992): 1421–26; and David Owen, *Balkan Odyssey* (London: Victor Gollancz, 1995). Another good account covering the period until mid-1992 can be found in Marc Weller, "The International Response to the Dissolution of the Socialist Federal Republic of Yugoslavia," *American Journal of International Law* 86 (July 1992): 569–607. Note that the European Community was renamed the European Union on 1 November 1993 in the wake of the Maastricht agreement.

36. Overviews of the ICFY can be found in "United Nations: Secretary-General Report on the International Conference on the Former Yugoslavia, November 11, 1992," *International Legal Materials* 31 (1992): 1549–94; and "Report of the Steering Committee of the International Conference on the Former Yugoslavia," RU 8/7/93 S/26066: Co-Chairmen's Report, *Balkan Odyssey* CD-ROM.

37. "Treaty Provisions for the Convention, 4 November 1991," PI 4/11/91: EC Conference Draft Convention," *Balkan Odyssey* CD-ROM.

38. "Statement of Principles for New Constitutional Arrangements for Bosnia and Herzegovina, Sarajevo, 18 March 1992," PI 18/3/92: Statement of Principles, *Balkan Odyssey* CD-ROM. This version of the document was agreed on in Sarajevo on 18 March after talks in Brussels on 7 March reconvened following the February Lisbon meetings.

39. "Statement of Principles."

40. As Silber and Little note, during the Lisbon talks of February 1992, "canton" was the new catchword, and "every Serb and Croat politician in Bosnia seemed to have a copy of the Swiss constitution in his office." Laura Silber and Alan Little, *The Death of Yugoslavia* (London: Penguin, 1995), 241.

41. Mladen Klemenčić, "Territorial Proposals for the Settlement of the War in Bosnia-Hercegovina," ed. Martin Pratt and Clive Schofield, International Boundaries Research Unit *Boundary and Territory Briefing* 1 (3) 1994, 41. The map of the 1991 census can be found in ibid., 24; and Owen, *Balkan Odyssey*, 64–65. Ethnographic cartography is necessarily politicized. For a detailed account of such maps with respect to the former Yugoslav republic of Macedonia, see H. R. Wilson, *Maps and Politics: A Review of the Ethnographic Cartography of Macedonia* (Liverpool: University of Liverpool Press, 1951).

42. Klemenčić, "Territorial Proposals," 37.

43. "Statement of Principles," Annex 3. This process was supposed to result in a proposal by 15 May 1992, but the onset of the war meant that the first Cutiliero map was the only product of these negotiations.

44. Klemenčić, "Territorial Proposals," 37.

45. "U.S. Policymakers on Bosnia Admit Errors in Opposing Partition in 1992," *New York Times*, 29 August 1993. This article contains the view of one anonymous state department official that, contrary to the EC's position, it was U.S. policy to encourage Izetbegović to repudiate the partition plan. This was contradicted by a letter to the paper from Warren Zimmerman, the U.S. ambassador in Belgrade, who met with Izetbegović after the Lisbon talks. See "Bosnian About Face," *New York Times*, 30 September 1993.

46. Klemenčić, "Territorial Proposals," 44.

47. "Proposed Provisional Rules of Procedure, LC/CI (REVISE) 25 August 1992," in "Documents regarding the Conflict in Yugoslavia," 1531.

48. "Statement of Principles, LC/C2 (FINAL) 26 August 1992," in "Documents regarding the Conflict in Yugoslavia," 1533–34.

49. "Statement on Bosnia, LC/C5 (FINAL) 27 August 1992," in "Documents regarding the Conflict in Yugoslavia," 1537–38.

50. "Secretary-General Report on the International Conference on the Former Yugoslavia, November 11, 1992," *International Legal Materials* 31 (1992): 1552.

51. Ibid., 1554, 1559.

52. Ibid., 1559.

53. "ICFY Working Paper on Constitutional Options," PI 4/10/92: Constitutional Options, *Balkan Odyssey* CD-ROM.

54. "Secretary-General Report on the International Conference on the Former Yugoslavia," 1560.

55. Ibid.

56. "ICFY Working Paper on Constitutional Options."

57. "Secretary-General Report on the International Conference on the Former Yugoslavia," 1560.

58. Ibid.

59. Ibid., 1561.

60. Ibid.

61. Ibid., 1562.

62. Ibid.

63. Ibid., 1563.

64. Ibid., 1585, 1591.

65. "Text of Interview with Lord David Owen on the Future of the Balkans."

66. Owen, *Balkan Odyssey*, 39.

67. "Vance-Owen Plan," PI: Text of VOPP Part 1, *Balkan Odyssey* CD-ROM.

68. Klemenčić, "Territorial Proposals," 46–49.

69. Owen, *Balkan Odyssey*, 104.

70. Ibid., 38.

71. Ibid., 63.

72. "Text of Interview with Lord David Owen on the Future of the Balkans."

73. Owen, *Balkan Odyssey*, 49, 58. The abandonment of the London Principles through these means is also noted by Kasim Trnka, "The Degradation of the Bosnian Peace Negotiations," in *Why Bosnia? Writings on the Balkan War*, ed. Rabia Ali and Lawrence Lifschultz (Stony Creek, Conn.: Pamphleteer's Press, 1993). An interesting pictorial manifestation of Owen's notion of equivalence can be found in the photographs of destroyed religious buildings published in *Balkan Odyssey* (near 139). With one from each faith, and no contextualization of how, when, and by whom they were desecrated, the implication is that each community was as bad as the other. But as chapter 4 made clear, when it comes to cultural destruction, the question of responsibility differs markedly among the communities. Moreover, this way of understanding the conflict is a sharp change from Owen's original intervention in the issue — a letter to John Major in August 1992 prior to his appointment as a negotiator — in which he argued in terms of the Holocaust. Ibid., 15.

74. See, in particular, the lengthy but partial account of the oft-cited question of responsibility for the February 1994 mortar attack on a Sarajevo marketplace that killed nearly seventy civilians. Owen, *Balkan Odyssey*, 260–62. For an account of this incident that doubts much of Owen's, see Silber and Little, *The Death of Yugoslavia*, 343–45.

75. Quoted in Owen, *Balkan Odyssey*, 32.

76. Ibid., 33.

77. Ibid.

78. Ibid., 342–43.

79. Klemenčić, "Territorial Proposals," 51–53.

80. Owen's frustration with the changes in U.S. policy are discussed in detail in *Balkan Odyssey*, chapter 4.

81. See Tore Bringa, *Being Muslim the Bosnian Way: Identity and Community in a Central Bosnian Village* (Princeton: Princeton University Press, 1995), 240 n.

82. Kemel Kurspahic, "Is There a Future?" in *Why Bosnia?* ed. Ali and Lifschultz, 16. The same logic is noted in Drago Hedl, "The Croat Mini-State: Boban's Fortune and Zagreb's Folly," *WarReport* 21 (August/September 1993): 14–15; and Robert J. Donia and John V. A. Fine, *Bosnia and Hercegovina: A Tradition Betrayed* (London: Hurst and Company, 1994), 251.

83. See "U.S. and 4 Nations Join Plan to Curb Fighting in Bosnia," and "Diplomacy's Goal in Bosnia Seems Not Bold Action but Avoiding It," both in *New York Times*, 23 May 1993. These events are also discussed in "Report of the Steering Committee of the International Conference on the Former Yugoslavia," RU 8/7/93 S/26066: Co-Chairmen's Report, *Balkan Odyssey* CD-ROM.

84. Owen, *Balkan Odyssey*, 190.

85. Ibid., 191.

86. "Croat-Serb Constitutional Principles for Bosnia-Herzegovina," GE 23/6/93: Constitutional Principles, *Balkan Odyssey* CD-ROM.

87. "Former Yugoslavia: Report of Co-Chairmen's meetings of 15–16 June," CO 17/6/93: Co-Chairmen's Meeting, *Balkan Odyssey* CD-ROM.

88. "Co-Chairmen's Meeting with Presidents Milosevic and Tudjman: 17 July," CD 17/7/93: Tudjman, Milosevic Meeting, *Balkan Odyssey* CD-ROM.

89. "Statement Issued by Tudjman and Milosevic, Geneva, 17 July 1993," PI 17/7/93: Tudjman/Milosevic Statement, *Balkan Odyssey* CD-ROM.

90. For the 1991 talks, see Silber and Little, *The Death of Yugoslavia,* 143–44. This desire has been confirmed by Tudjman during a dinner in London in May 1995 and meetings with the NATO Secretary General a year later. See "Tudjman Mapped Out Future on City Menu," *The Times,* 7 August 1995; and "Tudjman Skeptical Bosnia Will Survive as State," *OMRI Daily Digest* 119 (19 June 1996).

91. Klemenčić, "Territorial Proposals," 57.

92. Owen, *Balkan Odyssey,* 197.

93. "Agreement Relating to Bosnia and Herzegovina," PI Union of Three Republics, Part 1, *Balkan Odyssey* CD-ROM.

94. "Analysis of Second Internal Draft of 29 July 1993," in Francis A. Boyle, *The Bosnian People Charge Genocide: Proceedings at the International Court of Justice Concerning Bosnia v. Serbia on the Prevention and Punishment of the Crime of Genocide* (Amherst, Mass.: Alethia Press, 1996), 239–45; and "Memorandum of Conversation, Palais Des Nations, Geneva, July 31, 1993," 247–49. The person identified in the memorandum is actually Paul Szasz.

95. "U.S. Policymakers on Bosnia Admit Errors in Opposing Partition in 1992," *New York Times,* 29 August 1993.

96. "Joint Declaration," CO 16/9/93: Serb-Muslim Agreement," *Balkan Odyssey* CD-ROM.

97. Owen, *Balkan Odyssey,* 227.

98. The EUAP was a Franco-German initiative, and is set out in "Klaus Kinkel and Alain Juppe, Letter to Belgian EU Presidency," PI 7/11/93: Claes, Kinkel, Juppe Letter, *Balkan Odyssey* CD-ROM.

99. "Former Yugoslavia: The Search for a Global Settlement," CO 1/11/93: Consultations since FAC, *Balkan Odyssey* CD-ROM.

100. This point is also made in "Bosnia Talks: A 3-Way Split," *New York Times,* 3 December 1993.

101. See also "ICFY Briefing Note on Origins of 51–49 Per Cent Territorial Division of Bosnia-Herzegovina as under Contact Group Map," CD 13/5/94: Origins of Territorial Division, *Balkan Odyssey* CD-ROM.

102. "U.S. Termed Ready to Press Bosnians to Accept Division," *New York Times,* 11 February 1994. The confederation agreement can be found in "Bosnia and Herzegovina-Croatia: Preliminary Agreement Concerning the Establishment of a Confederation, March 18, 1994," *International Legal Materials* 33 (1994): 605–18. In the end, this preliminary agreement was scrapped by the Bosnian government in 1995. Owen, *Balkan Odyssey,* 338.

103. "Washington Negotiations: Report to Co-Chairmen of Conversations with Szasz and Steiner from David Ludlow, 12 February 1994," CD 12/2/94: Report from Ludlow, *Balkan Odyssey* CD-ROM.

104. On cantonization, see Klemenčić, "Territorial Proposals," 67. On the two-republic notion, see "COREU from Lord Owen 2 March 1994: Muslim/Croat Negotiations Washington," CO 2/3/94: Washington Agreement, *Balkan Odyssey* CD-ROM.

105. "Bosnia and Herzegovina: Constitution of the Federation, March 18, 1994," *International Legal Materials* 33 (1994): 744.

106. Hayden, "Imagined Communities and Real Victims," 792; "Serbs Demand Constituent Nation Status in Bosnian Federation," *OMRI Daily Digest* 71 (10 April 1995), in BosNews, 10 April 1995.

107. "Bosnia and Herzegovina: Constitution of the Federation, March 18, 1994," 750–51, 777, 783.

108. Ibid., 752–53, 768.

109. Klemenčić, "Territorial Proposals," 69.

110. "Direct Governmental Involvement in the Search for a Negotiated Settlement to the Conflict in Bosnia and Herzegovina with Special Reference to the Work of the Contact Group September 1992–July 1994, Part 1," PI Contact Group Negotiations, *Balkan Odyssey* CD-ROM. This report, in five parts, is a detailed account by David Ludlow of Owen's staff, who participated in the Contact Group process, of the diplomacy and its details.

111. "Direct Governmental Involvement in the Search for a Negotiated Settlement," Part 3.

112. Ibid., Part 4.

113. Ibid.

114. "Discussions surrounding the Contact Group Map, 14 May 1994–6 February 1995, Part 3," AN 6/2/95: Contact Group Map Talks (Parts 1–3), *Balkan Odyssey* CD-ROM.

115. Ibid.

116. Owen, *Balkan Odyssey*, 296.

117. Ibid., 293, 304.

118. Ibid., 337.

119. "Tragic Cost of Allies' Hidden Hostility," *The Guardian*, 21 May 1996.

120. "Agreed Basic Principles, September 1995," PI 26/9/95: Agreed Basic Principles, *Balkan Odyssey* CD-ROM. For a highly critical analysis of the separatist logic of these principles, see Francis A. Boyle, Memorandum to the Parliament of the Republic of Bosnia and Herzegovina, "Agreement on Basic Principles in Geneva on 8 September 1995," 11 September 1995, in BosNet (Digest 394), 12 September 1995.

121. Paul Szasz, "Introductory Note," in "Bosnia and Herzegovina-Croatia-Yugoslavia: General Framework Agreement for Peace in Bosnia and Herzegovina with Annexes, Done at Paris, December 14, 1995," *International Legal Materials* 35 (1995): 76, 77.

122. Klemenčić, "Territorial Proposals," 71.

123. Zoran Pajic, "The Structures of Apartheid: The New Europe of Ethnic Division," *WarReport* 21 (August/September 1993): 3–4.

124. "Bosnia and Herzegovina-Croatia-Yugoslavia: General Framework Agreement for Peace in Bosnia and Herzegovina with Annexes," 118.

125. Ibid., 118, 120. An Agreement on Special and Parallel Relations between Republika Srpska and the Federal Republic of Yugoslavia was signed in Belgrade on 28 February 1997, drawing muted criticism from the High Representative Carl Bildt for its potential challenge to Bosnian sovereignty. BosNet (Digest 530), 6 March 1997.

126. See Article 5, part (v), of the constitution. According to a statement from the presidency of Bosnia Herzegovina, this committee was established on 10 March 1997. See BosNet (Digest 534), 15 March 1997.

127. Article 2(b)(iii), "Treaty Provisions for the Convention, 4 November 1991," PI 4/11/91: EC Conference Draft Convention," *Balkan Odyssey* CD-ROM.

128. "Secretary-General Report on the International Conference on the Former Yugoslavia," 1585, 1591.

129. These quotes are from a Reuters report in Tribunal Watch, 7 May 1996.

130. Owen, *Balkan Odyssey*, 123.

131. Klemenčić, "Territorial Proposals," 28–35.

132. Ibid., 41–42.

133. "Brief Explanations of the Proposal of Thirteen Regions in Bosnia-Herzegovina," paper submitted to the ICFY by the State delegation of the Republic of Bosnia-Herzegovina, 9 December 1992, GE 9/12/92: Proposal for 13 Regions, *Balkan Odyssey* CD-ROM.

134. Klemenčić, "Territorial Proposals," 51.

135. "Constitutional Instrument, Etc. (Submitted by Francis A. Boyle, 31 July 1993)," in Boyle, *The Bosnian People Charge Genocide*, 251.

136. Klemenčić, "Territorial Proposals," 66–67.

137. "Chop Up Bosnia?" *The Economist*, 19–25 April 1997; "Peace Troops Face 'From Here to Eternity' in Bosnia," *The Guardian*, 22 May 1997.

138. William E. Connolly, "Pluralism, Multiculturalism, and the Nation-State: Rethinking the Connections," *Journal of Political Ideologies* 1 (1996): 61.

139. Renata Salecl, *The Spoils of Freedom: Psychoanalysis and Feminism after the Fall of Socialism* (London: Routledge, 1994), 12. As Salecl notes, these formulations come from Etienne Balibar, "Is There a 'Neo-Racism'?" in Etienne Balibar and Immanuel Wallerstein, *Race, Nation, Class: Ambiguous Identities* (London: Verso, 1991).

140. Connolly, "Pluralism, Multiculturalism, and the Nation-State," 56.

141. Jean Baudrillard, *The Perfect Crime*, trans. Chris Turner (London: Verso, 1996), 137.

142. Mearsheimer's remark is reported in Yosef Lapid and Friedrich Kratochwil, "Revisiting the 'National': Toward an Identity Agenda in Neorealism," in *The Return of Culture and Identity in IR Theory*, ed. Yosef Lapid and Friedrich Kratochwil (Boulder: Lynne Rienner, 1996), 125 n.

6. Deconstruction and the Promise of Democracy

1. William E. Connolly, "Democracy and Territoriality," *Millennium: Journal of International Studies* 17 (winter 1991): 463–84.

2. Johan Schulte-Sasse and Linda Schulte-Sasse, "War, Otherness, and Illusionary Identifications with the State," *Cultural Critique* 19 (fall 1991): 78–83.

3. William S. Lind, "Defending Western Culture," *Foreign Policy* 84 (fall 1991): 40–50.

4. Robert Hughes, *The Culture of Complaint: The Fraying of America* (New York: New York Public Library and Oxford University Press, 1993), 13.

5. Verena Stolcke, "Talking Culture: New Boundaries, New Rhetorics of Exclusion in Europe," *Current Anthropology* 36 (February 1995): 2, 4, 8. For examples of national debates in France and Britain, see Gérard Noiriel, *The French Melting Pot: Immigration, Citizenship, and National Identity*, trans. Geoffroy de Laforcade (Minneapolis: University of Minnesota Press, 1996); and Kathryn A. Manzo, *Creating Boundaries: The Politics of Race and Nation* (Boulder: Lynne Rienner, 1996). The relationship between immigration debates and stories of national identity in the United States is argued in Roxanne Lynne Doty, "The Double-Writing of Statecraft: Exploring State Responses to Illegal Immigration," *Alternatives* 21 (April-June 1996): 171–89; and Michael J. Shapiro, "Narrating the Nation, Unwelcoming the Stranger: Anti-Immigration Policy in Contemporary America," *Alternatives* 22 (January-March 1997): 1–34.

6. See Robert J. C. Young, *Colonial Desire: Hybridity in Theory, Culture, and Race* (London: Routledge, 1995).

7. Hughes, *The Culture of Complaint*, 13; Arthur M. Schlesinger Jr., *The Disuniting of America: Reflections on a Multicultural Society* (New York: W. W. Norton, 1992).

8. Quoted in "Exuding Confidence, Serbian Nationalists Act As If War for Bosnia Is Won," *New York Times*, 23 May 1993, 12.

9. John J. Mearsheimer, "Shrink Bosnia to Save It," *New York Times*, 31 March 1993.

10. Henry A. Kissinger, "In Bosnia, 'Peacekeeping' Forces Will Be 'Peacemakers,'" *Los Angeles Times*, 16 May 1993.

11. Robert Bernasconi, "On Deconstructing Nostalgia for Community within the West: The Debate between Nancy and Blanchot," *Research in Phenomenology* 23 (1993): 3–21.

12. Zillah Eisenstein, *Hatreds: Racialized and Sexualized Conflicts in the Twenty-First Century* (New York: Routledge, 1996), chapter 3.

13. Young, *Colonial Desire*; Mark Duffield, "Symphony of the Damned: Racial Discourse, Complex Political Emergencies, and Humanitarian Aid," *Disasters* 20 (September 1996): 173–93; Arjun Appadurai, *Modernity at Large: Cultural Dimensions of Globalization* (Minneapolis: University of Minnesota Press, 1996), 15; and Rob Nixon, *Homelands, Harlem, and Hollywood: South African Culture and the World Beyond* (New York: Routledge, 1994), 205–11. This rich field of debate is well surveyed in *Multiculturalism: A Critical Reader*, ed. David Theo Goldberg (Cambridge, Mass.: Blackwell, 1994); and *Mapping Multiculturalism*, ed. Avery F. Gordon and Christopher Newfield (Minneapolis: University of Minnesota Press, 1996). For a productive invocation of "hybridity," see Néstor García Canclini, *Hybrid Cultures: Strategies for Entering and Leaving Modernity*, trans. Christopher L. Chiappari and Silvia L. López (Minneapolis: University of Minnesota Press, 1995).

14. For various considerations of the first proposition, see *The Identity in Question*, ed. John Rajchman (New York: Routledge, 1995); for the second, see Charles Taylor, "The Politics of Recognition," in *Multiculturalism and "The Politics of Recognition": An Essay by Charles Taylor*, ed. Amy Gutman (Princeton, N.J.: Princeton University Press, 1992). Taylor's argument is, in turn, the subject of examination in William E. Connolly, "Pluralism, Multiculturalism, and the Nation-State: Rethinking the Connections," *Journal of Political Ideologies* 1 (1996): 53–73.

15. Connolly, "Pluralism, Multiculturalism, and the Nation-State."

16. Thus, we read Owen's lament that "it is beyond dispute that a Yugoslav identity was developed in parts of the former Yugoslavia and the valiant struggle to keep a multi-ethnic identity alive in besieged Sarajevo will for many always be a benchmark *for what might have been.*" David Owen, *Balkan Odyssey* (London: Victor Gollancz, 1995), 37; emphasis added.

17. Jacques Derrida, *Specters of Marx: The State of the Debt, the Work of Mourning, and the New International*, trans. Peggy Kamuf (New York: Routledge: 1994), 82.

18. Jacques Derrida, "Some Statements and Truisms about Neologisms, Newisms, Postisms, Parasitisms, and Other Small Seismisms," trans. Anne Tomiche, in *The States of "Theory": History, Art, and Critical Discourse*, ed. David Carroll (Stanford: Stanford University Press, 1990), 85.

19. The relationship of these thinkers was evident in Derrida's funeral oration for Lévinas. See Jacques Derrida, "Adieu," trans. Pascale-Anne Brault and Michael Naas, *Critical Inquiry* 23 (autumn 1996): 1–10.

20. For a discussion of this thesis, see David Campbell and Michael Dillon, "The End of Philosophy and the End of International Relations," in *The Political Subject of Violence*, ed. David Campbell and Michael Dillon (Manchester: Manchester University Press, 1993).

21. Edith Wyschogrod, *Saints and Postmodernism: Revisioning Moral Philosophy* (Chicago: University of Chicago Press, 1990), 191. As Lévinas has argued, "Like the categorical imperative, axiology belongs to Logos." Emmanuel Lévinas, "Ideology and Idealism," in Emmanuel Lévinas, *The Lévinas Reader,* ed. Sean Hand (Oxford: Basil Blackwell, 1989), 237.

22. Emmanuel Lévinas, "Reflections on the Philosophy of Hitlerism," trans. Sean Hand, *Critical Inquiry* 17 (autumn 1990): 63.

23. Ibid.

24. Overviews can be found in Adriaan Peperzak, *To the Other: An Introduction to the Philosophy of Emmanuel Lévinas* (West Lafayette, Ind.: Purdue University Press, 1993); and John Llewelyn, *Emmanuel Lévinas: The Genealogy of Ethics* (London: Routledge, 1995).

25. Emmanuel Lévinas, "Signature," in *Difficult Freedom: Essays on Judaism,* trans. Sean Hand (Baltimore: Johns Hopkins University Press, 1990), 291.

26. Simon Critchley, *The Ethics of Deconstruction: Derrida and Lévinas* (Oxford: Basil Blackwell, 1992), 221.

27. See the discussion of "the Augustinian imperative," the belief that there is an intrinsic moral order, of either "high command" or "intrinsic pattern," in William E. Connolly, *The Augustinian Imperative: A Reflection on the Politics of Morality* (Newbury Park, Calif.: Sage, 1993).

28. For a similar argument, see Zygmunt Bauman, *Modernity and the Holocaust* (Ithaca, N.Y.: Cornell University Press, 1990).

29. Emmanuel Lévinas, "Freedom of Speech," in *Difficult Freedom,* 206. In an interview Lévinas observed that his "critique of the totality has come in fact after a political experience that we have not yet forgotten." Emmanuel Lévinas, *Ethics and Infinity: Conversations with Philippe Nemo,* trans. Richard Cohen (Pittsburgh: Duquesne University Press, 1985), 78–79.

30. Emmanuel Lévinas and Richard Kearney, "Dialogue with Emmanuel Lévinas," in *Face to Face with Lévinas,* ed. Richard A. Cohen (Albany: SUNY Press, 1986), 18–19.

31. Simon Critchley, "The Chiasmus: Lévinas, Derrida, and the Ethical Demand for Deconstruction," *Textual Practice* 3 (April 1989): 100.

32. Critchley, *The Ethics of Deconstruction,* 113–14.

33. Lévinas, "Politics After!" in *The Lévinas Reader,* ed. Hand, 279.

34. See Michael J. MacDonald, "'Jewgreek and Greekjew': The Concept of the Trace in Derrida and Lévinas," *Philosophy Today* 35 (fall 1991): 215–27.

35. Lévinas and Kearney, "Dialogue with Emmanuel Lévinas," 20.

36. Ibid.

37. Emmanuel Lévinas, *Otherwise than Being or Beyond Essence,* trans. Alphonso Lingis (The Hague: Martinus Nijhoff Publishers, 1981), 10; and Emmanuel Lévinas, *Totality and Infinity,* trans. Alphonso Lingis (Pittsburgh: Duquesne University Press, 1969), 48, 79.

38. Lévinas, *Otherwise than Being or Beyond Essence,* 10. To speak of Lévinas's thought operating in the space opened by Heidegger raises the difficult issue of the intellectual relationship between Lévinas and Heidegger. Although it is commonly understood to be antagonistic, and a question is often raised about Lévinas's understanding of Heidegger's ontology, it is possible to interpret the relationship in more complex terms. See Robert John Sheffler Manning, *Interpreting Otherwise than Heidegger: Emmanuel Lévinas's Ethics as First Philosophy* (Pittsburgh: Duquesne University Press, 1993). The most important analysis of Lévinas's representation of Heidegger's philosophy is Jacques Derrida, "Violence and Metaphysics: An Essay on the Thought of Emmanuel

Lévinas," in *Writing and Difference,* trans. Alan Bass (Chicago: University of Chicago Press, 1978).

39. Lévinas, *Ethics and Infinity,* 95. It is important to acknowledge, even if it is not explored here in the necessary depth, that Lévinas's rendering of the subject and alterity embodies a specific and problematic gendered positioning. See Critchley, *The Ethics of Deconstruction,* 129–41.

40. Emmanuel Lévinas, "Ethics as First Philosophy," in *The Lévinas Reader,* ed. Hand, 83–84.

41. Jacques Derrida, "Force of Law: The 'Mystical Foundations of Authority,'" in *Deconstruction and the Possibility of Justice,* ed. Drucilla Cornell, Michel Rosenfeld, and David Gray Carlson (New York: Routledge, 1992), 19.

42. Critchley, "The Chiasmus," 96.

43. Fabio Ciaramelli, "Lévinas's Ethical Discourse: Between Individuation and Universality," in *Re-reading Lévinas,* ed. Robert Bernasconi and Simon Critchley (Bloomington: Indiana University Press, 1991), 87. See also Lévinas, "Ideology and Idealism," 245; Lévinas, *Otherwise than Being or Beyond Essence,* 10.

44. Lévinas, "Ethics as First Philosophy," 82.

45. Lévinas, *Totality and Infinity,* 43.

46. Lévinas and Kearney, "Dialogue with Emmanuel Lévinas," 27.

47. Ciaramelli, "Lévinas's Ethical Discourse," 85.

48. "Transcendence is passing over to being's *other,* otherwise than being." Lévinas, *Otherwise than Being or Beyond Essence,* 3. Critchley speaks of the insights, interruptions, and alterity uncovered by a *clotural* reading as "moments of *ethical transcendence,* in a which a necessity other than that of ontology announces itself within the reading." Critchley, *The Ethics of Deconstruction,* 30.

49. Lévinas, "Signature," 293.

50. Lévinas, "The Philosophy of Hitlerism," 63.

51. Lévinas, *Otherwise than Being or Beyond Essence,* 59.

52. Ibid.

53. Ibid. "God" is an important figure and site in Lévinas's discourse, which, according to Lingis, is located in the ethical relation as "the very nonphenomenal force of the other." As such, Lévinas neither reinscribes "god's" ontotheological status nor avoids agreement with Nietzsche's account of the death of God. Alphonso Lingis, "Translator's Introduction," in Lévinas, *Otherwise than Being or Beyond Essence,* xxxiii; and Critchley, *The Ethics of Deconstruction,* 113–14.

54. Lévinas, *Otherwise than Being or Beyond Essence,* 127.

55. According to Derrida, Lévinas does talk in terms of a "'Jewish humanism,' whose basis is not 'the concept of man,' but rather the other; 'the extent of the right of the other.'" Quoted in Derrida, "Force of Law," 22. See also Critchley, *The Ethics of Deconstruction,* 221.

56. Lévinas, "Ideology and Idealism," 247.

57. Lévinas and Kearney, "Dialogue with Emmanuel Lévinas," 27.

58. For a guide, see *Traditions of International Ethics,* ed. Terry Nardin and David Mapel (Cambridge: Cambridge University Press, 1992).

59. Lévinas and Kearney, "Dialogue with Emmanuel Lévinas," 23.

60. Lévinas, "Ideology and Idealism," 247.

61. For the view that Lévinas's thought is good only for the individuated relationship with the Other, see George Salemohamed, "Of an Ethics That Cannot Be Used," *Economy and Society* 20 (February 1991): 120–29.

62. Critchley, *The Ethics of Deconstruction,* 220.

63. Lévinas, *Otherwise than Being or Beyond Essence*, 11, 87, 88, 128.

64. Ibid., 159.

65. Ibid., 157.

66. Lingis, "Translator's Introduction," in Lévinas, *Otherwise than Being or Beyond Essence*, xxxv.

67. Ibid.

68. Lévinas, "Ideology and Idealism," 247.

69. Kearney and Lévinas, "Dialogue with Emmanuel Lévinas," 21.

70. Lévinas, *Otherwise than Being or Beyond Essence*, 76.

71. Ibid., 78.

72. Ibid., 100–101.

73. Ibid., 81–82; emphasis added.

74. Kearney and Lévinas, "Dialogue with Emmanuel Lévinas," 21.

75. Ibid.

76. Lévinas, "Ideology and Idealism," 247.

77. Lévinas, *Otherwise than Being or Beyond Essence*, 161.

78. Lévinas, "The State of Israel and the Religion of Israel," in *The Lévinas Reader*, ed. Hand, 260.

79. This is not to suggest that the State of Israel is illegitimate. Instead, it is to draw attention to the particular ethical and historical claims through which Lévinas attempts to secure that legitimacy. For his views, see "The State of Israel and the Religion of Israel," "The State of Caesar and the State of David," and "Politics After!" in *The Lévinas Reader*, ed. Hand; and "From the Rise of Nihilism to the Carnal Jew," and "Exclusive Rights," in Lévinas, *Difficult Freedom*. According to one blunt assessment, "in his ethical justification of the politics of Israel, Lévinas reproduces the same 'logic' as Heidegger's attempt to ground National Socialism on fundamental ontology." Richard Beardsworth, *Derrida and the Political* (London: Routledge, 1996), 144.

80. Lévinas, "Ethics and Politics," in *The Lévinas Reader*, ed. Hand, 290, 293.

81. Ibid., 294.

82. Lévinas, *Otherwise than Being or Beyond Essence*, 159; emphasis added.

83. Lévinas, "Ethics and Politics," 291; and Lévinas, *Otherwise than Being or Beyond Essence*, 128; second emphasis added. Although a number of commentators have rightly remarked that the epigraph to *Otherwise than Being or Beyond Essence* is addressed to all victims of anti-Semitism, broadly understood it contains within it a limit. It reads, "To the memory of *those who were closest* among the six million assassinated by the National Socialists, and of the millions on millions of all confessions and all nations, victims of the same hatred of the other man, the same anti-semitism." However, that limit could mark a personal reflection, for nearly all of Lévinas's family in Lithuania were put to death in concentration camps. See Manning, *Interpreting Otherwise than Heidegger*, 11.

84. Kearney and Lévinas, "Dialogue with Emmanuel Lévinas," 29.

85. Ibid.

86. Ibid., 21.

87. Ibid., 29–30.

88. Critchley, *The Ethics of Deconstruction*, 233.

89. This bears considerable affinities with William Connolly's articulation of a "post-Nietzschean ethical sensibility," which seeks (among other things) to "expose artifice in hegemonic identities, and the definitions of otherness (evil) through which they propel their self-certainty... [and] to contest moral visions that suppress the constructed, contingent, relational character of identity with a positive alternative that

goes some distance in specifying the ideal of political life inspiring it." See Connolly, *The Augustinian Imperative*, 143–44.

90. Richard Kearney and Jacques Derrida, "Dialogue with Jacques Derrida," in Richard Kearney, *Dialogues with Contemporary Continental Thinkers: The Phenomenological Heritage* (Manchester: Manchester University Press, 1984), 117–18.

91. Ibid., 123–24.

92. Critchley, *The Ethics of Deconstruction*, 189.

93. Ibid., 223.

94. Derrida, "Force of Law," 14.

95. Jacques Derrida, "Like the Sound of the Sea Deep within a Shell: Paul de Man's War," trans. Peggy Kamuf, in *Responses: On Paul de Man's Wartime Journalism*, ed. Werner Hamacher, Neil Hertz, and Thomas Keenan (Lincoln: University of Nebraska Press, 1989), 155.

96. Thomas Keenan, "Deconstruction and the Impossibility of Justice," *Cardozo Law Review* 11, 5–6 (July/August 1990): 1681.

97. Jacques Derrida, *The Other Heading: Reflections on Today's Europe*, trans. Pascale-Anne Brault and Michael B. Naas (Bloomington: Indiana University Press, 1992), 44–45.

98. Critchley, *The Ethics of Deconstruction*, 199.

99. Jacques Derrida, "Afterword: Toward an Ethic of Discussion," in Derrida, *Limited Inc* (Evanston, Ill.: Northwestern University Press, 1988), 115.

100. Ibid., 116.

101. Ibid., 148.

102. Ibid., 116. See the discussion in John Llewelyn, "Responsibility with Indecidability," in *Derrida: A Critical Reader*, ed. David Wood (Oxford: Blackwell, 1992), especially 93–94.

103. Critchley, *The Ethics of Deconstruction*, 199.

104. Derrida, "Force of Law," 14–15.

105. Ibid., 22.

106. Ibid., 24.

107. Ibid., 24–25.

108. Ibid., 26.

109. Ibid., 28; emphasis added.

110. Ibid.

111. Derrida, *The Other Heading*, 6.

112. Derrida, "Force of Law," 28.

113. Derrida, *The Other Heading*, 41.

114. Derrida, "Force of Law," 28; emphasis added.

115. Kearney and Derrida, "Dialogue with Jacques Derrida," 119; emphasis added.

116. Ibid., 120.

117. Derrida, *The Other Heading*, 15.

118. Ibid., 38–39.

119. Ibid., 41; emphasis added.

120. Ibid., 44.

121. Ibid.

122. Ibid., 76–79; first emphasis added.

123. Kearney and Lévinas, "Dialogue with Emmanuel Lévinas," 28.

124. Critchley, *The Ethics of Deconstruction*, 199, 200.

125. As Derrida observes, in pursuing what is possible to its impossible limits, we must recognize that "beyond these identified territories of juridico-politicization

on the grand geopolitical scale, beyond all self-serving interpretations, beyond all determined and particular reappropriations of law, other areas must constantly open up that at first seem like secondary or marginal areas." Derrida, "Force of Law," 28. These marginal areas could be thought of in terms of civil society and its networks of power, instances of which are discussed in the next chapter.

126. See, for example, Francis Fukuyama, *The End of History and the Last Man* (New York: The Free Press, 1992).

127. See, for example, Steve Chan, "Mirror, Mirror on the Wall . . . Are the Freer Countries More Pacific?" *Journal of Conflict Resolution* 28 (December 1984): 617–48; David A. Lake, "Powerful Pacificists: Democratic States and Wars," *American Political Science Review* 86 (1992), 24–37; and Carol R. Ember, Melvin Ember, and Bruce Russett, "Peace between Participatory Polities: A Cross-Cultural Test of the 'Democracies Rarely Fight Each Other' Hypothesis," *World Politics* 44 (July 1992): 573–99.

128. Slavoj Žižak, "East Europe's Republics of Gilead," in *Dimensions of Radical Democracy: Pluralism, Citizenship, Community*, ed. Chantal Mouffe (London: Verso, 1992), 193, 210.

129. Vanessa Vasic Janekovic and Anthony Borden, "National Parties and the Plans for Division," *WarReport* 16 (November/December 1992): 8–9.

130. See, for example, Fukuyama, *The End of History*, 43; and Gregory Foessedal, *The Democratic Imperative: Exporting the American Revolution* (New York: Basic Books, 1989), 34.

131. See Robert Latham, "Democracy and War-Making: Locating the International Liberal Context," *Millennium: Journal of International Studies* 22 (summer 1993): 139–64.

132. The last point has been addressed from a variety of perspectives by the contributors to *The Political Subject of Violence*, ed. Campbell and Dillon.

133. David Held, "Democracy and Globalization," *Alternatives* 16 (1991): 201–8; and David Held, "Sites of Power, Problems of Democracy," *Alternatives* 19 (spring 1994): 221–36.

134. Paul Hirst, "Associative Democracy," *Dissent* (spring 1994): 241–47.

135. Claude Lefort, *Democracy and Political Theory*, trans. David Macey (Minneapolis: University of Minnesota Press, 1988), chapter 11. It is important to stress that Lefort's argument concerns the contrasting political logic between these forms and does not claim that democracy was either the necessary or historical successor to Christendom or the ancien régime. For a good critical discussion of Lefort's arguments, see Simon Critchley, "Re-tracing the Political: Politics and Community in the Work of Philippe Lacoue-Labarthe and Jean-Luc Nancy," in *The Political Subject of Violence*, ed. Campbell and Dillon, 78–82.

136. Lefort, *Democracy and Political Theory*, 17–19.

137. Ibid., 226.

138. Ibid., 34.

139. Renata Salecl, "Democracy and Violence," *New Formations* 14 (summer 1991): 17–26.

140. Connolly, "Democracy and Territoriality," 477.

141. Ibid., 477–78.

142. I take this to be the theme of Nietzsche's reflections on this topic. See, especially, Friedrich Nietzsche, *The Will to Power*, trans. Walter Kaufmann and R. J. Hollingdale (New York: Vintage Books, 1967), book 1.

143. Eric Hobsbawm, "Barbarism: A User's Guide," *New Left Review* 206 (July/August 1994): 45.

144. Derrida, "Force of Law."

145. Geoffrey Bennington and Jacques Derrida, *Jacques Derrida*, trans. Geoffrey Bennington (Chicago: University of Chicago Press, 1993), 310.

146. Ernesto Laclau, introduction to *The Making of Political Identities*, ed. Ernesto Laclau (London and New York: Verso, 1994), 1–5, at 5.

147. Rodolphe Gasché, *Inventions of Difference* (Cambridge: Harvard University Press, 1994), 2.

148. Judith Butler, *Bodies That Matter: On the Discursive Limits of "Sex"* (New York: Routledge, 1993), 2. See the discussion of iterability in Judith Butler, *Excitable Speech: A Politics of the Performative* (New York: Routledge, 1997), 147–52.

149. Bennington and Derrida, *Jacques Derrida*, 64. The concept of iterability was first articulated in "Signature, Event, Context," in Jacques Derrida, *Margins of Philosophy*, trans. Alan Bass (Chicago: University of Chicago Press, 1982); and developed in Derrida, *Limited Inc.*

150. Laclau, introduction to *The Making of Political Identities*, 2.

151. Ernesto Laclau and Chantal Mouffe, *Hegemony and Socialist Strategy: Towards a Radical Democratic Politics*, trans. Winston Moore and Paul Cammack (London: Verso, 1985), 166–67.

152. Ibid., 4–5.

153. For the charge of a relationship by homology rather than argument, see Stephen K. White, *Political Theory and Postmodernism* (Cambridge: Cambridge University Press, 1991), 50.

154. Derrida, *Specters of Marx*, 59.

155. Derrida, *The Other Heading*, 78.

156. Derrida, *Specters of Marx*, 65.

157. This Derridean notion of democracy is also considered in Critchley, *The Ethics of Deconstruction*, especially 188–247.

158. See William E. Connolly, *The Ethos of Pluralization* (Minneapolis: University of Minnesota Press, 1995). Appreciating the temporality of the relationship between aporia and judgment is central to understanding the political significance of deconstructive thought. Beardsworth, *Derrida and the Political*, xiv.

159. Derrida, *Specters of Marx*, 169. For discussions of possible institutional arrangements, see Held, "Democracy and Globalization"; Hirst, "Associative Democracy"; and—at least insofar as the nonterritorialization of democracy through non-statist movements constitutes an institutional arrangement—William E. Connolly, *Identity/Difference: Democratic Negotiations of Political Paradox* (Ithaca, N.Y.: Cornell University Press, 1991), chapter 5.

160. Chantal Mouffe, *The Return of the Political* (New York: Verso, 1993), 8. See also Albert O. Hirschman, "Social Conflicts as Pillars of Democratic Market Society," *Political Theory* 22 (May 1994): 203–18. This involves an understanding of the social marked by the importance of antagonism and articulation, such as that in Laclau and Mouffe, *Hegemony and Socialist Strategy*.

161. Derrida, *The Other Heading*, 6.

162. Lefort, *Democracy and Political Theory*, 233. Lefort is using (and I am following him in this use) the concept of *totalitarianism* to signify a range of political initiatives that seek to foreclose on the openness of the social enabled by democracy. See Laclau and Mouffe, *Hegemony and Socialist Strategy*, 187.

163. Laclau, *New Reflections on the Revolution of Our Time* (London: Verso, 1990), 187; and Connolly, *The Ethos of Pluralization*.

164. Derrida, "Force of Law," 28.

165. Derrida, *Specters of Marx*, 92.

166. Ibid., 89.

167. Ibid., 90.

168. Laclau, *New Reflections on the Revolution of Our Times*, 214–15, 225; and Ernesto Laclau, *Emancipation(s)* (London: Verso, 1996).

169. Connolly, *The Ethos of Pluralization*.

170. For this point with regard to pluralism, see ibid., and the contributions to *Dimensions of Radical Democracy*, ed. Mouffe.

171. "Epilogue to the 1993 Edition: Modernity, Territorial Democracy, and the Problem of Evil," in William E. Connolly, *Political Theory and Modernity* (Ithaca, N.Y.: Cornell University Press, 1993), 178.

172. Ghassan Hage, "Locating Multiculturalism's Other: A Critique of Practical Tolerance," *New Formations* 24 (winter 1994): 19.

173. This is enshrined in the document for a post–Cold War Europe: see Conference on Security and Cooperation in Europe, "Charter of Paris for a New Europe," *International Legal Materials* 30 (January 1991): 195.

7. Bosnia and the Practice of Democracy

1. Homi Bhabha, *The Location of Culture* (New York: Routledge, 1994), 5.

2. Robert M. Hayden, "Imagined Communities and Real Victims: Self-Determination and Ethnic Cleansing in Yugoslavia," *American Ethnologist* 23, 4 (1996): 796. For "an elegy to the death of an idea . . . that within Europe, in Bosnia, a multiethnic people could exist in peace and tolerance," see *The Black Book of Bosnia: The Consequences of Appeasement*, ed. Nader Mousavizadeh (New York: Basic Books, 1996), xi. Of course, if the politically delimited notion of "tolerance" is exposed by the Bosnian war, then, in terms of the discussion in the previous chapter, that aspect at least may be a positive.

3. Hayden, "Imagined Communities and Real Victims," 783.

4. Population figures for postwar Bosnia are notoriously problematic, but even the data that Hayden uses to support his reluctant conclusion demonstrate this point. Ibid., 795–96.

5. Tone Bringa, *Being Muslim the Bosnian Way: Identity and Community in a Central Bosnian Village* (Princeton, N.J.: Princeton University Press, 1995). It should be emphasized that the poststructuralist political theorizations allied with Bringa's ethnography come from my reading and are not found, at least in those terms, in Bringa's study. However, the political implications for the war of Bosnian/Muslim identity detailed by Bringa are supported by others. See, for example, Renata Salecl, "The Crisis of Identity and the Struggle for New Hegemony in the Former Yugoslavia," in *The Making of Political Identities*, ed. Ernesto Laclau (London and New York: Verso, 1994), especially 228–30.

6. Bringa, *Being Muslim the Bosnian Way*, 3.

7. Other political moments can also be thought in these terms. See, for example, the reading of indigenous legal politics in Australia provided in Paul Patton, "Mabo, Freedom, and the Politics of Difference," *Australian Journal of Political Science* 30 (1995): 108–19. Patton's excellent account goes beyond Derrida to draw on Deleuze because of the claimed limits to the negative and critical gestures of deconstruction. The argument of this book, in relation to Bosnia, is designed to illustrate that deconstructive thought already goes beyond such a reading.

8. Bringa, *Being Muslim the Bosnian Way*, 20. See also Peter F. Sugar, *Southeastern Europe under Ottoman Rule, 1354–1804* (Seattle: University of Washington Press, 1977), chapter 2.

9. Bringa, *Being Muslim the Bosnian Way*, 21.

10. Ibid., 83.

11. Ibid., 18.

12. Ibid., 16.

13. Ibid., chapter 6.

14. Ibid., 27.

15. Ibid., 21.

16. Ibid., 22. See also Cornelia Sorabj, "A Very Modern War: Terror and Territory in Bosnia-Hercegovina," in *War: A Cruel Necessity*, ed. Robert A. Hinde and Helen E. Watson (London: I. B. Tauris, 1995), 87–91.

17. Bringa, *Being Muslim the Bosnian Way*, 25.

18. Ibid., 27. These census changes also reflected transformations in the nationalities policy as embodied in the constitutional changes between 1963 and 1974 (see the discussion in chapter 4).

19. Ibid., 29.

20. Ibid., 10, 29.

21. See Robert M. Hayden, "Constitutional Nationalism in the Formerly Yugoslav Republics," *Slavic Review* 51 (1992): 654–73; Hayden, "Imagined Communities and Real Victims," 790–92; and Bringa, *Being Muslim the Bosnian Way*, 26, 237 n.

22. Bringa, *Being Muslim the Bosnian Way*, 29.

23. Ibid., 34.

24. Ibid., 31.

25. Ibid., 34–36.

26. Ibid., 36.

27. Ibid., 30.

28. Ibid., 32.

29. "Lack of Political Concept Makes Bosnia's Position Difficult," BosNet (Digest 15) (electronic bulletin board), 9 January 1996.

30. Zoran Pajic, "Salvaging the Bosnian Ideal," *WarReport* 15 (October 1992): 1.

31. Salecl, "The Crisis of Identity and the Struggle for New Hegemony in the Former Yugoslavia," 225.

32. Yahya M. Sadowski, "Bosnia's Muslims: A Fundamentalist Threat?" *Brookings Review* 13 (January 1995).

33. Warren Zimmerman, "The Captive Mind," *New York Review of Books*, 2 February 1995, 6.

34. See the comprehensive indictment of the international community's conduct of these elections in International Crisis Group, *Elections in Bosnia and Herzegovina* (London: ICG, 22 September 1996).

35. International Crisis Group, *Why the Bosnian Elections Must Be Postponed*, Report Number 14 (London: ICG, 14 August 1996), section III(A). The UNHCR figures are cited here.

36. Samantha Power, "Mostar Postcard—Run for Your Lives," *The New Republic*, 9 September 1996.

37. "UN Sounds Alarm at Voter Intimidation in Bosnia," *The Guardian*, 12 August 1996.

38. According to the ICG, the vast majority of displaced Bosniacs and Croats (nearly 76 percent) registered to vote in their 1991 districts, while many others expressed the intention to travel personally on election day to cast their ballots. Only 24 percent of Bosnian Serbs did likewise, though the number would have been much higher had the reported intimidation by Republika Srpska, Federal Republic of Yugoslavia (FRY),

and Republic of Serbia officials not taken place. See International Crisis Group, *Elections in Bosnia and Herzegovina* ("Disenfranchisement of Refugees").

39. "Bosnian Serbs Apologize for Voter Manipulation, *OMRI Daily Digest* 160 (19 August 1996); and International Crisis Group, "ICG Cautions against Further Electoral Engineering in the Run-up to the Municipal Elections," press release, 4 December 1996.

40. Helsinki Citizen's Assembly, *Report of hCa Mission to Bosnia and Herzegovina 28 February-6 March 1996* (The Hague: hCa Western Liaison Office, 1996).

41. "UK Funds Serb War Criminal," *The Guardian*, 5 September 1996; " 'Corners Cut' in Race to Stage Bosnian Polls," *The Guardian*, 6 September 1996. These articles prompted a letter to the editor from Raznatović/Arkan that reprised familiar themes in order to plead his innocence. "Arkan: I am no war criminal," *The Guardian*, 14 September 1996.

42. Aid from the British government for reconstruction in Prijedor has been channeled through groups controlled by Bosnian Serbs who were involved in the detention camps at Omarska and Prijedor. Human Rights Watch, *The Unindicted: Reaping the Rewards of Ethnic Cleansing*, Research Report 9, 1 (January 1997).

43. "Thugs Kill Bosnia's Election Hopes," *The Guardian*, 23 August 1996.

44. International Crisis Group, *Elections in Bosnia and Herzegovina* ("Election Day, Results and Conclusions").

45. Quoted in "Bosnian Leaders Rally Diaspora Vote," *The Guardian*, 29 August 1996. Another aspect of tactical voting was that many of those who would have preferred the overtly multicultural Party for Bosnia's Haris Silajdžić rather than the SDA's Izetbegović cast ballots for the latter so as to ensure the chairmanship of Bosnia's joint presidency was not won by the Bosnian Serb they regarded as "the master ethnic cleanser," Momcilo Krajisnik. See "Three Colours: Black," *The Guardian*, 20 August 1996.

46. These statistics come from the 30 September 1996 final election results released by the Organization for Cooperation and Security in Europe, and obtained from the OSCE World Wide Web site. It is not known what proportion of this vote comes from former residents of territories now in Republika Srpska, exercising their right to vote according to their residence in the 1991 census, compared to those who are currently resident in Republika Srpska. That there are those who fit the latter category is not in doubt. See "Bosnia Village Left behind the Lines," *The Independent*, 2 April 1996.

47. See the Constitution of the Bosnian Republic in "Bosnia and Herzegovina-Croatia-Yugoslavia: General Framework Agreement for Peace in Bosnia and Herzegovina with Annexes," *International Legal Materials* 35 (1996): 118–23. The constitutional nationalism of the entities — where the federation is home to "Bosniacs and Croats, as constituent peoples (along with others)," and Republika Srpska is said to be based in "the inalienable and untransferable natural right of the Serbian nation to self-determination" — is discussed in Hayden, "Imagined Communities and Real Victims," 791–92.

48. Nedjo Milicevic, "Assembling the Bosnian House of Cards," *WarReport* 44 (August 1996): 22–23; and "Refugee's Dream May Be Nightmare for Izetbegovic," *The Guardian*, 3 September 1996.

49. "General Framework Agreement for Peace in Bosnia and Herzegovina with Annexes," Annex 7, Article 1(I) and 1(iii), 137.

50. A large number of media reports detail these points. For example, on the hostilities that have marked the practical implementation of Annex 7, see the commentaries in *Oslobodjenje* by Zija Dizdarevic (30 April 1996) and Gojko Beric (6 May 1996), *BosNet* (Digest 152), 13 May 1996. A press release by the German NGO the Society for Threatened Peoples, issued in Sanski Most/Gottingen on 29 April 1996, details IFOR's thwarting of their attempt to have 150 Bosnians exiled from Prijedor and now living

in Munich return home for a visit. Posted in *BosNet* (Digest 145), 4 May 1996. Authorities of the Croatian republic of "Herceg-Bosnia" — an entity in the federation that the Dayton agreement was supposed to have extinguished — have resisted large-scale Muslim visits and have removed local authorities deemed to be too lenient when negotiating with Bosniacs. See "Muslim Refugees Prevented from Visiting Stolac," *OMRI Daily Digest* 104 (29 May 1996); and "Croats Sack Mayor for Being Too Yielding to Bosniaks," *BosNet* (Digest 190), 11 June 1996. In a similar vein, Bosnian/Muslim authorities in the federation have used bureaucratic requirements to delay the return of Croats to Travnik. See "Travnik Croats Go Home," *OMRI Daily Digest* 116 (14 June 1996).

51. "Muslim Returnees Open Pandora's Box," *The Guardian*, 30 September 1996. A similar set of incidents in the town of Gajevi produced armed combat between refugees wanting to return home without international permission, and those who sought to repel them. "Second Day of Bosnia Fighting Is Worst since '95 Pact," *New York Times*, 13 November 1996.

52. The equal apportionment of blame by the international authorities is evident in a Reuters report, "Bosnian Factions Manipulate Frustrated Refugees," Tribunal Watch (electronic bulletin board), 23 April 1996; while the clash between popular desires and official nationalists is described in "Along an Ethnic Fault Line, Bosnians Fear Hard-Liners," *New York Times*, 1 June 1996; and "Moderate Bosnian Serbs Plot in Secrecy for Unity," *New York Times*, 31 July 1996.

53. "One Small Homecoming Brings a Flicker to the Bosnian Darkness," *The Guardian*, 5 February 1996.

54. Quoted in Daniel Warner, "Voluntary Repatriation and the Meaning of Return to Home: A Critique of Liberal Mathematics," *Journal of Refugee Studies* 7 (1994): 168.

55. "Germany to Deport Bosnian Refugees," *The Guardian*, 20 September 1996. According to UNHCR, only some 10,000 of the 520,000 refugees who have returned have been allowed to reenter areas in which "their ethnicity is not a majority." BosNet (Digest 573), 6 May 1997.

56. Derrida writes of a "hospitality without reserve" in *Specters of Marx: The State of the Debt, the Work of Mourning, and the New International*, trans. Peggy Kamuf (New York: Routledge: 1994), 65.

57. "UN Gives Up on Bosnian Refugees Going Home," *OMRI Daily Digest* 137 (17 July 1996). This conclusion was denied by the UNHCR. See "UNHCR Denies It Accepts Ethnic Cleansing," *OMRI Special Report: Pursuing Balkan Peace* 1, 30 (30 July 1996).

58. "Serbs Blew Up Refugee Homes," *The Guardian*, 7 November 1996; and "Defiantly, Bosnian Serbs Blow Up Muslims' Homes," *New York Times*, 7 November 1996.

59. "Muslim Police Torch Serb Homes?" BosNet (Digest 405), 7 November 1996.

60. "Blasts Shake Foundation of Bosnian Peace Plan, *Los Angeles Times*, 18 November 1996.

61. "Winking at Karadzic," *New York Times*, 28 October 1996. On other cases, see "War Criminals Serve Openly with Bosnian Serb Police," *OMRI Daily Digest* 210 (30 October 1996). The long-standing knowledge of these individuals' whereabouts, and the freedom of movement they have enjoyed even in areas controlled by IFOR, is well detailed in *OMRI Special Report: Pursuing Balkan Peace* 1, 44 (5 November 1996). See also the report of the Coalition for International Justice cited in "Rights Group Says Bosnian Suspects Flaunt Freedom," *New York Times*, 26 November 1996. To overcome this problem, the United States has recommended that a special police force to pursue war criminals be trained and deployed. However, it is hard to see what, in the absence of a greater sense of responsibility, such a force could achieve that the resources

of NATO's Implementation Force (IFOR), Stabilization Force (SFOR), and the International Police Task Force (IPTF), were they to be deployed differently, could not, as Operation Tango demonstrated. See "U.S. Urges Formation of Special Police Unit for War Crimes Duty," *Washington Post*, 18 December 1996; and "The Dance of Death," *The Guardian*, 12 July 1997.

62. Human Rights Watch, *Bosnia-Hercegovina: The Continuing Influence of Bosnia's Warlords*, Research Report 8 (17 D), December 1996. HRW has also protested against the mistreatment of individuals suspected of war crimes in federation territory, especially the Una Sana canton. See the HRW press release of 31 March 1997 in BosNet (Digest 550), 2 April 1997.

63. *OMRI Special Report: Pursuing Balkan Peace* 1, 49 (10 December 1996).

64. "Serbs Go Home to Bosnia Village, Defying Leaders," *New York Times*, 8 December 1996.

65. See the letter to the Bosnian Interior Minister from the Society for Threatened Peoples, in BosNet (Digest 464), 11 December 1996.

66. "Bosnian Federal Government Policy Resettles Muslim Refugees in Sarajevo," *OMRI Daily Digest* 105 (30 May 1996).

67. "Muslims in Sarajevo Take Over Homes of Serbs Who Fled the War," *New York Times*, 1 June 1996; "Housing: A Tool to Further Ethnic Division," *Liberation*, 28 August 1996. The rebukes come from Andras Riedlmayer, "Silent Ethnic Cleansing in Sarajevo," BosNet (Digest 217), 3 June 1996; and the Forced Migration Project of the Open Society Institute, New York, in BosNet (Digest 487), 13 January 1997.

68. "Bosnian Muslim Ruling Party Names Candidates for Council of Ministers," BosNet (Digest 463), 11 December 1996; and *OMRI Special Report: Pursuing Balkan Peace* 1, 29 (23 July 1996).

69. "Sarajevo Journal: Is the Grinch Running Bosnia's Government?" *New York Times*, 1 January 1997. Izetbegović opened this controversy with an open letter in January 1996 on the "false" symbol of Grandfather Frost. In written answers to the many responses this attracted, he argued that his point was that while Muslims should not accept this figure as representative of "their" culture, they should always respect the symbols of "other" cultures. This attitude only licensed greater intolerance of "us" versus "them" — thereby illustrating the limits of liberal tolerance as the medium for the relationship with the other — and cost Izetbegović a great deal of support, even from "Muslims." Our neighbors in Tuzla cited this issue as one of the reasons why they had doubts about the president and his politics. In more serious manifestations of communal tension during the 1996–97 holiday season, a mosque was fired upon in the Sarajevo suburb of Hrasnica, a Catholic priest was beaten by two men and told he had no place in Bosnia's capital, and a tear gas canister was thrown into an Orthodox church in the city. "Tear Gas Thrown during Orthodox Christmas Service in Sarajevo," *OMRI Daily Digest* 5 (8 January 1997).

70. Senad Pecanin, "Planning for Partition," *WarReport* 51 (May 1997), 6.

71. David Rieff, *Slaughterhouse: Bosnia and the Failure of the West* (New York: Simon and Schuster, 1995), 216.

72. For a range of articles and papers dealing with this information, see the contributions to the conference "Data Conflicts: Eastern Europe and the Geopolitics of Cyberspace," 13–15 December 1996, Potsdam, Germany, which was organized by Thomas Keenan and Thomas Y. Levin of Princeton University. Some are available at http://www.quintessenz.at/Dataconflicts.

73. On the openness of the Bosnian/Muslim media to opposition perspectives, and an assessment of the relative closure of the others, see the reports of the Bosnia

Media Monitoring Project. Begun on 5 June 1996, these reports were available on the Internet and published in *WarReport* (London: Institute for War and Peace Reporting, 1996). An overview can be found in Mark Wheeler, *Monitoring the Media: The Bosnian Elections 1996* (London: Institute for War and Peace Reporting, 1996).

74. International Crisis Group, *Elections in Bosnia and Herzegovina* ("Campaign," section 2(c)(iii)).

75. "Serb Fighter Now Fights Ruling Party in Bosnia," *New York Times,* 2 August 1996; "Independent Media in Republika Srpska Resist Government Pressure," *OMRI Daily Digest* 210 (30 October 1996); *The B&H Media Fortnight in Review: 6–19 January,* in BosNet (Digest 508), 29 January 1997.

76. Michel Foucault, "What Is Enlightenment?" in *The Foucault Reader,* ed. Paul Rabinow (New York: Pantheon Books, 1984), 50. See also Arjun Appadurai, *Modernity at Large: Cultural Dimensions of Globalization* (Minneapolis: University of Minnesota Press, 1996).

77. For a meditation on the notion of an "archive," see Jacques Derrida, *Archive Fever: A Freudian Impression,* trans. Eric Prenowitz (Chicago: University of Chicago Press, 1996). For an account of the intense postwar struggle over historical memory in Bosnia — which details what bodies like the International Criminal Tribunal for the Former Yugoslavia (ICTY) are up against — see "Never Again, Again: After the Peace, the War against Memory," *New York Times,* 13 January 1996. This struggle takes place in many sites, such as the debate over what should become of the destroyed National Library in Sarajevo. See "Bosnia's Postwar Battle: Library Is at Heart of Debate on Future," *New York Times,* 10 January 1996.

78. Because the ICTY cannot conduct trials in absentia, and because there were at the time of its inception doubts about the prospects of those indicted being handed over, the tribunal's statute provides for Rule 61 hearings, whereby evidence upon which the indictment is based can be publicly presented. Although such hearings do not lead to a judgment, the Trial Chamber is asked to determine whether "there are reasonable grounds for believing that the accused have committed any or all of the crimes of which they are indicated." In the case of the Rule 61 hearings against Karadžić and Mladić in June and July 1996, the Trial Chamber was so persuaded of the reasonable grounds that they invited the prosecutor to consider broadening the charge of genocide. Mirko Klarin, "Almost in the Dock," *WarReport* 44 (August 1996): 9–11. On the Erdemovic conviction, see Mirko Klarin, "Crisis Time in The Hague," *Tribunal* 4 (June/July 1996): 1–2.

79. On the financial problems facing the tribunal, see Tom Warrick, "Money Troubles," *Tribunal* 7 (February/March 1997): 8. The inadequate support for crucial activities such as the excavation of mass graves prompted the resignation of the UN envoy for missing persons in Bosnia. "UN's Bosnian Envoy Resigns," *The Guardian,* 27 March 1997.

80. Zoran Pajic, "UN Trusteeship Can Halt Ethnic Ghettoes," *YugoFax* 11 (7 May 1992): 1; "Alternative Paths to Peace," *WarReport* 14 (September 1992): 3; Zarko Puhovski, "A UN Protectorate a Pre-requisite for a Political Solution," *WarReport* 15 (October 1992): 15; "Bosnian Anti-war Activists Issue Peace Declaration," *New Statesmen and Society,* 18 June 1993; and Mary Kaldor, "Protect Bosnia," *The Nation,* 22 March 1993; Zoran Pajic, "Partition and Beyond," *WarReport* 38 (November/December 1995): 18–19.

81. See Anthony Borden's letter in the exchange with Richard Falk, *The Nation,* 21 February 1994.

82. See *hCa UK Newsletter* (spring 1996).

83. See, for example, Asbjørn Eide, "In Search of Constructive Solutions to Secession," in *Modern Law of Self-Determination,* ed. Christian Tomuschat (The Hague:

Martinus Nijhoff, 1993); and Ruth Lapidoth, *Autonomy: Flexible Solutions to Ethnic Conflict* (Washington, D.C.: United States Institute of Peace Press, 1996). For a discussion of the idea of special zones, see Gidon Gottlieb, "Nations without States," *Foreign Affairs* 73 (May/June 1994): 100–112. The Serb Civic Council (SGV) in Bosnia proposed, for example, that Sarajevo be a federal district with nonethnic municipalities to ensure its multicultural population was politically recognized. See "SGV—Sarajevo Should Be Union of Municipalities with Special Status," BosNet (Digest 57), 7 February 1996. Although the Croatian government turned down autonomy demands by Croatian Serbs in 1990–91, it has proposed what is described as a "surprisingly generous deal for Serbs" that offers full educational and cultural autonomy, along with political measures to match, as part of the reintegration of Eastern Slavonia into Croatia. See Drago Hedl, "A Pleasant Surprise," *WarReport* 48 (January/February 1997): 7.

84. For the colonial trap in trusteeship arrangements, see the enthusiastic endorsement of Paul Johnson, "Colonialism's Back—and Not a Moment Too Soon," *New York Times Magazine*, 18 April 1993.

85. "Mostar Elections Come Off Smoothly," *OMRI Special Report: Pursuing Balkan Peace* 1, 26 (2 July 1996). An overview can be found in Jelena Lovric, "Mostar Unbridged," *WarReport* 39 (February/March 1996): 6–7. Post-Dayton outbreaks of ethnic cleansing, and the continuing lack of an international response, are described in "Croatian Police Force Out Muslims," *The Guardian*, 12 February 1997; "Combined Forces Stretched to Rescue Mrs. Puzic's Undies," *The Guardian*, 13 February 1997; and Hamza Baksic, "The Same Old Story," *WarReport* 49 (March 1997): 5–6.

86. For details of some of the annual citizen's assemblies organized by hCa, which bring together people from across ethnic/national divides, see Anthony Borden, "Citizen's Forum," *WarReport* 16 (November/December 1992): 20; "Final Statement," Fourth Helsinki Citizen's Assembly, Tuzla, Bosnia-Herzegovina, 19–22 October 1995 (Prague: hCa International, 1995); and Radha Kumar, "Assembling in Tuzla," *WarReport* 38 (November/December 1995): 52–53.

87. See Charles Taylor, "Modes of Civil Society," *Public Culture* 3 (fall 1990): 95–132 (including Partha Chatterjee's critical response); Craig Calhoun, "Civil Society and the Public Sphere," *Public Culture* 5 (winter 1993): 267–80; *Civil Society: Challenging Western Models*, ed. Chris Hann and Elizabeth Dunn (London: Routledge, 1996); and Michael J. Shapiro, "Bowling Blind: Post Liberal Civil Society and the Worlds of Neo-Tocquevillean Social Theory," *Theory and Event* 1 (March 1997) (available at http://muse.jhu.edu/journals/theory_&_event/).

88. Paul Stubbs, "Nationalism, Globalization, and Civil Society in Croatia and Slovenia," *Research in Social Movements, Conflict and Change* 19 (1996): 1–26. For another argument, based on the Slovene experience, that "civil society" is not inherently democratic, see Tomaz Mastnak, "Civil Society at War," *WarReport* 16 (November/December 1992): 7.

89. Many details of these groups came from meetings with their representatives in Tuzla during July/August 1996. Published references include Helsinki Citizen's Assembly, *Report of hCa Mission to Bosnia and Herzegovina 28 February-6 March 1996*; various contributions to the *hCa Quarterly* 15/16 (winter/spring 1996); "Bosnian Independent Intellectuals Visit Rump Yugoslavia," *OMRI Special Report: Pursuing Balkan Peace* 1, 6 (13 February 1996); Report of the *Citizens Alternative Parliament of Bosnia and Herzegovina*, Constituent Assembly, Tuzla, 31 August 1996; and Report of the Third General Assembly of the Tuzla Citizen's Forum, 15 March 1997, in BosNet (Digest 548), 31 March 1997.

90. Shapiro, "Bowling Blind," paragraph 5.

91. "Bosnian Refugees Organize across Ethnic Lines," *OMRI Daily Digest* 210 (30 October 1996).

92. "Trials and Error for a Bosnian Solution," *The Guardian*, 7 September 1996.

93. "Bosnian Government Threatens to Close Down Arizona Market," *OMRI Special Report: Pursuing Balkan Peace* 1, 36 (10 September 1996); "Bosnians Burying Their Differences, with Money," *New York Times*, 17 October 1996; and "Bosnian 'Mission Creep' Yields Positive Results," BosNet (Digest 400), 4 November 1996. I saw the Arizona market while traveling between Tuzla and Zagreb in August 1996, and can testify to both its size and mixed population, which is evident from the various entities' car registration plates on show.

94. "Bosnian Serbs Veto Cross-Border Bus Routes," *OMRI Daily Digest* 101 (24 May 1996); and "Serbs Continue to Harass Cross-Border Bus Line," *OMRI Daily Digest* 110 (6 June 1996).

95. Slavoj Žižek, "Es Gibt Keinen Staat in Europa," available at http://lois.kud-fp.si/nsk, the *Neue Slowenische Kunst* World Wide Web site.

96. William E. Connolly, "Drugs, the Nation, and Free Lancing: Decoding the Moral Universe of William Bennett," *Theory and Event* 1 (March 1997): note 20.

97. Gillian Rose, "Spatialities of 'Community,' Power, and Change: The Imagined Geographies of Community Arts Projects," *Cultural Studies* 11 (1997): 14. Another version of Rose's argument is published in *Geographies of Resistance*, ed. Steve Pile and Michael Keith (London: Routledge, 1997). Such concerns could, for example, place greater emphasis on cities rather than states as the loci of community. See Peter Taylor, "Territorial Absolutism and Its Evasions," *Geography Research Forum* 16 (1996): 9–10.

98. "Nietzsche and the Machine: Interview with Jacques Derrida by Richard Beardsworth," *Journal of Nietzsche Studies* 7 (spring 1994): 47–48; emphasis added. See also Derrida, *Specters of Marx*, 84–85.

99. Alphonso Lingis, *The Community of Those Who Have Nothing in Common* (Bloomington: Indiana University Press, 1994), x.

100. Foucault's argument that we bore responsibility for the fate of Vietnamese refugees stranded in international waters enunciated the rights and duties that flowed from this. See the discussion in Tom Keenan, "The 'Paradox' of Knowledge and Power: Reading Foucault on a Bias," *Political Theory* 15 (February 1987): 20–22.

101. Derrida, *Specters of Marx*, 35. Likewise, Gasché argues that "a responsible discourse on responsibility can indeed only assert itself in the mode of a 'perhaps.'" Rodolphe Gasché, *Inventions of Difference* (Cambridge: Harvard University Press, 1994), 228.

102. Ernesto Laclau, *Reflections on the New Revolution of Our Time* (London: Verso, 1990), 187.

Note on Sources

1. For a discussion that demonstrates the corroboration of key points in an argument such as this, see the note on sources in Michael Sells, *The Bridge Betrayed: Religion and Genocide in Bosnia* (Berkeley: University of California Press, 1996), 157–64. The Community of Bosnia Foundation, with which Sells is associated, and which operates an informative World Wide Web site, can be reached at http://www.haverford.edu/.

2. On the language question, see Robert D. Greenberg, "The Politics of Dialects among Serbs, Croats, and Muslims in the Former Yugoslavia," *East European Politics and Societies* 10 (fall 1996): 393–415.

Index

David Campbell is professor of international politics at the University of Newcastle. He has also taught at Keele University and the Johns Hopkins University. Campbell is the author of, among other works, *Writing Security: United States Foreign Policy and the Politics of Identity* (Minnesota, 1992; revised edition, 1998) and *Politics without Principle: Sovereignty, Ethics, and the Narratives of the Gulf War.*